Global Public P....

WOLFGANG H. REINICKE

GLOBAL PUBLIC POLICY

Governing without Government?

BROOKINGS INSTITUTION PRESS
Washington, D.C.

Library of Congress Cataloging-in-Publication data

Reinicke, Wolfgang, H.
    Global public policy : governing without government? / Wolfgang
H. Reinicke.
    p. cm.
    Includes bibliographical references and index.
    ISBN 0-8157-7390-0 (cloth)
    1. International economic integration. 2. Economic policy. 3.
Policy sciences. I. Title.
    HF1418.5 .R446 1998
    337—ddc21   98-8941
                                                                          CIP

9 8 7 6 5 4 3 2 1

The paper used in this publication meets the minimum requirements
of the American National Standard for Information Sciences—
Permanence of Paper for Printed Library Materials, ANSI Z39-48-1984.

Typeset in Times Roman

Composition by Linda C. Humphrey
Arlington, Virginia

Printed by R. R. Donnelley and Sons Co.
Harrisonburg, Virginia

℔ THE BROOKINGS INSTITUTION

The Brookings Institution is an independent organization devoted to nonpartisan research, education, and publication in economics, government, foreign policy, and the social sciences generally. Its principal purposes are to aid in the development of sound public policies and to promote public understanding of issues of national importance.

The Institution was founded on December 8, 1927, to merge the activities of the Institute for Government Research, founded in 1916, the Institute of Economics, founded in 1922, and the Robert Brookings Graduate School of Economics and Government, founded in 1924.

The Board of Trustees is responsible for the general administration of the Institution, while the immediate direction of the policies, program, and staff is vested in the President, assisted by an advisory committee of the officers and staff. The by-laws of the Institution state: "It is the function of the Trustees to make possible the conduct of scientific research, and publication, under the most favorable conditions, and to safeguard the independence of the research staff in the pursuit of their studies and in the publication of the results of such studies. It is not a part of their function to determine, control, or influence the conduct of particular investigations or the conclusions reached."

The President bears final responsibility for the decision to publish a manuscript as a Brookings book. In reaching his judgment on the competence, accuracy, and objectivity of each study, the President is advised by the director of the appropriate research program and weighs the views of a panel of expert outside readers who report to him in confidence on the quality of the work. Publication of a work signifies that it is deemed a competent treatment worthy of public consideration but does not imply endorsement of conclusions or recommendations.

The Institution maintains its position of neutrality on issues of public policy in order to safeguard the intellectual freedom of the staff. Hence interpretations or conclusions in Brookings publications should be understood to be solely those of the authors and should not be attributed to the Institution, to its trustees, officers, or other staff members, or to the organizations that support its research.

To
my wife, Kirsten,
and
my children, Sophia and Cristoph

Foreword

DURING THE LAST DECADE *globalization* has become a fashionable term among policymakers and academics alike. It is repeatedly invoked to legitimize a policy decision, promote a policy prescription, or explain a policy outcome. No doubt it will occupy the attention of policymakers well into the next century. Yet despite the term's frequent use, little systematic analysis has been done on the sources, measurement, and implications of globalization for public policy.

In this book, Wolfgang H. Reinicke, until recently a fellow at Brookings, currently a nonresident senior fellow in the Brookings Foreign Policy Studies program and senior economist in the World Bank's Corporate Strategy Group, analyzes economic globalization and examines its implications for public policy. Although national responses, as suggested on both ends of the political spectrum in the United States and elsewhere, are flawed, they have grown in popularity and threaten to infiltrate mainstream policy discourse. To avoid a backlash against globalization when responding to the economic, social, and even security challenges that it inevitably involves, public policy—including its principles, instruments, and institutions—will have to undergo a fundamental reconstruction. Global public policy—not world government, but a network of public, private, nongovernmental, national, regional, and international organizations—provides an alternative and promising framework.

vii

viii FOREWORD

Reinicke offers three case studies that cover a broad range of today's global challenges: the need for global supervision of banking and finance; for concerted efforts to control money laundering, the engine of global criminal networks; and for management of dual-use technology trade. The book shows how the principles of global public policy have the potential to improve the capacities of governments to deal with the challenges of the twenty-first century.

The author wishes to acknowledge the many insightful and constructive comments, criticisms, and suggestions of his colleagues at the Brookings Institution, as well as James Rosenau and two anonymous reviewers of the manuscript. To the extent that the author was able to follow their recommendations, the result has been a better book. To the extent that he could not, he offers his apologies. Finally, the author would like to offer a special thanks to his wife, Kirsten, for her endless patience and encouragement, valuable ideas, and insightful comments during the course of his research.

Christopher Dall, the author's research assistant for the duration of this project, deserves special recognition for his efforts and success in tracking down valuable information and sources, maintaining several databases, and acting as a constant sounding board for the arguments developed in the book. Jan-Martin Witte, Karla Nieting, Lee Merwin, Andrea Duskas, and Claude Zullo also provided valuable research assistance. Karla Nieting, Megan de Long, and Stacey Knobler prepared draft manuscripts.

Michael Treadway edited the book, and Bridget Butkevich and Maya Dragicevic verified its factual content. Deborah Styles and Nancy Davidson shepherded the book through the production process. Ellen Garshick proofread the pages, and Deborah Patton provided the index.

The Brookings Institution gratefully acknowledges the financial support of the John D. and Catherine T. MacArthur Foundation.

The views expressed in this book are solely those of the author and should not be ascribed to the persons or organizations mentioned above, or to the trustees, officers or other staff members of the Brookings Institution.

MICHAEL H. ARMACOST
President

April 1998
Washington, D.C.

Contents

Figures

Introduction

We live in a world that is already in fact very different from the one which we have begun to comprehend, and by the time our comprehension has caught up with the new reality, the world is likely to be even more drastically different in ways that today may seem unthinkable.

—Zbigniew Brzezinski, *Out of Control*

FOR GOVERNMENT OFFICIALS—politicians and bureaucrats alike—Brzezinski's candid and perceptive observation can only arouse a great deal of discomfort.[1] For it implies, first, that change in our social and economic reality has outpaced change in the political institutions and processes in which that reality was once embedded. Equally important, Brzezinski's remark is a warning to all in the political arena that this reality will continue to change at such a pace that the only constant they are likely to be able to rely on is change itself.

Yet policymakers have been offered little advice on how to respond to this situation. Instead, there has been much "conceptual timidity,"[2] which is by no means limited to the United States. Even our rhetoric has elegantly muted the issue, labeling this new, more turbulent era by merely prefacing the familiar "cold war" with a "post." But terms such as "post," "new," or "future" give policymakers little substantive guidance and have no practical value. The "Post-[Cold War World] is what we call something when no one has figured out what it is."[3] Yet the very meaning of history implies that we have begun moving, if only drifting forward to the past, falling back on old stereotypes and the familiar policies associated with them. To be sure, there has been much talk about globalization, the future of sovereignty, the nation-state, and other such grand themes. But without a greater effort to understand the origin and nature of the current global transformation and its implications for public

1

policy, we will continue to react to events rather than act to shape the future course of world politics. Such passivity will leave our societies vulnerable to the risks that change will undoubtedly bring, while forgoing the gains that a more active policymaking could realize.

We tend to mark historical time with reference to evident discontinuities—watershed events that—with or without the benefit of hindsight—signal the end of a period in international relations. Thus much attention continues to be focused on the end of the cold war and how this historic event has affected and will continue to affect the international system. Some have escaped this somewhat blindered perspective and reminded us that the cold war was not the only thing that shaped the international system in the aftermath of World War II.[4] Liberal economic internationalism had an equal if not greater influence in structuring relations among states. This order, too, is beginning to unravel as multilateral institutions and principles lose their appeal.[5] Thus other changes in the international system, until recently less noticed yet no less dramatic, pre-date the end of the bipolar system and present an equal if not greater challenge to the international system, as they erode the structures that shaped the post–World War II international order. Indeed, the globalization of production and consumption, driven by the growing importance of technology and information processing, continues to transform our lives much more than the end of the cold war ever could.

Even the cold war's end can itself be seen as a result of economic globalization. Rapid technological innovation, the information revolution, and the deep integration of national market economies all contributed to its demise, and all are closely associated with the phenomenon of globalization, from which the centrally planned economies were for the most part excluded.[6] Quite revealing in this context is a statement made in 1983 by the chief of staff of the Soviet armed forces to an American visitor, who reported the conversation a decade later: "In the U.S. . . . small children—-even before they begin school—play with computers. Computers are everywhere in America. Here we don't even have computers in every office of the Defense Ministry. And for reasons you know well, we cannot make computers widely available in our society . . . . We will never be able to catch up with you in modern arms until we have an economic revolution. And the question is whether we can have an economic revolution without a political revolution."[7]

Thus the globalization of the world economy and the political, social, and other pressures that it created may well have been one of the primary causes of the end of the bipolar system. Globalization is therefore likely to be instrumental in determining whatever international structure will replace that system. This by no means implies that the collapse of communism did not have an important influence on these underlying forces. Rather, the end of the cold war should be viewed against the background of this already existing dynamic in the international system. Globalization, although it received relatively little attention at the time, was already a powerful force in the 1980s. But in the early 1990s it was unleashed from the constraints of the cold war, and now it has the potential to expand in geographic scope, challenging governments in a growing number of policy domains over which they once had firm control.

The many transnational challenges faced by nation-states today are a good example of this dynamic. Environmental pollution and natural resource depletion, financial integration and its associated risks, rising global inequality and the population explosion, global crime manifested in the trafficking of drugs, arms, and illicit dual-use technology—all these ills were with us during the cold war but were overshadowed by the constraints and opportunities posed by the bipolar conflict. Now they have surged to the top of the international policy agenda, not only because the end of the cold war allows policymakers to focus on these problems, but also because the deeper integration of the world economy is likely to accentuate many of them and change the context within which we need to seek solutions to them.

But economic globalization, although often treated as an irreversible trend, is by no means a foregone conclusion.[8] It is important to remember that what has been characterized as an essentially economic phenomenon takes place in a social, political, legal, and cultural setting—national and international—that has the capacity to slow and even reverse global economic trends. Thus, while economic, technological, political, and other forces have both facilitated and promoted globalization, many industrial societies are also witnessing the rise of social, political, and cultural forces working in the opposite direction.[9] At the level of domestic politics this countertrend has found its expression in the new economic nationalism and a politics of cultural identity, both of which reject closer international integration and link many of the problems these societies face, especially the social ones, to globalization.[10] Internationally, a growing number of "chaos theorists" have predicted a clash of civilizations, as Western values and norms attempt to impose themselves on other societies through the medium of globalization.[11]

Moreover, the empirical evidence on economic globalization reveals a sharp North-South divide, as many industrializing countries remain excluded. In fact, notwithstanding some spectacular growth rates in the 1980s, especially in east Asia, incomes per capita declined in almost seventy countries during the same period.[12] The globalization of communication, information, transportation, and other related activities has led many to resurrect the metaphor of the global village, which connotes a sense of unity and common heritage. But today's global village is sharply divided along several lines that are a potential source of global conflict.[13] If by "village" one means "community," in what sense can one speak of a village in which the assets of the 358 wealthiest villagers exceed the combined annual income of almost half the rest?[14] No social entity could possibly sustain such levels of inequality for long without considerable coercion. The rising tensions between globalization and the sociopolitical environment in which it is embedded must be addressed, lest they erupt and make globalization a source of overt conflict—domestic and international—rather than of peace and prosperity.

The purpose of this study is to contribute to the ongoing debate on globalization and its implications by examining the sources of conflict arising from the growing tension between globalization and governance and its institutions. From this analysis the book develops policy responses that policymakers can use to address these tensions, turning what is increasingly perceived as the threat of globalization into an opportunity.

This study operationalizes the amorphous term *governance* by defining it as the ability of a government to exercise public policy, which in turn is defined conventionally as "the governing policy within a community as embodied in its legislative and judicial enactments which serve as a basis for determining what acts are to be regarded as contrary to the public good."[15] Following Theodore Lowi's seminal article, this definition can be can be further refined by dividing public policy into three broad functional areas: distributive, regulatory, and redistributive.[16] The focus of this study is on the regulatory and supervisory dimension of public policy. It examines how economic globalization has compromised governments' ability to regulate and supervise a variety of economic activities or, following from the earlier definition, to preserve what is in the public's interest by providing public goods. However, this by no means implies that the analytical framework developed here cannot be applied to the two other domains, especially the redistributive one, which has received much attention during recent years.[17] The book uses three case studies—on the globalization of finance, crime, and dual-use technology flows—to examine the challenges that globalization presents for public regulation and supervision and how policymakers have responded. The choice of cases allows the analysis to cover a broad array of public policy issues, ranging from economic to traditional security issues, while emphasizing the growing role of transnational criminal activities.

Empirically, few would doubt that globalization is a real phenomenon, now encompassing most of the established industrial economies of the Organization for Economic Cooperation and Development (OECD) and a rising number of emerging markets.[18] Virtually all of the manufacturing sector and a growing range of service industries, including wholesale and retail trade, transport and communications, finance and business, and personal services, are either directly involved or indirectly but significantly affected. These sectors and services collectively account on average for about 70 percent of the gross domestic products (GDPs) of the Group of Seven countries (the seven largest OECD economies); the proportions in other OECD countries are similar.[19]

Chapter 1 defines and then fleshes out the concept of economic globalization by approaching it from several vantage points. The chapter first takes several empirical measures of the importance of globalization in financial services and manufacturing. These measures show that both the geography and the nature of cross-border economic activity differentiate globalization from economic interdependence, a term that became prominent in the early 1970s. The chapter then analyzes the various causes of globalization and how the relative weight of these has shifted over time. The chapter then examines the degree to which this dynamic has taken on truly global proportions. Finally, it considers the degree to which globalization is really a new trend—a common assumption that some have questioned recently.

A preliminary overview concludes that, although the term *globalization* has entered wide use, the phenomenon itself is still not well understood. Often invoked but seldom described, let alone defined, globalization has only recently captured the attention of political elites.[20] In fact, there is no commonly held definition, let alone a comprehensive conceptual framework, that would enable decisionmakers to consider the possible implications of globalization for public policy, and thus better understand some of the sources of the frictions observed to accompany it. *Globalization* has been applied to different institutions: the economy itself, the market, an industry, a sector, or a firm. The term has been used to describe a trend, a strategy, a condition, and a structure. But whatever aspect one focuses on, in most cases globalization appears to be understood as a continuous process of increasing cross-border economic flows, both financial and real, leading, according to some, to greater economic interdependence among formerly distinct national economies.[21] In this frame of reference, *globalization* and *interdependence* are used interchangeably, and globalization becomes no more than the relabeling of a phenomenon that has already received much attention in the field of international political economy.

This creates something of a paradox: a concept that, on one hand, is generally understood as a mere *quantitative* intensification of an ongoing trend dating back to the 1960s is also used, on the other hand, to refer to a fundamental *qualitative* transformation of the international system, leading to the end of the nation-state and justifying politically and socially difficult reforms in many countries around the world. Which understanding is the valid one has important implications for policy. If globalization means faster but still incremental change, there is little need or incentive for governments to reassess either their own role, or that of the institutions and principles that have governed the world economy since the end of World War II. If instead globalization denotes radical, sweeping transformation, it must be possible and necessary to differentiate between interdependence and globalization not only empirically but also at a more formal, conceptual level. Such a differentiation would provide the foundation upon which policymakers could reassess the role of government and governance under conditions of globalization.

Chapter 2 develops such a conceptual differentiation by introducing two distinctions concerning the concept of sovereignty. The first is between legal and operational sovereignty. Neither interdependence nor globalization can challenge the de jure or *legal* sovereignty of a nation-state. If anything, they challenge the de facto or *operational* sovereignty of a government, that is, its ability to conduct public policy. The second distinction is between internal and external sovereignty. The *internal* dimension depicts the relationship between the state and civil society and, in the economic realm, between the public and the private sector, both these pairs being functional opposites. Following Max Weber, a government is internally sovereign if it enjoys a monopoly of the legitimate power over a defined territory and its population.[22] The *external* dimension of sovereignty portrays relationships among states, these being functional equivalents, in the international system. In contrast to internal sovereignty, where the state is the central authority within its borders, external sovereignty has as its main characteristic the absence of a central authority. As Thomas Hobbes formulated it, anarchy is the constitutive rule of the international system.

This differentiation between internal and external sovereignty, based on the fact that they characterize entirely different relationships, is central to the analytical distinction between interdependence and globalization. Interdependence denotes a condition of mutual sensitivity and vulnerability among states in the international system, the source of which is external or systemic. Economic interdependence is generally understood as a challenge to the operational dimension of external sovereignty. In response to this challenge, governments since World War II have for the most part followed the principles of liberal macroeconomic internationalism, endorsing the stepwise but reciprocal reduction of their external economic sovereignty by lowering tariff barriers and relaxing capital controls.

The concept of external sovereignty loses much of its significance in an examination of the public policy implications of globalization. Globalization is for the most part a corporate-level phenomenon. It entails the application of new forms of industrial organization such as flexible manufacturing, coupled with the cross-border movement of increasingly intangible capital (including finance, technology, information, and the ownership or control of assets). This spatial reorganization of corporate activity leads to the emergence of a single, integrated economic geography defined by the reach of corporate industrial networks and their financial relationships. These networks and relationships cut across multiple political geographies, challenging the operational dimension of *internal* sovereignty, as governments no longer have a monopoly of the legitimate power over the territory within which these private sector actors organize themselves.[23] Globalization both integrates economically *and* fragments politically.

The fact that this political fragmentation threatens only the operational aspects of internal sovereignty in no way minimizes the challenge. In a democracy, sovereignty, in particular its internal dimension, is popular. Thus the threat to a government's ability to exercise internal sovereignty implies a threat not to the rules and institutions of democracy but to its effectiveness and efficiency. Citizens may continue to exercise their legal right to vote, but the power of that vote to shape public policy outcomes decreases with the decline in operational internal sovereignty. Ultimately, a persistent weakness and failure of internal operational sovereignty could lead to a questioning of the institutions and processes of democracy itself. This dynamic is not the only explanation for the exhaustion of democracy and the declining trust in institutions of governance, but it is an important contributing factor.

Governments will no doubt have to come with up with a response to globalization. Their basic options are discussed in chapter 3. In principle, policymakers have three strategies at their disposal: defensive intervention, offensive intervention, and global public policy. The first two continue to equate internal sovereignty with the territorial integrity of the nation-state. *Defensive intervention* relies on such economic measures as tariff and nontariff barriers or capital controls that force companies to reorganize along national lines much as they did before adopting global strategies. If such economic nationalism fails to arouse broad popular support, its political counterpart—territorial secession and partition—may do so. This political strategy, aimed at regaining internal sovereignty, has gained in popularity during the past decade.

Alternatively, policymakers may use *offensive intervention*. With this strategy, states themselves become global competitors by vying to provide within their respective territories the most attractive economic geography for corporations. Subsidies are used as a national policy tool to gain competitive advantage, and competitive deregulation has become common among financial centers and, more recently, among national tax jurisdictions. Politically, the popularity of offensive intervention has increased as policymakers attempt to broaden the reach of their internal sovereignty to match the economic geography of global corporate networks by relying on the extraterritorial application of internal sovereignty. In practice, however, both are in the long run very costly and politically unsustainable. They are bound to fail.

This raises the prospect of a third strategy, global public policy. This response reverses the adjustment path of the two geographies by placing the principal burden of adjustment on the political geography. However, this does *not* imply the formation of a global government—an unrealistic and impractical solution. Rather, global public policy decouples the operational aspects of internal sovereignty (governance) from its territorial foundation (the nation-state) and its institutional environment (the government). The institutional, operational, and political implications of such a decoupling are discussed.

Chapters 4, 5, and 6 examine the application of global public policy in three illustrative case studies. The financial services industry, the subject of chapter 4, is particularly useful to examine. Globalization has progressed a long way in this industry, making global financial markets "pioneers" in global public policy. The successes and failures in regulating and supervising the global financial services industry over the past fifteen years provide a rich empirical background. This history shows that policymakers are being forced to adapt many of their traditional tools of governance in order to respond to a rapidly evolving, technology-driven, and ever more complex global industry. So-called mixed (public and private, or government and self-) regulation, based on disclosure and coupled with stronger internal corporate controls, is becoming one of the core principles of global public policy in this field. As it does so it is altering corporate-government relations, as traditional lines of demarcation between the public and the private spheres are not only being redefined but becoming increasingly blurred, necessitating the formation of public-private partnerships in the management of global governance.

The case examined in chapter 5 stays within the domain of global finance, but considers another development that also requires the attention of public policy, namely, the growth of transnational criminal organizations. No doubt global crime has expanded with the end of the cold war. But transnational criminal cartels have benefited even more from the emergence of global networks in communications, information processing, and transportation, but especially in finance. The fight against money laundering is a crucial front in the war against global crime. The experience with U.S. efforts to combat money laundering reveals the need not only for a truly global approach to the problem, but also for a change in the incipient international efforts made to date. This redirection of effort must include a new public-private partnership to implement global anti–money laundering standards. Global public policy in this domain will not succeed unless such standards can be enforced. Both the International Monetary Fund and the World Bank will have to play a crucial role in that enforcement.

Chapter 6 stays in the domain of transnational crime but adds to it the security dimension. This case study examines the public policy implications of globalization for industries dealing in dual-use goods and technologies. Dual-use goods are defined broadly as goods that can be used for productive purposes in the civilian economy or for the development or enhancement of offensive military capabilities. Except for a very few items, a strategy of denying dual-use technology to would-be purchasers has been rendered all but impossible by the changing nature of warfare; by the role of technology, information, and communication in driving globalization; and by the sheer volume of cross-border economic activity. If it does anything, a strategy of denial only provides a false sense of security, increasing the risks of proliferation.

Drawing on the other two case studies, chapter 6 develops a basic structure for a dual-use regulatory regime that responds not only to the public interest aspects of security, but also to other and competing public and private interests that shape dual-use technology trade in today's world economy. This regime would be embodied in a proposed convention on the transfer of dual-use technology. Rather than denying technology, participants in the convention adopt a degree of transparency regarding both the transfer and the application of dual-use goods and technologies that induces the industry to behave in ways that conform to the norms of the mixed regulatory regime. Although the regime does provide for sanctions against nonparticipants, it recognizes the limitations of sanctions and instead assigns an important role to the international financial institutions to provide incentives that promote compliance.

The conclusion suggests a number of policy initiatives for global public policy. The world economy consists of a growing number of corporate networks. The current state of global governance, however, resembles at best a loose set of cross-national policy patchworks, conspicuous for their missing links and unnecessary overlaps. If global public policy is to become a viable alternative to interventionism, governments need to ensure that these patchworks evolve into networks of governance. The conclusion then takes a broader look at the likely impact of globalization on the international system. Given the still-limited reach of globalization, international relations at the end of the twentieth century are characterized by the coexistence of interdependence and globalization. Combining the two in a meaningful and constructive way will be the central challenge of international relations in the coming years, with wide-ranging repercussions on concepts such as international security—both its meaning and the institutions that provide it.

CHAPTER 1

Globalization of Economic Activity: Definition, Sources, Measurement, and Limits

THE ANALYSIS in this chapter focuses on the economic dimension of globalization—the globalization of economic activity.[1] Use of the term *globalization* has experienced explosive growth,[2] yet it is seldom defined. The words *interdependence* and *globalization* are often used interchangeably, and we have yet to determine the distinguishing features of globalization that differentiate it from interdependence.[3] This chapter defines the concept of globalization, identifies its sources, and provides an empirical overview.

Definition and Sources

The widespread and growing interest in globalization has already given rise to a number of different definitions and a number of different approaches to its analysis.[4] From the perspective of this study, the most important element in defining globalization is that it originated as—and remains—a largely *microeconomic* process. This is in contrast to the notion of interdependence, which is conceptualized and understood mostly in *macroeconomic* terms.[5] Globalization finds its origin in the changing pattern of " . . . transborder operations of firms undertaken to organise their development, production, sourcing, marketing and financing activities."[6] Heightened competition at home and abroad has led not

11

only to new developments in corporate and industrial organization, such as flexible manufacturing, but also to the cross-border movement of increasingly intangible capital, such as finance, technology, knowledge, information, and the ownership or control of assets.[7] These enable firms to establish a presence in foreign markets, realize efficiencies, and (in a process sometimes referred to as global localization) customize products for local markets.[8] Globalizing firms acquire a much wider array of inputs and support services from abroad, allowing them to take advantage of the specialization and expertise available in other locations while at the same time acquiring the knowledge and expertise to produce in local markets.

Increased economic interdependence has narrowed the distance between sovereign nations and regions, requiring closer cooperation in national macroeconomic management. Globalization, in contrast, represents the integration of an international dimension into the very organizational structure and strategic behavior of companies. It allows companies to enhance their competitive position by creating an integrated, cross-border corporate network, a "global web" of interconnected nodes in which value and wealth are generated and distributed.[9] This represents a shift from what Michael Porter has called a "multidomestic" industrial strategy, in which a company serves multiple independent local markets, to a global industrial strategy, which entails a vertical division of labor in the production of finished and intermediate goods.[10] In a multidomestic industry, competition in different countries is largely independent. Often the rationale for foreign operations is to overcome a variety of barriers, including tariffs and high costs in such areas as transportation and communication. In a global industry, however, a firm's competitive position in one country depends significantly upon its performance in other countries. A global firm is not a loose aggregation of national firms, but instead is governed by a set of globally integrated strategies that rationalize the allocation of all resources across the entire market spectrum.[11] Not only is such an organizational structure spread geographically across multiple national territories, but its geometry continues to change as companies adjust to changing economic and political conditions.[12]

This form of cross-border activity allows corporations to enter new markets along the entire length of the product cycle, and thus to exploit their technological and organizational advantages, reducing both costs and risks.[13] To succeed in an increasingly competitive environment, corporations must widen and deepen their operations, to produce and sell goods across a wider spectrum of markets, customizing their products in each.[14] As a result, their international engagement becomes more complex, going beyond arm's-length trade and traditional foreign direct investment (FDI) through new production facilities (so-called greenfield investment). A global corporate presence implies the globalization of almost all functional aspects of a firm—management, finance, research and development (R&D), marketing—as both the sources and the destinations of business operations expand.[15]

These developments further segment an increasing number of the firm's operations into separate activities carried out in different countries—what Paul Krugman has called "slicing up the value-added chain."[16] Often this strategy no longer involves the diversion of some activities to countries with lower factor costs. On the contrary, location decisions are often driven by an increasing structural similarity and a convergence of technical capacities across developed countries, heightening competition among firms located in these countries. Thus, in developing a global strategy, firms seek to locate their activities in regions with strong infrastructure externalities, such as a highly skilled supply of labor and well-developed commercial, technological, and information infrastructures. This leads to collaboration in R&D, which in turn provides global firms with access to experience and expertise that no single company or country can provide.

Underlying many of the changes taking place in the real sector of the economy has been the ongoing development of a globally integrated market for capital. The linkages between these two markets—the financial market and the market for goods and nonfinancial services—are complex. Developments in the former directly influence developments in the latter, but the reverse is also true: changes in firm structure and operation will have an impact on the financial economy. But the process is by no means synchronous, and globalization has proceeded in different ways and at varying speeds through each market.

Initially, in the 1970s, it was changes in the real economy, in the form of multinational manufacturing enterprises aggressively expanding their international presence, that drove changes in the financial sector. Banks responded to these challenges by following their corporate customers abroad, establishing overseas branch networks, and expanding their cross-border banking capabilities.[17] This was also the genesis of some early financial innovations, such as foreign exchange derivatives, which evolved out of multinationals' needs to better manage the exchange rate risks of operating overseas.[18] More recently the causality of the relationship has reversed itself somewhat, with the rapid globalization of financial markets now driving many of the changes taking place in the real sector.

However, the fact that we now witness a general trend toward the internal and external reorganization of corporate activity should in no way imply a homogenization of corporate strategies and operations around the globe—a trend often associated in people's minds with globalization. On the contrary, national differences explained by variations in historical experience (such as the length of time during which a country experienced the Industrial Revolution) and in the role of government in supporting or restraining the global aspirations of domestic corporations as well as differences across industrial sectors in their approach to globalization, continue to lead companies along divergent paths as they reorganize their cross-border activities. Such activities include financing, supply structures and trading, R&D, and investment.[19] In addition, local conditions on both the supply and the demand side that companies are likely to confront as they expand will lead to variations in their strategies, even though the overall goal in each case is to improve competitiveness.[20] Thus, for the foreseeable future, the idea of best practice will continue to be shaped by both home- and host-country factors, reminding us that this is an evolving process in a multistructured environment that defies short-term generalizations.

In addition to the consistent mutual reinforcement of trends in the globalization of manufacturing and finance, a number of common factors have induced companies—financial and manufacturing alike—to adopt global strategies. Two are of particular importance here. The first can be summarized as the liberalization and deregulation of international economic activity. Since its inception in 1948, the General Agreement on Tariffs and Trade has served as a forum for a series of eight multilateral negotiations, leading to the progressive reduction of tariff barriers.[21] This international regime facilitated corporate cross-border activity by reducing the costs of establishing a global network of corporate interaction, while creating a more predictable international environment through such principles as most-favored-nation status and the norm of reciprocity.[22] The success of these multilateral trade negotiations in reducing traditional tariff barriers and thereby facilitating increased transborder economic activity is most clearly reflected in the emergence of a new trade policy agenda, which focuses on such issues as market access and, more generally, nontariff barriers or behind-the-border issues, which today are seen as the principal impediment to further economic integration.[23] Many countries also weakened or even dismantled barriers to FDI and reduced other constraints on foreign ownership.[24] Finally, as a response to the stagflation of the 1970s, countries also deregulated in the area of competition policy. This encouraged cross-border horizontal mergers in industries other than financial services, especially transportation and communications, which facilitated new forms of cooperation among firms.[25] The lowering of trade barriers and the removal of restrictions on investment flows, together with other initiatives geared toward the liberalization of real economic activity, were also important factors encouraging companies to adopt global strategies, because they reduced companies' uncertainty about future market access.[26]

Deregulation and liberalization of international finance centered primarily on the lifting of currency and credit controls that countries had erected to prevent damaging speculative challenges to the Bretton Woods system of pegged exchange rates. After the collapse of the Bretton Woods system in 1971, the logic for such controls gradually unraveled. Governments moved to dismantle barriers to capital flows, both to facilitate the inflows that would allow them to fund deficit spending and to avoid the outflows that could result from capital moving to less regulated foreign markets. In those countries where change was slow in coming, multinationals increasingly adopted strategies of exit and evasion, using their global presence to channel financial flows to other, more favorable regulatory environments.[27] What followed, not surprisingly, was a process of competitive deregulation across the major financial markets throughout the 1970s and 1980s, as each country sought to protect its share of worldwide financial business. Between 1974 and 1984 France, Germany, Japan, the United Kingdom, and the United States eliminated virtually all of their foreign exchange controls. At the same time, measures were taken to phase out interest rate ceilings, reduce or eliminate withholding taxes on interest rate payments to nonresidents, and open domestic financial markets to foreign financial institutions.[28] As a result, by the early 1990s the restrictive Bretton Woods financial order had been completely overturned, and an almost fully liberal pattern of financial relations had emerged among the advanced industrial states, giving market operators a degree of freedom unparalleled since the 1920s.[29]

Technology, the second principal force fostering globalization, has had a twofold impact: through advances in a variety of technologies that find wide application in daily business operations, and through the rapidly declining costs of many technologies. These factors have propelled globalization in several ways.[30] For example, technological evolution has in a number of instances driven the deregulation and liberalization of economic activity, as public policy officials have struggled to keep up with the speed of innovation (especially in the case of financial services), or as modern technology in such areas as telecommunications has simply eluded regulatory efforts or rendered them too costly.

Moreover, technological innovation itself is a rich source of new products and services, especially the financial services that create international business opportunities. Computer-driven financial innovations such as twenty-four-hour trading, program trading, online trading, and electronic settlement have provided the hardware and software that now make it possible to move huge sums of money around the globe in intervals often measured in seconds. Similarly, it is hard to imagine how the market for derivatives, today a core component of the global capital market, could have grown as rapidly as it has without computers. Of equal importance are the advances in information technology that have greatly aided the gathering and distribution of political and economic data. Large-scale information networks have given individual investors access to the detailed knowledge traditionally monopolized by banks, with their strong customer ties and research departments. These networks have been a powerful force behind investor engagement in foreign capital markets, where background financial and political information has been notoriously difficult to root out. The modern portfolio manager, or indeed anyone with an Internet connection, can now tap into a stream of data transmitted around the globe by a host of information vendors.

This improved technical capability and the diffusion and decline of the costs associated with computing (especially data management), communications, information collection and storage, and transportation technologies have also led to a reduction in geographic constraints in a number of phases of the product life cycle. This, in turn, has allowed manufacturers to rationalize their operations, centralizing or decentralizing in the most effective way by organizing and managing operations on a global scale while dispersing their activities to exploit local specialization and expertise. A key example of this has been the drive by some multinationals to divide up their global operations along functional and business lines, subordinating the role of geographic units.[31]

The rapid international diffusion of microelectronics-based information technologies, especially the application of microprocessors to new products and processes in transportation and communications, has led to instantaneous worldwide information flows both within corporate entities (through so-called intranets) and between them, as well as between suppliers and customers (via the Internet). This process has created access to knowledge about new products, services, and business opportunities, stimulating competition on an increasingly global scale.[32] At the same time, declining costs have allowed firms to exploit their competitive advantage on a wider geographic scale.

Finally, the sources on which companies rely to acquire these technologies have themselves become increasingly global. The rapid growth of knowledge-intensive industries, characterized by rising R&D costs, a quickening pace of innovation, and a shortening of product life cycles, has forced firms to expand beyond their home-country borders, to search out and exploit new products and technologies more rapidly and on a wider scale. This allows them to recoup R&D expenditures more quickly and has made the development of new products more responsive to consumer needs, all of which has increased the importance of consumer-oriented services.[33] Companies can pursue any of a number of different strategies, including centralized internationalization, centrally directed decentralization, or the creation of an integrated R&D network.[34]

Meanwhile the costs and risks of developing new technologies are increasingly leading firms to collaborate in R&D and to market the resulting products jointly. This has led to the emergence of global patterns of R&D whereby firms not only share costs but also make more efficient use of growing and diverse sources of scientific input, helping them meet an increasingly globalized competition.[35] Moreover, the creation of productive knowledge generates its own diffusion, since centers of innovation cannot isolate themselves without losing much of their innovative capacity. Communicating knowledge in a global network is therefore also part of a strategy to keep up-to-date without complicating proprietary control.[36] Of course, companies can use a variety of strategies to spread R&D activities among a number of countries, and for the most part information has been distributed among countries asymmetrically.[37] There are indications, however, that as developing countries have improved their infrastructure, including the supply of inexpensive skilled labor, an increasing number of firms have begun to locate some of their R&D activities there.[38] The relative importance of these factors has shifted over time, but there is no doubt that, since the late 1980s, technological change and innovation have been by far the most important factors in determining the course of globalization and the challenges it has created for public policy.

Measurement

One cannot capture the extent and impact of globalization through quantitative measures alone, such as increases in FDI, international trade, and cross-border financial flows. Rather, as the definition of globalization offered above indicates, one must also take into account changes in the organizational logic of companies and in corporate behavior. In manufacturing, the changing geographic concentration and composition of FDI (in mergers and acquisitions versus greenfield investment) and trade (finished versus intermediate products) and the rise of interfirm strategic alliances reflect such qualitative changes. In the financial markets globalization is best captured by the phenomenon of securitization, which has fundamentally altered the nature of international finance. However, as will become apparent, data on some of these indicators of globalization remain scant, and data from different sources are not always compatible. Moreover, given that an examination of global corporate strategies entails a microeconomic analysis, data collection efforts to date have relied on industry surveys and other similar methods, including media surveys. Thus national and international organizations should be permitted and indeed encouraged to make every effort to enhance their capacity to monitor global economic activity to permit a better understanding of its dynamics and of its policy implications.

Foreign Direct Investment

The strongest evidence of the globalization of industry comes from the rapid growth and geographic deconcentration of FDI flows since the early to mid-1980s. Between 1985 and 1990, worldwide FDI *flows* rose at an average annual rate of 31 percent, nearly three times faster than global trade or output (figure 1-1). Over the same period the global *stock* of foreign investment also rose dramatically, from $700 billion to $1.7 trillion, almost doubling as a share of world output.[39] Although this growth was somewhat checked by the onset of the global recession during the early 1990s, more recent figures indicate that FDI flows have

Figure 1-1. *Global Output, Trade, and Foreign Direct Investment,*
1980–95

Index (1980 = 100)

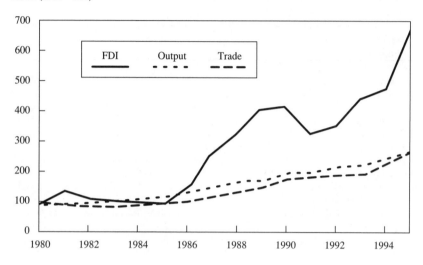

Sources: IMF, *Balance of Payments Statistics Yearbook* (Washington, various issues); *International Financial Statistics,* CD-ROM and various issues; World Bank, *World Tables,* various issues; and World Bank, *World Development Indicators,* CD-ROM.

now rebounded to their prerecession highs. Estimates for 1996 put worldwide FDI flows that year at $350 billion, which if accurate would eclipse the previous high posted in 1995.[40] It is widely recognized today that FDI, with its associated effects on international trade, international capital markets, and the transfer of technology, knowledge, ownership, and control, has become the principal vehicle of the deeper integration of the world economy.

Transnational corporations number at least 45,000 parent firms, which in turn control over 280,000 foreign affiliates worldwide.[41] In 1994, they accounted for roughly one-third of global product.[42] Reflecting the more rapid growth of FDI than trade in the mid- and late 1980s, sales of foreign affiliates during this period increased at a consistently faster rate than global exports. By 1995 these sales were estimated to be somewhere in the neighborhood of $7.0 trillion, equivalent to 115 percent of total world exports of merchandise and commercial services.[43] Not surprisingly, many economies have come to rely heavily on the increasing

Table 1-1. *Degree of Transnationalization of U.S. Nonbank Transnational Corporations, by Sector, 1983–91*

Percent

Sector	1983	1985	1988	1991
Assets				
Primary	69.5	72.1	74.4	80.1
Secondary	19.4	18.5	21.2	22.9
Tertiary	18.1	16.8	19.5	23.7
Sales				
Primary	79.3	78.8	73.2	83.5
Secondary	25.0	23.9	29.6	31.8
Tertiary	27.0	24.9	28.1	29.3
Employment				
Primary	69.2	69.8	68.9	78.0
Secondary	28.3	28.7	29.3	30.2
Tertiary	18.7	18.8	20.2	22.4

Source: UNCTAD, Division on Transnational Corporations and Investment, based on U.S. Department of Commerce, *U.S. Direct Investment Abroad: Operations of U.S. Parent Companies and Their Foreign Affiliates* (GPO, various issues), as found in UNCTAD, *World Investment Report: Transnational Corporations, Employment and the Workplace* (Geneva, 1994), p. 135, table III.10.

number of jobs provided by these foreign affiliates, many of which are highly paid, highly skilled positions.[44] But the networks of multinational enterprises have become not only larger and more prolific, but also more globalized, generally increasing their foreign operations as a proportion of total business (table 1-1).

One notable feature of the rapid expansion of FDI has been the prominent role of mergers and acquisitions (M&As). Although it is difficult to say exactly what proportion of FDI is attributable to M&As rather than greenfield investment, these transactions represent a growing share of all investment flows and are consequently a good barometer for predicting the movement of FDI as a whole.[45] Estimates of the dollar value of M&As vary considerably, but most sources agree that 1996 was yet another record year, with one estimate putting the total at $263 billion, up from $237 billion in 1995.[46] To a large extent the rapid growth of M&A activity in the late 1980s and again in the mid-1990s has been a result of firms wanting to establish a global presence and to protect, consolidate, and advance that presence. Such reorganizations often involve selling off assets that do not belong to the firm's core business, while acquiring technical know-how, brand names, and supplier and distribution networks—all assets likely to enhance the firm's competitiveness in a particular sector worldwide. Domestic producers have seen their protected markets eaten away by imports and the local production of foreign multinationals, compelling them also to invest abroad to diversify their sales. Rather than achieve this through greenfield investment, many firms have found it cheaper and far quicker to merge with or simply acquire a foreign company (often a competitor). Not only have the development of new financial instruments and the deregulation of capital markets made it easier for firms to finance their rapid international expansion, but M&As in the financial services industry itself have been one the largest categories.[47]

The pattern and composition of FDI confirm that a change has taken place in the corporate strategy of multinationals that is characteristic of globalization. First, a large share of the FDI explosion and the growth in M&As during the mid- and late 1980s was directly attributable to a surge of investment flows into developed rather than developing economies. Although the bulk of this investment still came from other developed countries, the sources of flows within this group became more varied, with Japan in particular joining the ranks of major foreign investors.[48] This trend differs significantly from that in earlier periods, when the United States dominated investment outflows, and either resource-rich or low-wage industrializing countries were the primary target.[49]

Second, as the geographic orientation of FDI has shifted, so has its composition. Increasingly, FDI (particularly that originating in developed countries) has shifted away from primary industries (resource extraction and agriculture) and basic manufacturing to high-value-added, knowledge- and R&D-intensive manufacturing, and to an increasing number of service industries. Data compiled by the U.S. Department of Commerce show that the share of U.S. investment stock abroad accounted for by investments in primary industries fell from 15 percent of the total in 1985 to roughly 7 percent in 1994. In their place, the stock of investment in tertiary (service) industries has risen, from 41 percent in 1985 to 52 percent in 1994.[50] Together these trends confirm the growing propensity of multinational enterprises to adopt a global strategy, consolidating and rationalizing their operations across a growing number of national markets with comparable technical capacities and broad structural similarities.

International Interfirm Collaboration

The internalization of assets and activities through cross-border M&As and other forms of FDI are not the only way a firm can gain global exposure on both the supply and the demand side. To an ever greater extent, firms that desire a global presence are achieving it through minority stakes in foreign firms or through nonequity vehicles, mainly in the form of international alliances and collaboration agreements, in functional areas ranging from R&D to sales and marketing.[51] These arrangements may be horizontal, linking firms in different industries, or vertical, linking firms at different stages of production in the same industry. In general, collaboration enables firms to undertake projects that exceed the technical and financial resources of any one firm, or allows them access to each other's markets even in the face of investment and regulatory impediments to foreign firms. Alliances are most common in trade- and technology-intensive manufacturing industries such as automobiles, aerospace, computers and semiconductors, and telecommunications.[52]

These agreements can take a variety of forms ranging from joint ventures to licensing deals to research consortia to supply arrangements.[53] Some are very tightly focused, enabling a firm to achieve a specific tactical goal, such as breaking into a new market or achieving its sales objective for a given export market. Others are more long term and can be quite far-reaching in scope, leading in many cases to a gradual merging of corporate identities and an eventual buyout of one partner by the other.

National statistical offices do not collect data on interfirm collaboration, and most measures of this trend are as a result assembled from a mixture of surveys and media reports. One such survey recently estimated that "the top 1,000 U.S. firms now draw nearly 6 per cent of their revenues from alliances, a fourfold increase since 1987."[54] Perhaps the most comprehensive effort to date to gather data on interfirm collaboration is a database maintained by the Maastricht Economic Research Institute on Innovation and Technology (MERIT).[55] The MERIT data document a sharp increase in cross-border interfirm alliances starting in the early 1980s and peaking toward the end of the decade. Thus there were 86 such alliances in the period 1973–76, 177 during 1977–80, 509 during 1981–84, and 988 during 1985–88.[56] Figures for the 1990s suggest that despite a general decline in the number of new interfirm agreements, demand for these agreements in at least three high-technology sectors—

biotechnology, information technology, and new materials—has been similar to that exhibited in the mid-1980s.[57]

The motivations for cross-border interfirm collaboration largely parallel those for FDI, with a few exceptions. Most notably, firms that collaborate often do so because it is cheaper and quicker than globalizing through FDI. This calculation has been sharpened by the increasingly competitive nature of global markets. As was discussed above, growing competition requires that companies maintain some form of corporate presence in more than one country, and small and medium-size enterprises can often only do this through low-cost alliances and collaboration agreements.[58]

Developments in technology-intensive industries have also increased the attractiveness of interfirm collaboration. As already discussed, the rapid pace of innovation in these industries and the high costs of keeping up make alliances a useful way of defraying spiraling R&D expenses.[59] This observation is borne out by figures from the MERIT database, which show that alliances are largely concentrated in the fields of information technology and biotechnology, where R&D costs loom large in total production costs (figure 1-2). Finally, in cases where firm nationality is an issue, for example where governments have erected barriers to foreign investment in the form of antitrust laws or restrictions on foreign ownership, collaborative linkages give allied firms the political advantage of being a local firm almost anywhere. This provides another means of overcoming national political boundaries in what from a firm's perspective is a global market.

Changing Patterns of International Trade

The rapid growth of international trade has been one of the most salient features of the postwar economic landscape. In virtually every year since 1950, growth of world merchandise trade has exceeded that of world merchandise output. Trade has expanded at an average annual rate of slightly more than 6 percent over that period, compared with only 4 percent for world output.[60] Not surprisingly, when asked what globalization means to them, most people will immediately point to these increasing trade linkages between countries. Trade and globalization, at least in the public mind, are synonymous.

But this is only partly true. As mentioned at the beginning of the chapter, globalization is much more than the quantitative intensification

Figure 1-2. *Composition of Domestic and International Strategic Technology Alliances, by Industry, 1990–93*

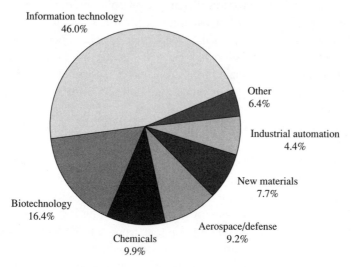

Source: Maastricht Economic Research Institute on Innovation and Technology—Cooperative Agreements and Technology Indicators (MERIT-CATI) database.

of a preexisting trend. Indeed, if globalization were just a question of the quantity of trade, the contemporary experience would be little different from that of the early years of this century, when many countries experienced levels of trade almost equal (in proportion to output) to today's. Rather, *globalization* properly refers also to a qualitative change in the organization and nature of trade. It is not just how much countries trade with each other that is important, but also the way in which this trade is structured: what goods and services are traded, and between whom they are traded.

Since the 1960s two forms of trade have progressively come to dominate the cross-border flow of goods, and to a lesser extent that of services. These are intrafirm trade and trade related to the international sourcing of intermediate inputs.[61] Both forms are implicitly tied to globalization and reflect the progressive structuring of international trade around the operations of global corporations and international interfirm arrangements for production and supply. As will become apparent, both forms of trade have increasingly little in common with the standard textbook case of comparative advantage.[62]

INTRAFIRM TRADE. Intrafirm trade (IFT), defined as trade between operations of the same multinational in different countries, is the most overt example of how trade associated with the globalization of companies has displaced the traditional concept of trade as an exchange between two unrelated parties (so-called arm's-length trade). In effect, IFT amounts to a substitution of these market-based arm's-length transactions by internal, nonmarket transactions within the multinational firm. A simple example would be the shipment of truck axles from a General Motors (GM) plant in the United States to another GM affiliate in Brazil. Although the transaction would be counted as a U.S. export, the goods never leave the corporate "boundaries" of GM, and the price of the sale is not determined in the open market as an arm's-length export would be. Instead, the transaction occurs at a notional transfer price, which may or may not be similar to the price of the same or similar goods on the open market. In many cases, equivalent open-market transactions for the product do not even exist.

Motives for IFT vary but include the desire of multinationals to rationalize and integrate their activities across different countries, the presence of market imperfections and high transaction costs, and government policies affecting taxes, tariffs, competition, and investment.[63] Another motivation is the fact that intangible assets such as R&D, industrial expertise, and knowledge related to one firm's operations cannot be easily transferred to another through market mechanisms. IFT may also be the response of a multinational to a change in exchange rates. For example, a multinational with production and marketing operations on both sides of an exchange rate can choose to increase production in the country whose currency is depreciating and therefore whose relative production costs are falling. The increased output is then shipped to the country with the appreciating currency, where relative costs have risen, and sold through the existing sales network, insulating the company from the exchange rate fluctuation.[64]

Data on IFT are notoriously limited and reduce both the geographic breadth of the analysis and the extent to which one can draw any firm conclusions.[65] At a basic level, the fact that IFT is valued according to a multinational's internal transfer pricing introduces considerable uncertainty into the measurement of IFT, as firms may over- or underinvoice an intrafirm transaction to avoid taxes.[66] The only comprehensive set of data on IFT available is for the United States only and is compiled by the U.S. Department of Commerce. The data extend only as far back as 1982 on a continuous basis. Not surprisingly, the result is that the extent of this form of trade is often underappreciated, and to date relatively little is known about its causes and consequences.

IFT is an important component of U.S. trade. In 1995, the latest date for which figures are available, IFT accounted for 36 percent of U.S. exports of goods and 43 percent of imports.[67] Because IFT is more concentrated in U.S. imports than in exports, it accounts for a disproportionately large share of the U.S. trade deficit.[68] In 1995, 71 percent of the U.S. merchandise trade deficit was attributable to IFT, whereas IFT's share of total U.S. trade was only 40 percent.[69]

Two additional features of the U.S. data on IFT stand out. First, total IFT (exports and imports combined) increased at an annual average rate of about 9 percent between 1982 and 1995, only slightly above the rate of increase for total trade, which grew at a fraction over 8 percent during the same period. As a result, the share of IFT in total U.S. trade increased only marginally over the space of these twelve years. This finding is somewhat paradoxical given the previously noted explosion of foreign investment flows beginning in the mid-1980s, much of which was in the form of foreign investment in the U.S. economy. Although FDI does not have to result in IFT, FDI can promote trade, including IFT, through the import and export activities of foreign affiliates, and in a number of cases variations in the volume and direction of IFT have been found to be consistent with variations in the distribution of FDI.[70] Why, then, has the IFT share of U.S. trade not increased in tandem with the recent expansion of FDI?

One explanation might be that much of the FDI over this period was directed at expanding the local production capabilities of multinationals' foreign affiliates. This form of trade-destroying FDI might actually lead to a decrease in IFT as foreign affiliates produce locally many of the intermediate inputs formerly supplied by the parent company. Ironically, as the foreign affiliate increases its ability to produce locally, it may in turn become a source of intermediate inputs for other affiliates in the same company network. Returning to the earlier example, this would be equivalent to one of GM's British affiliates supplying inputs for another affiliate in Germany that had previously been supplied through exports from the United States. From GM's perspective the level of IFT is unchanged, but because this trade no longer crosses the U.S. border, it is no longer counted as a U.S. intrafirm export. That this shifting of production away from the parent company is a common practice is to some extent borne out by data from the operations of U.S. multinationals, which show affiliate-affiliate IFT to have grown faster than parent-affiliate IFT over the 1982–95 period.

The second notable feature of U.S. IFT is its increasing role in the exports and imports of U.S. parent companies. By 1994 IFT accounted for almost 46 percent of all U.S. parents' trade, up from 33 percent in 1982.[71] This is a quite different picture from IFT's share in total trade, which, as noted earlier, has remained flat. The difference here concerns the movement of the two baselines. Whereas total trade has increased at about the same pace as IFT since 1982, trade associated with U.S. parents has shown a pronounced decline, from 57 percent of their total trade in 1982 to 47 percent in 1994.[72] What these various measures seem to indicate is that, even as their trading operations have declined as a share of total trade, U.S. multinationals have become tighter, more globally integrated units, internalizing an ever-increasing share of their cross-border transactions.

Besides the United States, only one other country, Japan, collects time-series data on IFT. Unfortunately, the Japanese data are extremely limited, and their lack of coverage makes any comparison with U.S. figures impossible. What can be determined is that, for the limited number of Japanese multinationals surveyed, IFT plays an important role and nearly doubled as a share of their total trade between 1980 and 1993.[73]

INTERNATIONAL SOURCING OF INTERMEDIATE INPUTS. The second way in which globalization has come to structure international trade is through the expansion of international sourcing. This term is used here to describe a range of practices that have as their central theme the disaggregation of the production process into a number of stages, spread across a number of countries. Included under this heading are intraindustry trade, defined as two-way trade in similar manufactured products, and the concept of "slicing up the value-added chain."[74] All of these concepts capture, from slightly different angles, the process by which firms now seek to harness internationally the benefits of product differentiation and economies of scale.

One way of conceptualizing the changes resulting from international sourcing is to look at how export transactions have changed over the years. Typically, goods that in the past were associated with a single export transaction, the transfer of the finished good to the foreign market, are today often the object of numerous trade transactions. Thus, a good may be assembled in one country from components produced in other countries, and these in turn may be assembled from subcomponents produced in yet other countries. As a result, the trade involved in the global production of a finished good may easily be several times the value added through all the stages of its production.[75] Among the forces driving this trend, the most important are the declining costs of computing, communication, and transportation; the growing complexity of modern manufacturing; and the adoption of new forms of production.

Although there are obvious differences between international sourcing and IFT—the latter is by definition limited to multinationals—the two concepts often overlap, and their effects on the structure and nature of international trade can be quite similar. To continue with the example of GM, that company's intrafirm trade with its affiliate in Germany is also a case of international sourcing and, in all likelihood, of intraindustry trade. Even when international sourcing takes place outside of an intrafirm network, it may still share many of the same characteristics as IFT, because a large proportion of international sourcing is conducted by firms linked through interfirm partnerships, alliances, and joint ventures. Typically these linkages are a response to the demands of modern production techniques, such as flexible production and just-in-time delivery, and are intended to ensure the availability, quality, and price of intermediate inputs. The resulting collaborative relationships are often non-price-regulated, require relatively secure long-term commitments, and favor mutual feedback of information. Increasingly, suppliers even play an active role in designing the products they supply.[76] As in the case of IFT, much of the trade within these network organizations is effectively off-market and bears little resemblance to the classic textbook model of international trade. A prominent example of this trend is the cross-border operations of the Japanese *keiretsu,* or interlinked business groups.

Data from the Organization for Economic Cooperation and Development (OECD) suggest that international sourcing has been growing rapidly since the early 1970s. As table 1-2 shows, the ratio of goods sourced abroad to goods sourced domestically increased in each of the survey countries, with the largest increases generally occurring in the most recent years. Evidence from intraindustry trade paints a similar picture, with similarly substantial increases over the last three decades. By 1991 as many as fourteen members of the OECD had intraindustry trade ratios of over 50 percent for trade within the OECD area, whereas only two countries had ratios that high in 1964.[77] Predictably, levels of international sourcing vary greatly across industries. The chemical and

Table 1-2. *Ratio of Imported to Domestic Sourcing of Intermediate Inputs for Six OECD Countries*

Percent

Country	Early 1970s	Mid- to late 1970s	Mid-1980s
Canada	34	37	50
France	21	25	38
Germany	n.a.	21	34
Japan	5	6	7
United Kingdom	16	32	37
United States	7	8	13

Source: David Levy, "International Production and Sourcing: Trends and Issues," *STI Review,* no. 13 (December 1993), p. 31, table 1.

n.a. Not available.

pharmaceutical industries, for instance, do not rely heavily on intermediate inputs because many of their critical technologies are associated with processes, which are hard to outsource. The computer industry, however, is extremely dependent on outsourcing, because few companies can cope with the spiraling costs of keeping up with the many different technologies that go into the manufacture of computers.

Financial Services

As mentioned above, cross-border activity in the financial services industry has been increasing for many decades, in parallel with increasing interdependence in the real economy. This process received an additional stimulus with the collapse of the Bretton Woods system of pegged exchange rates in 1971. The last fifteen years, however, have witnessed both an acceleration and a qualitative transformation. In addition to an international market for bank-intermediated debt, which has existed for some time, there are now international markets for foreign exchange, bonds, and, increasingly, equities. Today when we talk of financial globalization we are referring to the creation of a global pool of highly liquid capital that can move quickly and freely between countries and assets. The major actors in this landscape are a relatively small number of highly capitalized financial conglomerates operating in a range of markets across a number of locations.

The most remarkable development in the international financial sector has been the tremendous growth in international financial flows, and

Figure 1-3. *Global Trade, Foreign Direct Investment, and Portfolio Investment Flows, 1980–95*

Index (1980 = 100)

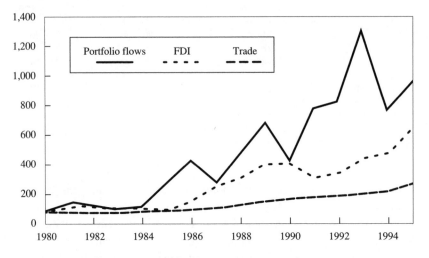

Sources: IMF, *Balance of Payments Statistics Yearbook* (Washington, various issues) and *International Financial Statistics,* CD-ROM and various issues; World Bank, *World Tables,* various issues; and World Bank, *World Development Indicators,* CD-ROM.

specifically in portfolio flows, which represent the cross-border purchase of bonds and equities. As figure 1-3 shows, the expansion of these flows has outstripped even the rapid growth of FDI and international trade. The main causes of this trend have been deregulation, technological innovation, and the almost universal desire of governments to run large current account deficits. Aggregate transactions, which represent the sum of all trading rather than the net purchase of portfolio instruments, have grown even faster, as innovations such as computer-controlled and online trading have sharply increased the number of international transactions executed in the world's bond and stock markets each day. In the United Kingdom the volume of these transactions had reached a staggering 1,000 percent of GDP by 1993.[78] All of this activity has resulted in a ballooning of the foreign exchange markets, which by 1995 were estimated to be handling nearly $1.2 trillion each day. By comparison, the total foreign exchange reserves of all governments (which represent their ability to intervene in the foreign exchange markets) stood at a little over $670 billion.[79]

Figure 1-4. *Cross-Border Trading in Equities, 1979–95*

Trillions of U.S. dollars   Percent

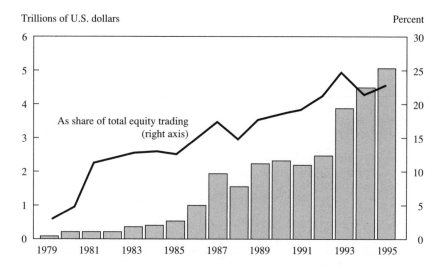

Source: Baring Securities, *The Financial Silk Road . . . A Fifth Wave of Global Money, Cross Border Equity Flows,* vol. 2 (London, July 1995), p. 12, fig. 3.

As financial flows grow ever larger, many capital markets are becoming more integrated. In most cases, international financial transactions have grown as fast as or faster than domestic activity, resulting in increasing foreign penetration and the integration of separate national financial markets. Figure 1-4, which charts the growth of cross-border equity trading as a share of total (domestic and cross-border) equity trading, indicates the extent to which equity markets have become integrated. By 1995 it was estimated that one in five equity transactions worldwide was made by or on behalf of a foreign investor.[80] The evidence from government bond markets is similar, with foreign investors in many countries increasing their holdings of government debt relative to domestic investors (table 1-3).[81] In the United States, which saw the share of government debt in the hands of foreign investors decline briefly in the early 1990s, the share of marketable debt held by foreigners amounted to 33 percent in 1996.[82]

Another way of looking at capital market integration is to measure the extent to which returns on similar assets traded in different markets have been equalized.[83] If financial markets are indeed fully integrated, the returns to capital in the form of interest rates should be roughly equal

Table 1-3. *Foreign Holdings of Central Government Debt in Six OECD Countries, 1980–92[a]*

Percent of total debt outstanding

Country	1980	1986	1992
United States[b]	21.04	16.44	19.36
Germany[c]	9.14	20.22	26.28
France[d]	. . .	0.84	42.61
Sweden[e]	27.97	28.00	45.75
United Kingdom[f]	8.89	9.78	17.43
Canada[g]	13.87	17.61	24.51

Source: Adapted from International Monetary Fund, *International Capital Markets: Developments, Prospects, and Policy Issues* (September 1994), pp. 40-41, table 7.

a. Data are as of March 31 for the United Kingdom, and as of December 31 for all other countries.

b. Securities are valued at par. Holdings of debt include foreign accounts and international accounts.

c. Data for 1980 and 1986 include debt of the federal government, the Equalization of Burdens Fund, the ERP Special Fund, the Länder governments, and local authorities. Data for 1992 include debt of the federal government, the German Unity Fund, the Debt-Processing Fund, the ERP Special Fund, and the Länder governments and local authorities (including those of eastern Germany). Data exclude mutual indebtedness of public authorities and holdings of the Bundesbank.

d. Data represent holdings of central government securities, excluding Bank of France holdings.

e. Data represent holdings of national debt, excluding the holdings of the Riksbank, other state institutions and funds, and the National Pension Insurance Fund. Data for 1980 and 1986 include debt held by all holders abroad; data for 1992 include external debt in kronor and debt in foreign currency.

f. Data represent total market holdings of gilts (U.K. government securities).

g. Data include Government of Canada direct securities and loans (underlying outstanding amounts are at par value), excluding holdings of securities by the Bank of Canada and in Government of Canada accounts.

across their borders. A number of these "law-of-one-price" tests exist, and at least two indicate that there has been considerable capital market integration over the last fifteen years. The first test compares yields on similar onshore and offshore (Eurocurrency) deposits in the same currency. These yields converged markedly during the 1980s, suggesting a move toward closer integration. The second test takes this one step further by measuring the yields (adjusted for foreign exchange risk) on similar deposits in different currencies. Here again there has been a convergence, especially in the currencies of the industrial countries and other countries that have removed capital controls. That there are limits to capital market integration is revealed by two further tests, which subject the law of one price to somewhat more rigorous assumptions. First, in a integrated capital market one would expect yields on deposits in different currencies to be similar, even without adjustment for foreign exchange risk. Second, if capital market integration indeed holds, one would also expect a convergence of real as well as nominal yields. In both cases, results indicate that the current level of international financial integration falls short of what would be expected in a truly integrated financial market.

To this point the discussion has focused largely on quantitative measures of the size and integration of the global capital market. Significantly, however, this quantitative sketch describes only part of the changes brought about by globalization. As seen earlier in the discussion of its impact on the manufacturing sector, globalization is as much a qualitative as a quantitative transformation. In manufacturing this is evidenced by changes in the organizational logic of companies and in corporate behavior, which are captured by looking at the direction and composition of foreign trade and investment and the rise of interfirm strategic alliances. In finance it is best captured by the phenomenon of securitization, the rise of derivative markets, and the institutionalization of saving and investment, which together have not only increased the size of international financial markets but changed their very nature.

SECURITIZATION. *Securitization* broadly describes the process by which financial intermediation—the bringing together of savers and borrowers—has been moving rapidly from banks to capital markets. This process has been evident in some form or another since the early 1980s. In its earliest guise, securitization referred simply to the issuance of debt securities as relatively close substitutes for bank credit. Rather than obtaining financing from banks, companies would issue bonds, commercial paper, and medium-term notes to meet their borrowing needs. More recently, the term has become associated specifically with the process of converting cash flows from certain assets, such as home mortgages or loans to foreign governments, into tradable securities.[84] Today securities are not just alternatives to bank loans but, in the case of asset- and mortgage-backed securities, actually *are* bank loans that have been repackaged.

Securitization first developed as a reaction to the economic uncertainty engendered by high rates of inflation as well as volatile interest and exchange rates. Because securities were much more flexible than bank loans and could more easily be tailored to investors' needs, they offered savers and investors greater protection from the economic gyrations that followed the

Table 1-4. *Private Sector Capital Outflows from Major Industrialized Countries, Annual Average, 1975–95*

Outflows	1975–79	1980–84	1985–89	1990–94	1990	1991	1992	1993	1994	1995[a]
	Billions of dollars									
Equities	3.3	10.4	37.5	88.7	22.9	91.9	51.1	166.1	111.7	80.0
Bonds	9.1	31.4	139.3	181.7	128.7	187.6	199.7	271.6	120.9	250.0
Total portfolio investment	12.4	41.8	176.8	270.4	151.6	279.5	250.8	437.7	232.6	330.0
Direct investment	34.7	41.0	128.4	176.8	209.5	165.5	158.9	152.5	197.8	215.0
Banking (excluding interbank)	46.2	38.7	23.5	45.0	39.9	7.2	65.3	63.9	48.5	55.0
Total	93.3	121.5	328.7	492.2	401.0	452.2	475.0	654.1	478.9	600.0
	Percent of total									
Equities	3.5	8.6	11.4	18.0	5.7	20.3	10.8	25.4	23.3	13.3
Bonds	9.8	25.8	42.4	36.9	32.1	41.5	42.0	41.5	25.2	41.7
Total portfolio investment	13.3	34.4	53.8	54.9	37.8	61.8	52.8	66.9	48.6	55.0
Direct investment	37.2	33.7	39.1	35.9	52.2	36.6	33.5	23.3	41.3	35.8
Banking (excluding interbank)	49.5	31.9	7.1	9.1	10.0	1.6	13.7	9.8	10.1	9.2

Source: Baring Securities, *The Financial Silk Road . . . A Fifth Wave of Global Money: Cross Border Equity Flows*, vol. 2 (London, July 1995), p. 9, table 2.
a. Estimated.

collapse of the Bretton Woods system of pegged exchange rates and the two oil crises of the 1970s. Increasingly, however, cost has become securitization's main advantage over bank loans, as securities markets are now able to intermediate funds at a fraction of the cost of banks.

Securitization is fundamentally altering the system of international financial intermediation. Some sense of the changes taking place is given in table 1-4, which displays a breakdown of capital outflows from the OECD countries over a twenty-year period. During this time the relative importance of portfolio flows and banking flows has been almost completely reversed, with portfolio flows now occupying the dominant position.[85] This trend is likely to continue. It is estimated that by 1992, in the United States alone, the stock of securitized mortgages, loans, and asset-backed commercial paper stood at $1 trillion and had been growing at a compound annual growth rate of 34 percent for the previous four years.[86] As barriers to financial integration come down, more and more of these securitized domestic assets will be traded across borders and find their way into the portfolios of foreign investors.

This is precisely why securitization is so important to financial globalization. Securitization drives the pricing and market availability of assets that were previously nontradable. As these nontradables are turned into securities, they become linked to the global pool of liquid capital and can then be freely bought and sold internationally. As a result, it is now possible for a Japanese pension company to buy U.S. residential mortgages, for a German insurance company to invest in corporate loans made by a British bank, or for a U.S. investment bank to trade in pools of developing-country debt formerly held as bank loans.

The move to securitization does not mean that banks will cease to play a role in international finance. Stock-in-trade banking services such as deposit taking and payment services will remain important. However, as their traditional lending functions are gradually usurped by capital markets, banks will be forced to develop new revenue sources. The growing importance to banks' balance sheets of fee-based income and proprietary trading are the first examples of this shift in emphasis.[87]

DERIVATIVES. Another novel and important feature of the financial services industry, related to securitization, has been the emergence of financial derivatives markets, which in recent years have developed as powerful parallels to the underlying currency, bond, and equity markets. Currency spot transactions have given rise to currency derivatives, bond

Table 1-5. *Markets for Selected Financial Derivative Instruments, 1989–96*

Billions of U.S. dollars, notional amounts outstanding at year-end

Instrument	1989	1990	1991	1992	1993	1994	1995	1996
Exchange-traded instruments	1,766.6	2,290.2	3,519.3	4,634.4	7,771.1	8,862.5	9,188.2	9,884.2
Interest rate futures	1,200.8	1,454.5	2,156.7	2,913.0	4,958.7	5,777.6	5,863.4	5,431.1
Interest rate options[a]	387.9	599.5	1,072.6	1,385.4	2,362.4	2,623.6	2,741.8	3,277.8
Currency futures	15.9	16.9	18.3	26.5	34.7	40.1	38.3	50.3
Currency options[a]	50.2	56.5	62.9	71.1	75.6	55.6	43.2	46.5
Stock market index futures	41.3	69.1	76.0	79.8	110.0	127.3	172.2	198.6
Stock market index options[a]	70.6	93.7	132.8	158.6	229.7	238.3	329.3	380.2
Over-the-counter instruments[b]	n.a.	3,450.3	4,449.4	5,345.7	8,474.6	11,303.2	17,712.6	24,292.0
Interest rate swaps	1,502.6	2,311.5	3,065.1	3,850.8	6,177.3	8,815.6	12,810.7	n.a.
Currency swaps[c]	449.1	577.5	807.2	860.4	899.6	914.8	1,197.4	n.a.
Other swap-related derivatives[d]	n.a.	561.3	577.2	634.5	1,397.6	1,572.8	3,704.5	n.a.

Sources: Futures Industry Association, various futures and options exchanges, calculations by the International Swaps and Derivatives Association (ISDA) and the Bank for International Settlements, as found in Bank for International Settlements, *65th Annual Report, 1st April 1994–31st March 1995* (Basle, June 12, 1995), p. 184, table VIII.10; and Bank for International Settlements, *67th Annual Report, 1st April 1996–31st March 1997* (Basle, June 9, 1997), p. 131, table VII.5.

n.a. Not available.

a. Calls and puts.

b. Data collected by ISDA only; the two sides of contracts between ISDA members are reported once only.

c. Adjusted for reporting of both currencies, including cross-currency interest rate swaps.

d. Caps, collars, floors, and swaptions.

markets have spawned interest rate derivatives, and equity markets are now mirrored in equity-based derivatives. The growth of these derivative instruments has been dramatic, far outstripping that in any of the under-lying markets (table 1-5). The consequences of this trend for interna-tional financial integration have been particularly significant.

Perhaps most important, derivatives (financial instruments whose prices are derived from the underlying financial asset) help investors better manage the risk of cross-border activities by unbundling that risk into its various constituent elements. An investor purchasing equity in a foreign oil producer would, for instance, be exposed not only to the operating risk of the company but also to currency risk, the risk of petroleum price fluctua-tions, and liquidity risk. Derivatives allow the investor to disaggregate these risks and take on only those that he or she is willing to bear. The cur-rency risk can be hedged through a currency swap, the future price of petroleum can be locked in using petroleum futures, and the potential liq-uidity risk of the equity can be managed through an equity swap.[88]

Beyond their utility in risk management or hedging, derivatives are powerful tools for cross-border speculation. Currency options, for instance, allow large investors to place large bets on the movement of a currency for a fraction of the cost of holding a comparable position in dollars or yen. Similarly, stock index derivatives enable speculators to take positions on the movement of foreign equity markets without acquiring any foreign stock. Although all these parallel markets are linked to a stock market in some country, or to a national currency, their location is simply a function of where a demand develops, or where a conducive regulatory environment can be found, irrespective of national borders. Thus, the largest market for options on German government bonds is in London, as the activities of Barings trader Nick Leeson revealed. Significant speculation on the Nikkei 225 (an index of Japan-ese equities) takes place in Singapore, and trading in Japanese bond futures takes place in Chicago. Ultimately, the proliferation of these instruments and markets has had a powerful arbitraging effect, bringing both prices and regulations across borders closer together.

INSTITUTIONALIZATION. Increasingly, the leading actors in the global financial market are not banks or other financial firms trading for their own accounts (rather than acting as intermediaries), but large institu-tional investors such as pension funds, mutual funds, and life insurance companies. Propelled by the gradual aging of industrialized-country populations and their consequent higher levels of saving, these institutions have rapidly increased their share of household assets.[89]

Not only do institutional investors invest heavily in stocks and bonds, but they also favor a geographic spread of their investments in order to reduce risk.[90] Although a considerable number of these investors are still subject to prudential safeguards that place conditions on the quantity or quality of their foreign holdings, these safeguards have gradually been eased.[91] Table 1-6 illustrates how almost all types of institutional investors in a number of countries have internationalized their portfolios over the last decade. The shifts illustrated in the table become more significant when one considers the enormous sums that many such funds now control. In the United States alone, the combined holdings of all pension funds more than quadrupled between 1980 and the end of 1993, at which point they stood at $3.5 trillion.[92] U.S. mutual funds have grown even faster, boosting their capital under management ninefold in the same period, to $2.1 trillion.[93] Given these figures, the seemingly innocuous $3^{1}/_{2}$-percentage-point increase in the foreign holdings of U.S. mutual funds between 1991 and 1993 shown in the table translates into a startling dollar increase of almost $49 billion.[94] Because many of these funds contain numerous relatively small contributions from unsophisticated investors who would not normally consider making overseas investments, they play a key role in the internationalization of assets that would otherwise have been invested domestically.

What effect the greater presence of institutional investors will ultimately have on the international capital market is unclear. However, as a result of the growing influence that these large investors exert on the structure and operation of financial systems, it is generally recognized that public policy needs to take a closer look at both the functioning and the regulation of these institutions.[95] The presence of global institutional equity investors and shareholders is already being felt in the real sector. As global capital markets become increasingly integrated, investment capital or equity will naturally tend to flow to those companies that are the most efficient and therefore the most profitable, irrespective of their nationality or where they are located. In response to shareholders' demands for globally competitive returns on capital, these corporations will seek to press their competitive advantages on a worldwide scale. Companies that are inefficient and exposed to competition from these best-practice firms will face pressure from their shareholders to adapt: to become more productive, to reduce costs, and ultimately to adopt best-

Table 1-6. *Institutional Investors' Holdings of Foreign Securities,*
by Type and Country of Investor, 1980–93
Percent of investor's total assets

Type and country of investor	1980	1988	1990	1991	1992	1993
Pension funds						
Germany	n.a.	3.8	4.5	4.5	4.3	4.5
Japan	0.5	6.3	7.2	8.4	8.4	9.0
United Kingdom	10.1	16.5	18.0	20.8	22.0	19.7
United States	0.7	2.7	4.2	4.1	4.6	5.7
Life insurance companies						
Germany	0.6	0.6	1.0	1.0	n.a.	n.a.
Japan	2.7	14.2	13.5	12.5	11.4	9.0
United Kingdom	5.5	9.5	10.8	12.4	12.7	11.6
United States	4.1	3.6	3.6	3.6	3.7	n.a.
Mutual funds						
Germany	n.a.	n.a.	56.3	53.5	47.6	45.2
Japan[a]	n.a.	9.1	7.9	13.0	9.9	n.a.
United Kingdom	n.a.	n.a.	37.1	39.2	37.9	36.0
United States	n.a.	n.a.	n.a.	6.6	n.a.	10.1

Sources: Bank of Japan, *Economic Statistics Monthly,* various issues; Bisignano (1994); Chuhan (1994); European Federation of Investment Funds and Companies; International Monetary Fund, *International Financial Statistics;* InterSec Research Corporation; United Kingdom, Central Statistics Office, *Financial Statistics,* various issues; United States, Board of Governors of the Federal Reserve System, *Flow of Funds Accounts,* various issues; IMF staff estimates, as found in IMF, *International Capital Markets: Developments, Prospects, and Policy Issues* (Washington, August 1995), p. 168, table II.7.
    n.a. Not available.
    a. Investment trusts.

practice techniques themselves.[96] Those that do not will see their investor support disappear and will face liquidation or takeover. The global capital market thus becomes one important additional mechanism by which global capitalism (or globalization) is transmitted around the real sector, from firm to firm and industry to industry.

Limits to Globalization: Sectoral, Geographic, and Historical

The concept of globalization can be further specified. First, from a contemporary perspective, a more disaggregated analysis of the data pre-

Table 1-7. *Patterns of the Globalization of Trade in Selected Industries in the OECD Countries, 1993*

Percent

Industry	Trade as a share of sales		International sourcing as a share of total	IFT as share of total trade
	Finished products	Intermediate products		
Pharmaceuticals	10	8	10–30	70
Computers	26	14	20–60	50–80
Semiconductors	20	n.a.	10–40	70
Motor vehicles	21	13	25–35	50–80
Consumer electronics	55	30	10–40	30–50
Nonferrous metals	21	21[a]	30–50	30
Steel	27	35–45[b]	15–25	5–10
Clothing	25–30	25–30[c]	10–40	5–10

Source: OECD, Industry Division compilation; elaborated from data sources used for the sector case studies, as found in OECD, *Globalisation of Industry: Overview and Sector Reports* (Paris, 1996), p. 49, table 1.21.

n.a. Not available.

a. Unwrought aluminum.

b. Iron ore, coking coal, and scrap.

c. Textiles.

sented above shows that the instruments that corporations use to pursue global strategies vary across sectors, and that the geographic scope of those strategies is more limited than the term *global* would lead one to believe. For example, science-based industries such as pharmaceuticals, computers, and semiconductors exhibit the strongest tendencies toward globalization. They are characterized by high levels of intrafirm trade and large flows of direct investment, and they account for a large proportion of all interfirm collaborative agreements for development purposes. They are followed by scale-intensive industries such as automobiles and consumer electronics, which exhibit somewhat lower levels of FDI and affiliate sales, similar levels of IFT, and a high level of interfirm collaborative agreements for purposes of production. The apparent outliers here are industries such as steel, clothing, and nonferrous metals, which are resource- and labor-intensive. With the exception of nonferrous metals, these industries exhibit broadly lower levels on most indicators of globalization (tables 1-7 and 1-8).[97]

As far as geographic scope is concerned, it can be shown that, as of the early 1990s, the term *globalization* does not accurately reflect economic reality. If one takes "the end of geography" (to use Richard O'Brien's phrase)[98] to be synonymous with globalization, evidence suggests that globalization is not yet truly global: many countries are not yet part of the global economy but remain mired in geography, participating only at the very edges of globalized corporate networks.[99] Indeed, on all the various indicators used to measure globalization, the world remains sharply divided along North-South lines.[100] This has led to a situation where "the risk of exclusion from the growth dynamics of globalization in the developed countries is significant."[101]

Thus, as of 1994 a total of 74 percent of global FDI *stocks* resided in the OECD countries (excluding Mexico), only a little less than the 77 percent recorded in 1980. In fact, as already discussed, the OECD share of inward FDI *flows* actually increased over much of the last decade, indicating that globalization has been deepening but not widening.[102] Not surprisingly, these same trends also come through in data on mergers and acquisitions. Between 1986 and 1994 companies located in OECD countries were the targets of 86 percent of all cross-border M&A deals.[103] Similarly, 91 percent of all international technology alliances formed between 1980 and 1989 were between companies from the United States, Europe, or Japan.[104] Finally, the OECD countries dominate IFT flows, accounting for 76 percent of U.S. IFT in 1992, substantially more than their 59 percent share of total U.S. merchandise trade in the same year.

It is true that in the last few years developing countries have become somewhat more integrated into the global economy. This is evident from an examination of FDI flow data since the early 1990s. In 1993, for example, developing countries' share of worldwide FDI inflows rose to 40 percent, while their share of M&A deals rose to 23 percent. There is also some anecdotal evidence that a number of newly industrialized countries have become important locations for interfirm collaborative alliances. However, these figures should be interpreted with care, as they are liable to short-term influences and thus may not necessarily reflect a sustainable trend.[105] Thus in 1995, for example, the FDI share going to developing countries dropped again, to 30 percent. In addition, much of the future trend of FDI to developing countries will depend not only on further market-opening measures but also on the degree to which their governments put in place a legal infrastructure to protect foreign investment, in the form of property rights, patent protection, and provisions safeguarding the repatriation of profits.

Table 1-8. *Patterns of the Globalization of Foreign Direct Investment and Cooperative Agreements in Selected Industries in the OECD Countries, 1993*

Percent

Industry	Foreign direct investment				Cooperative agreements (share of total)		
	FDI flows as share of gross fixed capital formation	Affiliates' sales as share of total sales	M&As as share of operations	Equity participation as share of operations	For development purposes	For production purposes	For marketing purposes
Pharmaceuticals	50–70	40–50	52	48	38–68	13–29	19–41
Computers	30–40	50–60	43	57	50–70	15–28	17–32
Semiconductors	15–25	20–25	39	61	n.a.	n.a.	n.a.
Motor vehicles	15–25	10–20	33	67	24–48	39–66	9–20
Consumer electronics	20–35	20–30	39	61	24–40	36–62	12–33
Nonferrous metals[a]	20–35	15–25	45	55	n.a.	n.a.	n.a.
Steel	5–10	15–25	72	28	n.a.	n.a.	n.a.
Clothing[b]	15–20	5–15	n.a.	n.a.	n.a.	n.a.	n.a.

Source: OECD, Industry Division compilation; data sources used for the sector case studies. as found in OECD, *Globalization of Industry: Overview and Sector Reports* (Paris, 1996), p. 49, table 1.21.

n.a. Not available.

a. The somewhat higher FDI component in the nonferrous metals industry is explained by the fact that companies active in this industry are also involved in advanced materials research, which requires direct investment to diversify horizontally. The high level of M&A activity in the steel industry is explained by extensive rationalization in the face of declining demand and competition and continued scope for consolidation, as concentration is not very high. See OECD, *Globalization of Industry, Overview and Sector Reports*, p. 50.

b. Cooperative agreements in the clothing industry are limited in number and scope.

Moreover, the bulk of these investments as well as of interfirm alliances went to a few select middle-income countries in Asia, Latin America, and most recently eastern Europe. For instance, in 1996 only ten countries accounted for 76 percent of all FDI flows to non-OECD economies (a group numbering well over 100 countries).[106] Not all of this investment should be considered an integral part of corporations' global strategy. This is especially the case for China, which in 1995 alone absorbed 38 percent of all investments to non-OECD countries; much of that investment was in labor-intensive, low-technology manufacturing.[107] Controlling for the opening of both China and the former Soviet bloc, which attracted almost no investment prior to 1985, the share of foreign direct investment going to the developing world, which on average amounted to 26 percent between 1981 and 1985, dropped to 14 percent in 1995.[108]

A similar division can be observed in the domain of global finance. In 1996, 140 of the 166 developing countries accounted for as little as 5 percent of private capital flows to developing countries.[109] Thus recent trends in net portfolio investment to the developing world as a whole mask the extent to which most of these countries effectively participate in the cross-border market for stocks and bonds. For instance, it is estimated that in 1993 gross foreign equity trading totaled slightly more than $3.8 trillion, of which developing countries and other emerging markets accounted for just over 11 percent—a substantial increase over previous years, yet still a relatively small share.[110] Although data on total cross-border trading or holding of bonds are more elusive, figures for international bonds (those offered in the Euromarkets) are readily available. In 1995 total stocks of outstanding international bonds and Euronotes, excluding issues by international institutions, stood at approximately $2.5 trillion; 14 percent of these consisted of issues originating in the developing world.[111] Where possible, a disaggregation of these foreign equity and international bond transactions reveals the same concentration of activity in a small number of countries that was evident in the data on FDI. Thus, of the $430 billion in emerging market equities traded in 1993, 30 percent was in equities from Hong Kong and Singapore.[112] Similarly, over half the stocks of international bonds and Euronotes placed by emerging market issuers in 1993 were accounted for by a small number of offshore banking centers such as Hong Kong, Singapore, the Netherlands Antilles, and the Cayman Islands.[113]

In addition to these sectoral and geographic limits, a number of commentators, taking a longer historical perspective, have characterized the current infatuation with globalization as "our modern myopia."[114] They correctly remind us that this is not the first time that the world economy has experienced such high levels of economic integration.[115] However, some have gone even further and concluded that the novelty of the current phase of international economic integration is much less than generally assumed.[116] This argument is most often made by comparison with the period 1870–1913, a time often referred to as "the golden age of international economy."[117] During this period a combination of declining transport costs, stable exchange rates, relatively low tariff rates, and few restrictions on the flow of capital and people across borders ensured that cross-border economic activity (both financial and real) reached impressive levels even by the standards of the late 1980s.

A number of these claims have been disputed by more recent historical analyses, which do not support the notion of a golden economic age of growth and rapid convergence. These analyses conclude that such descriptions are "a myth that romanticizes the nineteenth century and makes free trade almost into a sacred doctrine" and "ignores or forgets the fact that until the early 1960s the commercial history of the developed countries was almost entirely one of protectionism."[118]

But even if we understand the internationalization of economic activity since World War II as a continuation of the trend before World War I, a number of important changes have taken place, especially in the last decade, that distinguish the current process from previous phases, with important implications for contemporary public policy responses to the globalization of corporate activity.[119] To begin with, and using the aggregate data usually cited in these long-term comparisons, the level of international economic activity has now gone beyond anything witnessed in the golden age. Moreover, these comparisons consider merchandise trade only and do not include trade in services, which makes up an increasing share of total trade in most industrialized countries.[120] As a share of world output, the stock of FDI has now caught up with the levels posted in 1913 (9 percent in 1993). Furthermore, given the many new investment opportunities that the end of the cold war has created in many parts of the world, the FDI growth rate is likely to stay well above the rate of growth in output (barring a major international conflict), thus increasing the share even further.

More important, as in the case of distinguishing globalization from interdependence, a historical comparison should also go beyond mere aggregate data, to examine the nature, composition, and scope of international economic activity and consider the political environment within which it is embedded. Starting with the international financial markets, a number of factors stand out.[121] First, from about 1880 until the outbreak of World War I, exchange rates between most major economies were fixed under the gold standard, in sharp contrast with the increasing exchange rate volatility that followed the move to freely floating rates in 1973. The confidence and predictability engendered by the gold standard encouraged investors to view domestic and international assets as largely substitutable.[122] Although the advent of hedging and exchange rate derivatives has worked to alleviate some of the uncertainty since the collapse of Bretton Woods, these instruments are not without cost, nor do they make international investing wholly predictable. Derivatives require the presence of someone willing and able to stand on the other side of a transaction and bear the risk that the other party seeks to avoid (for a price, of course). Questions must also be raised about the comparability of interest rate differentials as a measure of financial market integration across two periods with markedly different interest rate elasticities.

A second difference concerns the breadth and depth of current capital flows when compared with those of the prewar decades. Before 1914 foreign investment was limited largely to a handful of countries, among which the United Kingdom was the dominant actor, accounting for half of all overseas investment. At the same time, the greater part of these early international capital flows, and even of portfolio flows, tended to be concentrated in relatively long-term investments, often in developing countries and primarily in public infrastructure projects.[123] These trends stand in sharp contrast to the current international financial landscape, which is characterized by a larger and less concentrated group of capital exporters and the use of a much broader array of investment vehicles.

Turning to FDI, the aggregate figures cited earlier hide many differences between investment flows today and those at the turn of the century. One important development has been the increasing geographic diffusion of FDI, in terms of both host and home countries. This is particularly true of outward FDI: ownership of this investment is now concentrated far less in the hands of a few source countries than in 1914 or even 1960 (figure 1-5). In addition, an increasing number of newly industrialized economies, primarily in Asia, have joined the ranks of significant foreign direct investors. Moreover, as indicated earlier, there has also been a clear shift away from investment in resource-based primary production (such as agriculture and mining) and traditional

Figure 1-5. *Concentration of Global Foreign Direct Investment Stock, by Country of Origin, 1914, 1960, 1996ᵃ*

Percent of total (cumulative)

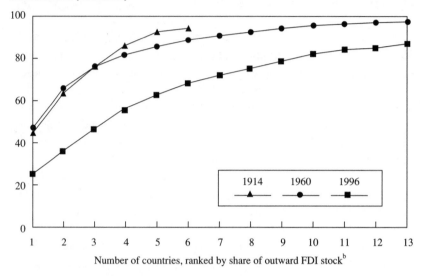

Number of countries, ranked by share of outward FDI stockᵇ

Sources: John H. Dunning, *Multinational Enterprises and the Global Economy* (New York: Addison-Wesley, 1993), p. 117, table 5.1; and UNCTAD, *World Investment Report 1997: Transnational Corporations, Market Structure and Competition Policy* (United Nations, 1997), pp. 319–24, annex table B.4.

a. Figures for 1996 are estimates.

b. Data for 1914 are limited to only the six largest foreign investors, which were the United Kingdom, the United States, France, Germany, the Netherlands, and Russia.

manufacturing toward high technology and other knowledge-intensive investments.[124] This has led to a change in the spatial pattern of FDI outflows in terms of both geographic scope, which is now focused on the industrialized countries, and the direction of the flows, which today are often two-way, rather than one-way as in 1870–1913. Given the type of investment, international production in the golden age was organized mostly along vertical lines, with relatively simple, hierarchical modes of integration. Today international production is horizontally networked among comparable production units, and the backward and forward linkages of FDI in the host economies, reflected in employment and sales, are much more extensive. Considerable differences in trade patterns are also evident, as the share of commodity trade has declined at the expense of manufacturing, and with that, as was shown above, the structure of trade has shifted from interindustry to intraindustry and intrafirm trade.[125]

Finally, and most important, one cannot ignore the fact that in the nineteenth century the world economy was much more integrated politically than at any time since World War II, providing an entirely different political context for cross-border economic transactions. Thus a considerable amount of cross-border flows both during the golden age and directly before and after it were not "international" in the sense of transactions across the borders of sovereign states, but were in fact flows within existing or recently dissolved colonial networks.[126] Investment data from the interwar period suggest that through 1938 almost half of the major colonial powers' foreign investments were concentrated within their own empires.[127] Often these flows were international in name only and shared few of the characteristics commonly associated with cross-border flows of goods or capital today. Tariff and nontariff barriers, for instance, were not commonly an issue between countries or territories that effectively shared a common government.[128] Under such conditions foreign investment was also made much easier. A familiarity with colonial administrations, as well as the presence of close economic ties between colony and colonizer, which often extended to a common currency, ensured that colonial investors avoided many of the political and financial risks usually associated with FDI. These experiences stand in sharp contrast to the postwar international economy, which has required an elaborate international institutional framework among sovereign states as well as several decades of slow and often painstaking negotiations to achieve the same degree of economic integration. These differences in the political structure of the international system should also be kept in mind when comparing the two periods.

If we are prepared to keep these differences in mind, however, history does have one important lesson to teach us. Interaction among national economies has been far from constant, characterized by distinct periods of integration and disintegration.[129] This serves as a reminder that international economic integration is by no means a foregone conclusion. Rather, even before the golden age ended, policymakers found themselves at a critical juncture, having to choose from a number of strategic options at their disposal. As the next chapter will show, globalization has given rise to a set of policy challenges that has placed policymakers once again at a crossroads. They must again choose from among a number of strategic options that are laid out in chapter 3, and their choice will have lasting consequences for the world economy and for international relations.

To sum up, this chapter has drawn out the specific features of globalization and, in so doing, distinguished it qualitatively from economic interdependence. Such a distinction justifies a more formal inquiry into the implications of globalization for public policy, which is the focus of the next chapter. This chapter has defined globalization as a primarily microeconomic phenomenon driven by firms responding to an increasingly competitive international environment. This environment was brought about by government deregulation and liberalization in both the financial and the real sectors of national economies, and by the advancement, rapid diffusion, and declining costs of modern technologies, especially in the areas of communication and transportation.

The instruments of choice for firms' global strategies and expansion have been FDI and international interfirm collaboration. Over time these forms of corporate international engagement have led to changes in the way firms organize their development, production, sourcing, marketing, and financing. The clearest evidence of this has been the changing nature of international trade over the last two decades, best exemplified by the increasing importance of both international sourcing and IFT. Taken together, these various factors have given rise to the compelling and now-familiar image of the globalized firm as an integrated international production system. Within such a system the nationality of firms and the borders between states are increasingly blurred. Global firms use their international networks to shuttle inputs and outputs—tangible and, increasingly, intangible—seamlessly among geographically dispersed facilities. Production in many cases is stateless, associated more with a virtual network of intermediate goods providers and subassembly suppliers than with any single factory floor.

One important policy conclusion that emerges from this analysis is that economic globalization should not automatically be equated with the globalization of the *market* economy, or with the emergence of a global *market*. As has been shown, much of the shifts in the aggregate measures that define recent cross-border economic activity reflects changes in the way firms are organizing their operations. Often this involves the internalization or quasi internalization of previously external activities, processes that were once subject to the operations of market forces. As far as FDI is concerned, a common mistake has been to equate net flows with a transfer of productive resources in one direction or another. Globalization, and with it the rising importance of M&As within total FDI flows, suggests, however, that even the largest single investment in any given year "may represent nothing more than a change of ownership, with no effect on resource allocation between the two countries."[130] Turning to trade, recall that IFT does not represent trade between two unrelated economic actors but rather a transfer within a single corporate entity—it is off-market trade. Moreover, with globalization, an increasing part of international trade is generated by nonequity relations among firms, such as producer-supplier links and marketing agreements such as franchising. These forms of collaboration and quasi integration between independent firms increase the amount of international off-market trade even further.[131]

Concerns have also been raised about the growing number and spread of interfirm collaborative agreements, which blur the traditional line between competition and cooperation. In general, policymakers' concern relates to the danger of powerful global oligopolies emerging and the lack of a framework for public policy to regulate these cross-border alliances and their activities.[132] As one study on the relationship between technology and globalization concludes, "as a result, in a growing number of industries in manufacturing and services, the prevailing form of supply structure is world oligopoly. This raises novel and previously unaddressed problems relating to the measurement of international concentration and possibly its control in the face of possible dangers of international cartelization."[133]

This internalization of market activities associated with the emergence of a global production structure is central to an examination of the public policy implications of globalization. Under conditions of interdependence, national economies—subject to domestic structures of governance—were linked primarily through markets at the macroeconomic level. This interaction among national economies was structured by the rules and principles of the Bretton Woods institutions. Globalization has led to the emergence of a parallel, even competing, set of linkages at the level of production. This explains the qualitative change of cross-border economic flows, to which public policy for the most part has yet to respond. Confirming this lack of global public policy, one study goes further and suggests that private sector actors themselves have begun to respond. Thus the "world wide growth of [corporate] networks and interfirm alliances reflects a more or less explicit resolve to regulate, at the microeconomic level, the sometimes devastating effects of competition."[134]

Developing in tandem with the process of real sector globalization, and at times driving it, has been the progressive globalization of financial markets. Unfettered and increasing capital flows coupled with the emergence of new financial techniques (securitization), instruments (derivatives), and actors (institutional investors) have created a financial landscape that makes it far easier for firms to realize their global aspirations. Spurred on by the liberalization of financial regulations and the lifting of capital controls, foreign investors today have much greater freedom in managing their investments; meanwhile new risk management techniques enable them to take on the risks that they feel capable of managing and to hedge those that they are unwilling to accept. In this way the global capital market has become a core force, breaking down the barriers to real sector globalization and creating the conditions for an accelerated flow of goods and technology overseas.

But the qualitative transformation of international financial intermediation has also altered the challenges facing public policy and the environment within which public policymaking takes place. Some of these challenges, such as how to manage the risks inherent in global foreign exchange markets, are made more pronounced by the sheer volume of cross-border flows brought about by globalization. Others, however, are new and present policymakers with unique concerns. In particular, securitization and the proliferation of derivatives have made "trading" a major component of many financial and even nonfinancial firms' operations. This in turn has forced policymakers to focus their attention on the concept of market risk—the danger that a particular counterparty may suffer catastrophic losses through unexpected general market price and interest rate changes—as opposed to credit risk, which was the focus of regulators during the earlier period.

In addition, the establishment of parallel derivative markets for most financial instruments, and the fact that many of these markets are located in a different country from where transactions in the underlying assets take place, now demand that regulators cooperate across borders if they are to police these markets adequately. Finally, the increasing international orientation of institutional investors and the power that they can bring to bear on newly emerging capital markets raises powerful questions about the desirability and volatility of certain capital flows. As will be discussed at greater length in chapter 4, this not only requires that policymakers in different countries cooperate to a much greater degree than before, but also indicates that financial markets are likely to continue to adjust to external conditions and changing technological developments, thereby exerting great pressure on public policy to continue to respond to this fast-changing environment. Chapter 2 will examine the implications of globalization for public policy and lay out the choices that governments have in responding to them.

CHAPTER 2

Globalization and Public Policy: An Analytical Framework

THIS CHAPTER develops a conceptual framework that links globalization and public policymaking. It is probably fair to say that the perception is widespread among policymakers and the general public that globalization has weakened the sovereignty of governments. Indeed, some have gone so far as to state that globalization will lead to the disappearance of states as primary organizing actors in the international system.[1] Given the powerful role that the nation-state has played in organizing social, economic, political, cultural, and other activities within its borders ever since the Industrial Revolution, the implications of such a withering away of the state, should it come to pass, would be profound to say the least. It is therefore inconceivable that states and governments will simply disappear from the landscape of politics in general, and of international relations in particular. States are not "up for grabs." After all, no viable alternative institutional form to organize contemporary political life has yet been put forward, however inefficient and ineffective the current form may have become.[2]

Yet some would argue that the significance of states relative to that of other social organizations such as multinational enterprises, nongovernmental organizations, and international organizations has been declining as a result of interdependence and globalization, leading to considerable tension between state and nonstate actors.[3] Others have taken the opposite tack, suggesting that the metaphor of a powerless state is a myth and a convenient policy tool for politicians, left and right, seeking to justify politically difficult adjustments. As evidence that the state remains a powerful force, they point to the considerable and rising share of government spending as a percentage of GDP among the established industrial countries.[4]

Such a perspective, however, confuses the issue at hand. The state, by virtue of its formal powers, can raise taxes and increase spending and thus increase its weight in the national economy. But this by no means implies that its ability to conduct public policy for the economy and society at large has remained the same. On the contrary, it is an indication that, in order to maintain their operational capacity and fulfill their mandate to provide public goods and act in the public interest, governments in an increasingly open world economy need more resources rather than fewer.[5]

A more interesting and, from a policy perspective, more promising question is how states and governments might react to the phenomenon of globalization and any potential challenge to their sovereignty arising from it. Just how does globalization challenge a government's sovereignty? How, if at all, does that challenge differ from the challenge of economic interdependence, which is also widely considered to dilute sovereignty? Will states—which, next to markets, remain by far the most powerful form of social organization in the modern world—resist being swept aside by globalization? Do governments have different options in responding to globalization? What are those options, how do they differ, and what will be their consequences? And if states were to disappear in the long run, what, if anything, would replace them?

Clearly, national governments will have great influence over the process by which tensions between public policies and globalization are resolved. Prior choices about how to organize and institutionalize political life limit the options available in the medium term. Thus, unlike a purely utilitarian or functionalist perspective, which would predict a withering away of the state, a more realistic scenario posits that the implications of globalization for public policymaking—whatever the outcome—will be path-dependent and thus mediated by the primary form of political organization in the world today: the modern territorial and democratic state.[6]

Following from the empirical discussion in chapter 1, the analytical framework developed here also draws a distinction between interdependence and globalization. At the root of the distinction lies a differentiation between *external* and *internal sovereignty*. Both are relational concepts. But whereas the former focuses on a state's external environment and characterizes relations among states within the international system, the latter depicts a state's setting within its own territory, characterizing, for example, relations between a government and its citizens, the economy, or other, more narrowly defined groups and institutions. From the perspective of this study, public policy is defined as the principal instrument by which governments operationalize internal sovereignty both in a constitutive and in an executive sense.

Challenges to a state's external sovereignty have of course been the central focus in the study of international relations. So far the same cannot be said of internal sovereignty, which has remained the focus of students of domestic politics. The globalization of industrial activity calls this conventional division of labor into question and suggests that the concept of internal sovereignty will become a central theme of the study of world political economy. The globalization of industry presents a fundamental challenge to states' ability to exercise internal sovereignty. Among other things this is reflected in the fact that, increasingly, what are conventionally considered domestic policy issues, that is, matters of internal sovereignty, are being drawn into or reappear in discussion and deliberations on matters of foreign policy. When Theodore J. Lowi wrote his seminal article in the late 1960s, categorizing public policy into three functional areas, he stated that he did not include foreign policy in his categories because "in many ways it is not part of the same universe."[7] Such a rigid separation may have been possible at the time, but it is no longer possible today. Contemporary theories of international relations do not draw a distinction between internal and external sovereignty. As a result, these theories fail to appreciate the nature of the transformation that globalization entails for the international system, and in particular for the interests and motivation of its primary actors, the world's nation-states.

Interdependence: Challenges to External Sovereignty

The study of the increasing interdependence of national economies and the associated emergence of a world economy has become one of the core areas of research in the field of international relations. The popularity of interdependence as an analytical concept increased considerably with the publication of *Power and Interdependence* by Robert Keohane and

Joseph Nye Jr.[8] They coined the term *complex interdependence* to characterize a condition in which independent states are connected by an increasing number of channels—political, social, economic, cultural, and others. They and other authors argued that complex interdependence led to a weakening of security issues, which had been the dominant set of issues defining the relationships among states in the international system.

Much has been written since then about complex interdependence, and the concept has been refined and even further redefined.[9] The central proposition, however, has remained the same: interdependence, or mutual dependence, implies sensitivity or vulnerability to an external force.[10] The units to be studied when examining and measuring interdependence are territorially bound, sovereign nation-states. International interdependence thus denotes a condition of mutual sensitivity and vulnerability among states in the international system. From the perspective of each state, the source of this sensitivity and vulnerability is *external*.

As discussed in the previous chapter, *economic* interdependence is characterized by an increasing flow of goods, services, and capital across borders. This increased flow is due to variations in countries' resource endowments, such as capital, labor, and natural resources, and differences in countries' stage of industrialization, among other factors. All these factors lead to an increasing international specialization and division of labor among national economies, which is then reflected in the pattern and composition of international trade and finance.

However, despite this expanded flow of goods, services, and capital across borders, national frameworks for policymaking under conditions of interdependence remain for the most part separate from the international arena. In other words, the increased interaction of national economies due to rising specialization leads to heightened interdependence, or, as is often argued, simply dependence, yet national governments remain the principal center of political and economic power as well as the locus of decisionmaking. Economic events in other countries do not have a direct and immediate impact on the domestic economy but are filtered through a set of policy boundaries, the effectiveness of which begins at, but does not reach beyond, the territory of the domestic economy.

It is helpful to introduce two distinctions that are often overlooked when considering the implications of interdependence on sovereignty. First, although it may be implicitly assumed, it is seldom spelled out that interdependence challenges not de jure or legal sovereignty, but de facto or operational sovereignty. In other words, it is not the legal concept of sovereignty that is being challenged, but the ability of states to practice that concept in the daily affairs of politics.[11] This distinction is important. If interdependence were to challenge the legal sovereignty of states, it would also by definition challenge the notion that the international system is anarchic (legal sovereignty being the basis for anarchy), a condition that lies at the heart of the dominant schools in international relations: realism and liberalism (these are discussed further below).

Second, and more important, it is helpful to distinguish between an internal and an external dimension of sovereignty. Accordingly, sovereignty "combines a description of attributes with various emotive concerns for or against limitations on the *internal* and *external* discretion of the state."[12] Hedley Bull puts it succinctly in *The Anarchical Society*: "On the one hand, states assert, in relation to this territory and population, what might be called internal sovereignty, which means supremacy over all other authorities within that territory and population. On the other hand, they assert what might be called external sovereignty, by which is meant not supremacy but independence of outside authorities."[13] In each case, as John Ruggie has put it, "it [sovereignty] signifies a form of legitimation that pertains to a system of relations.[14] The concept of sovereignty did not start out with this double meaning attached to it. Rather, the term originated from the need to justify "the king being the master of his new modern kingdom, absolute internally" and only later became "the justification of equality of such sovereigns in the international community . . . a theory of sovereign states."[15] Going back to the fourteenth century, the concept almost exclusively referred to the internal dimension and initially served as a form of legitimation of central state authority against competing domestic claimants.[16]

Later this internal dimension also figured prominently in Max Weber's definition of the state as enjoying a monopoly of the legitimate use of force over a given territory and population.[17] It came to refer to a central legal and administrative structure, as well as its decisionmaking process, that forms a polity which defines a network of institutional ties, behavioral regularities, and values that bind together public and private actors, who participate in implementing authoritative decisions.[18] Put slightly differently, internal sovereignty refers to the formulation, implementation, and maintenance of a legal, economic, political, and social order that allows individuals to peacefully coexist and interact in a relatively predictable environment.

Over the years, the concept of internal sovereignty evolved into constitutional, democratic governance. "Subjects" became "citizens," and as far as internal sovereignty is concerned, the concepts of citizenship and inclusiveness became central constitutive elements in shaping a state's identity. Internal sovereignty came to describe the relationship between a democratically elected government and society at large. Modern internal sovereignty refers to popular sovereignty. Internal sovereignty is bestowed upon the "rulers" at regular intervals through the electoral process and is thereafter subject to pluralistic and/or corporate structures of decisionmaking. As will be shown below, these links among internal sovereignty, democracy, and inclusive plurality are of great importance when analyzing the relationship between globalization and public policy.

In operational terms, internal sovereignty in today's modern democracy means the ability of a government to formulate, implement, and manage public policy. Thus, in terms of this inquiry, which focuses on the regulatory and rule-making dimension of public policymaking, governments exercise internal sovereignty when they make laws and regulations, decide on the best and most effective ways to implement those laws and regulations, and monitor compliance with them. A threat to a country's operational internal sovereignty implies a threat to its ability to conduct public policy. With respect to the economy, the legal dimension of internal sovereignty becomes operational when governments collect taxes or regulate private sector activities, assuming that the boundaries that define the relationship between the public and the private sector are both stable and symmetric.

The external dimension of the concept of sovereignty goes back to Thomas Hobbes. In contrast to internal sovereignty, external sovereignty implies the absence of a supreme authority and therefore the independence of states in the international system. External sovereignty is the logical consequence of Hobbes' position that there is no security in domestic anarchy. Thus Hobbes solved the problem of domestic anarchy by "exporting" it to the international system. External sovereignty is the central constitutive rule of the international system.[19] States are mutually exclusive and disjointed and follow the principle of self-help.[20] Identity formation by states (such as the development of interests, beliefs, and expectations) in the presence of anarchy is primarily concerned with the maintenance of their own security. The international system is competitive and individualistic, and security in the absence of central rule is the responsibility of each country individually.[21] External economic sovereignty is operationalized, for example, when countries collect tariffs or devalue or revalue their currencies.

It can now be seen that the two concepts of sovereignty are closely related. The rationale for external sovereignty would not exist in the absence of internal sovereignty. Indeed, it is unlikely that a state could exist for long relying solely on external sovereignty.[22] Suffice it to say here that, given the nature of the origin of external sovereignty, any threat to it would ultimately also affect its internal counterpart. Similarly, a sustained challenge to a country's internal sovereignty will eventually affect its external sovereignty.

As currently conceptualized, territoriality is central to both notions of sovereignty. External sovereignty is based on the principle of mutual exclusion, and it is this principle that defines territoriality in the international system.[23] With a few exceptions, such as the global commons, the international system is fully determined. As far as internal sovereignty is concerned, the assertion of final authority within a given territory is the very basis for its existence and legitimacy as well as its ability to be inclusive by generating a sense of identity and belonging.

But even though external and internal sovereignty are closely related and rely on the principle of territoriality as a common and defining characteristic, it is important to keep in mind that they are diametrically opposed, with respect to both the principles by which they operate and the purpose for which they came into existence. Any attempt by a single state to establish ultimate authority in the international system will be and always has been fiercely contested by others. But at home a government's authority is supreme and largely uncontested. Second, although states interact internationally with each other on the basis of mutually respected exclusion, inclusiveness is essential for both the effectiveness and the legitimacy of a government domestically. Third, whereas domestically the identity or purpose of government is to represent the collective interest, or the common or public good, internationally states need to fend for their own individual interests. Fourth, as a relational concept, external sovereignty refers to functional equivalents, namely, states, whereas internal sovereignty refers to functional opposites, namely, the public and the private domains. Fifth, the common attribute of territoriality individuates in the international system, but spatially delineates a collective at the domestic level. Given these two different roles or collective meanings attached to the two forms of sovereignty, it follows that states have a dual identity derived from their differing institutional roles at the domestic and the international level. Each of these roles generates different sets of interests and expectations, responding to a different environment and different actors. These roles have been kept separate even under conditions of interdependence.[24]

One of the major theoretical debates of the last decade between realists and liberals in the field of international relations has revolved around the concept of interdependence, in particular its meaning and significance for the interests, and subsequently, the behavior of states in the international political and economic system.[25] At the risk of oversimplifying this ongoing discussion, the two positions can be described as follows. Realists, or neorealists as they have been called in the most recent round of the debate, maintain that states' interests and behavior in the international system are shaped by the system's *structure,* which is characterized by the absence of a central power. The organizing principle is anarchy, which promotes competition and conflict among states and restrains their desire to cooperate with other states, even when there is a clear recognition that they have joint interests.[26] Liberals or neoliberals, on the other hand, while recognizing and even accepting the inevitability of the anarchic structure of the international system, argue that *process* can under certain circumstances lead to cooperation among states. ("Process" here refers to interaction among states, which allows for learning by them—that is, by policymakers and bureaucrats—as a result of that interaction.) In addition, the neoliberal perspective attributes to international institutions the ability to facilitate interaction and provide an environment conducive to both learning and reciprocity among states.[27]

In liberal theorizing, states seek to maximize absolute gains in the international system. That other states might gain as well is not an impediment to cooperation. The major impediment is cheating, which results in free riding in the international system.[28] Realists disagree, arguing that states do worry about the gains of other states. For realists, states perceive gains in relative terms: a state is unlikely to cooperate if another state is likely to gain more than it does, even if the first state would also benefit.[29] As a result, international institutions cannot have the mediating and facilitating effect on cooperation that liberals claim they do, and in a neorealist view of the international system one is likely to witness far less cooperation among states than the neoliberal approach would predict.

Yet as much as these two theoretical schools may differ on states' responses to increased interdependence, and thus on the promise of international cooperation and the role of institutions in facilitating cooperation, their approaches also—and this is central to the analysis—have a number of fundamental and important methodological and conceptual commonalities. Most important, both schools take a "rationalist" approach to international relations, which implies that the identities and interests of states are predetermined exogenously and cannot change. Another shared concept is that states are unitary, self-interested actors coexisting in an anarchic environment. Hence, although the two schools differ on how states behave in an anarchic environment, they do not differ on the fundamental interests and identities of states in such an environment.[30]

This theoretical correspondence of neorealist and neoliberal views of states' interests, identities, and their anarchic surroundings also translates into a shared understanding of the nature and purpose of sovereignty in the international system, and how sovereignty is affected by economic interdependence. For both schools the origin of the challenge to a state's operational sovereignty is considered external, or "systemic," as it is often called. Interdependence describes the sensitivity of one nation to events occurring in another, and vice versa. The dynamic forces, the external pressures that states experience as a result of interdependence, originate in the international system, which is composed of other states. To what degree and in what form these external forces subsequently get refracted at national borders and are filtered into the domestic system—in other words, how vulnerable states are and how they respond to this vulnerability—is a source of dispute between the two schools.

Neoliberals, again, emphasize the absolute gains that can be derived from cooperation.[31] In the realm of economic interdependence, those gains are said to be achieved by reducing tariff barriers and capital controls—a reduction in the external dimension of sovereignty—in order to facilitate the free flow of goods and services so that intercountry specialization based on the principle of comparative advantage can be furthered. If common ground for a reduction of external barriers between two or more countries can be established, there is a basis for cooperation.

Cooperation will succeed and the gains from increased economic interdependence will be realized, in the neoliberal view, if other states do not cheat on previously agreed-upon arrangements to lower external barriers. Such an agreement to reduce and thus limit external sovereignty is rationalized by the principles of nondiscrimination and reciprocity—in other words, by a comparable reduction in the external sovereignty of all other states that are party to the agreement. Institutionalized forms of international cooperation are often referred to as international regimes, which are defined rather broadly as "sets of implicit or explicit principles, norms, rules, and decision-making procedures around which actors' expectations converge in a given area of international relations."[32]

Thus neoliberals acknowledge the neorealist claim that states compete in an anarchic international system, but suggest that they do so in a cooperative and reciprocal fashion, which alters their perception of risk and changes their incentive structure by reducing uncertainty, providing information, and lowering transaction costs. To the question of whether states do or do not lose external sovereignty in this process, the neoliberal answer would be "both." They do lose external sovereignty in absolute terms as economic borders are lowered, but they do not lose external sovereignty relative to other states, which lower their borders likewise, in line with the principle of reciprocity.[33] In substantive terms, this process, which will be called *cooperative competition,* is embedded in international regimes and evolves from each country's dominant domestic private sector coalitions, whose interests are projected by governments into international negotiations and the multilateral agreements that emerge from them.[34] Thus governments under conditions of cooperative competition do not necessarily represent the general public interest, but often only the dominant private sector interests in the international system, ensuring that those interests can be addressed once an agreement has been struck. This applies even to such cases as free trade, which, contrary to a widespread perception, is not in itself a public good according to the standard Samuelsonian definition of nonexcludability and joint supply.[35]

Neorealists, on the other hand, argue that the promise of absolute gains, although a necessary condition for cooperation, is not a sufficient one.[36] For these realists what ultimately determines whether or not states cooperate with other states is the relative gains to each, that is, how cooperation affects each state's position in the international system vis-à-vis other states. Because not all states can be relative gainers, realists argue, cooperation is unlikely to occur, and when it does is highly unstable and short-lived. For realists the international system is characterized by what is called here *adversarial competition,* which they argue is the only way to preserve external sovereignty.

Both schools acknowledge that states are structural and functional equals that compete in the international system and pursue similar interests. However, the terms on which that competition takes place and the ways in which states respond to a challenge to their external sovereignty vary. Neorealists see states as primarily adversarial, reluctant to concede external sovereignty. Neoliberals argue that states will cooperate if the potential joint gains resulting from greater economic interdependence can be realized, even though in absolute terms they will have to concede some of their external sovereignty. But while the two schools differ on the outcome of state interaction in the international system, they do not differ on the source. Both explain the success or failure of cooperation by pointing to external developments: changes in the position or behavior of other states in the international system.

This brief review sets the stage for a discussion of globalization and its implications for sovereignty and public policy. However, one cannot resist pointing to the empirical evidence of the world economy, which seems to confirm that individual governments, in relations to date involving both the real and the financial sectors, have by and large tended to follow a strategy of cooperative competition. They have relinquished some of their external sovereignty in absolute terms, while at the same time using international regimes to ensure that they do not lose external sovereignty in relative terms. Of course, this is not to say that adversarial competition has vanished from the field of international relations. Adversarial competition remains a policy option that states have on many occasions threatened to use, and in some cases have used, when cooperative competition has failed.

Globalization: Challenges to Internal Sovereignty

As was stated in the introduction, if there is no formal difference between interdependence and globalization, governments have little need or incentive to reassess their own role in view of globalization, or to reassess the purpose and principles of the institutions that have governed the world economy since the end of World War II. However, if such a distinction can be drawn, it provides the conceptual basis for a reassessment of the role of government and governance in an emerging global economy.

Chapter 1 described the characteristic features of globalization from an empirical perspective. Based on the discussion in the previous section, it is now possible to draw a formal, analytical distinction.[37] According to one definition, globalization in its pure form is a process that subsumes and rearticulates national economies into the global economy through cross-national processes and transactions. These processes and transactions take on an autonomous role in a consolidated global marketplace for production, distribution, and consumption. According to this view, the global economy dominates national economies existing within it.[38] Although certainly helpful for comprehending the fundamental and historic transformation that the world political economy is undergoing, such broad macrostructural definitions do not capture the central difference between globalization and interdependence. Nor are they necessarily specific enough to allow for a comprehensive examination of the policy implications that globalization may entail for policymakers.

It was shown in chapter 1 that globalization is an industry-level, microeconomic phenomenon. Cooperative competition among governments during the 1960s and 1970s—and its outcomes, liberalization and cross-border deregulation—were important preconditions for the strategic corporate decisions that now drive the geographic expansion of foreign direct investment and the rising incidence of intrafirm trade, international sourcing, and interfirm collaborative agreements. But increasing interdependence alone does not capture this process. Indeed, unlike in the case of interdependence, governments for the most part have not yet become involved in the dynamics of globalization. Recall that globalization was defined as a strategic decision to divide a growing number of functional aspects of the product life cycle, including R&D, production, marketing, and even disposal of a product, into different segments across a variety of structurally similar national economies, and that this decision often involves the internalization or quasi internalization into a single corporate entity of activities formerly conducted as market transactions across two distinct firms in distinct national economies. As an economic dynamic, therefore, globalization differs from interdependence in that it subsumes or internalizes into its own institutional structure economic activities that previously took place between national markets, that is, between distinct economic *and* political units. For a global as opposed to an international firm, foreign presence is no longer one of several elements in determining the firm's competitive advantage; it has become a precondition for participation in a particular industrial sector. Globalization has become an intrinsic structural characteristic of an industry.[39]

As national borders no longer encompass sufficient territory to function as self-contained markets for global companies, the spatial structure and dynamics that delineate the geography of private sector economic activities are becoming decoupled from the territorial structure and dynamics that define political geography, that is, the territorially bound nation-state and its power of decisionmaking within the economy. Territoriality, the defining characteristic of internal and external sovereignty, becomes "unbundled."[40] Whereas the political geography that defines markets continues to be structured by mutual exclusion, the economic geography on the basis of which these markets function has become increasingly inclusive, defying the territorially fixed nature of the nation-state by creating its own, nonterritorial space. Keeping in mind the geographic and sectoral limitations of globalization discussed in chapter 1, national boundaries to an increasing degree no longer mediate market exchanges but instead merely register internal corporate flows. These off-market transactions are often misleadingly treated as exchanges in such conventional measures as trade statistics and foreign exchange rates. To be sure, the management of interdependence was an important precursor to this development, but interdependence no longer adequately describes the structure of the international system or the challenges that emanate from it.

Quantitatively, this inadequacy of national markets manifests itself in the various empirical indicators of globalization examined in chapter 1. In the financial services industry it is probably best reflected in the fact that the financial intermediation of both credit and, more recently, market risk no longer takes place within national financial markets, but instead relies on a much broader and more fluid geographic space. The increasingly widespread phenomenon of parallel derivative markets is probably the most vivid example. The changing composition of international trade—caused by the rising importance of intrafirm trade and long-term supplier relationships, or the fact that global sales of the affiliates of multinationals have for some time exceeded world exports—reflects the increasing disjuncture between the economic geography of globalization and the political geography of a world economy structured by nation-states.

Qualitatively, this disjuncture, or mismatch, between political and economic geography does not challenge the external sovereignty of states. It cannot. Rather, by altering the spatial relationship between the private and the public sector, global corporate networks challenge the internal sovereignty of states. Specifically, since the organizational logic of globalization induces corporations to seek the fusion of multiple, formerly segmented national markets into a single whole, it generates an economic geography that subsumes multiple political geographies. As a result, a government no longer has a monopoly of legitimate power over the territory within which corporations organize themselves. The greater the mismatch between political and economic geography, the more difficult it will be for national governments to act in an inclusive manner, allowing individuals to coexist and interact in a relatively predictable environment. This leads to the heightened perception of risk and insecurity widely observed in our societies.

For example, a government's ability to provide such security for economic activity depends crucially on access to a constant stream of information about the activity of economic actors—a stream that is not always easy to maintain. Information asymmetries have always been one reason why policymakers find it difficult to keep up with the changing nature of the marketplace. But globalization has led to a sharp increase in these asymmetries, making it almost impossible for governments to maintain even a minimum amount of crucial information.[41] Moreover, as far as regulatory and supervisory policies are concerned, globalization has led to an acceleration of the regulatory dialectic, in which public and private actors engage in a continuous contest, the former trying to constrain the latter while the latter tries to escape those constraints. This dialectic not only is fiscally wasteful but rarely achieves its goal. Similarly, as globalization progresses, governments will find it increasingly difficult to assess and collect taxes, since they lack crucial information about the activity of those they seek to tax.

In other words, the unbundling of political and economic geography brought about by globalization has created a structural imbalance, and possibly even a disjuncture, between the public and the private spheres of society. Governments and governance, which continue to be bounded by territoriality, can no longer project their policymaking capacity over the territory within which a global industry (on the supply side) and, to an increasing degree, a global community of consumers (on the demand side) operate.[42] Globalization not only integrates along one dimension, the economic or private; it also fragments along another, the political or public.

This is not to say that private sector actors necessarily and always make a deliberate effort to circumvent and outrace government efforts to control them. Rather, each geography, the economic and the political, follows a set of fundamentally different operational logics. Political systems, at least in their contemporary form as nation-states, are boundary-maintaining systems. Indeed, their legitimacy is derived from their ability to maintain boundaries. Markets, although dependent for their creation on political power and local economic networks, do not depend, once in operation, on the presence of territorial boundaries.[43] Given the expansive nature of globalization, the spatial symmetry between the public and the private is disappearing. From a historical perspective this raises a number of important questions about the long-term future of the nation-state. After all, it was precisely the superior ability of the nation-state to establish internal sovereignty—to consolidate the public and private spheres into a single territorial entity—that allowed it to outmaneuver institutional and organizational competitors such as city-states and city-leagues in the organization of political and economic life at the end of the feudal era.[44] The concluding chapter of this study will address this issue at greater length.

At this point it is important to recall the earlier distinction between legal and operational sovereignty. Like interdependence, globalization does not and cannot in any way challenge the *legal* internal sovereignty of a government. Globalization challenges internal *operational* sovereignty, and it is important for the subsequent discussion to keep this distinction in mind. Thus, just as states became increasingly sensitive and vulnerable to the actions of other states as increasing interdependence weakened their external operational sovereignty, so their internal operational sovereignty is being undermined by globalization, as territorially bounded governments can no longer project their power and policymaking capacity over the territory within which a global industry operates.[45]

Recall that the empirical examination of globalization in chapter 1 showed that the globalization of industry (financial services and manufacturing alike) is not necessarily equivalent to the globalization of the market economy. From the previous analysis of the divergent paths of political and economic geographies, this point can now be made at a more formal and general level. One can only confuse globalization with the rise of the global market economy if one understands a market economy (national, regional, or global) as an almost idealized arrangement in which rational, self-interested economic agents interact free of any constraints, political but also legal or of some other form, and are minimally affected by social relations, their history, traditions, culture, or other factors. In this atomized, undersocialized, and depoliticized conception of human action, the market economy and its geography would be a separate, differentiated sphere of modern society, unrelated to the broader historical, political, and social environment and their geographies, in which the market economy is embedded.[46] Economic rationality would prevail over political, social, and judicial rationality.

Notwithstanding the fact that economic rationality is an essential component of a market economy, the latter is of course more than a loosely structured agglomeration of individual economic actors freely expressing their preferences in pursuit of their individual or private interests, generating Pareto-superior or even Pareto-optimal outcomes for themselves. A market economy is a complex organization, based not only on the interaction of individual economic preferences but also on the presence of a collective or public interest that relies on relatively stable social relationships and patterns of behavior, legal norms and mechanisms, political forces and institutions, and, increasingly, ecological and resource constraints. All of these interact in a structured manner to produce the relatively consistent behavior characteristic of any large institution. Thus a market economy is a form of social organization—indeed it is the *principal* form of social organization that shapes industrial democracies. It is a highly complex system that forms a social whole but functions through a network of constituent parts.

It is true that economic interactions are the most visible of these constituent parts and the most closely associated with the wealth-generating potential of market exchange, that is, the pursuit of private interests. Economic interactions are the source of the spontaneity for which markets are well known. But that wealth-generating potential would not always be utilized, and indeed would be at high risk and would often fail, were it not for a broad set of legal and administrative parameters and a variety of social norms that give market economies a certain constructive character—a foundation, a collective or public good, that allows the market economy to perform its integrative function. For example, the institutions of a market economy and the transactions undertaken within them depend on the presence of trust—a collective good—which market processes themselves cannot provide.[47] The social organization of trust is thus an important constituent element of a market economy and has to be developed by means other than economic exchange. If anything, it should be a precondition of economic exchange.

Markets are also firmly embedded in a network of organizations governed by legally binding administrative rules and regulations, which in turn are shaped by political forces. At the macrostructural level this network of organizations ensures the smooth and efficient interaction of participants in a market, and when necessary it employs legal means to enforce certain behaviors. At the microstructural level organizations often perform the function of aggregating and intermediating the interests of persons and groups in the market, and representing these interests to policymakers. Chambers of commerce, labor unions, trade and business associations, and consumer groups are all vital elements of a modern market economy.

Thus the risk associated with the spontaneity of economic exchange and the pursuit of private interests would be too great without some constructive foundation and a stabilizing framework that can provide collective goods and meet the public interest. Similarly, the constructive foundation and the stability that these collective goods create would be of little tangible value unless one could point to the wealth and income generated by the spontaneous interaction of individual economic actors pursuing their individual interests. Societies can place too much emphasis on either of these constituent elements. Too much emphasis on the constructive aspects of a market economy is likely to stifle its dynamism, while an overemphasis on spontaneity can turn dynamism into turbulence and chaos. Managing such a complex organization and its constituent parts, that is, deciding which issues will be resolved by individual choice and decisionmaking and to what degree (the market being the principal mechanism), and which should be resolved by collective choice and decisionmaking, balancing public and private interests, and to what degree, is what public policymaking at the national level is all about. It presumes the ability of a government to exercise internal sovereignty.[48]

Following from the above, the unbundling of the political (legal, social, cultural) and economic geographies brought about by globalization has created an imbalance and possibly even a disjuncture between the two central constituent spheres of the market economy. Since the operational capacity of governments to exercise internal sovereignty depends on considerable correspondence between the two spheres, globalization has severely weakened the ability of governments to provide public goods and act in the public interest. Moreover, as has already been discussed, in many countries today sovereignty, in particular its internal dimension, is popular, legitimized at regular intervals through the electoral process. As a result, any threat to a government's internal operational sovereignty implies, by definition, a threat to the effectiveness of democracy itself. In other words, although individuals may exercise their legal right to vote, the power or influence of that vote in shaping public policy has decreased with the decline in operational internal sovereignty and will continue to do so. Ultimately, a persistent weakness and failure of internal sovereignty, therefore, will lead to a questioning of the institutions and processes of democracy itself.

Although this dynamic is certainly not the only explanation for the exhaustion of democracy and the declining trust in institutions of governance and political leaders in many countries, it certainly should be considered an important contributing factor.[49] In addition, it explains the increasing popular resentment against deeper economic integration, which ultimately threatens the process of globalization itself, as nationalism and the politics of identity provide a simplistic but easy, and therefore powerful, response to a complex, historic transformation of the economic (although not yet the political) landscape in which industrial societies coexist. In the words of one commentator, "Too much democracy kills the market, because the people, or an authority acting in their name, take all the decisions collectively, leaving nothing to the individual. But too much market may also kill democracy. If every choice is left to the market, the right to vote becomes meaningless, because the people you elect have no power to change anything."[50]

Taken together, then, the globalization of industry presents a challenge to the capacity of governments to govern. But this challenge to their ability to conduct public policy is not an external challenge. It does not emanate from another state, as usually conceptualized in the standard approaches to the study of international relations, and in particular of international interdependence, which focuses on external sovereignty.[51] Rather, the challenge comes from within each country, as economic networks (legal and illegal alike) increasingly operate in a nonterritorial functional space that defies individual territorialities and thus internal sovereignties. Although this space has no center politically, it is highly integrated at the microeconomic level, creating what has been called a *"space-of-flows* operating in real time which exists alongside the *space-of-places,"* also referred to as national but interdependent economies.[52] This space-of-flows, a growing part of which consists of cyberflows as electronic finance and commerce continue to gain in importance, is characterized by a set of mutually reinforcing cross-national networks pertaining to technology transfer, the processing and dissemination of knowledge and information, financial intermediation, transport, and, last but not least, research and development. These networks form the backbone of global corporate operations and thus of an emerging global manufacturing and services economy. Accordingly, the global economy is not located in another place or at a different level; it *is* another place.[53] Thus, although national boundaries have remained points of contact as well as points of separation between political systems, they no longer perform those functions in the strategies of global corporations or the consumption patterns of individuals, notwithstanding that there might be other factors that constrain their spatial horizon. Finally, given the close linkage between internal sovereignty and democracy, globalization not only undermines the effectiveness and efficiency of governments but weakens the legitimacy of democratic institutions and the democratic process itself.

How are governments to respond to this challenge? As the next chapter will show, they have a number of options. Global public policy, the pooling and collective operationalization of internal sovereignty, is one such option. But for global public policy to succeed, national governments have to agree to commit themselves to an unprecedented amount of cooperation. It is unprecedented because, contrary to the neoliberal vision of cooperative competition, where states lose some of their external sovereignty in absolute terms, there is no "space" for external sovereignty if global public policy is to succeed. More specifically, given the causal relationship between the two dimensions of sovereignty, external sovereignty ceases to exist among those states in those functional domains in which they agree to operationalize internal sovereignty collectively.

This need for cooperation among governments on a scale and depth not yet witnessed represents the central analytical challenge for global public policy and brings the discussion back to the debate between realists and liberals over the prospects for cooperation in the international system. However, given the focus of both on external sovereignty, neither realism nor liberalism can be very helpful in examining the policy implications of globalization, nor can either predict the prospects for cooperation under conditions of globalization. Indeed, the fact that the globalization of industry has transformed internal sovereignty from a domestic into a global policy issue has profound implications for this debate. As long as the international system was characterized solely by the dynamics of interdependence, the preservation of external sovereignty was the dominant and singular interest of states in the international system, and shaped their identity. And even though neoliberals argued that the nature of the ensuing competition among states was likely to be cooperative, they had to concede the causal powers of anarchy to the neorealists, as the interests of states were exogenously given and could not change.[54]

Globalization alters this one-dimensional constellation of state interests and identity in the international system. It introduces the possibility of change in the formulation and subsequent administration of those interests, neither of which was possible in neorealist or neoliberal thinking. By elevating internal sovereignty to the rank of a global policy issue, the international system, and with it the collectivity of externally sovereign states, is confronted with the management and resolution of this second, equally important determinant of states' overall identity. States no longer exhibit a singular systemic identity—the preservation of external sovereignty—but have to rely on the international system to achieve internal sovereignty as well. Given that for the foreseeable future the international system will continue to be characterized by exclusiveness, and thus anarchy (primarily of course to preserve legal external sovereignty), the only way for governments to achieve inclusiveness, and thus internal sovereignty, is to pool, and thus share, internal sovereignty in those sectors in which globalization has undermined the effectiveness and efficiency of internal sovereignty at the national level.

Therefore, the anarchic structure of the international system does not necessarily cause states to compete in order to maintain their external sovereignty, but it could induce them to cooperate to realize their internal sovereignty. It follows that state interests and identities in the international system are no longer determined a priori, as suggested by the neorealist approach and conceded by neoliberals, but instead may vary (cooperative competition versus competitive cooperation) depending on the issue under consideration. Neoliberals no longer need to concede the causal properties of anarchy to the neorealists. It is true that, under conditions of interdependence, anarchy causes competition among states seeking to preserve external sovereignty. But as shown above, under conditions of globalization, anarchy would be highly detrimental to a state's ability to realize one crucial aspect, if not *the* crucial aspect, of its identity.[55]

If the deeper integration of the world economy is to continue, cooperation is the *only* way to maintain internal sovereignty. Cooperation thus becomes vital to the constitution of states, their interests, and their identities.[56] Just as competition was rational for state engagement in the international system under interdependence, so the need to cooperate motivates states' behavior under conditions of globalization. *Anarchy is no longer just the outcome of, but also the cause for state interests in the international system.* The same reasoning that led neorealists to characterize the international system as competitive (internal sovereignty cannot be achieved under conditions of anarchy at the domestic level, and therefore anarchy must be "exported") now leads to the conclusion that the international system should be cooperative, because one central dimension, a state's identity, can only be achieved collectively.[57]

What is the role of external sovereignty in such a context? Can it still have any meaning? Is there still room for anarchy in the international system? Recall from the discussion at the beginning of this chapter that the principal rationale for the existence of external sovereignty was the desire to establish internal sovereignty in a territorially fixed geographic space—the state. The concept of global public policy, however, is based on a strategy whereby some dimensions of internal sovereignty at the operational level are territorially delinked and functionally disaggregated. "Internal" thus no longer refers to territory but to the spatial extension within which global companies pursue their activities, cutting across a number of externally sovereign territories. Since "internal" no longer refers to territory, external sovereignty, as a heuristic device, loses its utility in the context of globalization.

Put differently, the purpose of external sovereignty was to ensure monopoly power over decisionmaking within a particular territory and to prevent outside interference. Its rationale was conditioned on the fact that internal sovereignty was operationalized territorially. Since internal sovereignty can no longer be achieved in a territorial context, external sovereignty becomes redundant. It has effectively lost its meaning. In fact, since external sovereignty is the central precondition for anarchy, it is to be avoided, as countries would then be unable to cooperate to achieve internal sovereignty. As will be discussed later, however, globalization remains a limited phenomenon. External sovereignty remains an appropriate conceptual tool. Even the collectivity of states that agree to pool their internal sovereignty on a particular policy issue remains externally sovereign (legally and operationally), with respect to each other in other policy domains and to third states in the same policy domain. How likely is it that countries would be willing to abandon their external operational sovereignty?[58] As will be shown in the first and last case studies, this is not as unlikely as one might at first be inclined to believe. The reason is obvious: the incentive for relinquishing external operational sovereignty is the hope of safeguarding its internal counterpart.

To sum up, the discussion on the debate between neorealists and neoliberals characterized the dynamics of interdependence as one of cooperative competition. States relying on the institutional and rule-based infrastructure of the world economy agreed to facilitate international economic exchange by reducing barriers to cross-border flows of goods, services, and capital. The behavior of states in the international system reflected the interests of the dominant domestic private sector coalitions. The goal was to enhance international economic competition, albeit in a reciprocal, that is, cooperative fashion.

Chapter 1 showed that the management of economic interdependence followed an agreed set of principles, emphasizing the reciprocal lowering of cross-border barriers to both real and financial flows. Managing economic interdependence in this way was considered an important precondition for globalization to occur. The mere presence of globalization thus confirms that cooperative competition has occurred. At the same time, however, cooperative competition has created new challenges for states, transforming their identity, interests, and thus behavior in the international system. To preserve the internal dimension of their sovereignty under conditions of globalization, states (barring other responses, which will be discussed in the next chapter) will *have* to cooperate to represent their own interests in the international system and thus preserve their own legitimacy and identity, and indeed rationalize their very existence.

In contrast to the case of interdependence, under conditions of globalization it is cooperation rather than competition that motivates states' global engagement and explains their behavior in the international system. However, given that countries differ over both what is and what is not in the public interest, as well as over how that interest can be best achieved (for more on that see chapter 3), the process or method by which states establish cooperation is likely to be on competitive terms. Whereas *cooperative competition* among states best captures the dynamics of interdependence, globalization inverts that formula and induces *competitive cooperation*. It is important to note, however, that "competition" here does not refer to the outcome of the interaction or to the type of order within which individual actors interact, but to the method or process by which a cooperative order is achieved. Thus competition here should be understood as a bargaining process, ultimately resulting in a cooperative agreement that defines global public policy, that is, the rules and procedures by which internal sovereignty is achieved and maintained in the global economy.

From a behavioral perspective, states' actions may not be all that different when they cooperate, in the case of interdependence, or compete, in the case of globalization. The crucial difference is the interests involved, their purpose, and the outcome of each process: private sector competition in the former, public sector cooperation in the latter. This change in purpose will have a profound impact. Take the case of the Bretton Woods institutions and the other international organizations originally designed to manage interdependence. Rather than promoting the progressive liberalization of cross-border economic flows, which within the established industrial economies has been quite successful, these institutions will have to address the consequences of that liberalization, following the principle of global public policy. This requires considerable change in their mandate and organization.

Given the nature of the challenge that globalization presents to national governments, it seems unlikely that they will not respond. But global public policy is not the only way in which governments can regain or maintain internal sovereignty. On the contrary, as the next chapter will demonstrate, a variety of other strategies can achieve the same goal. However, they cannot do so without jeopardizing not only continued international economic integration but indeed the entire postwar international economic order.

CHAPTER 3

Policy Responses:
Matching Economic and
Political Geography

IF POLICYMAKERS want to retain or regain internal operational sovereignty, they need to ensure that they can maintain or reestablish a considerable degree of symmetry between the political and economic geographies in those sectors affected by globalization. Such an adjustment is most needed where globalization has reached the point at which national public policies have lost their effectiveness and can no longer prevent market failure, or where they have become increasingly inefficient as globalization raises the marginal cost of maintaining internal sovereignty.

In principle there are three possible strategies for reestablishing congruence between political and economic geography. Two of these equate political geography with the continued territorial integrity of the nation-state and attempt to impose that same territorial definition upon the organizational logic and economic geography of corporations. These strategies will be referred to here as defensive and offensive intervention. The third strategy is global public policy. Unlike the other two strategies, global public policy is compatible with the economic geography of globalization. This will require not only considerable adjustment on the part of the national and international institutions, processes, and elites currently charged with public policymaking but also the engagement of new actors.

Defensive Intervention

Policymakers can intervene defensively or offensively in globalization. By maintaining or resurrecting barriers to globalization through protective economic measures such as tariff and nontariff barriers, capital controls, or other national regulatory measures in the domains of transport, communications, and information, *defensive intervention* would in principle return internal sovereignty to the national government. This, in turn, would force companies to reorganize along national lines, much as they did before they adopted global strategies.

To date, defensive intervention has not yet been employed on a large scale, but some have warned that the world risks being engulfed by "a returning tide of protectionism and nationalism of the worst kind."[1] Pressures to intervene defensively became evident during the long and painful Uruguay Round negotiations of the General Agreement on Tariffs and Trade: the round was successfully concluded only after some ambitious liberalization proposals were withdrawn. Today most countries are reluctant to support a new multilateral trade round to further liberalize international trade. There is also evidence that nontariff barriers, including increasing reliance on antidumping measures, have taken on a more prominent role in the industrialized countries. Many of these barriers will be far more difficult to remove than the tariffs they replace.[2] Concern is also growing that the dispute settlement mechanism of the World Trade Organization (WTO) may be used as a more subtle form of defensive intervention:[3] during the first two and a half years of its existence, dispute settlement panels were convened in one hundred cases.[4]

Finally, an increasing number of countries have witnessed a popular backlash against deeper economic integration at the regional and the global level. In Europe this reaction has found its expression in the nationalist campaigns and party platforms of Jimmy Goldsmith in the United Kingdom, Jean-Marie Le Pen in France, Jörg Haider in Austria, and others across the continent.[5] In the United States calls for defensive intervention have grown considerably during the last few years against a background of stagnating wages for unskilled workers and growing income inequality, even though evidence of a causal relationship between these developments and globalization remains disputed.[6] Led by such politically diverse figures as Patrick Buchanan, Ross Perot, and Ralph Nader, this economic nationalist agenda has created unusual political coalitions around the desire to preserve the national identity. This agenda calls (to varying degrees depending on the spokesperson) for tariff barriers on a broad variety of imports, a "social tariff" on manufactured goods from developing countries, curbs on immigration, taxation on consumption of foreign goods, curbs on the activities of multinational enterprises, and the ending of all foreign aid and support of the World Bank and the International Monetary Fund.[7] Although protectionist sentiments have been around a long time, these more recent efforts have found an increasing resonance in Congress and among the general public. They have had a direct impact on the political process, slowing down the administration's international trade agenda (for example, the expansion of the North American Free Trade Agreement) and leading prominent members of the Republican party to tone down their free-trade rhetoric.[8] The agenda is also characterized by a strong anti-big-business sentiment that accuses "corporate executioners" of "worship[ping] at the altar of efficiency" and laying off American workers.[9]

More recently, arguments over the United States' deeper involvement in regional and global economic integration efforts and institutions erupted during the debate over the ratification of the Uruguay Round in 1994, the 1996 presidential race, and the failure to ensure fast track negotiating authority in the fall of 1997. The Uruguay Round agreement included the charter of the newly established WTO, making that body the new arbiter of international trade disputes, with power to enforce trade rulings against its members. Opponents of the WTO decried it as a new form of world government and attacked what they saw as the autocratic nature of the ratification process.[10] After Buchanan's departure from the presidential race, both major party candidates carefully avoided international economic topics. One reason was that the margin of difference between the two on these issues was negligible. But their silence also reflected the inability of both camps to develop a coherent, clear rebuttal to the case for defensive intervention, especially when put as cogently as it was by Buchanan: "If this city [Washington] of parasites that produces nothing ever had to experience the social and economic disruption of factories shut down and jobs gone it would be howling for protectionism."[11] The presidential debate on how the United States would prepare itself for the twenty-first century thus sidestepped one of the core issues that should have been addressed, and that is unlikely to go away as global integration continues.[12]

Offensive Intervention

An alternative strategy to defensive intervention is *offensive intervention*. Here countries themselves become global competitors, striving to provide the most attractive environment possible for the strategies of global companies within their own territorial boundaries, or to lobby other countries on behalf of their domestic corporations in support of their overseas strategies.[13] In the early 1990s offensive intervention was advocated by some geoeconomists, who argued that in a post–cold war world, economic competition would replace military competition.[14] Although the notion of economic warfare has declined in popularity somewhat over the years, some of its aspects—especially the notion of "national" competitiveness—continue to influence the public policy debate and popular thinking in many of the established industrial countries.

Offensive intervention can take place through a variety of economic channels. For example, a government concerned only with gaining competitive advantage for domestic companies could deregulate an industry or lower taxes to attract business activity into its territory. As the first case study, in chapter 4, will show, such a dynamic developed in world financial markets during the 1980s. Similarly, tax competition among national jurisdictions has been present for some time. Yet national governments have only recently acknowledged that fiscal dumping undermines their internal sovereignty: in 1997 the member governments of the Organization for Economic Cooperation and Development (OECD) asked the organization to "develop measures to counter the distorting impact of harmful tax competition on investment and financing decisions."[15]

Other avenues of offensive intervention include subsidies, aggressive export promotion campaigns, generous export insurance guarantees, and the tying of foreign aid to exports. Illegal activities such as bribes and other forms of corruption are no longer excluded. Subsidies grew by 27 percent from 1989 to 1993 in the OECD area.[16] In many countries it has become common practice for politicians to lobby abroad on behalf of the domestic private sector.[17] In the United States such lobbying became official policy with a renewed emphasis on export promotion programs during the first term of the Clinton administration. The justification given by administration officials—that "Washington is merely a late entrant in a game long played by other governments, notably in Europe and Japan"—is hard to dismiss.[18] Not surprisingly, the United States, through political pressure including the personal intervention of Presi-

dent Clinton, scored some spectacular successes, such as the 1994 decision by Saudia Arabia to replace its ailing national airline fleet exclusively with planes from the Boeing Company and McDonnell Douglas
Corporation.[19] Shortly thereafter Saudi Arabia awarded a contract to
AT&T to upgrade the kingdom's telecommunications network, despite
claims by several European competitors that they had made better
offers.[20] These deals, in which the United States outmaneuvered Europeans who were also applying political pressure, were among the largest
in each industry's history.

Regarding illegal activities, a confidential 1995 report by the U.S.
Department of Commerce stated that, over a period of twenty months,
bribes had been used by foreign countries to edge out U.S. competitors
on $36 billion worth of international business deals. The report predicted
that during the next decade over $1 trillion in similar projects would
come up for bid, and suggested that the United States develop an export
promotion strategy equally as aggressive as those of its competitors in
Europe and Japan.[21]

The increasing use of offensive intervention has also been reflected in
a growing reliance on national intelligence agencies in the gathering of
economic information.[22] Economic spying is now widespread among the
United States, Japan, and the countries of the European Union: the
United States has become a major target of industrial espionage, and its
own intelligence agencies have been involved in several well-publicized
incidents.[23] Institutional and bureaucratic politics no doubt also play a
role, as intelligence agencies struggle to redefine their role in a new
global environment. According to the inspector general at the Central
Intelligence Agency, Frederick Hitz, the agency could play an important
role in "leveling the playing field for our companies to do business
abroad."[24] With each of these instruments, used singly or in combination,
legally or illegally, policymakers hope to regain internal sovereignty and
thus influence the economic success of private sector actors within the
territory over which they have jurisdiction.

Intervention can be taken further if the national jurisdiction to which
it is applied is inappropriate or cannot address the particular challenge at
hand. Under these circumstances political rather than economic instruments are used in an effort to reassert internal sovereignty. For example,
policymakers intervene offensively through the extraterritorial application of national law, unilaterally seeking to broaden the reach of their
internal sovereignty to match the economic geography of global corpo-

rate networks. In the United States one of the more prominent examples was California's attempt to impose its unitary tax code on companies such as the Barclays Group and Colgate-Palmolive Company; examples at the federal level include the Helms-Burton Act and the Iran-Libya Sanctions Act.[25]

Obviously for most countries this option is only theoretical. Offensive political intervention is likely to be used only by countries or regions that are politically powerful and economically large enough to expect that other countries might yield to their pressure. Yet another form of intervention can be applied if the territoriality for which intervention is suggested fails to generate sufficient support for either defensive or offensive intervention, but does find backing at the regional or state level. It should therefore come as no surprise when local or regional elites, raising the specter of globalization and the ensuing loss of identity, try to assert greater territorial independence. In its extreme form this type of interventionism—whose motivation can be either offensive, as in the case of the Northern League in Italy, or defensive, as in the case of the separatist movement in the Canadian province of Quebec—can amount to the secession of a region or the partition of a country, redefining territoriality in the hope of regaining internal sovereignty.[26]

Intervention in Practice

These four strategies to regain internal operational sovereignty are not necessarily mutually exclusive. A government could intervene to protect its industry from competition while at the same time waging an aggressive export promotion campaign for that very same industry abroad, or threatening to impose its internal sovereignty on an industry worldwide. German companies have long argued that the perpetuation of stringent multilateral export control regulations on machine tools during the 1980s and 1990s, even after the cold war had ended, could only be explained by the uncompetitiveness of the U.S. machine tool industry. Yet at the same time German policymakers have long resisted the loosening of export controls on certain telecommunications equipment, such as fiber optics, where the U.S. industry dominates the market.

Its advocates' rhetoric notwithstanding, these different forms of intervention have only been used in a limited fashion so far. The reason is simple: they will achieve their goal only at great cost, or not at all. If applied in a more sustained fashion, offensive or defensive intervention will not only bring globalization to a halt but also jeopardize the achievements of interdependence, and so undermine the stability of the world economy. Under the current norms of the international economic system, defensive intervention by one country, even when designed to preserve internal sovereignty, is most likely to lead to retaliation by others, resulting in the progressive disintegration of the world economy, with all the economic, social, and political costs that that would entail.[27] Defensive interventionists like Buchanan, who claim they will "make America the enterprise zone of the industrial world," forget that in such a world the United States would no longer be a privileged "zone" within an integrated world economy, having surrounded itself with high tariffs while its companies have been shut out from markets overseas.[28]

The use of offensive strategies, such as subsidizing an industry with the sole purpose of gaining competitive advantage, will not advance integration either, but rather will divert scarce public funds from important public policy goals. This has already happened in the United States, where in recent years the debate over the economic "war among the states" and the associated waste of public funds for private purposes has sharpened.[29] Apart from being bad public policy, offensive intervention will also provoke retaliation. Indeed, the export promotion offensive initiated by the Clinton administration was justified by Under Secretary of Commerce for International Trade Jeffrey E. Garten with the comment that "they [Europe and Japan] should not have started the ball rolling." Not surprisingly, the Europeans pledged to intensify their own efforts at export promotion once it became clear that their private sector had lost out to Boeing, McDonnell Douglas, and AT&T.[30] As one commentator put it, offensive intervention has an "inherent beggar-thy-neighbor dynamic that can only lead to provocation, escalation and retaliation among the major industrial nations. An approach that consciously uses market intervention to capture a significant share of . . . industries for one's own country, if legitimated for any particular state, becomes a fair game for all."[31] As a result, competitive subsidization will have only marginal effects, in addition to being expensive and fiscally wasteful.

Few would question that countries benefit from increasing the productivity of their industries, especially if they are able to ensure that these benefits are distributed widely. No doubt governments can play an important role here by helping raise the level of education, improve infrastructure, support research and development, and encourage structural reform. But when the notion of competitiveness, which is often used as a synonym for productivity, is attached to entire nations and measured in relative terms, by comparing one nation's competitiveness with another's, international economic integration risks becoming a win-lose, zero-sum game, creating highly unstable relationships and a never-ending struggle to gain the upper hand. Today's comparative advantage may become tomorrow's competitive drag. Concern over competitiveness shifts the focus of policymakers from the country's absolute performance and living standards toward its position relative to other countries. As one commentator aptly observed, an overemphasis by the industrialized countries on national competitiveness is:

> doomed to frustration, since technological catch-up and liberal policy reform mean that emerging market economies are almost certainly bound to grow faster than the United States or the European Union, which will consequently have steadily shrinking shares of world GNP and trade. Britain has had to get used to relative decline for a century or more. . . . Such relativities should be a matter of indifference but in practice states, like individuals, are often more agitated by differential than absolute performance.[32]

An emphasis on relative national competitiveness can thus encourage wasteful government spending and misguided public policies, by leading policymakers to become fixated on developments in other countries rather than on their own country's needs. It is also likely to lead to protectionism.[33] Countries that do not succeed at offensive intervention, yet are determined to intervene, have little choice but to fall back on its defensive counterpart. Finally, if policymakers were to rely on deregulation as the principal tool to increase national competitiveness, and other countries were to respond in kind, the ensuing process of competitive deregulation would not generate the desired outcome either. Rather, internal sovereignty would progressively diminish, defeating the original purpose of the policy.

Redefining political geography through territorial adjustment may generate greater consensus on any of the above strategies and give the appearance of greater control over policy. Yet partition of a country focuses exclusively on the external dimension of sovereignty. In no way does it insulate governments, old or new, from the challenges of globalization. If anything, it makes them more vulnerable. Extraterritoriality is no friend of deeper integration either. It disregards the territorial constraints of internal sovereignty and, by definition, invades the political geography of other nations, challenging their internal sovereignty. Whatever the merits of the approach taken by the United States, as, for example, in the case of Helms-Burton, other countries will not tolerate this imposition of U.S. internal sovereignty upon their own. They will retaliate by imposing their own internal sovereignty on the economic geography defined by the issue at hand. This creates not only confusing but conflicting layers of internal sovereignties in the space-of-flows, resulting in no governance at all and leaving the private sector in a state of confusion, while having little or no effect on the countries that are the target of the policy. Unilaterally imposing internal sovereignty on a global policy issue sets a dangerous procedural precedent for handling the many similar issues that are likely to crowd the agenda of international politics in the twenty-first century.

Finally, even if defensive and offensive economic intervention appeared feasible in theory, there is mounting evidence that international economic integration has already come so far that both forms of intervention have lost their practical effectiveness in a globalizing economic environment. Global firms, with the help of flexible networks that spread across borders, are in a much better position to circumvent or absorb the costs that a resurgence of restrictive trade measures would impose upon them.[34] In many instances they may even be able to profit from such measures. Corporate strategic alliances and cross-investment have made it very difficult to promote, subsidize, or protect "domestic" firms to the exclusion of others. This undermines the ability of public policies to capture territorially the external economies from such offensive interventions as state-sponsored innovation and technology policies. Similarly, where governments have erected barriers to foreign investment in the form of antitrust laws or restrictions on foreign ownership, collaborative linkages give allied firms the political advantage of being a local firm almost anywhere, again overcoming national political boundaries in what from a firm's perspective is a global market.

Not only have defensive and offensive intervention become less effective and more difficult; they are also likely to have unintended consequences that could even accelerate globalization. For example, in an environment of high capital mobility, measures of intervention in trade will exert a direct impact on the volume and direction of investment flows. All forms of defensive intervention in trade, be they tariffs, quotas, nontariff barriers, or gray-area or other regulatory measures, are likely to induce foreign investment in protected markets, defying the restrictive objective of these measures. This phenomenon is likely to gain even greater importance with the conclusion of the international investment agreement currently being negotiated in the OECD.[35] To take another example, a study on the effect of U.S. antidumping policy in reducing import competition showed that the biggest winners may not be the industries that initiate the complaints, but exporters abroad who gain orders at the expense of competitors accused of dumping.[36] The same applies to offensive intervention. Thus, local content rules, discriminatory government procurement practices, and subsidies, although favoring domestic producers in the short run, will also lead foreign producers to establish local production facilities and engage in mergers, so that the nationality of a company is no longer an obstacle to access to these territorially restricted benefits.[37] Indeed, when a few years ago legislation was pending in the United States to treat foreign companies differently from U.S. companies in government research and development programs, the measure was opposed by the U.S. private sector because "narrow eligibility criteria discourage beneficial foreign investment, invite retaliation against U.S. exporters and U.S. companies doing business abroad."[38]

To sum up, all forms of defensive and offensive intervention reemphasize territoriality as an ordering principle of international relations. As such they respond only indirectly to the challenge to internal sovereignty by relying on and attributing renewed weight and importance to external sovereignty—a condition that integration has worked so hard to overcome and that, with the end of the cold war, appeared to have been secured. All these forms of intervention are at odds with globalization and will only succeed if the achievements of interdependence are undone. Thus, defensive and offensive intervention not only would halt and reverse the trend toward globalization, but would also amount to an assault on the established principles of cooperative competition and its norms and institutions, which, as discussed in chapter 2, have been and remain the cornerstones of economic interdependence. Moreover, given the limited effect that these strategies will have on the actual behavior of corporate actors, they are likely to reinforce a sense of political fragmentation, as globalization will continue to progress, worsening the paralysis of current public policies.

Yet even though these interventionist strategies cannot answer for any sustained period the challenge that globalization presents to national governments, they should not be dismissed as inoperable in a political context. They are attractive and popular, as they provide policymakers the appearance of control, while the rhetoric used in their advocacy induces a feeling of security against the declining effectiveness of internal sovereignty. And, as was shown, it is not difficult to find evidence that the use of interventionist strategies is increasing in a number of countries. Unless policymakers are given a viable alternative, governments, notwithstanding the longer-term economic and political consequences, may soon be forced to employ one or a combination of defensive and offensive interventions, as the continued loss of internal operational sovereignty not only calls their legitimacy into question but leads to a further erosion of belief in the institutions of democratic governance, and ultimately to the breakdown of the political and social consensus that internal sovereignty is supposed to uphold.

Global Public Policy

The scenario just outlined makes it all the more imperative that policymakers, the private sector, and the general public focus their attention on the third strategy, global public policy. In principle, global public policy can avoid many of the pitfalls of both forms of intervention. In practice, however, it requires a considerable adjustment on behalf of both the actors and institutions in charge of public policy, and those who have an interest and a stake in its outcome. Global public policy differs from both interventionist strategies in that it reverses the adjustment path between the two geographies by realigning the political with the economic geography. Rather than trying to force the economic geography of globalization to adjust to the political geography of interdependence, global public policy alters the political geography in a way that can both accommodate economic globalization and at the same time allow countries to continue to exercise internal sovereignty. Under these circumstances, the reach and management of internal sovereignty are no longer defined by territoriality, but rather by the spatial extension of globalization, that is, on a functional or sectoral basis. As discussed in the previous chapter, global public policy requires a qualitatively new form of cooperation among countries, as the reach of internal sovereignty is defined by the structure of global corporate networks. Given their focus on external sovereignty, neither realism nor liberalism was helpful in rationalizing this type of cooperation, as states' interests and identities in the international system now go beyond the mere defense of external sovereignty. But global public policy also raises a number of institutional and procedural challenges, which are discussed below. Most important, it will be necessary to demonstrate that the operational aspects of internal sovereignty can indeed be decoupled from territoriality, its formal legal counterpart.

One central challenge is the fact that what is and what is not in the collective or public interest often differs across countries. Hence, for global public policy to be successful, not only would participating societies have to show a willingness to cooperate in the establishment of internal sovereignty; in practice they would have to recognize and accept others' notion of the collective interest and others' definition of the public good. Given that the definition of the public space in each society is the product of a lengthy historical process dating back to at least the Industrial Revolution, and has been shaped by experiences unique to that society, sometimes reflecting cultural attributes, this is a difficult task to say the least. Moreover, different perceptions of the public's interest often result from differences in level of economic development. This needs to be taken into consideration when developing common responses to global problems that reach beyond the OECD. For example, although the industrialized countries are rightly concerned about environmental pollution at the local, regional, and global levels and rank environmental protection among the most important common goods, they cannot necessarily expect developing countries to have the same set of priorities, one of the dominant themes surrounding the negotiations at the Framework Convention on Climate Change in Kyoto.

Even if participating countries could agree on a set of policy issues that they consider to belong in the public domain, and that can only be adequately addressed at the global level, they may still differ on what action to take. Constitutional, cultural, political, intellectual, institutional, bureaucratic, scientific, and other differences and idiosyncrasies, which are often deeply historically rooted, are likely to lead different countries to prefer different strategies on a given issue.[39] Again, policy resolution may require that long-established practices of domestic public policymaking be adjusted to achieve the desired results.

These two examples give an indication of some of the impediments that policymakers are likely to encounter in their domestic environments when embarking on such an ambitious project. Global public policy is

likely to challenge deeply entrenched economic, political, and bureaucratic interests, and in other circumstances it may simply lack broader
support from a society that prefers the status quo to a new environment
that is still vague and often ill defined.

Implementing Global Public Policy

In considering strategies to ease the implementation of global public
policy in a given industry, one approach should be dismissed right at the
outset. Global public policy cannot and does not imply the establishment
of a global government. Such a top-heavy, imposed construct reflects an
overly simplistic adherence to the outmoded notion of territoriality and
the inflexible institutions associated with it, both of which are not very
relevant to the particular issues raised by globalization. A global government would be not only utopian, as it would require states to abdicate
both their internal and external sovereignty in an operational *and* a
formal sense, but unsustainable as well. Both from the perspective of
administrative efficiency and effectiveness, and from the perspective of
political legitimacy and accountability, this option is unrealistic. Rather,
global public policy, if it is to succeed, has to be able to respond continuously both to the changing economic geography of globalization and to
changing functional requirements. No global government could possibly
meet such expectations. Global public policy must be sufficiently adap-
tive to respond to a process of mutual learning among states about each
other's systems of public policymaking. It must also be able to tolerate
some continued diversity of public policymaking among national
systems, while ensuring sufficient cohesion to meet the common good in
a global context.

The key to what may seem at first a contradictory policy prescription
is that *governance*—a social function crucial for the operation of any
market economy, whether national, regional, or global—does not have to
be equated with *government*.[40] This insight provides the cornerstone for
a more promising strategy for global public policy, namely, the delinking
of some elements of the operational aspects of internal sovereignty (governance) from its territorial foundation (the nation-state) and its institutional and legal environment (the government), and their reapplication
on a sectoral—that is, functional—basis. Such a strategy would cut
across national boundaries in order to match up the political geography

of an industry with its economic counterpart, defined by what chapter 2 referred to as the space-of-flows.

This delinking of sovereignty from its territorial and institutional environment relies on the notion that sovereignty in its operational form, and ultimately even in its legal form, is divisible.[41] This divisibility of sovereignty is embedded in the principle of subsidiarity, which implies that economic decisions such as levying taxes, undertaking public expenditures, and regulating the behavior of private sector actors should be made by lower-level jurisdictions unless a clear rationale can be given for assigning them to higher-level jurisdictions.[42] Subsidiarity is also firmly anchored in the U.S. Constitution and formally became part of the European Community with the conclusion of Maastricht Treaty, which established the European Union.[43] A decision to invoke subsidiarity is often a matter of political calculation, and is thus often contested. In both the United States and the European Union the ultimate judgment of the appropriate level of authority or sovereignty rests with the judiciary: with the U.S. Supreme Court and the European Court of Justice, respectively. Given that global public policy addresses the operational and not the formal dimension of internal sovereignty, the need for legal recourse in the case of global public policy is not evident but falls within the domain of "soft" international law.[44] Thus global public policy will be structured around so-called legally nonbinding international instruments. Besides requiring implementation by the participating nations individually, this puts great emphasis on two aspects of global public policy that are crucial to its success: compliance and enforcement. These will be discussed in greater detail in the case studies.

Despite the fact that subsidiarity is not only employed as a technical term but also frequently used as a political instrument, it is helpful for purposes of this study to provide a more differentiated use of this concept. This is especially the case as far as the operational dimension of internal sovereignty is concerned. The concept of subsidiarity allows a more detailed examination of the various strategies that policymakers can adopt to operationalize internal sovereignty in the space-of-flows.

For example, the option to invoke subsidiarity should be explored during all three phases of the public policymaking process: policy identification and agenda setting, policy formulation, and policy implementation. It is also possible to differentiate between *functional* and *structural subsidiarity*.[45] Thus it happens not uncommonly that, from a functional perspective, a given public policy issue, in particular in the realm of economic regulation, is best addressed by formulating global standards, keeping in mind of course that what one calls "global" may well be not entirely so. A global approach avoids an uneven playing field and thus is an important precondition for the private sector to agree to such an arrangement. It can also help prevent regulatory arbitrage by private sector actors, which is likely to deteriorate into offensive intervention as governments face increasing great pressure to deregulate. But taking a global perspective in policy formulation does not imply that both the initial agenda setting and the subsequent policy implementation cannot be delegated to lower administrative levels—regional, national, or local. Subsidiarity here brings the policy process closer to those who have an interest in the outcome and makes use of existing bureaucratic structures and institutions. In fact, as long as formal sovereignty remains in the hands of national authorities, policy implementation will have to be located at the national or the subnational level.

To help articulate the notion that governance does not necessarily imply government, it is helpful to introduce a distinction between *vertical* and *horizontal subsidiarity*.[46] This can be achieved by using the term subsidiarity in a much broader sense. "Sub" no longer just refers to the narrow spatial context of policymaking at a lower policy level as we know it from the European Union or the Tenth Amendment to the U.S. Constitution. It is used in a functional sense and refers to any actor or institution that is in the best position to support the operationalization of internal sovereignty in the global context. In seeking to improve the legitimacy, acceptability, efficiency, and effectiveness of public policies, *vertical subsidiarity* delegates public policymaking to other public sector actors at both lower and higher levels of governance. In terms of globalization, this refers mainly to international institutions. However, this does not mean that local actors may not play an important role in enforcing and monitoring globally agreed rules and standards. Vertical subsidiarity, especially with regard to the distinction between function and structure, works both ways and provides practical guidance to the often quoted line, "Think globally, act locally." *Horizontal subsidiarity* seeks the same improvements as the vertical variant by delegating, or "outsourcing," part, but not all, of public policymaking to nonstate actors: for example, to businesses and their associations, labor groups, nongovernmental and nonprofit organizations, consumer groups, foundations, and other interested parties, or a combination thereof. These actors have a direct stake in the outcome of public policy. More important, their range of activity is not bound by a particular territory, which frees them from the constraints of territoriality in external or internal sovereignty. In addition, these actors' better information, knowledge and understanding of increasingly complex, technology-driven, and fast-changing public policy issues will generate greater acceptability and legitimacy for global public policy. Such public-private partnerships initiated by invoking horizontal subsidiarity will also produce a more efficient and effective policy process for the design and implementation of public policies for a particular global industry. Finally, horizontal subsidiarity encourages mutual learning among national public policy systems, an important precondition for achieving greater cooperation among them.

Both vertical and horizontal subsidiarity can be employed as early as the phase of *policy identification* and the setting of a policy agenda. Horizontal subsidiarity should play an important role in policy identification. A broad-based dialogue among national governments and relevant nonstate actors as well as subnational administrative units and relevant nonstate actors should be initiated to identify global policy issues of common concern. In setting the policy agenda, structural subsidiarity should be used extensively, even for issues that are global from a functional perspective, so that the dialogue can take place at both the national and the subnational level.

Later, at the stage of global public *policy formulation,* it will be necessary in many cases to develop and agree on a joint policy formula. Such a formula has to be quite detailed, for example setting specific quantitative indicators, targets, or levels. Joint policy formulation avoids creating an uneven playing field, which is important for the reasons already discussed.[47] But although policy is developed for a collective of countries, parties to the formulation process should explore the possibility of allowing a certain degree of flexibility, so that countries can retain some idiosyncratic elements of their own national approach. For the global financial services industry such functional subsidiarity has proved critical in the development of joint formulas (see chapter 4). Although such differences can create minor bumps in the playing field, other parties to the agreement should consider them an acceptable price to pay.

How and to what extent governments want to use the partnership approach and involve nonstate actors in the formulation of joint policies has to be decided on a case-by-case basis. Nonstate actors may be granted actual voting rights, for example, or may be limited to an advisory role. Whatever form it takes, their participation may lead to cross-national partnership coalitions between state and nonstate actors, or encourage the intensification of global issue coalitions. As will be shown, this can help facilitate compromise among governments by exposing bureaucratic and institutional rivalries that have little or nothing to do with the issue at hand, but can prevent the issue from being resolved.

Policy implementation is the third phase. Structural subsidiarity should be applied as widely here as during the phase of policy identification. This not only avoids unnecessary duplication of bureaucratic activities, but also allows implementation to be closer to the economic activity to be regulated, again reducing the potential for information asymmetries. The possibility that differences in national and subnational structures and mechanisms of implementation will lead to an uneven playing field cannot be excluded, however. Implementation therefore needs to be monitored and may require some adjustments to domestic public policymaking structures.

The various applications of subsidiarity mentioned above are already being practiced in some form or another, with different degrees of success. Thus vertical subsidiarity will remain a central element of global public policy as long as formal internal sovereignty remains bounded by territoriality. Many internationally agreed-upon obligations are subsequently written into domestic law. An exception is the European Union, where some aspects of formal internal sovereignty have indeed been transferred from the member states to Brussels. The dispute settlement mechanism of the WTO is another example where some elements of formal sovereignty are emerging at the global level, although with a rather broad array of escape clauses.

Horizontal subsidiarity is also practiced in the setting of international standards through the International Organization for Standardization, and in the field of international environmental cooperation. An example of the latter is the participation of both environmental groups and industry in the OECD's policy deliberations on international trade and the environment. The International Labour Organisation has long-established procedures for horizontal subsidiarity as well. It is also generally recognized that the World Bank has endorsed the partnership idea and initiated more regular contact with the broader private sector, and with nongovernmental organizations and other nonprofit communities, and has begun to include them in both policy identification and implementation. Another instance of horizontal subsidiarity, although less institutionalized, was the negotiations surrounding the global climate treaty, which culminated in the Earth Summit in Rio de Janeiro in 1992. Never before then had nonstate actors been so deeply involved in both the setting of the agenda and the negotiation of an international agreement.[48] At the same time, however, greater reliance on horizontal subsidiarity has in many instances remained more of a reactive and ad hoc policy response to increased pressure from nonstate actors. It does not yet represent the systematic and comprehensive policy response that, this study argues, economic globalization calls for and which is further developed below.

The introduction of horizontal subsidiarity during policy implementation is probably the most innovative and most controversial strategy to separate the operational aspect of internal sovereignty from its formal counterpart. Yet it could turn out to be the most promising strategy and therefore deserves greater attention. Taking again the case of regulatory policy, an extreme version of horizontal subsidiarity would amount to self-regulation. Governments would retain the monopoly of formulating regulatory policy for a particular global industry, but would delegate all implementation and enforcement of the regulations to the industry at which the policy is directed. Although possible in theory, such an arrangement is unlikely. As will be shown, a mixed regulatory strategy is more realistic. Here some, but not all, of the implementation process (data collection, monitoring, and supervision) is delegated to a regulatory organization in which both the public and the private sectors are represented. Even some enforcement and disciplinary activity could under certain circumstances be delegated to this mixed regulatory organization. The exact composition of "self" in this partly public, partly self-regulatory scheme remains to be determined. Thus which nonstate actors get involved in this scheme should be decided on a case-by-case basis. However, following the general practice of public policy, all those who have a stake in the outcome should have formal access.

Less controversial are two other forms of horizontal subsidiarity that have gained in prominence during the last few years but are still underutilized and deserve much greater attention, especially as far as the transnational dimension is concerned. The first involves the so-called third sector, which lies at the interface of the private and the public spheres, composed of institutions that are private in form but public in purpose.[49] It is not inconceivable that existing or newly created third-sector organizations could take on certain roles in global public policymaking. At a minimum they could act as mediators between opposing interests on a given functional issue. The second form involves the individual at large—the "global citizen"—who can have substantial influence over the behavior of global economic actors on both the supply and the demand side, as an investor and a consumer, respectively.

The three forms of horizontal subsidiarity just outlined are not mutually exclusive, and a combination of all three may well be the most effective and efficient form of creating new partnerships for improving global public policymaking. This is especially the case if outsourcing to nonstate actors relies to a greater degree on market or incentive-based approaches, which, as has been demonstrated in the national context, are often much more transparent and cost efficient and, most important, more effective.[50]

Horizontal Subsidiarity: A Case Study

Here it may be helpful to describe in some detail the structure and dynamics of horizontal subsidiarity. In the United States the securities industry and its regulator the Securities and Exchange Commission (SEC) have long relied on a mixed regulatory structure to monitor the activities of the National Association of Securities Dealers (NASD), the private sector organization that regulates the over-the-counter securities market.[51] The case of the NASD is particularly instructive for two reasons. First, it provides insights into the structure and mandate of an organization whose success depends critically on its ability to accommodate very large numbers of participants and transactions, to evaluate large amounts of data in a short time, and to detect fraudulent behavior—all of which the NASD does through the use of sophisticated computer technologies. Given the scope and purpose of global public policy, the ability to accommodate large numbers and detect fraudulent behavior is a necessary although not sufficient condition for any global regulatory effort. Second, the example of the NASD highlights some of the weaknesses and dangers in setting up an organization that manages under one roof both public and private interests—thus anticipating criticisms that will certainly arise in response to proposals for global public policy.

The NASD was established for the purpose of cooperating with regulators in their efforts to prevent improper transactions in the securities market.[52] Pursuant to the provisions of federal law, the NASD adopts, administers, and enforces the rules governing the securities industry. These rules must be designed to promote just and equitable principles of trade, and to meet other statutory requirements. The SEC supervises the NASD's operations and is authorized to review all its disciplinary actions and decisions.[53] In addition, the NASD carries out its regulatory responsibility through a variety of activities including the following: member education; on-site examinations of member firms; cooperative programs with government agencies and industry organizations that solve problems affecting investors, public companies, and member firms; forums for investors and members to arbitrate disputes; and, most important for the purposes of this study, continuous automated surveillance of the markets it operates. The SEC has the right to review applications for membership in the NASD and examine any changes made in the rules by the NASD Board of Governors, and it ensures criminal enforcement of violations. In conjunction with all of these activities, the NASD requires the registration of all securities brokers and dealers, and it maintains a detailed file containing professional and personal data as a means of protecting the integrity of the organization.[54]

The National Association of Securities Dealers Automated Quotations (NASDAQ) system is a computerized system that provides price information on the stocks of thousands of companies to broker dealers.[55] To prevent unlawful activity, the NASD continuously monitors securities trading through this system. Using sophisticated hardware and specialized software, NASDAQ's monitoring system tracks price quotes generated daily across the country, flagging any unusual price and volume movements.[56] If changes in an indicator such as volume, price, or quote spread cannot be explained by the system's mathematical model, it automatically triggers an alert.[57] The automated surveillance software is essential for detecting possible insider trading or other questionable trading patterns, and it continues to be refined.[58] In 1995 the market surveillance system triggered 7,859 online price and volume alerts, leading to 221 formal investigations and the referral of 113 cases to the SEC for further examination or prosecution.[59]

The recent history of the NASD also highlights some of the dangers inherent in relying on public-private partnerships when developing frameworks for global public policy. In 1994 a well-publicized study suggested that NASDAQ dealers kept trading spreads, and thus profit margins, too wide, furthering their own private interests at the expense of the investing public's interest.[60] These allegations prompted investigations by the SEC and the Department of Justice in late 1994 into NASD rules and their enforcement.[61]

In a preemptive move, the NASD itself, at the suggestion of SEC chairman Arthur Levitt, responded by appointing a high-profile commission headed by former senator Warren B. Rudman to examine the market's operation.[62] The commission's review was limited largely to issues of public governance and avoided issues subject to the ongoing investigation by the SEC and the Justice Department. Nevertheless, since the two categories were implicitly linked, it was hoped that any recommendations made by the commission in one category would ease the pressure on the NASD by public authorities.

The report of the NASD Select Committee on Structure and Governance, the "Rudman Report," released in the fall of 1995, made two criticisms—both revealing considerable organizational and structural weaknesses in the NASD—that seem particularly relevant for this study.[63] First, the report found that the association's regulatory and enforcement division was both understaffed and underfinanced. As a result, only 2 percent of all investor complaints made in 1994 resulted in disciplinary action against brokers or securities firms.[64] Second, the report stated that the NASD was paying too much attention to private interests and not enough to the public's interest. The commission pointed to the fact that although the NASD and NASDAQ have separate boards of directors, both boards have traditionally been dominated by representatives of NASDAQ firms. In 1995, for example, ten of the fifteen members of the NASDAQ board and twenty-one of the twenty-six members of the NASD board were officials from NASDAQ market makers. The report also strongly criticized the housing of both operation and oversight of the market in a single unit. The commission suggested that the enforcement and disciplinary activities of NASDAQ be separated from the operation of the market. This was to be achieved by creating a new entity called NASD Regulation Inc., which would be responsible for all regulatory issues concerning NASDAQ. As before, the operation of the market would remain the responsibility of the NASDAQ board of directors. Under the new scheme both NASD Regulation Inc. and the NASDAQ board would be overseen by the NASD. To deal with the problem of insider overrepresentation on the boards, the Rudman commission recommended that, in the case of the NASD board, the majority (60 percent, or five members) should come from the public at large. The ratio recommended for the other two boards was 50 percent. Furthermore, the staff of the three operations should not overlap. In addition, to further serve the public's interest, the report recommended that the NASD create an ombudsman position to handle complaints from small investors and set up an internal oversight office to police itself.

With investigations by the SEC and the Justice Department pending, the NASD was quick to respond to most of the Rudman commission's recommendations. Within a month the NASD board approved the suggestion to create a separate regulatory subsidiary.[65] The association shied away from the commission's exact numerical recommendations for board membership, but it claimed that, in principle, it would adhere to the recommendation to increase the public's representation.[66] The NASD also announced that it would increase its regulatory budget considerably.[67] To further signal its intention to rectify the system's shortcomings, the NASD hired a top-rank regulator to become the first head of the new independent regulatory division.[68]

On completion of their own investigations, both the SEC and the Justice Department also concluded that the existing NASD system was biased against the public's interest. The SEC charged that there was insufficient transparency and disclosure for small investors, and it instituted several rules designed to ensure greater public access to trading information and thus put individual investors on a more equal footing with dealers and market makers.[69] Despite efforts to soften the SEC's criticism, in mid-1996 the NASD was publicly censured by the SEC for failing "to comply with certain NASD rules and, without reasonable justification or excuse, fail[ing] to enforce compliance with the Exchange Act, the rules and regulations thereunder and its own rules."[70] In addition, in response to the public censure, which hurt the image and standing of NASDAQ relative to competing exchanges, the NASD agreed to institute a variety of new procedures, as well as to spend an additional $100 million over the next five years to "enhance its system for market surveillance, including the development of an enhanced audit trail, surveillance, enforcement and internal audit."[71]

For its part, the Justice Department "found substantial evidence of coercion and other misconduct in this industry."[72] The NASD was able to avoid the accusation of price fixing and thus escape criminal charges, but had to submit to a number of new procedures. These include random taping of conversations on over-the-counter trading desks, spot checks of tapes and trading activity by regulators, stepped-up monitoring of NASDAQ traders through the designation of an antitrust compliance officer, and the filing of quarterly reports with the Justice Department to certify compliance. In addition, "the Justice Department will be able to force Wall Street firms to secretly tape traders suspected of violating the rules."[73]

It remains to be seen whether all of these actions will suffice to redress the balance between the public and the private interest in this mixed regulatory organization. In fact, a number of commentators have suggested that the actions taken may not be enough, especially if there is no enhanced enforcement effort by the regulators themselves.[74] The important point for this study, however, is that, when establishing an industry organization responsible for the implementation of global public policy, policymakers must ensure that its structure and rules do not entail a bias against the public interest. This is not because of anybody's preference of the public over private interests, but rather because experience shows that sooner or later market failure will occur, and a costly and complicated restructuring will have to follow. This not only reduces the faith of the public in horizontal subsidiarity as an alternative means of operationalizing internal sovereignty, but it also hurts the image of the private sector in the eyes of the general public, which is likely to turn elsewhere to meet its interest—in this case to other stock exchanges such as the New York Stock Exchange.

Implications for Policy

The experience of the NASD shows that mixed regulation, with the participation of all interested parties, offers a number of advantages over traditional public regulation that are particularly relevant for global public policy. The most important of these are briefly spelled out here and developed at greater length in the case studies. First, mixed regulation is likely to provide an incentive to industry to participate in a framework for global public policy, since it promises some regulatory relief— not necessarily in the form of deregulation, which may or may not be an outcome, but through a process of reregulation that leads to administrative streamlining, shorter time lags, and simplification. Second, if a global mixed regulatory organization agrees to accept responsibility for part of policy implementation, differences among national bureaucracies and their resistance to change (not always due to the regulatory issue at hand, but often the result of bureaucratic politics) are of less and possibly no relevance to finding a global solution.[75]

Third, information asymmetries between regulators and the regulated, already a common source of regulatory and consequently of government failure at the national level, are likely to be an even greater problem in a global setting.[76] Mixed regulation will lead to a considerable reduction of these asymmetries. By involving nonstate actors in the public policy-making process, information gathering is no longer restricted to the national but can take place in the global network, allowing regulations to be applied in a more effective and efficient way and avoiding the regulatory dialectic discussed in chapter 2.[77]

Fourth, given the high technological intensity of most global industries and the fact that new technologies are being introduced at a rapid pace, a mixed regulatory regime is in a better position to assess the regulatory implications of such a rapidly and constantly changing public policy environment, and to suggest and implement appropriate adjustments. Moreover, the incentives that delegating part of the regulatory activity creates could lead to innovative approaches to the prevention of market failure. For example, it may encourage an industry to alter product specifications at the research and development or the design stage to such a degree that the need for regulation is reduced or even eliminated. As in the policy identification phase, the exact structure, participants, and rules of policy implementation depend on the public policy issue under consideration and therefore need to be decided on a case-by-case basis. The first step for policymakers should be to initiate a dialogue among all parties involved, to explore the possibility of setting up a global public policy regime in the sector in question.

The degree to which public-private partnerships can be used at any of the three phases of policymaking, but especially during the last one, depends of course on the willingness of nonstate actors (especially industry) to take on some of the regulatory responsibilities conventionally performed by state actors and execute those responsibilities in a professional and ethical manner. In principle, nothing argues against such an approach, although in practice some may question the wisdom of an arrangement that puts the pursuit of both public and private interests under the care of the same institution. One way for public authorities to reduce the risk of self-regulatory failure is to require greater transparency of industrial activity. As the case studies will discuss in greater detail, applying strict principles of disclosure-based regulation is one important way to allow public sector and other nonstate actors to review industry activity on a regular and timely basis, and thus reduce the risk of market failure under conditions of mixed regulation.[78]

In addition to providing extensive disclosure, private sector actors must be asked to contribute to the success of horizontal subsidiarity by improving their internal control and risk management structures in ways that reduce or even eliminate the chance of market failure. These efforts must cover both the organization itself and those who use it to engage in illegal activities. Numerous examples in the areas of financial risk, environmental pollution, and export controls come to mind. The case studies will address some of these. Much will therefore depend on the willingness and ability of private sector actors to participate in this effort and make the necessary adjustments in a responsible and reliable fashion.

There will no doubt be opponents to such an arrangement. The business community will resist the intrusiveness of the disclosure rules and the cost of internal reform, but it should consider the alternative. Given that governments will not allow their internal sovereignty to be undermined, the only available alternative—defensive intervention—imposes a much higher cost on business. Citizen groups will raise questions about the degree of trust given to the private sector in executing public functions, but they should consider that they are likely to have greater and more direct influence over public policy under such an arrangement than under either of the two interventionist strategies.

But although the principle of horizontal subsidiarity can address the organizational challenge of separating operational internal sovereignty from its formal dimension, it brings with it other potential problems. As mentioned in chapter 2, internal sovereignty presumes popular sovereignty, that is, the legitimation of public policies at regular intervals through democratic elections. Yet by decoupling the process and practice of internal sovereignty from its territorial base, global public policy runs the risk of undermining popular sovereignty and thus the democratic nature of the policymaking process even further.

The problem of democratic control arises with respect to both vertical and horizontal subsidiarity. Starting with vertical subsidiarity, the problem of democratic control is not new. It has become an issue in the context of European integration (where it is also known as the "democratic deficit"), and more recently with respect to the North American Free Trade Agreement, the ratification of the Uruguay Round, and the debate over fast track.[79] Concerns over the democratic deficit become particularly acute when some aspects of public policymaking are delegated to international organizations, which in a number of cases has already occurred and will have to continue if internal sovereignty is to be preserved. At present, most international institutions that would be charged with implementing global public policy do not meet the most minimal standards of popular sovereignty. This raises doubts about the accountability and legitimacy of global public policy, and therefore enhancing popular sovereignty should become part of the reform agenda of these institutions. If new institutions to deal with global public policy issues are to be created, the potential for democratic deficit in their operation will have to be taken into account.[80] It is not sufficient to rely on the fact that, ultimately, formal internal sovereignty will be applied when an international agreement is subjected to national ratification procedures. As will be shown in chapter 4, the pressure on national legislatures to acquiesce in an internationally negotiated agreement is considerable and reduces the option for exercising democratic control.

Concerns over a democratic deficit should also be taken seriously because it is often used as the second pillar in the antiglobalization rhetoric of defensive interventionists, who call for, among other things, withdrawal from the WTO because it undermines national sovereignty.[81] Thus protectionist forces can easily disguise their agenda by hiding it behind concerns about a democratic deficit, and achieve their goals indirectly by appealing to democratic principles and procedures of domestic public policymaking. The analytical framework developed here allows one to expose and isolate such forces, first by showing that the claim of loss of sovereignty is false, and second by addressing the problem of the democratic deficit itself. Turning first to the issue of sovereignty, we can now see that, unlike under the General Agreement on Tariffs and Trade, which embodied a mutually agreed reduction in external economic sovereignty, many of the new issues on which the WTO focuses (competition policy, trade and environmental or social standards, dispute settlement mechanisms, and others) have been raised in an effort to maintain or even regain sovereignty. However, it is the internal dimension of sovereignty, the one challenged by globalization, with which these efforts are concerned.

Second, protectionists can be isolated by addressing the problem of a democratic deficit. In the context of vertical subsidiarity, greater emphasis should be placed on its structural aspects, that is, the delegation of some aspects of policymaking to lower administrative levels, where established democratic structures are in place, without impeding the goal of functional equivalence as in the case of regulatory policy issues, for example. This not only brings the policy process closer to those who have an interest in the outcome, but can make use of an already existing bureaucracy. In fact, as long as formal sovereignty remains in the hands of national authorities, policy implementation will have to be located at the national or the subnational level. It will, however, be necessary to establish the relevant linkages between the local, national, and global policymaking levels. For the moment, nongovernmental organizations have become the principal actors in the definition of global interests and are becoming an important force in the realization of structural and horizontal subsidiarity.[82] Yet it is much too early to predict the final outcome of what must be considered a modest change in that direction.

With regard to horizontal subsidiarity it becomes immediately obvious that the involvement of nonstate actors itself contributes to a reduction in the democratic deficit. However, once an international organization has decided to outsource part of the policymaking process to nonstate actors, it must ensure that all parties that have an interest in the issue also have access to the process, thus avoiding the weaknesses and problems that became apparent in the investigations surrounding the NASD's decisionmaking. If the necessary institutional and operational guidelines are adhered to, horizontal subsidiarity will lead to an increase in accountability and accessibility compared with current international decisionmaking processes.

The case studies in the following chapters will apply the conceptual framework developed here in a more detailed and concrete policy context. The choice of cases reflects the wide spectrum of public policy issues—economic and security issues alike—where globalization has led governments to reconsider the preference ordering of their interests (from cooperative competition to competitive cooperation) and to which they are now forced to respond.

CHAPTER 4

Global Financial Markets: Pioneers in Global Public Policy

THIS IS THE FIRST of three case studies that seek to probe the success and limitations of governments' attempts to construct global public policy responses to the challenges of globalization. As was shown in chapter 1, one of the central features of globalization has been the rapid expansion of international financial activity during the last decade. Financial markets are today larger and more liquid than at any other time in history. Increasingly, this is resulting in deeper levels of financial integration, as the distinction between domestic and international markets becomes blurred. To succeed in this environment, major financial firms have become global actors with interests and operations in all the world's major financial centers.

Together with the increasing opportunities that globalization offers borrowers, investors, and financial intermediaries has come a series of challenges to the internal sovereignty of national governments and in particular their regulatory authorities.[1] Some argue that financial integration is causing governments to lose power over their own economies. The example most often cited is that of the worldwide foreign exchange markets and the constraints they place on central bankers' and finance ministers' ability to control exchange rates. In addition, not only do the growing powers of national and international bond markets limit the flexibility of governments to chart independent fiscal and monetary policies, but governments also find themselves more constrained in what they can spend, as raising money is not as straightforward as it once was. Moreover, financial integration and footloose capital have combined to make taxation an international rather than a domestic issue. Not only is it difficult to determine where a global company should be taxed; even in cases where jurisdiction can be agreed on, many companies are easily able to reshuffle their tax liabilities from countries with higher to those with lower rates of taxation. Finally, new technologies and financial instruments such as derivatives and electronic cash are threatening to undermine even those tools that governments still have at their disposal to control the economy and the behavior of economic actors.

Despite the widespread attention these issues have received, the reaction by governments has so far been slow and difficult to coordinate. At present the available empirical evidence is insufficient to allow a thorough assessment of the evolving relationship among national governments, international institutions, and nonstate actors as they respond to globalization.[2] An exception, however, can be found in efforts among the Group of Ten (G-10) countries to develop international regulatory standards under the auspices of the Basle Committee on Banking Supervision.[3] The origin, evolution, and aftermath of the so-called Basle Accord provide a rich empirical ground for examining the complex relationships between actors participating in an effort to establish a global public policy framework. This chapter undertakes such an examination, placing the Basle Accord in the context of the analytical and policy framework developed in chapters 2 and 3.

Concluded in 1988,[4] the Basle Accord was initially hailed as a major success. However, it soon became obvious that the policy framework it established was too centralized and inflexible. The new regime was unable to respond to the dynamics of a continuously evolving global financial services industry, as the integration of national financial industries progressed and new financial instruments transformed the business. In addition, the global financial services industry was hit by two major scandals that revealed fundamental loopholes and shortcomings in the framework.

The Basle Accord: Anatomy of a Global Regulatory Agreement

In the early 1970s the volatile international macroeconomic environment and the possibility that some industrializing countries might fail to

honor their debts undermined public confidence in financial markets—
both domestic and international.[5] When confidence was further eroded in
1974 by several well-publicized bank failures that had international
repercussions, bank regulators for the first time acknowledged publicly
the need for international cooperation in the field of bank supervision.[6]
Regulators attributed these failures to a failure of bank supervision to
keep pace with the increasing international integration of the financial
services industry. In the words of Peter Cooke, the second chairman of
the Basle Committee, "There was, in effect, a supervisory vacuum in this
new global market which needed to be filled. Neither the supervisors, nor
indeed the banks themselves, had fully appreciated the degree to which
the banking environment was changing in character and the new and
increasing risks involved in international business. Supervisors were still
very much domestically oriented within the framework of different
national banking systems."[7]

The Basle Committee on Banking Regulations and Supervisory Practices was established at the end of 1974 by central bank governors of the
G-10 industrialized countries plus Luxembourg. In the committee's first
decade, representatives of the member countries supported a series of
principles for supervising banks' international operations, in the hope of
making the international banking system more stable.[8] Later, in the aftermath of the collapse of Bank of Credit and Commerce International
(BCCI), these principles were once again revised with the understanding
that globally active banks would be policed on a worldwide basis by a
single home-country bank regulator, and would thus be unable to evade
what policymakers believed was a tightly coordinated web of national
bank regulations.[9]

Another issue that drew the attention of bank regulators was the maintenance of adequate levels of capital by banks—a cornerstone of a sound
and stable financial system. Multilateral efforts to both raise and harmonize capital adequacy standards among the leading industrial nations had
started in the late 1970s.[10] Although members of the Basle Committee
were highly skeptical of the prospects of harmonizing regulatory standards across countries, they also felt that making the effort was critical
to the stability of the international financial system. Divergent capital
requirements in different countries, they believed, would have adverse
prudential effects, as weaker standards in one country would force other
countries to intervene offensively, lowering their standards in an effort to
protect the competitive standing of their banks. The result would be a

cycle of competitive deregulation. The difficulties that harmonization was likely to face were best described by George Blunden, Governor of the Bank of England and the Basle Committee's first chairman:

> In spite of the trend towards integration of banking systems across international frontiers, there are still . . . great variations in national banking systems. Even if these distinctive national characteristics did not exist, it would not be possible to move towards the integration of national banking supervisory systems into an internationally coherent system, without the creation of a new supra-national supervisory authority. The banking system of a country is central to the management and efficiency of its economy; its supervision will inevitably be a jealously guarded national prerogative. Its subordination to an international authority is a highly unlikely development, which would require a degree of political commitment which neither exists nor is conceivable in the near future.[11]

Blunden's statement laid out the two difficulties that any attempt at global public policy in this domain would face. First, there were wide variations in participants' definitions of what is and is not in the public interest, even in the area of bank regulation. Second, members of the G-10 were unlikely to delegate the degree of operational sovereignty necessary for such an agreement to come to fruition.

Over the next ten years the member countries of the committee engaged in what often seemed a frustrating and slow negotiating process to harmonize their capital standards. When the committee finally announced its agreement in July 1988, it was considered a major accomplishment of international regulatory cooperation. Yet this global public policy effort was helped by a unique set of *domestic* political circumstances and economic forces in one of the member countries, the United States. These circumstances, coupled with the United States' political and economic power, inspired and drove the negotiations to the eventual conclusion of an agreement.

U.S. bank regulators (the Federal Reserve, the Comptroller of the Currency, and the Federal Deposit Insurance Corporation, or FDIC) had been concerned about declining bank capital ratios—domestic and international—for some time. Securitization (see chapter 1) and the growing competitive strength of European and Japanese banks had sharply eroded U.S. commercial banks' competitive positions in both domestic and international financial markets.[12] As the large U.S. money center banks responded to this challenge by engaging in riskier behavior, particularly in the form of highly leveraged loans, their capital base deteriorated sharply.[13] Meanwhile, during the 1970s the number of bank failures had begun to rise again after a long period of stability stretching back to the 1930s. Several unprecedented failures of billion-dollar banks raised the concerns of policymakers and the public, as the average size of banks needing assistance from the Federal Reserve or the FDIC also grew.[14]

Regulators and Congress agreed in principle that some response to this challenge to internal sovereignty was necessary.[15] At the same time, however, they disagreed over the proper extent of the new regulation. Despite congressional concerns that higher capital standards should apply to all banks, the Federal Reserve succumbed to pressure from the large money center banks and excluded them, for the most part, from the new, more stringent regulations with regard to capital standards. This situation changed drastically with the eruption of the Latin American debt crisis in 1982. In addition to exposing the low capital ratios of the money center banks, the debt crisis propelled Congress into a powerful bargaining position with respect to both the banks and their regulators.[16] The U.S. contribution to the international rescue package, which consisted of an increase in International Monetary Fund (IMF) quotas, required congressional approval. During the course of a series of hearings, a consensus developed within Congress that the regulators had been insufficiently alerted to the unfolding international debt crisis and had wrongly allowed the money center banks to delay enforcement of the higher capital standards. Proper enforcement, Congress felt, would have protected the U.S. economy from the repercussions of the debt crisis. Congressional sentiment toward the regulators was probably best expressed by Senator William Proxmire (D-Wisc.), who asked at one of the hearings, "Where were our bank regulators? . . . [T]hey did everything except what they are paid to do, and that is to regulate."[17]

After some initial resistance (which highlighted the international competitive pressure felt by the money center banks and their fear of the additional costs that carrying more capital implied), the Federal Reserve and the Comptroller of the Currency responded to congressional pressure and committed themselves to more stringent and clearly defined numerical targets for *all* banks. Within weeks the IMF quota increase passed the legislature. Throughout this process the banks, especially the large, internationally active ones, had fiercely resisted further regulatory encroachment by either Congress or the regulators. Indeed, earlier in the year they had successfully challenged the internal sovereignty of regulators to enforce any capital standards.[18] Congress, determined to ensure that what many legislators considered an "international bailout for adventurous U.S. bankers"[19] would not happen again, recognized that further legislation was necessary to strengthen the internal sovereignty of bank regulators by furnishing them with sufficient statutory power, and to codify the commitment by regulators to increase and enforce capital standards for all banks.

U.S. policymakers were at the same time coming to the realization that strengthening domestic regulatory powers alone would be insufficient to safeguard the U.S. financial system from another international financial crisis. Domestic supervision could only be effective in the context of a multinational agreement on capital adequacy standards. The globalization of the financial services industry had progressed to the point where higher capital standards in the United States alone could not insulate the U.S. system from a crisis in another financial market. The economic geography of the financial services industry had become decoupled from the political geography of U.S. bank regulation, and a financial crisis outside U.S. jurisdiction could easily harm the country's banking system. Moreover, legislators, particularly those from states like California and New York, where most of the money center banks are located, were sympathetic to the banks' arguments that defensive intervention in the form of a unilateral strengthening of capital standards would not only fail to achieve the goal of financial stability, but would also undermine the competitive position of U.S. banks in the global financial services industry.

The money center banks received strong support for their arguments from one of their regulators, the Federal Reserve. According to former Federal Reserve chairman Paul Volcker:

> There are intense competitive pressures in these markets, and this is an area where it is important, to the degree possible, to have a common international approach . . . . I would also note that—not as any kind of excuse, but as a fact—banks undoubtedly have felt under very heavy pressure internationally, and carrying more capital is a cost. From the viewpoint of an individual institution, if it feels its competitors, particularly in this business which is literally worldwide, have a competitive advantage, this is not an atmosphere in which it is easy to get capital.[20]

Higher U.S. standards, in other words, would lead to further erosion of market share, weakening the financial strength of U.S. banks and contributing to future domestic and international financial crises.

In light of these concerns, in 1983 Congress passed the International Lending Supervisory Act (ILSA).[21] Recognizing the de facto separation of the economic geography of the financial services industry from the political geography of U.S. bank regulation, ILSA directed the Federal Reserve chairman and the secretary of the Treasury to "encourage governments, central banks, and regulatory authorities of other major banking countries to work toward maintaining, and where appropriate strengthening, the capital bases of banking institutions involved in international lending."[22] Noting that unilateral action might put U.S. banks on an uneven playing field, ILSA also asked regulators to seek an international agreement on harmonized capital adequacy standards within the framework of the Basle Committee. Regulators were required to report back to Congress within a year on the progress toward such an agreement. ILSA thus created considerable political pressure from both Congress and the private sector for U.S. regulators to persuade their counterparts in the G-10 to develop a global public policy framework for the regulation of capital standards.

Over the next three years the Basle Committee engaged in a lengthy and often tedious effort to develop a common approach to the regulation and level of capital standards.[23] These efforts were accompanied by rising concerns, now voiced publicly, about the increasing integration of global financial markets and the lack of any complementary regulatory structure.[24] In general, officials concurred on "the importance of a high degree of supervisory co-operation in an increasingly global marketplace" and that "there was a broad measure of agreement on what should constitute the constituents of capital . . . ."[25]

Yet although a model for convergence was beginning to take shape, there was no clear sense of how to transform technical agreements achieved within the committee into actual applications in national banking systems. At a meeting in Basle in early 1986, central bankers commented that it seemed unlikely that standard capital requirements would be introduced. Given the committee's lack of political authority and its inability to enforce new rules on the maintenance of capital, any such political initiative would have to come from one or several committee members. However, most national regulators continued to face considerable opposition from strongly entrenched interests in their banking industries at home.[26] Only those governments that either faced little domestic opposition or whose banking industries actually had an interest in an international agreement were likely to take the necessary initiative.

The United States was such a member. As already noted, U.S. regulators were in the midst of reconsidering their own measurement techniques and had put forward a proposal in 1986 which deliberately considered the work done in Basle and incorporated some elements to minimize any potential differences with national standards in case an international agreement ever became a reality. Moreover, broadening the debate to include the global dimension of bank regulation imposed no political cost. On the contrary, by seeking such an agreement, policymakers were able to counter the banks' charges of an uneven playing field and satisfy private sector and congressional demands that U.S. regulatory policy not be conducted in isolation from other national banking systems.

As one banker put it, "While capital is important it should be emphasized that American banks must compete with banks around the world. Some of these banks have no or low capital requirements. It is essential that the U.S. banking system is competitive in the world marketplace in order to finance U.S. exports and U.S. industry in general."[27] As domestic pressure grew, U.S. officials, in particular at the Federal Reserve, became increasingly impatient with the slow progress of the Basle Committee. The issue of competitive inequality had become so important that it was difficult to conceive of a policy solution that would separate the domestic regulation of U.S. capital standards from the ongoing global efforts in the Basle Committee.[28] For all practical purposes, defensive intervention— like offensive intervention before it—had become politically unacceptable. The only way for U.S. policymakers to strengthen their internal sovereignty was to ensure that the Basle Committee reached an agreement. Although private interests were not entirely neglected, policymakers' preference had shifted from *cooperative competition* to *competitive cooperation,* as they now insisted on the need for an international regulatory agreement.

To support its efforts, the United States needed an ally that would support its call for global action. It found such an ally in the Bank of England, which also had been a strong proponent of an agreement.[29] A series of confidential bilateral negotiations was concluded in January 1987 and led to an agreement between the two countries. The agreement was hailed as a major event in international supervisory cooperation and a step toward international consistency that would minimize the distortion in international competition.[30] It called for the convergence of supervisory policy and capital adequacy assessments among countries with major banking centers and invited other countries to join on an individual basis. At the same time, the accord specified that if the Basle Committee did not reach a prompt agreement among the major industrial countries, the United States and the United Kingdom would proceed alone with their bilateral harmonization plan.[31]

In addition, during the next several months the United States and the United Kingdom increased the pressure on other countries to join the agreement. In a statement to Congress, Paul Volcker noted that the United States had:

> . . . not applied extraterritorially U.S. bank capital standards on a consolidated basis to foreign banking organizations seeking to expand in the United States. However, the U.S./U.K. risk-based capital proposal represents a step forward toward a more consistent and equitable international norm for assessing capital adequacy. For this reason, we believe such a framework can, under appropriate circumstances, assist in evaluating the capital positions of foreign banks applying to acquire U.S. institutions.

Asked specifically about the possibility of applying mandated reciprocity, Volcker suggested that U.S. regulators "could move in that direction."[32] In essence, the United States threatened to project its definition of its own internal sovereignty onto other countries by calculating the capital standards of foreign banks in the United States on a consolidated basis and deciding whether they met U.S. standards and were thus eligible to acquire U.S. banking institutions. This form of pressure was specifically directed at the Japanese, whose inclusion in the agreement was considered essential.

However, the United States and the United Kingdom also intensified their informal contacts with other members of the Basle Committee to examine the possibility of a broader agreement, the chances of which had increased for a number of reasons.[33] The threat of retaliatory action by the United States allowed other members of the Basle Committee to take the political initiative both at home and in the committee and intensify their efforts to reach an agreement.[34] Within their countries, the debate over restructuring capital adequacy regulation was now given greater urgency by the potential negative repercussions of U.S. retaliatory action. For its part, the Basle Committee itself saw its reputation and role in the field of global public policy challenged, if not undermined. Failure to reach an agreement would cast doubt on the committee's institutional capacity to function effectively, with respect to both past commitments and future challenges. To regain the initiative, the committee imposed on itself a deadline for the end of 1987 and used the U.S.-U.K. agreement as a foundation to be expanded to encompass the other member countries—a tremendous task, given the complexity of designing an internationally acceptable definition of capital adequacy.[35]

The greatest challenge was reaching an agreement with the Japanese. By 1987 Japan had become a formidable force in international financial markets, and committee members realized that they needed to convince Japan to be part of the agreement or else risk a major backlash from the private sector in their own countries. (U.S. regulators had already approached the Japanese on a bilateral basis in late 1986.) But substantial differences with regard to the definition of bank capital remained between the Japanese and the other members.[36] Again the United States used its political and economic power to exert pressure on Japan, threatening to exclude large Japanese banks from the U.S. market for financial services.[37]

In response, Japan took a first step toward breaking the impasse by announcing that, in principle, it would go along with the U.S.-U.K. accord. Several more meetings were held during the spring and summer of 1987, amid escalating concern on the part of regulators over the rapid pace of structural change in global financial markets and their own increasing inability to supervise the international activities of banks.[38] Over this period the changing identity of states and interests of policymakers associated with this new environment were reflected in the 1987 annual report of the Bank for International Settlements (BIS). Accordingly, the liberalization of national financial markets that had occurred since the early 1980s had not always had beneficial effects, and the report noted, "Capital market liberalization may even have had harmful effects on the real economy."[39] The report concluded that these developments made it even more crucial for countries to adopt only those regulatory responses that were achieved in a cooperative effort among national authorities.[40]

In December 1987 the central bank governors of the member countries announced that they had agreed on a common approach to the issue of capital adequacy and its measurement.[41] As expected, banks and legislators in the G-10 countries were critical of the agreement. In the United States, ironically, the same congressional committee that in 1983 had called on regulators to "cause banking institutions to achieve and maintain adequate capital by establishing minimum capital levels" and that asked the three U.S. regulatory agencies to "encourage governments, central banks, and regulatory authorities of other major banking countries to work toward maintaining, and where appropriate strengthening, the capital bases of banking institutions" scheduled hearings on the competitive implications of the agreement.[42] The majority of the House Banking Committee members, while approving the fact that an agreement had been struck, were critical of many of its aspects.

U.S. regulators responded quickly and displayed a remarkable degree of harmony and cooperation in defending most elements of the Basle Accord (the FDIC did, however, take some exception to the applicability of the agreement to small rural banks). Although prepared to consider some of Congress's criticisms, they were not willing to introduce any major changes that would require renegotiating the agreement. Having endured the long and delicate negotiations and made the difficult compromises necessary to achieve an agreement among the ten most powerful economies in the world, U.S. officials realized that the domestic competitive concerns of a relative few but politically important banks would not be taken seriously by their colleagues on the Basle Committee. Any unilateral maneuver would lead not only to criticism from the other regulators on the committee, but to strong private sector opposition in the other countries, thus jeopardizing the entire agreement.

Pressure on the Federal Reserve from both Congress and the private sector, which accused the agency of "betraying" U.S. banks, continued to mount. But the regulators remained firm in their determination not to jeopardize the larger objective of the entire enterprise, namely, an international agreement to reestablish their internal sovereignty. Only one day after Representative Charles E. Schumer (D-N.Y.) sent to Alan Greenspan (who succeeded Volcker as Federal Reserve chairman) a letter signed by thirty of the fifty members of the House Banking Committee, predicting that the standards would have a "devastating impact on the international competitiveness of the largest American banks,"[43] one commentator aptly described the regulators' position as follows: "It is not the technicalities that are important here, but the recognition that the world's finance is no longer carried on by separate national banking systems dealing with each other at arms' length. It is dominated by multinational institutions that will soon have grown entirely beyond the reach of country-by-country regulation, unless the world's regulators can get together to enforce these kinds of rules."[44] When the Basle Committee announced its final version of the report in July 1988, its central features were reaffirmed.

The Lessons of Basle

This short history of the Basle Accord provides a useful context for examining the dynamics involved in one domain of global public policymaking and highlights a number of issues that are important to keep in mind when considering other global public policy initiatives. One important difference between this and the other cases should be noted, however: the participation of nongovernmental actors in the various policymaking stages is limited in this case to one set of interests. Unlike other domains of global public policy, such as international trade, where issues of environmental protection, labor standards, and even human rights enter the picture, and others where conflicting interest groups have become deeply involved in setting the global agenda and determining the eventual policy outcome, nongovernmental participation in the area of international finance has been limited mostly to the financial services industry.[45] In many ways this absence of other interest groups reflects the state of domestic public policymaking in the area of banking and finance. The absence of conflict among domestic interests in the Basle case greatly facilitated the conclusion of an agreement. But the relative ease with which this occurred, with respect to both process and timing, also means that this case is in this respect not comparable to other domains that would benefit from a move toward global public policy.

The lack of participation by other interest groups in the policy formulation stage, however, does not necessarily mean that they were not affected by the policy outcome. Indeed the Basle Accord, and in particular the risk weights it assigned to different groups of assets for purposes of determining a financial institution's capital base, did have a profound effect on the broader public in the participating countries and led to charges that the weighting scheme was biased.[46] But once the agreement had been reached, it was not exposed to the usual domestic public policymaking processes in the United States. Once a delicate compromise had been achieved in Basle, the fundamentals of the agreement could not be altered to accommodate national concerns without jeopardizing the entire exercise of global regulatory harmonization. Given the need for a global agreement to stabilize global financial markets, the margins of public policymaking at the domestic level had shrunk considerably.

This loss of accountability at the domestic level was not compensated for at the international level. To the contrary, both the agenda to be discussed in Basle and the process by which the final compromise was achieved suffered from a democratic deficit. This does not necessarily imply a deliberate effort to escape accountability. Rather, the postwar international institutional structure was built to accommodate an international economic system based on economic interdependence, which, from a public policy perspective, is best accommodated by facilitating intergovernmental relations and therefore did not have to be particularly concerned about its democratic attributes.[47] The issue of the democratic deficit was rarely relevant, since most public policymaking remained within the boundaries of the national political economy.[48]

At the same time, were it not for the presence of a democratic deficit, a compromise may have been struck too late, or not at all. More specifically, the factors that contributed significantly to the agreement's eventual passage were the complexity and abstractness of the issues involved (which accounted for the lack of broader public interest); the fact that the negotiations took place among central bankers, who even at the domestic level are usually insulated from day-to-day politics; the presence (as already noted) of only one primary interest group trying to influence the outcome; and, once a compromise had been struck, the ability of regulators to point to the fragility and international nature of the Accord when pressured by domestic legislatures (in particular in the United States) to revise it.

This is not to say that the absence of accountability and transparency in global decisionmaking is necessarily a welcome development, but only that the presence of a democratic deficit contributed significantly to the timely conclusion of an agreement, and consequently to the prevention of what many officials believed could become a global financial crisis—a policy outcome clearly in the public interest of all the G-10 countries. To explain such an outcome, it is important to recall from chapter 2 that under conditions of globalization the preference ordering of states in the international system shifts. In the United States, this change in preference ordering (from cooperative competition to competitive cooperation) was confirmed when U.S. regulators, whose internal sovereignty would have been severely undermined by a failure of the Basle process, successfully resisted pressure from both Congress, which took the side of the private sector, and the private sector itself to succumb to their particular interests. Given the change in preference ordering on the part of regulators, whose internal sovereignty and legitimacy were threatened by the globalization of finance, the probability of reaching an international agreement that actually served the larger public interest was increased considerably. This is encouraging, but more empirical evidence is needed before drawing the general conclusion that such changes in preference ranking will be the norm. Yet there is no doubt that this difficult trade-off between democratic accountability and efficiency in global public policymaking will become one of the defining issues in the debate over the benefits and drawbacks of globalization.

The history of the Basle Accord suggests two strategies by which the likelihood of a democratic deficit could be reduced. First, issues could be addressed early, in the nascent stages of their development, to allow more time for resolution. Under pressure from domestic legislatures to change elements of the Accord, regulators from the G-10 repeatedly pointed to the threat of a global financial crisis that required quick and decisive action and did not allow for an extended debate. Early warning mechanisms that rely on increased transparency of private sector activities, as well as on a formal and regular exchange of information among regulators so as to allow proactive rather than reactive engagement, with the emphasis on prevention, are therefore essential to ensure sufficient public debate and hence the legitimacy of global policymaking.

Second, the more vertical subsidiarity built into an agreement—in other words, the more flexibility it can offer participating countries without compromising its ultimate purpose—the more it can be adapted to each country's national financial system. The negotiations surrounding the Basle Accord reflected differing and deeply rooted perspectives on the role of finance in society, different attitudes toward risk (individual and social), and other country-specific characteristics, which have their origin both in broad historical developments such as the speed of industrialization and the experience (or lack thereof) of particular national or international financial crises.

The Basle Accord applied vertical subsidiarity both in its functional and in its structural form. First, a two-tier definition of capital was adopted. The definition of tier-one or core capital, which had to constitute at least 50 percent of a bank's total capital, was the same in all countries and strictly limited. The definition of tier-two or secondary capital, however, allowed for the inclusion of all other elements of capital admitted in the various national supervisory schemes. This provided for functional subsidiarity. The advantage of the two-tier formula was that it could accommodate continued differences in definitions among countries.[49] Second, interpretation and implementation of the Accord were left to the discretion of national regulatory authorities, with the provision that authorities would stick closely to the standards agreed upon in Basle. This provided structural subsidiarity. The use of both functional and structural subsidiarity was instrumental in concluding an agreement that would enhance the operational internal sovereignty of all bank regulators while preserving the formal internal sovereignty of each. This reduced the impression that the agreement represented the imposition of an international standard on domestic financial systems by some foreign, remote, and obscure bureaucracy.[50]

The anatomy of the Basle Accord raises yet another important issue not often brought up in discussions on globalization, namely, the end of sovereignty and the disappearance of states. Despite its global application, the Accord originated in the domestic political context of a single member of the Basle Committee, the United States. Its eventual success was due to a unique set of domestic and international political circumstances, and the primary force behind the agreement was the national interests of the world's leading political and economic power, which led it to take on a leadership role in promulgating international regulatory harmonization. State power and sovereignty (operational and formal) not only played a central role in promulgating the agreement but were strengthened as a result of it.

However, to speak with one voice abroad and take on a leadership role in the Basle Committee, the United States first had to come to an agreement at home. It took the Latin American debt crisis to shift political power from regulators to Congress and allow it to enforce a unified and coherent domestic approach to capital adequacy regulation.[51] Although in this case the shifting constellation of political forces helped clear the way toward an agreement, the history of the Basle Accord demonstrates that a highly dispersed and decentralized domestic decisionmaking structure may impede quick and decisive action at the international level. More important, a more centralized and unified policymaking network will allow a country or a small group of countries to take the initiative at the global level and thus shape the specific agenda according to its own interests.

Ultimately it was the political and economic power of the United States, in particular the threat to cut off access to its financial markets, that facilitated the compromise. This fact is important to remember when one considers to what degree the Basle Accord and other policy responses to the globalization of financial markets can be considered precedents for other global public policy initiatives. The Basle Accord also shows that global public policy does not have to start as a truly multilateral effort. It was the formation of a bilateral agreement—the U.S.-U.K. alliance—and the message it sent to other G-10 members and their domestic constituents, especially financial institutions, as well as to the Basle Committee itself, that led to success. What started out in the traditional fashion of great power politics ended in a generally acceptable compromise.

Indeed, as the G-10 soon came to realize, the regulatory standard they had established for themselves soon began to spread to other financial markets. First, other countries, especially those with emerging financial markets, began to adopt the Basle standards and to integrate them into their domestic regulatory and supervisory practices.[52] Second, and more important, in an interesting demonstration of horizontal subsidiarity, financial institutions outside the G-10 began to adopt the standards voluntarily, often because they were pressured by existing or potential customers to do so.[53]

In summary, so far this analysis of the Basle Accord has confirmed the validity of the conceptual framework developed in chapter 2. In the wake of the increasing globalization of the financial services industry, domestic public policy concerns such as the prudential regulation and supervision of financial institutions can no longer be addressed effectively within the political geography of national financial markets. As globalization intensifies, states will have to pool their operational sovereignty if they are to continue to conduct public policy in this area at all. In fact, unless they cooperate, economic integration will most likely stall or even regress, as the eventual eruption of an international financial crisis would lend support to those political forces calling for defensive intervention.[54] However, the shift in the preference ordering of countries does not imply that private interests have to be neglected entirely. To the contrary, the U.S. commercial banks did not have to endure the unilateral imposition of higher capital controls, but instead were joined by their strongest competitors in the G-10 countries.

Beyond Basle: New Challenges Facing Global Public Policy

From the perspective of public policy, one of the most challenging aspects of the financial services industry is the speed at which it has changed in recent years. Driving this change has been an almost continuous process of financial product innovation and new pricing and risk management techniques. These innovations, which rely on an ever more sophisticated use of technology, are themselves driven by two forces. The first is a highly competitive business environment, in which each financial institution constantly tries to gain an advantage, however temporary, over its rivals. The second is change in the domestic and the international regulatory environment. Often even before a new regulation has been put in place, financial institutions seek loopholes or create new products that allow them to circumvent it. The resulting dynamic between public officials and the industry—what chapter 2 called the regulatory dialectic—engages regulators and financial institutions in a continuous contest, the former trying to constrain the latter while the latter tries to escape those constraints.[55] In addition, a lack of information, or of timely information, about new developments in financial markets creates an information asymmetry that leaves regulators at a constant disadvantage relative to the industry. As one official put it, "Bank supervisors rarely have the opportunity of anticipating new trends and determining their direction. In most cases they have to be content with putting changes which have already taken place on an orderly basis."[56]

It should not be too surprising, then, that by the time regulators from the G-10 announced the final agreement on capital adequacy in the summer of 1988, new challenges to the stability of the global financial system were already looming. In fact, both the regulators and the private sector began to realize that the new public policy framework was inadequate, in part because of changes in the nature of banking itself, and more generally, because of the functional consolidation of the financial services industry, which had led to the emergence of so-called financial conglomerates.

The explosive growth of the exchange-traded derivatives markets and the largely unregulated over-the-counter derivatives market stands out. Indeed, it was in part the capital adequacy standards of 1988, with their focus on credit risk, that prompted banks to shift from their traditional lending activities into so-called off-balance-sheet activities such as derivatives and other securitized instruments not covered by the 1988 agreements.[57] These changes could be observed in the G-10 countries and beyond, but they were most pronounced in the United States.[58]

In light of the developments in the derivatives markets, the Basle Committee recognized that its formula focused too much on credit risk and too little on market and operational risks.[59] Over the next few years a series of intense discussions within the committee, but also, and in particular, between regulators and the private sector, got under way; this effort culminated in what amounted to a radical change in the global public policy framework developed in the late 1980s. To accommodate the changes that had taken place in the markets, in April 1993 the Basle Committee issued for comment a proposal on a capital standard based on market risk.[60] But the private sector sharply criticized the proposed reforms as too complex for smaller institutions to manage, and too difficult for the public to understand, yet too crude for banks already active in the derivatives market using much more sophisticated risk management techniques.[61] In the ensuing debate over the future of global regulatory arrangements, regulators came to realize that there was only one way they could hope to control what, by 1994, had become a rapidly evolving and ever more complex industry: they would have to not only engage the private sector to a much larger degree in the agenda setting and formulation of global public policy, but also make extensive use of public-private partnerships during implementation.

Momentum toward a new approach accelerated considerably with the collapse of a major U.K. bank, the Barings Group, in February 1995. This debacle, which occurred with little warning and with great speed, involved the extensive proprietary use of derivatives to establish large, highly leveraged positions in Nikkei 225 (Japanese equities) futures on the futures exchanges in Singapore and Osaka. Barings' collapse came on the heels of other financial crises involving derivatives, such as those of the government of Orange County, California, and the German firm Metallgesellschaft. The Barings collapse revealed three shortcomings that any attempt to establish a revised framework for global public policy would have to take into account. First, as late as the end of 1993 Barings had a capital ratio well in excess of the Basle Agreement's 8 percent requirement, and in January 1995 it was still considered a safe bank; the fact that Barings found itself in receivership only two months later could not but raise serious doubts about the adequacy of the regulatory system for capital requirements. Second, the collapse showed that internal controls at

Barings were totally inadequate to support the activities of its traders. And third, it was evidence that regulators in different countries had failed to communicate with each other to a degree sufficient to reduce at least in part the information asymmetry that globalization had created.

Against the background of these events and the shortcomings they revealed, the Basle Committee accelerated its efforts and in April 1995 issued for comment a proposal for an entirely new approach toward the regulation and calculation of banks' capital requirements. Banks for the first time in their history would be allowed to use their own internal risk management models, which they use for day-to-day trading and risk management, to determine their capital requirements.[62] Regulators would no longer impose or enforce strict, uniform, quantitative limits on the activities of banks. Rather, in a recognition of the growing complexity and innovative dynamism of the global financial services industry, the Basle Committee acknowledged that, provided certain qualitative and quantitative safeguards were present, the banks' own control and risk management mechanisms would prove superior to any that regulators could impose. The committee proposed to allow banks to use their own in-house risk models, also called value-at-risk (VAR) models, which are designed to assess and monitor market risk (the form of risk perceived to be the greatest threat arising from the emergence of the derivatives markets) and, on the basis of these models, to calculate their own capital charges.[63]

A detailed technical discussion of this new approach would go far beyond the scope of this chapter. But for purposes of this study, and in particular the theoretical framework laid out in chapter 2, it is important to note that regulators did not by any means entirely give up control over setting capital requirements. Rather, they proposed to outsource one important and highly complex function in the determination of capital standards to those actors better equipped, trained, and experienced to execute that function—the banks themselves. In so doing they eliminated a central cause of the information asymmetry that had hampered previous regulatory and supervisory efforts. But regulators also retained ultimate control over the determination of the capital requirements themselves. According to Tommasso Padoa-Schioppa, fifth chairman of the Basle Committee, "The model approach is a novelty in itself, so we must be conservative in the way we introduce it, at least initially."[64]

Under the proposal, banks would have to determine to a 99 percent probability that their capital at risk would not be greater than the capital charge, and would have to assume that they would hold the portfolio for at least ten trading days before liquidating it or adjusting its compensation.[65] The capital charge would be set as the highest level of the VAR that day or on any of the preceding sixty days. The resulting capital charge would be multiplied by a factor of at least three by the bank's regulator. This cushion is intended to compensate for the chance that markets will be more unstable than in the previous year, which is the time horizon used by banks in their modeling exercise. Moreover, in an effort to improve the quality of banks' risk assessment models, regulators would engage in a process called backtesting, which assesses the accuracy of a bank's model ex post. Backtesting is already widely used by banks. However, in a variation of that practice, regulators would impose a penalty—a so-called plus factor—by increasing the multiplier if banks' models turn out to have inaccurately predicted the performance of their portfolios. It is expected that this feature will give banks a considerable incentive to be as accurate as possible in their estimation techniques and thus in the calculation of the capital charge.

Banks applauded the regulators' recognition of the superiority of the banks' own risk assessment models, and they welcomed the ability to participate in the determination of capital requirements. But they were equally disappointed at the conservative approach that the committee had taken by imposing its own parameters on the risk assessment process. Indeed, the International Swaps and Derivatives Association (ISDA), an industry organization representing many banks affected by the proposal, suggested that the generic parameters that the committee had imposed—the sixty-day average to calculate risk, and the unusually high multiplier—were "unrealistically conservative."[66] The ISDA argued that the entire process of market risk measurement should be shifted to the banks—a move that would essentially amount to self-regulation.

As in 1988, however, the regulators did not give in to what they considered to be unrealistic demands, particularly with the memory still fresh of the highly publicized collapses or near collapses of financial institutions due to derivatives trading. When the committee announced its new rules in December 1995, to be implemented by the end of 1997, little had changed from the April proposal since the Committee had "been inclined to take a conservative approach in its choice of parameters . . . ."[67] Yet in light of the novelty of the new approach, the Committee also indicated that it reserved the right to apply some flexibility in accommodating the banks' concerns and that it " . . . reserve[d] the right to modify the specifications required for banks using models as more experience is gained."[68]

In general, the industry's reaction was one of disappointment that the regulators had not taken their criticisms more seriously. According to one comment, "The problem most people have with it [the multiplier] is that the number [three] is just plucked from the air."[69] If an internal model is accurately assessing a bank's risk, many bankers argued, it should not be necessary to multiply the resulting figure at all. As the final proposal showed, however, the regulators considered it prudent to maintain the multiplication factor because of the weaknesses of the models so far developed.

The evolution of global capital adequacy regulations follows the framework developed in chapter 3. In light of their increasing inability to keep up with the changing nature of the global financial services industry, and thus their continued inability to exercise internal sovereignty, policymakers needed to make some fundamental adjustment in the way they operationalized their internal sovereignty over the global financial services industry. They did so by making extensive use of public-private partnerships. In what many saw as a bold and even revolutionary move, regulators outsourced an important part of the regulatory process to the banks, taking advantage of the latter's superior capacity to assess risk, and thus reducing the information asymmetry, which by then had reached unacceptable levels. Reflecting the fundamental change in the nature of regulation, the chairman of the Basle Committee called it "a very big development in philosophy."[70] Indeed, to indicate the significance of the change and its direction toward partial self-regulation, Padoa-Schioppa drew the analogy of a taxpayer being asked to design his or her own tax form.[71]

Yet the Basle Committee stopped far short of full self-regulation and instead opted for mixed regulation, instituting a number of quantitative measures that would conform to the regulators' more risk-adverse posture. This reflected the change in governments' preference ordering that had taken place. However, in doing so they relied on yet another innovative set of methods to ensure compliance. First, to validate the quality of the models that banks use to assess their risk, regulators insisted on a considerable degree of disclosure with respect to those models. Second, to ensure that banks would not understate the VAR of their portfolios, they created a built-in incentive, the plus factor penalty, together with ex post disclosure, that would encourage banks to be as accurate as possible in their estimation of the VAR.

As discussed in chapter 3, horizontal subsidiarity through the outsourcing of certain aspects of the public policymaking process is a necessary condition for successful global public policy, but it may not be sufficient.[72] Two additional factors were listed as central to any effort at building a framework for global public policy. First, private sector actors not only must be *willing* to take on some of the responsibility of regulation, but must also be *able* to execute those responsibilities in a professional and ethical manner. Thus financial institutions must, at a minimum, have the organizational capacity, incentive structure, and corporate culture to take on such a role.

The Barings collapse confirmed that this is not always the case. Although initial accounts centered around the fraudulent activities of one of its employees, futures trader Nicholas Leeson, and evidence suggests that Leeson indeed was engaged in highly speculative transactions and deliberately tried to deceive his superiors, his actions were not the only reason for the group's failure.[73] They were compounded by totally inadequate internal communications, controls, and channels of accountability, as well as insufficient regulatory oversight by U.K. regulators and a lack of communication between regulators in the United Kingdom, Japan, and Singapore.

The most striking aspect of the lack of internal communication is that it was common knowledge on the futures markets that Barings was building an increasingly risky position. As one U.S. fund manager put it, "The futures community [had] known of this mega-position for about the last three months."[74] In New York the manager of one of the biggest hedge funds said that "news of Barings' purchase of contracts had been the subject of 'intense discussion' in the financial markets for at least two weeks," and short of completely inadequate in-house communications, it is inconceivable that senior management was unaware of these developments.[75]

Management's failure to prevent the demise of Barings also stemmed from Barings' flawed internal controls and channels of accountability. Leeson was responsible for both the trading and the settlement sides of the Singapore operations, which made it easier for him to conceal his contracts from his superiors. But senior management was made aware of this situation as early as 1992.[76] From the evidence so far available, it appears that such concerns were not passed on to Barings' external auditors, who almost certainly would have included them in the annual report on management systems and controls submitted to the Bank of England under U.K. bank regulations.

The Bank of England was praised for the way it handled the attempt to rescue Barings and managed to avoid any spillovers into the international financial system. It sent a clear signal to other market participants to contain the moral hazard problem always present in financial markets. At the same time, however, the Bank of England has drawn criticism for its poor oversight and has been partially blamed for the conglomerate's failure. First, supervisors never saw the internal audit report warning of Leeson's compromising position as head of both trading and settlements. This is a clear case of information asymmetry and calls into question the rigor with which the Bank of England carried out its job. Second, the U.K. Banking Act of 1987 and, more recently, the Large Credit Exposure directive of the European Union lay down rules governing allowable credit exposures for banks. They specify that a bank should not have a credit exposure of more than 25 percent of its equity capital in any one investment without the approval of its regulator, in this case the Bank of England. In Barings' case, funds from the bank were used to meet the margin requirements of Baring Futures in Singapore. The total capital of Barings Bank at that time was about £440 million. Against this, the bank apparently provided Leeson with £580 million (over 100 percent of its equity capital) to meet margin requirements. Given the apparently strict reporting requirements, the Bank of England should have known about this continuously rising exposure.

Finally, although the Bank of England had not been informed that Barings' Singapore office's positions were rising too quickly and too high, it could have indirectly picked up signals from the London money markets. At least one U.K. bank noticed that Barings had been drawing on credit facilities as of the end of January, about two weeks before its collapse. The Bank of England's apparent failure to notice this development despite its role in the money markets raises questions about its ability to detect the emergence of a crisis. In other words, the Barings collapse was not a case of information asymmetry; information was readily available but was not used or was misinterpreted. This episode would tend to support those who argue for greater horizontal subsidiarity. Since other market participants noticed Barings' use of credit facilities, they might have intervened earlier had they been assigned part of the regulatory responsibilities.

This brief review of government failure in the Barings case leaves no doubt that mixed regulation in banking will only be as effective as supervisors' ability to judge the banks' own activities. Thus, to validate the

VAR risk assessment models, regulators themselves will have to acquire these models and become proficient in the use of sophisticated modeling techniques. Moreover, unless regulators have had sufficient training and experience, they will lack the credibility and legitimacy to impose penalties on individual financial institutions if, for example, backtesting leads to the conclusion that an institution underestimated its VAR and the plus factor should be imposed.

An even greater threat to the success of mixed regulation is that private sector actors may be unprepared to take on regulatory responsibility. Such a shift of responsibility requires, above all, considerable improvement in internal risk management and clear lines of internal authority and responsibility at the level of the individual institution. Having a top-rated risk measurement model but a poor risk management and control process could be worse than having a poor internal VAR model but good risk control. At the broadest level, therefore, a financial institution should state clearly what it hopes to achieve in using such innovative instruments as derivatives. What is the firm's philosophy? Where does it believe the use of these financial instruments is appropriate? Where is it not? Only with a clear definition of the purpose of using derivatives can management procedures to achieve that purpose be worked out in detail and properly implemented.

These more detailed management decisions should be reflected in a company's corporate culture and, in particular, its compensation structure. The huge bonus payments received by the most successful traders have become a crucial element of risk management. Since traders like Nicholas Leeson are accustomed to winning huge payouts if they are successful, but losing no more than their jobs if they are not, they have few incentives to pursue more cautious strategies. A few banks have introduced so-called risk-adjusted performance measures, which make compensation depend not just on the profits a trader brings in but also on the amount of risk to which he or she exposes a bank. It is too soon, however, to evaluate the success of this change.[77]

In addition to requiring adjustments in corporate culture, the success of mixed regulation will depend critically on substantial changes in the internal organizational structure of firms.[78] Who is responsible for managing the risk profile? Who takes the positions, who values them, and who evaluates the bank's exposure? What are the trading limits, and who enforces them? How does the control architecture work? These are all questions that need to be answered, and the answers need to be made available to bank staff. To ensure that all those involved in the management of risk are sufficiently accountable, an institution should consider designating these responsibilities to a newly created senior management position: the risk management officer. Finally, although many companies do have internal auditors, they are not always as independent as they should be of the audited. It is very important that they be independent. The transactions they must review are often quite technical and highly complex, but internal auditors should not rely on the traders who make the transactions for the inputs into their own calculations. Making auditors truly independent may require not only substantial investments in systems and state-of-the-art technology, but also—as with the regulators—the recruitment of highly specialized professionals.

The 1996 amendments to the Basle Accord address some of these issues by establishing a set of qualitative organizational standards.[79] Banks have to meet these standards before they are permitted to use internal risk models. Subsequently, the extent to which banks meet these qualitative criteria will influence the level at which supervisory authorities set the multiplication factor.[80] But the amendments do not spell out exactly how regulators will verify that banks meet these qualitative standards on a regular basis. There is no provision for an external audit, for example, that could assess the state of internal risk management. Progress in this area has been limited and is concentrated among a few large U.S. banks.[81] This was confirmed by a recent survey conducted by the Group of Thirty to determine how many dealers would follow the recommendations on sound risk issued by the same group in a report a year earlier. The results were anything but encouraging.[82]

The Basle Committee also stated that, in return for being delegated an important part of the regulatory process, banks would be required to disclose a substantial part of their internal risk management activities: "In order to gain additional information and comfort with the results produced by internal models, supervisory authorities reserve the right to require banks wishing to use internal models to perform testing exercises and to provide any other information necessary to check the validity of banks' models."[83] Central to increased levels of transparency, however, are the disclosure rules governing the activities of these institutions. According to a former chairman of the U.S. Securities and Exchange Commission (SEC), "[T]he disclosure rules . . . when I was there were not adequate."[84] At a minimum, disclosure requirements need to show each firm's approach to risk, its track record in risk management, and its aggregate risk posture, to reduce information asymmetry and allow for a more proactive and efficient approach to prudential supervision. Finally, large financial institutions may be able to implement and maintain elaborate and complex internal controls with relative ease. However, the high fixed costs that such an operation would require would place a big burden on smaller institutions, impairing their already weakened competitive position even further.

One possible solution would be the establishment of a nonprofit organization—private in form but public in purpose—that would act as an intermediary between industry and regulators. The principal function of such a mixed regulatory and supervisory organization, which could be modeled on the National Association of Securities Dealers (see chapter 3), would be to monitor and enforce the quantitative and, in particular, the qualitative standards set by the Basle Committee.[85] It could even be responsible for the imposition of sanctions and penalties if industry norms are violated. For large banks, which run their own control units, the role of such an organization would be equivalent to that of an external auditor. Smaller banks, on the other hand, given the cost of such an operation, may want to delegate the implementation and management of its internal risk control system to such an organization for a fee. In addition, in a fast-changing market such an organization could serve as an exchange of information on the latest regulatory developments affecting financial institutions. The organization could even perform an educational function by taking on the responsibility of training bank employees in modern sophisticated risk management techniques.[86]

The premise behind the success of such an organization is that financial institutions, individually and as an industry, have an interest in maintaining a good reputation. As one private sector representative stated, "[I]t would be hard to overstate [reputation's] importance to a firm that seeks to thrive over the long term. Reputation is the major source of franchise value in any firm. Reputation is exceedingly difficult to establish and maintain but exceedingly easy to destroy. Consider the importance of reputation in the minds of our clients . . . . After all you can't take a swap for a test drive."[87] Regulators and the industry should explore the possibility of establishing such an organization.

This additional reliance on public-private partnerships, supported by significant, lasting, and verifiable adjustments in the internal organizational structure and corporate culture of financial institutions, would go far toward laying the foundation for a new global public policy framework, except for one additional and important element. As the 1996 Basle amendments indicate, national regulators will remain in charge of a considerable part of all three stages of the policy process. To operationalize their internal sovereignty at the global level, however, regulators need to be able to rely on an institutional network that allows for regular and timely interaction and permits the exchange of information, sometimes even information of a proprietary nature.

Again, the collapse of Barings is helpful to demonstrate that such an information network among regulators will be essential in making global public policy succeed. Although responsibility for consolidated supervision rests with the Bank of England, the activities of Baring Futures in London and Singapore were also under the scrutiny of the U.K. Securities and Futures Authority and Singapore's International Monetary Exchange (SIMEX), respectively. Any worries on the part of SIMEX officials about Barings' futures activities could and should have been reported to Barings' consolidated regulator, the Bank of England. Instead, SIMEX officials, in a rather unusual move, contacted Barings' treasurer in London to express concerns about the positions Leeson had built up.[88]

Questions must also be raised about the extent of communication and even coordination between the Osaka and Singapore futures exchanges. It appears that SIMEX officials were aware of the positions Leeson was taking on the Osaka exchange after the Kobe earthquake. Had they been in direct communication with the Osaka exchange, these officials should have realized that the trader's long positions in Singapore were not offset by short positions in Osaka.[89] At the same time, it is important to remember that Leeson's original assignment was to engage in arbitrage: to profit from price differences for the same product on the two exchanges. These price differences were at least in part due to different margin requirements for futures transactions: margins were 9 percent in Osaka but only 1 percent in Singapore. Considering the degree to which the trading that resulted from Barings' regulatory arbitrage also generated income for the two exchanges, it was in their interest to maintain those differences.[90] As one recent IMF study concludes, "If information about Barings' activities had passed freely among its five supervisors . . . then it would have been possible to obtain a consolidated picture of Barings' exposure and the failure may well not have occurred."[91]

Clearly, regulators have to improve the current level of cooperation in this area if they want to succeed in containing global financial crises. In addition to overcoming "vertical" information asymmetries, that is, those between market participants and regulators, they now also face the challenge of "horizontal" asymmetries, or insufficient contact and cooperation among regulators themselves in different countries. But the challenge of developing standards and practices for a more regular and timely exchange of information has been complicated by the blurring of borders between different segments of the financial services industry since the mid-1980s, which has led to the development of financial conglomerates.[92]

A financial conglomerate is defined as a group of companies under common control whose exclusive or predominant activities consist of providing services in at least two different financial sectors (for example, banking, securities, and insurance).[93] For regulators, financial conglomerates add another layer of complexity. Their efforts to overcome horizontal information asymmetries must no longer extend merely across countries but also across different functions. One of the main risks associated with conglomerates is so-called contagion risk: not only will losses in one activity reduce the amount of capital available to support other parts of the operation, but problems in one segment of the conglomerate may affect the confidence of customers dealing with other segments of the same institution. Yet another risk that is often mentioned is known as double-gearing, which occurs when the capital of the group as a whole is less than the sum of its parts if the same capital is used in different parts of the group to support business.[94]

In the presence of these and other risks to which financial conglomerates are subject, an improved exchange of information among regulators will be instrumental in strengthening their ability to exercise internal sovereignty. However, initial progress has been slow, and at least some regulators have been frustrated with the scant progress made. Commenting on his experience with efforts to establish joint capital standards for derivatives, Richard C. Breeden, former chairman of the SEC, stated:

> The overall process is so difficult and involves so many trade offs that a common standard will tend not to be updated even when new developments make marginal changes desirable. In any event, as Chairman of the IOSCO Technical Committee, I had to endure endless discussions in which some European regulators sought to have the SEC slash its capital requirements. Aside from being utterly fruitless, these discussions tended to monopolize the staff and divert it from more important issues such as designing the best possible approach to a capital rule for derivative activities of U.S. broker-dealers.[95]

Convinced that greater cooperation was absolutely essential, the Basle Committee succeeded in setting up a multidisciplinary working group called the Tripartite Group of Banking, Insurance, and Securities Regulators, which met for the first time in February 1993 and presented some initial findings in early 1994.[96] Their conclusion, that risk assessment should be undertaken from a group perspective, meant that many of the same obstacles that had to be overcome during the initial Basle Accord negotiations would have to be remastered for an international regulatory agreement on financial conglomerates.[97] In its progress report, the group stated that it "is unanimous in advocating that there needs to be an assessment of capital on a group-wide basis, but there are differences of opinion as to the most appropriate approach."[98] This of course is highly reminiscent of statements made by the Basle Committee in the mid-1980s, when it recognized the need for action but realized that major political obstacles to an agreement on capital standards lay ahead.

This time, however, regulators acted more quickly. In July 1994 the Basle Committee and the Technical Committee of the International Organization of Securities Commissions (IOSCO) issued parallel papers containing guidelines for the risk management of derivative activities, but regulators were not too hopeful that quick progress could be made.[99] Here, too, action was accelerated by the Barings collapse. In May 1995 the two committees issued a joint framework for the reporting of derivatives-related information to supervisory authorities. The release of such a joint document is unprecedented in the history of global financial regulation and a noteworthy event for national standards. Finally, in November 1995 yet another joint report was released recommending the disclosure of information on the trading and derivative activities of banks and securities firms.[100] At a meeting of the Tripartite Group in Paris during July 1995, regulators, who as recently as three years before had been unable to agree on anything, decided to convert this informal gathering of supervisors into a permanent committee, the Joint Forum on Financial Conglomerates, as they recognized that the maintenance of internal sovereignty in this public policy domain, too, had become a systemic issue.[101] According to Andrew Large, the U.K. securities regulator for the Securities and Investment Board, "It is coming home to people that the international and the domestic agendas are becoming very much the same . . . . No one market supervisor has the full picture [of] groups that are operating globally."[102]

But although some progress has been made, other problems remain unsolved. Reflecting the more complex composition of the Tripartite Group, the progress report also concluded that authorities need the legal powers to share sensitive prudential information with regulators from other sectors at the national and, more important, the international level, which if implemented would result in the pooling of formal sovereignty. In addition, regulators noted the usefulness of a clearinghouse to both collect and disseminate information to all parties involved in the regulation of a conglomerate. Given the sensitivity of such information, a strict secrecy code would have to be put in place to ensure the trust of the private sector actors.

Although necessary, these provisions will, if implemented, undoubtedly create new legal and institutional hurdles that will not be easily overcome. In the legal arena, financial institutions would likely challenge this "internationalization" of proprietary information in national courts, which could delay the implementation of an agreement for years. Indeed, keeping in mind that the Basle Accord relies on national authorities to exercise formal sovereignty in enforcing such standards, one might well question the degree to which international law—under current circumstances—could not only take on such responsibilities but also enforce them. Another major difficulty is the difference in regulatory focus of bank and securities regulators. Bank regulators tend to focus on systemic risk issues, because banks are relatively more vulnerable to contagious collapses; securities regulators, on the other hand, tend to pay more attention to issues of investor protection.

As to the institutional hurdles, there are considerable structural and procedural differences between the Basle Committee and IOSCO, which as the umbrella organization for securities regulators would be responsible for the securities divisions of financial conglomerates.[103] Moreover, in addition to dealing with conflicting interests among participating nations, successful conclusion of an agreement on capital standards for financial conglomerates would also have to overcome competition and turf fights among national regulators, which no doubt would be carried over into the international forum. Again, a more consolidated financial regulatory structure at the national level is likely to promote conclusion of an international agreement.

It should not be too surprising, then, if these and a constant flow of new hurdles—legal, institutional, and political—lead to the conclusion that the United States, or for that matter other countries, should go their own way and follow the advice of former SEC chairman Breeden, quoted above. Yet Breeden, despite his apparent enthusiasm for unilateral action, during the same testimony also acknowledged that defensive intervention was no longer a policy option: "[T]his market is a global market that can easily shift transactions from one jurisdiction to another. Where a nation puts in place unilateral and ill-considered actions . . . market participants will swiftly move transactions to other venues and thereby render the action meaningless except as a jobs export program."[104]

In conclusion, as this chapter has shown, financial markets are indeed the pioneers of global public policy, as laid out in the previous chapter. In the course of the last fifteen years remarkable progress has been made in establishing a framework for the governance of the global financial services industry. Supervisors have relied on a set of innovative structures and mechanisms to overcome the challenge of governing without government in a fast-changing, complex environment. Policymakers have also undergone a learning process, and with the help of a number of formal and informal institutional arrangements they have become more effective and efficient. Whereas it took almost ten years to conclude the 1988 accord (which was only implemented in 1992), it took less than two years to develop the internal risk assessment approach. In the latter case, however, the occurrence of a number of financial crises helped accelerate the policymaking process. The current system is far from perfect, and policymakers must act fast to develop structures and coordinating mechanisms that will be sufficiently robust to withstand new crises. This will not be made easier by the fact that many new financial centers have emerged and that regulatory efforts can no longer be limited to the G-10. Rather, a wider multilateral forum will have to be found to ensure that the political geography of regulatory cooperation covers the economic geography of the global financial services industry.

Policymakers have recognized this fact and begun to respond. Thus in September 1996 the BIS agreed to offer membership to nine additional central banks and more are likely to follow.[105] Since none of the new members is expected to be allocated a seat on the eleven member board of the Bank, their influence will be limited.[106] However, there is a clear expectation that this enlargement will lead to increased cooperation preventing a repeat of financial crises.[107] In addition to enlarging its membership, the Basle Committee also issued twenty-five Core Principles for Effective Banking Supervision, which were developed in cooperation with other financial regulators around the world in the "hope that they would provide a useful mechanism for strengthening financial stability in all countries."[108] The principles were endorsed both at the June 1997 G-7(8) Denver Summit and the annual meetings of the World Bank and the IMF in September 1997 in Hong Kong. The implementation of the Principles will be reviewed at the next International Conference of Banking Supervisors to be held in 1998 and biennially thereafter.[109] Though certainly a start in the right direction, some have criticized the principles for being too unsubstantial and failing to recognize the weakness, or absence, of the appropriate legal and institutional environments in many developing countries necessary for the principles to be enforced.[110] At present there is no enforcement mechanism in place although "in the long run, banks from countries that do not apply these principles could find they are treated more harshly by supervisors in other countries when they try to open subsidiaries."[111] Both the expansion of the BIS and the agreement on the core principles came too late to have any effect on the financial crisis in Asia that erupted at the time this book went to press. Nevertheless the crisis should have eliminated any lingering doubts that both actions should not have been delayed so long.

This discussion has also shown that, if global public policy in financial markets is to succeed, the private sector will have to become intimately involved in its development, formulation, and implementation. This, however, presupposes a number of fundamental changes in both corporate culture and internal organizational structures, which will not always be easy to implement and in some cases—just as was the case with governments—imply a departure from conventional operations and methods. Here, too, much work needs to done. But to say that the governance of the global financial services industry may be better achieved with less direct involvement of government by no means implies that governments will wither away. To the contrary, what this chapter has shown is that, in defense of the formal aspects of their internal sovereignty, governments have joined forces with nonstate actors and have begun to outsource the operational aspects of their internal sovereignty in order to strengthen that very sovereignty and thus their own legitimacy.

It is too early to predict whether they will succeed. But it is difficult to imagine a return to the status quo ante. Public policy will never be the same in this domain of the global economy, as the line between public and private roles becomes more blurred, as so-called third-sector institutions take a more prominent role, and as technology-driven innovation makes public policy a fast-changing, increasingly complex target of governance. Finally, one question that arises from this discussion is whether the public policy challenge discussed in this chapter is unique. As the subsequent case studies will show, the answer is a resounding no, not only with respect to financial services but also as far manufacturing is concerned.

CHAPTER 5

Global Crime and Public Policy: The Case of Money Laundering

GLOBALIZATION HAS LED to a surge not only in legal but also in illegal transnational economic activity, presenting new challenges for public policy. Many of these challenges reach far beyond the economic realm, whether the financial or the real sector, to have broad social and political implications in both industrialized and developing countries.[1] Although the end of the cold war was a major factor in accelerating and broadening transnational criminal activities, their pervasiveness and dangers and increasingly international character were recognized long ago. There is general agreement that the liberalization of cross-border economic flows as well as rapid technological evolution are two of its principal causes.[2] According to U.S. Deputy Secretary of the Treasury Lawrence H. Summers, "[A]t the very moment that the world economy is expanding and integrating, creating vast new opportunities for business, so the technology and capacity at the disposal of criminals is greater than ever before."[3] The emergence of global networks of information and communication, transportation, and financial intermediation not only has allowed corporate actors to adopt a transnational perspective on many organizational and operational aspects of management, but also permits criminal organizations to attach themselves to and feed off of these legal, global networks. Criminals easily operate across multiple political and legal geographies, thus creating their own transborder networks that skillfully evade detection and prosecution. Organized crime has become predominantly border free, whereas law enforcement remains locked within fixed territorial legal frameworks.[4] According to one recent estimate, the gross global criminal product from organized crime and drug trafficking reached $1 trillion in 1996. Half that sum was generated in the United States, where the mafia's estimated criminal profits made it the twentieth-richest organization in the world, with an income greater than that of 150 countries.[5] But there is every indication that organized crime has been spreading around the world for decades. It has become a multipolar phenomenon, not unlike the trend in foreign direct investment between the 1960s and the 1990s, discussed in chapter 1.

Although no one would deny their fundamentally different nature and purpose, the behavioral characteristics of illegal and legal corporate networks, and thus the public policy challenges posed by them, share considerable similarities. One point of similarity is their *transnational* organization, best illustrated by the blend of corporate and criminal activity that characterizes the international criminal cartel based in Cali, Colombia. Crime multinationals, as some have called them, adapt easily to changing external circumstances, including government regulation and technological change.[6] Not only are these organizations highly mobile and fluid, but their practices are constantly evolving as they respond to changing markets, conditions, and demands. Obviously these criminals try to evade any form of public control while maximizing profits at acceptable levels of risk. At the institutional level one can observe global criminal conglomerates and various forms of strategic alliances emerging in response to the opportunities and new demand that globalization generates. Criminal organizations, like their legal counterparts, can benefit from synergies, establish their presence in local markets, coopt competitors, minimize risk, and break into protected markets.[7]

Nowhere have legal and illegal global networks become more intertwined than in global banking and capital markets, where money laundering has grown during the last decade to become one of the most pervasive international public policy problems.[8] There are no precise figures of the volume of money laundered worldwide. According to the Financial Action Task Force (FATF), an intergovernmental organization created in 1989, "efforts to arrive at a methodologically sound estimate of the size of the phenomenon have been flawed. However, it is generally agreed that it amounts to hundreds of billions of dollars annually."[9] The estimates that have been made range from $300 billion to $1 trillion. There is little doubt that the liberalization of cross-border financial flows and the revolution in information and communications technologies, applied to modern financial systems, have contributed significantly to the problem.

From a public policy perspective the fight against money laundering should be considered a particularly important component of the fight against global crime. A survey on transnational crime, conducted among governments and nongovernmental organizations in preparation for the United Nations Congress on the Prevention of Crime and Treatment of Offenders, held in Cairo in 1995, identified seventeen criminal categories. Among these, money laundering was ranked as the number-one problem.[10] According to a recent study by the U.S. Office of Technology Assessment, "Money laundering is one of the most critical problems facing law enforcement today. International crime probably cannot be controlled or reduced unless criminal organizations can be deprived of their illegal proceeds. At present they enjoy a swift, silent, almost risk-free pipeline for moving and hiding money. . . ."[11] Given its central position in the infrastructure of global crime, money laundering provides the lifeblood for all other criminal activities. Without the ability to launder the profits from crime, most if not all of the incentives for a broad range of illegal activities would disappear. Global criminal organizations are also most vulnerable at the point where their proceeds enter the legal financial system.[12] Therefore, a successful campaign against money laundering is likely to have widespread beneficial implications.

There are many important similarities between the effort to control global money laundering and the effort to regulate global financial markets, discussed in chapter 4. For example, like multinational financial institutions, money launderers do not challenge the territorial integrity of nation-states. On the contrary, they often benefit from protected national jurisdictions, which permit large-scale regulatory arbitrage. Likewise, all transnational criminal activities, including money laundering, challenge first and foremost the internal sovereignty of a country, not only where the financial system is concerned, but also on a broad range of economic, social, and political issues. Finally, policymakers have to contend with many of the same problems, such as regulatory dialectics, severe information asymmetries, and considerable variation across national regulatory regimes, that make any effort at cross-national cooperation quite difficult, yet essential for policy success.

Money laundering also adds to both the national and the global public policy effort a number of novel challenges that need to be confronted.

First, in order to detect illegal activities, any effort at control must be capable of acquiring and managing large amounts of data pertaining to the ever more complex financial flows that sophisticated launderers use to escape detection. Who should maintain jurisdiction over this information, and how such data should be collected, evaluated, and protected from illicit use, raise a number of important policy questions. Second, in the case of financial regulation, until the mid-1990s officials were able to manage global public policy within the Group of Ten, and only now are they beginning to expand this global regulatory forum to reflect the growing importance of emerging markets. Efforts to control money laundering will have to cast a wider net from the outset.

Indeed, the number of countries at risk to become the target of money launderers has been growing steadily since the late 1980s. Between 1995 and 1996 alone, the U.S. State Department, which ranks countries according to their risk of becoming the target of money laundering, upgraded its risk assessment of twenty-one countries, in eleven of which money laundering had been of no concern before.[13] In contrast, a small number of countries signed the Basle Agreement. The greater number of countries included in the domain of money laundering means that global public policy is likely to face additional obstacles. The size of the international collective that needs to agree to pool internal operational sovereignty is just one concern; others include matters of compliance and enforcement, as well as technical and financial support for governments in developing countries. One advantage, however, is that some of the organizations that have become involved in the campaign against money laundering (the Basle Committee, the International Organization of Securities Commissions, the Offshore Banking Supervisory Group, and others) have already dealt with global supervisory issues, and thus bring with them some possibly helpful institutional experience.

As far as policy responses are concerned, the options are essentially the same. However, it is unlikely—but not inconceivable—that a country would deliberately adopt a strategy of offensive intervention by relaxing its own national legislation against money laundering, accepting the presence of criminal organizations as the price of desirable capital inflows for the local economy.[14] Intervening offensively through the extraterritorial application of domestic law is quite clearly an option, and one that the United States has used on a number of occasions.[15] The best-known incident so far has been the capture, prosecution, and conviction of Panamanian strongman Manuel Noriega. However, most countries would take issue with a strategy that extends internal sovereignty in these matters beyond territorial boundaries; hence this type of offensive intervention is generally not considered a very constructive approach to achieve a global solution.[16] Defensive intervention, on the other hand, clearly is an option that can no longer be excluded. Despite the potential adverse consequences for international trade and capital flows, policymakers may feel increasing popular pressure to restrict capital inflows from around the world, especially if they are linked to the narcotics trade, with its attendant domestic social and economic costs. Nowhere has this conflict become more apparent than in U.S.-Mexican relations.[17] There is little doubt that in the United States such concerns have led to reconsideration of the benefits of the North American Free Trade Agreement and have thrown doubt on its further expansion, both substantive and geographic.

If offensive intervention in money laundering is a devil's bargain, and defensive intervention has the usual undesirable side effects, is there scope for global public policy in this area? International efforts to combat money laundering to date fall well short of such an ambitious undertaking. Yet there is little doubt that the nature of the problem makes this the only viable strategy compatible with the continued deepening of the global economy. To date few nations have had much experience with legislation at the national level to curb money laundering. This chapter therefore draws on the experience of the United States, which has by far the most elaborate legal and regulatory structure to fight money laundering. As will be shown, U.S. policymakers realized early on that they have little choice but to rely to a growing degree on horizontal subsidiarity if they want to contain this threat to their internal sovereignty.

U.S. Anti–Money Laundering Initiatives and the Emergence of Horizontal Subsidiarity

At the formal level, domestic efforts to establish internal sovereignty with respect to money laundering are relatively recent. Moreover, all such efforts reflect the constant struggle of regulators to maintain internal sovereignty as they try to catch up with a rapidly changing environment. Criminal organizations and their money brokers continue to develop increasingly sophisticated and complex laundering techniques, relying on a growing variety of financial and nonfinancial institutions, complicated cross-border transactions, and layering schemes that leave fewer and fewer traces. The resulting information asymmetries have drawn policymakers into a regulatory dialectic, forced to respond to these changing tactics on an almost continuous basis. In addition, rather than pursue individual lawbreakers, who are easily replaceable within a criminal organization, recent strategies emphasize the importance of disrupting the criminal network itself, for example by stemming the flow of profits and seizing assets. This approach promises far greater success, but it also requires additional information about the network, further contributing to the asymmetry.

The United States, where an estimated one-third of all money laundering takes place, has over the years established by far the most extensive set of laws and regulations to fight money laundering. This legislation dates back to the enactment of the Bank Secrecy Act of 1970 (BSA). The act requires financial institutions to ensure that adequate records are maintained of transactions that have a "high degree of usefulness in criminal, tax or regulatory investigations or proceedings."[18] Since then the legislature, the executive, and the judiciary have continuously amended the public policy framework. For example, in 1986 the Money Laundering Control Act for the first time made institutions and individuals criminally liable for knowingly participating in money laundering. In addition, the act covered a new and broader range of conduct and financial transactions that might facilitate the knowing concealment of the source or the existence of illegally obtained proceeds, and it criminalized the use and expenditure of such proceeds. Two years later, in 1988, the Anti–Drug Abuse Act further stiffened civil and criminal penalties for money laundering and gave the Treasury authority to require additional recordkeeping of currency transactions in certain geographic locations.

In 1990 Congress passed the Depository Institution Money Laundering Amendment Act, which further broadened the arsenal of instruments that federal authorities could use to investigate money laundering, by making it possible for them to share information with foreign regulatory agencies in the pursuit of launderers. The Housing and Community Development Act of 1992,[19] also known as the Annunzio-Wylie Anti–Money Laundering Act, strengthened the anti–money laundering agencies and imposed additional reporting requirements on banks. The law included a so-called safe-harbor provision to protect financial institutions against civil liability arising from suspicious transactions and possible money laundering charges.[20]

Beginning in the early 1990s, wire transfers through such networks as the Clearing House Interbank Payments System (CHIPS), Fedwire, and the Society for Worldwide Interbank Financial Telecommunications (SWIFT) emerged as the new tool for money launderers.[21] Congress responded to this new challenge by passing the Money Laundering Suppression Act (MLSA) in 1994, which broadened the attention of law enforcement officials to money transmitters, check cashing agencies, and other financial institutions.[22] Similar policymaking patterns can be observed in Australia, Canada, France, and other countries, all of which have made the fight against money laundering a public policy priority.[23] No doubt the public policy dynamics outlined above, reflecting long-standing information asymmetries and the resultant regulatory dialectics, are reminiscent of regulators' efforts to establish internal sovereignty in the area of prudential regulation and supervision. If anything, as the U.S. legislative history shows, the cycle between policy action and reaction is shorter in the case of money laundering, making policy formulation and implementation even more difficult, possibly ineffective, and thus inefficient.

With regard to the operational dimension of internal sovereignty, one difference from the previous case study should be noted at the outset. Unlike in the regulation of capital adequacy, policymakers charged with the fight against money laundering are not for the most part in a position to interact directly with the organizations or persons that either commit the crime or launder the profits it generates. Rather, they have to rely on indirect information provided by private sector actors operating knowingly or unknowingly as intermediaries. Thus, at the operational level of the fight against money laundering, horizontal subsidiarity is already an integral part of the policymaking process. Without the ability to collect and evaluate vital information, officials would be at a loss to operationalize internal sovereignty, that is, to ensure compliance by enforcing the numerous laws and administrative measures created for their support. Yet as will be shown, here, too, policymakers starting in the mid- to late 1980s were forced to adjust the policy framework, increasingly delegating operational tasks to private sector actors.

The principal mechanism through which regulators have gathered the information mandated by the BSA has been the Currency Transaction Report (CTR), which banks and other financial institutions must file for every cash transaction over $10,000. The aim of this requirement was to create a paper trail that would allow law enforcement agents to track the large cash transactions commonly associated with money laundering. In practice, however, the early results of the policy proved less than successful, as many financial institutions failed to comply with the reporting requirements. Instances in which customers could walk into a bank and, with a minimum of identification, make large deposits of cash, which were then not reported, were still not uncommon after the BSA went into effect. Banks were simply uneager to turn away this potential business by confronting the depositor with a series of detailed questions. The situation was exacerbated by lax enforcement on the part of regulators, who did not aggressively check bank procedures for compliance.[24] An additional problem was that banks had no standardized mechanism for conveying to law enforcement officers their own suspicions of depositors or transactions. Even in cases where banks were in a position to provide such intelligence, concerns about incurring liability from disclosing private customer information often prevented them from doing so.[25]

Policymakers initially responded by pushing for better compliance with BSA requirements. Increasingly, banks were now fined or given warnings for not filing CTRs.[26] Additionally, anti–money laundering legislation in 1986 and 1988 required financial institutions to establish and maintain reporting procedures that complied with the BSA, and imposed stronger penalties on insured banks and other financial institutions and their employees that willfully violated the recordkeeping regulations.[27] Also in 1994, a separate Internal Revenue Service reporting requirement was imposed, requiring businesses other than financial institutions— such as automobile dealers, commonly cited in conjunction with money laundering—to report cash transactions over $10,000.[28]

It soon became clear, however, that the steps taken thus far could not deal with the underlying problem that policymakers were facing and would continue to face in the future. The mere fact that financial intermediaries had to report more data, and that regulators had broadened their reach to those bank and nonbank institutions that had become the target of money launderers, did not by itself address the regulatory dialectic. At best these would turn out to be short-term solutions, initiating yet another policymaking cycle, at the end of which regulators would find themselves again lagging behind developments in the criminal marketplace. Clearly the system was much too inflexible, indiscriminately collecting information on every transaction over the $10,000 threshold.

This created huge amounts of data, most of which were never evaluated. And even if they had been evaluated, they would turn out to be of little value because the information provided was not specific enough.

Thus, although the legislative framework appeared to maintain internal sovereignty at the formal level, it could not be operationalized. Unless policymakers could reduce the information asymmetry, or in some cases even leapfrog ahead of the criminals, thus reversing the asymmetry, they would continue to fail to root out the problem. Without resorting to large-scale defensive intervention, which would be detrimental to the U.S. economy and to which many, including financial institutions themselves, would strongly object, policymakers needed to change the underlying division of labor between public and private sector actors. One way of doing this was to delegate not only the basic data gathering but also some of the evaluation to the private sector. In this way they could take advantage of the often highly individualized and detailed client information available in the marketplace that a standardized reporting could not possibly capture and that was beyond the reach of regulators, while protecting the privacy of the customer.

During the second half of the 1980s, pressure on policymakers to act increased for a number of other reasons. First, there was a growing recognition that, in light of the continued and even accelerating changes in banking and capital markets, coupled with the dramatic increase in cross-border financial flows and the further liberalization of world trade, the current system to fight money laundering would fall far behind developments and prove entirely inadequate to ensure internal sovereignty. Second, there was a growing awareness on the part of the public, the media, and political elites of the close causal linkage between money laundering and the growing inability of the United States to win the war against drugs, at home as well as abroad. Increasingly, the real "impetus for U.S. anti–money laundering legislation was the same for international initiatives—curtailing the drug trade."[29]

Finally, there was also increasing opposition, from both financial institutions and their clients reluctant to submit an ever-growing amount of proprietary information. Banks also criticized the BSA not only for being too costly and excessively bureaucratic, but also for setting up a power structure between the government and banks that gave the impression that banks were uninterested in curtailing illegal activities and thus indirectly supported the growing domestic drug problem and the violent crime associated with it. The private sector rejected this notion with increasing vehemence. One reason was the growing public awareness of the serious and widespread social, economic, and even security implications of continued failure to control money laundering. Thus money laundering not only presented a risk to the public at large, but now also created a "reputation risk" for financial institutions, which needed to be contained and, if possible, avoided altogether. Accordingly, banks argued that they had to become more careful about participating knowingly or unknowingly in channeling the proceeds from organized criminal activity.[30] A former Treasury official described the change in the following terms:

> I have been amazed at the changes in attitude in the industry since I first assumed the position as Deputy Assistant Treasury Secretary for Law Enforcement. At first, virtually all bankers were opposed to the intrusion of government regulation aimed at illegal money laundering activity. Today, either because of the enormity of the drug problem, or because of a greater sensitivity and awareness of the potential for abuse within the financial systems of this country, I have seen a much more active interest and participation in the drug war by bankers. . . . The role of the banker has changed and is changing. Financial privacy is not absolute. It is a Hobson's choice for the banker dealing with a customer that may be a bit shady; either report him to the IRS, or face the prospect of being personally involved in a sensational drug money laundering case. It is clear that bankers can no longer act in complacent ignorance of the world around them.[31]

In light of these developments, policymakers began in the late 1980s to initiate a number of changes in the reporting process that would change the structure of the policy framework itself. For example, the Anti–Drug Abuse Act of 1988 required that ". . . a national bank submit a Criminal Referral Form (CRF) upon the discovery of any known or suspected criminal violation committed against the bank or involving a financial transaction conducted through the bank."[32] Shortly thereafter, in 1990, the CTR was altered to allow bank employees to tick a box on the form if they felt that a cash transaction over $10,000 was suspicious. Both initiatives delegated a small part of actual policy implementation to the banks themselves, asking them to flag potential money laundering activities, based on information that regulators either did not have or, often, were incapable of spotting. Still, remaining bureaucratic (multiple agency reporting) and organizational (duplicate reporting) hurdles meant that the new system did not operate smoothly.[33] In addition, banks remained concerned about how much customer information they could divulge to regulators without fear of liability, and thus they were reluctant to use their newfound power. This was despite two amendments to the law on financial privacy rights, in 1986 and 1988, which protected banks from liability suits by their clients.

Policymakers responded in 1996 by further streamlining the reporting requirements and delegating additional responsibilities to the private sector. According to Stanley E. Morris, director of the Financial Crimes Enforcement Network (FinCEN) and one of the leading Treasury officials in the fight against money laundering, policymakers:

> . . . are going to "re-engineer" the environment for BSA compliance and enforcement and to do so fundamentally. We're going to treat banks, securities firms, money order sellers, and others through whom money launderers seek to move the proceeds of crimes as our allies and even partners. We're going to provide them with information and expertise. We're going to carefully monitor the flow of information in return. And we're going to move swiftly and decisively against wrong-doers.[34]

In an important move, policymakers agreed on one-stop shopping for banks seeking to report suspicious activity: banks now had to file just one standardized form, the Suspicious Activity Report (SAR), with the newly created FinCEN. Unlike the earlier CRFs, the new reports would be immediately accessible to other federal and state law enforcement agencies through an electronic data distribution network. More important, however, banks were now given considerable responsibility for determining whether or not a certain transaction was suspicious; at the same time the definition of suspicious activity was broadened. Thus the guidelines, which remain in place today, continue to require a bank to report transfers stemming from known illegal activity, but now also require banks to report a transaction when it does not appear to be part of a business contract or other lawful purpose, when it is outside a customer's normal transactions, and when the bank knows of no reasonable explanation for the transaction.[35] To meet this new standard, it was anticipated that banks would be forced to develop "collective knowledge" as to what behavior by their customers should be considered suspicious.[36]

In addition to directly involving banks in the evaluation of financial information, regulators took yet another step that recognized the banks' access to privileged information that would enable them to reduce the information asymmetry. By the early 1990s the volume of annual CTR filings had reached over 10 million, overwhelming attempts to investigate them all and making it difficult even to locate records needed to complete an investigation.[37] The vast majority of these filings involved legitimate commercial transactions that had nothing to do with money laundering.[38] In response, the MLSA of 1994 authorized the secretary of the treasury to introduce measures exempting from the CTR requirements any transactions ". . . which ha[ve] little or no value for law enforcement purposes. . . ."[39] In crafting the new exemption policy, the Treasury consulted regularly with industry representatives under the auspices of the Bank Secrecy Act Advisory Group, an institutionalized form of horizontal subsidiarity set up in March 1994 to advise the department on how to strengthen its anti–money laundering programs.[40] The subsequent interim rule, issued by FinCEN in early 1996, created so-called bright line tests, whereby banks could exempt whole categories of transactions from reporting requirements.[41] Exempted under the rule are banks' transactions with other banks; with any federal, state, or local government; with any listed corporation whose stock is traded on either the New York Stock Exchange, the American Stock Exchange, or the NASDAQ; and with any consolidated subsidiary of a listed corporation that files combined federal income tax returns.[42] These exemptions are expected to yield a reduction of almost 2 million in annual CTR filings, and an effort is under way to bring these numbers down even further by expanding banks' exemptions to include transactions with retail, wholesale, and service businesses. It is hoped that, by cutting down on these burdensome procedures, banks will be able to focus greater attention on information that is important to investigators, such as the reporting of suspicious activity.[43]

In sum, recognizing their growing inability to stem the tide of money laundering, and faced with increasing pressure from the private sector, policymakers have outsourced important operational aspects of internal sovereignty to financial institutions themselves. They felt that, by doing so, information central to policy success, and readily available, could be used much more effectively. Financial institutions no longer just collect and aggregate data before passing them on to regulators. Rather, by making a number of internal judgments, they have become directly involved in the evaluation of the information they collect. The exemptions allowed them to eliminate some information gathering altogether, making the process more efficient by reducing the burden for both public and private actors. In addition, for those transactions that were not exempt, financial institutions were asked to make certain preliminary judgments. This reduced even further the amount of data to be passed on to regulators. Moreover, and probably more important, by delegating part of the evaluation process to the financial institutions themselves, regulators got access to privileged and confidential information gained from the close, regular contacts that, for example, bank officers have with their clients. This information enables them to develop a more complete and individualized risk profile that more standardized collection methods could not capture.

The parallel between this and the previous case, which described the transformation of capital adequacy regulation from the centralized application of a rather simplistic, generalized, quantitative indicator to the decentralized, individual use of sophisticated value-at-risk (VAR) models, which emphasized also the quality of the individual portfolio, is obvious. Policymakers, realizing their inability to keep up with a rapidly changing external environment, turned to the industry itself to make preliminary risk assessments regarding the potential threat of money laundering. By tapping into information that regulators either found difficult to access or simply did not have, this change in policy was to reduce the information asymmetry while at the same time slowing down the regulatory dialectic.

However, as in the case of capital adequacy regulation, regulators did not just delegate greater responsibility to the private sector. They also strengthened their own resolve to ensure that the industry would have both the will and the ability to take on such a quasi-public function. As far as banks' willingness to cooperate was concerned, policymakers needed to narrow the gap between the banks' perception of the risk they faced (the private or reputation risk) and the risk of money laundering to society at large (the social risk). The greater the chances of a bank incurring a loss of reputation, heavy fines, and or some other punitive measure, the closer its assessment of risk would be to that of the public at large.

Thus, in April 1990, the Treasury Department announced the establishment of FinCEN. FinCEN was created as a financial intelligence unit, designed to "provide a governmentwide, multi-source intelligence and

analytical network in support of the detection, investigation, and prosecution of domestic and international money laundering and other financial crimes by Federal, state, local, and foreign law enforcement agencies."[44] Its primary purpose is to identify suspected offenders and to
report on trends and patterns in money laundering.[45] In addition, FinCEN
was to conduct and disseminate research and policy studies on money
laundering enforcement and to support government-wide law enforcement by providing tactical support for ongoing investigations.

To fulfill its primary mandate, FinCEN relies on a wealth of information. One set of data originates from the various reports discussed earlier,
which since 1994 have been directly and exclusively filed with
FinCEN.[46] The agency stores the data on its Financial Institution and
Regulatory Agencies Criminal Referral Enforcement System and automatically forwards SARs to the proper law enforcement agency. Another
data bank, the Source Database developed in house by FinCEN, compiles information on suspects as well as additional information collected
by FinCEN.[47] In addition, FinCEN accesses over twenty government and
commercial databases that contain information pertinent to its mission;
examples include the U.S. Department of Agriculture database, records
of foreign nationals purchasing U.S. property, and TRW-Sherlock and
other credit bureaus.[48]

To examine the information it gathers, FinCEN uses the FinCEN Artificial Intelligence System (FAIS). Installed in 1993, this system electronically links transactions and applies a set of thresholds and rules that can
detect patterns in transactions suggestive of money laundering.[49] FAIS
has steadily increased its efficiency, case load, and the number of positive
hits. As of January 1995, 20 million transactions had been entered and
linked, covering 3 million consolidated subjects and 2.5 million
accounts.[50] Some 200,000 new transactions are added every week. FAIS
has identified about $1 billion in potentially laundered funds, with 90
percent of feedback indicating that FAIS analysis has opened new cases
or provided relevant information to ongoing investigations.

There is thus little doubt that FinCEN has improved the internal sovereignty of policymakers. Besides consolidating data collection into a
single repository, it helps analysts determine what information is useful
and what should be discarded. Sourcing other open but also restricted-
access data banks and using artificial intelligence techniques to track historical patterns will further reduce the information asymmetry. Most
important, however, by relying on these alternative sources of informa-

tion, including classified intelligence, FinCEN creates incentives for banks to be diligent and accurate in their own assessment, narrowing the gap between private and social risk. In the words of FinCEN Director Stanley Morris, "we will exercise our very powerful authorities against those financial sector employees or institutions who choose not to cooperate with or who turn a blind eye to money launderers, rather than taking us up on the opportunity for mutual progress that we're creating."[51] In principle, this clearly resembles the practice of backtesting in the case of capital adequacy regulation, which was also introduced to generate an incentive structure for the private sector that was appropriate for the degree of horizontal subsidiarity it was granted.

Chapter 3 also argued that the private sector must have the capability, as well as the incentive, to exercise its newfound responsibility in a professional manner. As the case study in chapter 4 showed, regulators demanded that banks at a minimum have the organizational capacity and corporate culture to take on such a role, and it enforced that demand by establishing a set of internal qualitative standards that each organization had to meet before being granted permission to use VAR models. The goal of these standards was to improve internal management and establish clear lines of authority and responsibility.

In the case of money laundering, policymakers assigned this role to what were called know-your-customer (KYC) policies or programs.[52] These consist of a set of internal operational guidelines and standards designed to help financial institutions identify money launderers. They call on banks, for example, to verify the identity and business of account holders and create transaction profiles on them, in order to detect activity that is inconsistent with an account holder's business or income. Some go so far as to encourage bank employees to be on the lookout for suspicious body language and behavior.[53] The idea for KYC programs goes all the way back to the implementation of the BSA, yet for a long time it received little attention from the banks or the regulators.[54] It was only with the decision to rely to a greater degree on public-private partnerships that KYC policies suddenly reemerged as a core element in the fight against money laundering. Thus the MLSA of 1994 gave the Treasury the authority to develop and implement a KYC rule. Similarly, the Federal Reserve came to view KYC policies as "one of the most important, if not the most important, means by which financial institutions can hope to avoid criminal exposure to the institution by 'customers' who use the resources of the institution for illicit purposes . . . . The adoption of 'know your customer' guidelines . . . has proven extremely effective. . . ."[55] Indeed, since 1994 the KYC program administered by the Treasury has allowed banks to apply for additional exemptions from reporting requirements provided they meet the KYC rules developed by Treasury.[56]

Many of the changes examined above are too recent to allow an adequate assessment of their effectiveness. The new SARs, for example, were only released in October 1995. Meanwhile, a number of additional policy steps should be considered to strengthen the current policy framework and ensure that the greater reliance on public-private partnerships remains a success. First, policymakers must issue mandatory KYC standards for the financial services industry and other industries known to be targets of money laundering. The development of mandatory KYC policies for financial institutions has been tied up in the bureaucracy and the Bank Secrecy Advisory Group for over three years.[57] In this context it is noteworthy that the American Bankers Association has publicly stated that it supports "the concept of formalizing a 'know your customer policy.'"[58] One approach would be to use the voluntary standards mentioned above, which currently qualify institutions to apply for additional exemptions. Such a threshold, however, should not exclude the continued practice of giving added incentives to the private sector to institute even higher KYC standards in return for additional exemptions.

Second, in addition to mandatory KYC policies, the industry could be asked to install sophisticated internal monitoring systems that would automatically sound an alert in cases of potentially suspicious activity. Such an alert should lead to investigation by a designated manager responsible for BSA compliance. A number of banks have already begun to establish such internal control mechanisms. For example, to comply with regulations issued by the Department of the Treasury's Office of Foreign Assets Control (OFAC), which are designed to block wire transfers to and from rogue states and individuals, several U.S. banks have developed systems that screen incoming wire transfers against a list of suspect locations, organizations, and persons. If the sender or receiver matches an entry on the OFAC list, the transfer is stopped and investigated and, if necessary, canceled. In addition, a number of large U.S.-based multinational banks, in cooperation with commercial software vendors, have begun to implement sophisticated internal control mechanisms that go beyond OFAC requirements. For example, Chase Manhattan Bank has implemented a system that aggregates multiple currency transactions occurring on the same business day. The system's value is demonstrated by the fact that 65 percent of the CRFs filed by Chase are a direct result of investigations into activity flagged by the system.[59] Numerous software firms offer programs that permit banks to aggregate currency transactions over a fixed period of time and flag all those aggregations that exceed a specified threshold. In addition, these systems can mark individual accounts and automatically generate reports on their cash activities.[60] An added benefit of such systems, which FinCEN cannot provide, is real-time detection, so that the activity can be interrupted while in progress. Finally, it is recognized that a fully automated system will be far more efficient in the long run. Although the cost of implementing such a system is not high, at least in comparison with alternative compliance schemes, policymakers might consider some form of financial support for small and medium-size enterprises seeking to acquire them.

Third, under the Annunzio-Wylie Anti–Money Laundering Act of 1992, a bank's charter can be annulled, or its insurance by the Federal Deposit Insurance Corporation can be discontinued, if the bank is convicted of noncompliance. However, as one source indicated, "[t]hese sanctions are so powerful that, according to bank regulators, they are unlikely to be sought often."[61] This does not set a very good precedent for efforts to ensure compliance. Unless policymakers use these enforcement tools consistently and rigorously, the whole effort to narrow the gap between private and social risk will fail. To avoid charges of unfair treatment, nonfinancial institutions that violate the law should incur similar penalties. One option would be a liability clause that holds violators responsible for the broad range of damages created by money laundering. Here policymakers can rely on the considerable experience gained in establishing corporate and lender liability for environmental pollution.[62] In the early 1990s, for example, a U.S. court ruled that banks are liable for damages if they participate in the financial management of a facility to a degree indicating a capacity to influence the corporation's treatment of hazardous wastes.[63] Apart from the considerable financial damage that such liability threatens, it also links money laundering to its more tangible social consequences, such as drug-related violence and addiction. The threat of publicity and the associated shaming should further encourage compliance.

As the history of environmental liability suggests, banks may initially reject this role.[64] But this experience also shows that banks have learned to cope with the new and still emerging environment and have responded positively in various ways.[65] To cope with potential liabilities arising from environmental pollution, for example, financial institutions and insurance companies have begun to seek the services of special advisers, who coordinate and market pollution and environmental engineering programs, conduct environmental risk assessments, handle environmental claims, and provide feasibility studies for captive insurers.[66] If anything, then, liability in the case of money laundering is likely to improve KYC standards and encourage the installment of internal monitoring systems. Here, too, policymakers might consider an exemption clause, exonerating banks from liability if they have such internal controls in place.

Finally, although the creation of FinCEN has led to a considerable consolidation and concentration of the information flow from private to public sector actors, facilitating evaluation and further dissemination, no single institution is in charge of maintaining the information flow in the opposite direction. Private sector actors need to be informed on a variety of matters, including the latest developments in money laundering techniques, select intelligence information that could prove vital for detection of a money laundering scheme, and changes in legislation and KYC standards. Nor is any single institution responsible for training those personnel who will be responsible for compliance. Rather, at least a dozen bureaucracies and industry organizations currently take on such information and training functions, competing for the banks' attention. This makes the overall compliance effort appear overwhelming, creates confusion among the recipients, and leads to expensive duplication. It would be helpful to streamline and consolidate the process wherever possible. Indeed, policymakers might consider delegating many of these functions to an industry organization. In many ways such a mixed regulatory organization would amount to an institutionalization of the current BSA. It would still operate under the auspices of and draw upon the experience and information of the enforcement agencies. In addition, working in close cooperation with the government, it could propose and update KYC standards, monitor their implementation, and supervise the introduction of the internal computerized surveillance systems suggested earlier. Short of getting involved in criminal prosecution, they could also be charged with enforcement of the industry's anti–money laundering standard.

These suggestions may appear somewhat premature and far reaching, but one can identify a number of trends that are likely to move the debate in this direction. Moreover, given the perennial pressure on regulators to keep up with these trends, the suggestions made here may come just in time. For example, there is every indication that the range of financial institutions targeted by money launderers will spread. As one high-ranking U.S. official put it in the summer of 1996, "To the extent that we have really tightened up our regulation and our controls for banks, they [money launderers] have moved from bank to non-bank financial institutions, money exchange houses, and currency exchange houses."[67] Most recently this group was joined by a card club, which the Treasury now considers an important source of money laundering activities. The Treasury is proposing to include these clubs in the definition of financial institutions under the BSA in order to subject them to reporting requirements. In its 1997 report the FATF points to the continuing shift of money laundering activity from banking to nonbank financial institutions, as well as to nonfinancial businesses in the form of shell companies and such professions as accountants, lawyers, and notaries.[68]

There is every indication that money launderers have also infiltrated the international trading system and are laundering money through cash or bearer-negotiable instruments that are physically concealed in merchandise or in shipping containers, vessels, aircraft, and others; cash to product resale of consumer goods through brokers and import/export businesses; and fraudulent importations or exportations of commodities, for example, at inflated prices, and parallel transactions.[69] Between 1990 and 1994 alone, the world economy witnessed thirty-three regional trade agreements,[70] which will further compound the problem. Finally, in an effort to infiltrate the legal economy, transnational criminal organizations have also infiltrated privatization programs around the world. According to the UN Commission on Crime Prevention and Criminal Justice, these organizations have begun to acquire "state-owned banks and financial, telecommunications and other service [sector] institutions . . ." to the point where they "could start to control—if effective countermeasures are not quickly implemented—not only assets, but countries as well."[71]

Looking to the future, changes associated with the application of new technologies to the payment system threaten to add another dimension to this already complex picture. Going under various names, from e-money to digital cash to cyberpayments, these developments may give rise to a whole new set of institutions and transactions that criminals could use to circumvent controls on money laundering.[72] Although this technology is still in its infancy, a number of threats that it poses to the regulatory structure can already be identified. The development of digital or electronic money may promote financial disintermediation, replacing banks and other depository institutions with issuers of electronic credits or stored value cards.[73] Many of these new institutions will fall outside the range of those now covered by money laundering statutes. E-money and other electronic cash substitutes may also soon come to replace traditional notes and coins. Here the challenge for regulators will be to adapt regulations that have conventionally focused on tracking the movement of large amounts of cash through the financial system.

Whether and how these concerns are addressed will hinge to a large degree on the question of financial privacy. On one hand, the digitization of financial transactions holds the potential for greater regulatory oversight. Technically, it is not difficult to engineer electronic systems that would allow law enforcement officials to monitor financial transactions carried out using digital cash or over the Internet. On the other hand, the major selling point of electronic cash is that it is both secure and virtually anonymous. As a result, any built-in features that compromise this security or anonymity will make electronic transactions correspondingly less attractive. The potential conflict between these priorities has already been highlighted in the context of the U.S. debate on encryption standards, and many more battles will undoubtedly ensue before these issues are resolved.[74]

In light of this ongoing proliferation of private sector actors that are being drawn into the issue of money laundering, questions must be raised about the feasibility of expanding FinCEN's role. After all, even as policymakers were managing to reduce, through exemptions and SARs, the amount of information that FinCEN had to assess, the definition of what constitutes a financial institution had to be expanded, increasing the net burden on FinCEN. Already in 1993 FinCEN was dealing with over 250,000 institutions, all of which at that time fell under the BSA reporting requirements.[75] Besides raising organizational and administrative concerns, further expansion of FinCEN's powers would undoubtedly generate considerable resistance from both the industry and the general public. The former is likely to object on the grounds that it further exposes financial and nonfinancial institutions to charges of violating the Right to Financial Privacy Act—a constant concern throughout the history of the BSA. The latter has criticized FinCEN for having "ushered in the age of 'Big Brotherism' and government computer surveillance of personal finances."[76]

It is unlikely that any large-scale expansion of FinCEN's activities, especially as far as the nonfinancial sector is concerned, would be able to overcome this strong resistance.[77] Even if eventually it did, it would take years before such a system could be implemented, in light of the challenges it would face in the courts. In the meantime money launderers would be free to go about their business. In light of the above limits, it cannot be ruled out that further steps will have to be taken to allow policymakers to focus on the core challenge of enforcement and prosecution, while delegating additional aspects of policy implementation to others. The mixed regulatory institution suggested above is one possible answer, as under such a scheme much of the information-gathering activity would be taken out of public hands. This, however, presumes that private sector actors have both the will and the ability to support the mandate and the philosophy of such an organization.

Although challenges thus remain for policymakers in the coming years, the United States has no doubt made considerable progress in the fight against money laundering.[78] Most important, within ten years after money laundering was criminalized, it had become widely recognized that bringing this problem under control required engaging private sector actors and challenging them to participate actively in the policymaking process, and officials had taken a series of concrete steps to implement this strategy. Yet more needs to be done now that other private sector actors have become the target of illegal activities. This has led to a further increase in the number of agencies involved in the formulation of policy, making quick and decisive action ever more difficult, notwithstanding the efforts of the recently created Interagency Coordination Group that is coordinated through FinCEN.[79] But it is precisely the fact that money launderers have moved on to other shops that shows that the current strategy is effective. To sustain this accomplishment, it will be important to preserve the cooperation of the private sector while ensuring that the gap between private and social risk does not grow too large. The policy recommendations offered above are aimed at achieving that.

U.S. policymakers have also understood that unilateral action alone will not be enough. Already in the mid-1980s money laundering and organized crime had a considerable cross-border component. By the early 1990s participants in these activities had adopted the organizational logic of global corporations, marginalizing the role of territoriality except for purposes of jurisdictional arbitrage and to escape prosecution. The geography of money laundering became increasingly decoupled from its legal and political counterpart. Without a determined effort by national governments working collectively to match the geography of global crime and money laundering, they could not hope to succeed individually. The following section examines these collective efforts to combat money laundering and explores the possibilities and prospects for global public policy in this domain.

Toward a Global Anti–Money Laundering Regime

In reviewing international efforts to combat money laundering one is struck by the fact that there has been little or no time lag between national and global public policy efforts. In fact, just as in the case of global prudential bank regulation, one can observe with increasing frequency instances of "reverse engineering," in which an international convention or a legally nonbinding agreement serves as a leading point of reference, if not a model, for countries in the midst of building—or just beginning to build—their own domestic policy frameworks.[80] This is especially true as far as the United States is concerned. In 1988, only two years after money laundering had been criminalized, Congress passed the Anti-Drug Abuse Act, which in effect acknowledged that the problem could only be resolved collectively and asked the secretary of the treasury "to enter into negotiations with the appropriate financial supervisory agencies . . . to reach international agreements" on a variety of money laundering–related issues including "adequate record[keeping] of large United States currency transactions" by foreign banks and other financial institutions, and to "establish a mechanism whereby such records may be made available to United States law enforcement officials, . . . further cooperative efforts, voluntary information exchanges, the use of letters rogatory and mutual legal assistance treaties." The legislators also requested that the secretary submit within two years a report to Congress on the outcome of the negotiations.[81] No doubt the nature and purpose of this congressional action are reminiscent of the International Lending Supervisory Act of 1983, which initiated U.S. efforts to secure what came to be known as the Basle Agreement.

Also in 1988 the UN Convention against Illicit Traffic in Narcotic Drugs and Psychotropic Substances was adopted, which was the first of a number of multilateral efforts to draw attention to the problem. The convention laid the groundwork for efforts to combat money laundering by obliging the signatory states to criminalize the laundering of money from drug trafficking. To date, of the 185 UN member countries, 147 have signed the convention, and 136 have ratified it.[82] The Basle Committee in 1988 drafted and adopted the Basle Statement of Principles, which established a minimum set of operating standards or principles for bank management.[83] In June 1992 the Group of Ten endorsed the so-called Basle Code, which established new minimum standards to reduce banking malpractice. The Basle Code was a direct response to the collapse of the Bank of Commerce and Credit International and related illegal activities.[84] The code also addresses the sensitive issue of information sharing and encourages greater progress in this area.[85] The International Organization of Securities Commissions also issued a statement in 1992 acknowledging that money laundering "must be treated as a regulatory and enforcement priority."[86]

The European Union adopted a directive to curb money laundering in 1991.[87] What is noteworthy about this directive is that at the time the European Commission transmitted its proposal to the Council of Ministers for consideration and approval, in March 1990, money laundering was a criminal offense in only one member state. The fact that the initiative originated at the European level was a direct response to the integration of the European market for financial services, which required a more coordinated approach.[88] Another European initiative rests with the Council of Europe, which now includes many countries from central and eastern Europe. In 1990 the council adopted the Convention on Laundering, Search, Seizure, and Confiscation of Proceeds from Crime. But as of the fall of 1997 only eighteen of the forty members of the council had ratified the convention.[89]

To date, however, the most comprehensive and promising effort has been the creation of the Financial Action Task Force at the 1989 economic summit of the Group of Seven (G-7) nations in Paris.[90] The FATF is currently composed of the twenty-four members of the Organization for Economic Cooperation and Development (OECD)[91] plus Hong Kong[92] and Singapore, the Commission of the European Communities, and the Gulf Cooperation Council. Its secretariat is accredited with the OECD, much as the Basle Committee is accredited with the Bank for International Settlements. Its mandate, originally set for five years, was extended in 1994 and is currently due to expire in 1998–99.[93]

According to the Paris summit communiqué, the mandate of the task force is to "assess the results of cooperation already undertaken in order to prevent the utilization of the banking system and financial institutions for the purpose of money laundering, and to consider additional preventive efforts in this field, including the adaptation of the legal and regulatory systems so as to enhance multilateral judicial assistance."[94] It was clearly recognized that unless countries not only strengthened their national regulatory structures, but also adapted them around a commonly derived standard and developed a system of close cooperation and information exchange, money launderers would continue to exploit the growing disjuncture between territorially based legal systems and the nonterritorial character of international financial flows.

The FATF performs numerous functions. It has conducted a number of technical studies, generating considerable insight into the nature of the problem as well as exploring how different member jurisdictions have responded to it. The studies have included a cross-jurisdictional review of systems for reporting suspicious transactions; a cross-country analysis of the confiscation of the proceeds of crime; a comparison of customer identification systems; and a report on the challenges presented by cyberpayments. The task force also conducts an annual survey of money laundering methods and countermeasures, to keep members abreast of the latest developments. In addition, the FATF and its members conduct an extensive external relations program, which today covers all continents and is by far the most comprehensive effort of its kind at the global level, including the activities of the United Nations, which on many occasions has supported the FATF.

However, at the center of the FATF's work has been the development of Forty Recommendations that lay out the basic elements and conditions necessary for any public policy structure directed at the problem of money laundering. In addition to embracing the 1988 UN convention, the recommendations cover three core dimensions: the role of the national legal system, the role of the financial system, and the need to strengthen international cooperation. The rationale for establishing these recommendations rests on the recognition that members can no longer operationalize their internal sovereignty unilaterally, but instead need to adopt broadly comparable standards that they pledge to implement. Today these recommendations have developed into the single most important set of international norms in the fight against money laundering. So far they have been revised once, under the chairmanship of the United States during the seventh FATF session (FATF VII, 1995–96). That revision produced no major changes but did reflect the experience gained during the previous years and the new trends in money launder-ing discussed above.[95] For example, countries are now encouraged to introduce mandatory reporting of suspicious transactions by financial institutions; the Forty Recommendations were extended to nonfinancial businesses; and members were encouraged to focus attention on the implications for money laundering of new or developing technologies in electronic payments.

The change considered most important by the task force itself was the extension of the definition of money laundering beyond that related to narcotics trafficking to other serious crimes. This was done in response to indications that global criminal organizations are infiltrating other parts of the economy. According to the FATF, "there has been over-whelming evidence in FATF countries and throughout the rest of the world that non-drug predicate offences constitute an important and growing source of illegal wealth entering legitimate financial channels. Indeed, in some countries non-drug related crime constitutes the pre-dominant source of laundered proceeds."[96]

To achieve joint implementation of the group's recommendations, FATF members have instituted two monitoring devices: annual self-assessments and more detailed peer reviews, also called mutual evalua-tions, of each member's progress in implementing the recommendations. The latter include on-site examinations by anti–money laundering experts from other member states.[97] The task force describes the peer reviews as "an irreplaceable mechanism to expedite the enactment of money laundering countermeasures."[98] By the time FATF VI (1994–95) concluded, all member states had been the subject of one round of mutual evaluations, which focused on whether all members had ade-quately implemented the forty recommendations. FATF VII (1995–96) began the second round of peer reviews, which focuses on the more sen-sitive dimension of the "effectiveness of countermeasures in place."[99] To create a sense of continuity, the second round of evaluations also "checks any follow-up action taken in response to the suggestions for improve-ment made in the first round."[100]

FATF VII also marked the implementation of a FATF policy for non-complying members.[101] Such a policy had become necessary because of concern that the task force's mission and credibility were at stake if some members failed to make any progress toward implementing the recom-mendations. This concern arose especially with respect to the FATF's external relations program, which has become increasingly important as member policies have become more effective and geographic proliferation has accelerated. "Recognising that it could not expect others to do what certain of its members fail to do," the task force felt compelled to act.[102] According to the FATF, these measures "represent a graduated approach aimed at enhancing peer pressure."[103] To date the most significant case of public disciplinary action relates to Turkey, which by mid-September 1996, more than six years after the FATF was established, still had not passed any anti–money laundering legislation and whose compliance with the recommendations was judged "seriously deficient."[104]

The FATF's interaction with the private sector was close to nonexistent until 1996. This is all the more startling since the majority of recommendations in section 3 of its list (recommendations 8–29) focus on financial institutions, emphasizing the importance of reporting suspicious transactions and of KYC policies. The FATF recommends, for example, that banks develop transaction profiles and training programs for KYC policies, as well as external audits of their systems. Policies on maintaining records and sharing those records without fear of prosecution by the client, as well as the development of competent authorities to monitor and enforce the law and help financial institutions meet their obligations, are laid out. In light of recent developments, these recommendations are applied not only to banks but to any financial or nonfinancial institution that a money launderer could use as an intermediary.[105]

It took the chairmanship of the United States to initiate the first official contact between the FATF and the private sector. Given the increased reliance on horizontal subsidiarity in U.S. domestic policy, this should come as no surprise. In early 1996 the task force convened the first-ever meeting with representatives of the financial services industry and established a "Forum for Future Exchange." The purpose of the meeting was to solicit the advice and support of the world's financial community to ensure that the task force's efforts would take into full account the interests and priorities of the private sector.[106] More important, this meeting reflected a fundamental change in the FATF's policy, embracing the notion of horizontal subsidiarity at least with regard to agenda setting. Thus the goal for the FATF was to "establish a bridge between itself and the industry and to work in partnership with the private sector in combating money laundering."[107] As part of that interaction, the FATF carried out a study on the need for public officials to provide feedback to financial institutions reporting suspicious transactions.[108] The private sector also participated in the FATF's most recent study, on the money laundering threats posed by new payment technologies, and the task force sought the cooperation of financial institutions in its effort to secure the identification of the ordering client in electronic funds transfers through the SWIFT network.[109]

There is no doubt that the creation of the FATF reflects a realization by governments that internal sovereignty in the domain of money laundering can only be operationalized collectively. In addition, by instituting both the self-assessments and, in particular, the peer reviews, the task force was able not only to establish an important process of continued information exchange, but also to infuse a considerable degree of transparency and disclosure into its own organizational structure, which created a sense of trust and equal treatment among members. At the same time, policymakers recognized that harmonization of countries' legal systems, if possible at all, would be not only much more complex technically than establishing a single quantitative indicator, as in the case of the Basle Agreement, but politically very sensitive as well. Hence the relatively broad language used in the task force's recommendations, in combination with their legally nonbinding nature, allowed for not only structural but also a much greater degree of functional subsidiarity than did Basle's definition of tier-two capital. This approach gave national policymakers the flexibility necessary to implement the recommendations according to their differing legal traditions and constitutional arrangements, without abandoning the broader goal.

Operationalizing internal sovereignty at the global level is a matter of learning and custom. As such, the special studies, the self-assessments and peer reviews, and the annual meetings and other joint venues should all be considered not only as important mechanisms for ensuring a continued reduction in information asymmetry, both among regulators and between officials and the private sector, but also as a first and important step toward disclosure-based regulation, softening the hard shell of internal sovereignty. In addition, these initiatives have created a sense of community, mutual understanding, shared experience, and success among policymakers that is vital to sustain the effort and to allow the FATF to evolve over time, broadening its agenda, strengthening its resolve, and, most important, establishing a process of formal cooperation with the private sector. As far as cooperation among policymakers themselves is concerned, the FATF has moved beyond the global public policy community in the domain of global financial supervision; as the previous case study showed, supervisors have to develop closer ties if they are to establish a more regularized structure for information sharing.

Yet, as the FATF itself has acknowledged, much more needs to be done. For example, one can take issue with the FATF's relatively weak instruments to enforce internal sovereignty in the member countries. The task force will undoubtedly have to continue to strengthen its compliance and enforcement mechanisms. Yet another important future challenge concerns the FATF's ability to respond to the continued and rapid expansion of the geography of money laundering beyond the jurisdiction of its members. This, too, the members clearly recognize. As one recent task force study concludes, "A general observation drawn from the typologies exercises is that given the global nature of the money laundering phenomenon, geographic borders have become increasingly irrelevant. Launderers tend to move their activity to jurisdictions where there are few or weak anti–money laundering countermeasures."[110] If policymakers want to maintain internal sovereignty in the future, they urgently need to expand the reach of the task force.

So far, however, the history of FATF expansion has been relatively uneventful. After its initial creation in the wake of the 1989 G-7 summit, when the task force counted fifteen members, two successive enlargements in 1990 and 1991 brought it to its present size. According to some, this expansion was only achieved after considerable political pressure.[111] On several occasions prior to 1990 the issue of FATF expansion was put on the agenda, but any serious consideration of expansion was rejected outright. Thus the FATF III Annual Report stated, "FATF now has twenty eight members. For an organization that prides itself on its informality of procedure and ready ability to achieve consensus, this is clearly approaching the maximum membership possible. The FATF has, therefore, decided not to accept any new members for the time being."[112] FATF IV marked a slight change in tone. The task force stuck to its overall position that a significant increase in the size of the FATF would prejudice its flexibility and efficiency. But it did indicate that if it should someday decide to expand, such expansion would have to be "very limited."[113] Since 1994 the task force has pledged to review its policy on expansion, but no expansion has occurred. This was controversial, since a number of states had apparently indicated a desire to join.[114] Still, even the 1996–97 annual report continues to take a rather passive attitude toward enlargement, despite the clear recognition of the underlying contradiction between the task force's geographic constraints and the worldwide reach of global crime: "There is an absolute need for continuing action at the international level to deepen and widen the fight against money laundering. This vital issue will be fully addressed in the review of the FATF's future activities, structure and membership, which will take place in 1997–1998."[115]

One reason why the decision over expansion has been held up is the current uncertainty over the future of task force itself. The FATF is scheduled to be dissolved in 1999, when its present mandate expires. As a first step, therefore, member governments should renew their commitment now to extend the mandate for another five years, to 2004. Such an extension, however, would have to entail a commitment by the FATF to develop a medium-term strategy for both deepening and broadening its structure over the next five years. The rationale is obvious. Transnational organized crime will remain for the foreseeable future one of the major challenges to the international system. Unless governments can develop an adequate collective response to this threat to their internal sovereignty, the exploitation of an increasingly open international economic structure by criminal conglomerates will eventually threaten deeper integration, as policymakers are left with little choice but to resort to defensive intervention to protect their societies from organized crime and its consequences, both social and economic. As far as broadening the task force's structure is concerned, the general goal should be to extend the FATF's Forty Recommendations and both types of assessments to as many countries as possible. At a minimum it should cover all those states that are known to present a considerable risk and that are the preferred targets of money launderers. The latest U.S. State Department International Narcotics Control Strategy Report (INCSR) ranks sixty-four countries as high, medium-high, or medium priority concerns.[116] The governments of these countries should become the immediate target of a global strategy to expand the FATF's standards, keeping in mind that the group of priority countries is likely to grow over the next several years.[117]

The central challenge of any enlargement initiative is to find the appropriate balance between ensuring consistency of the standards currently applied and maintaining, if not increasing, their flexibility and diversity, which will be necessary to absorb new members. This can be achieved using the task force's Forty Recommendations as a minimum benchmark. However, rather than enlarge the FATF itself to a size that would render it inflexible, a more promising strategy would be to create regional FATFs, each of which would accommodate a smaller number of governments and which could address specific regional issues and in some cases be attached to regional integration projects already under way.

The FATF's current external relations strategy, to which considerable time and resources have already been devoted, provides a good starting point.[118] To date the most promising achievement of its external relations program is the formation of the Caribbean Financial Action Task Force (CFATF). Established during the early 1990s and modeled on the FATF, the CFATF became fully operational in 1994.[119] Its members have agreed to implement the Forty Recommendations as well as an additional nineteen recommendations specific to the region.[120] Originally the task force consisted of twenty-six governments from the Caribbean, including dependent territories. However, when the CFATF adopted a Memorandum of Understanding, which embodied its objectives, principles, functions, and terms of membership, at its council meeting in October 1996, eight countries did not sign. These countries are no longer considered members of the CFATF, even though they originally endorsed the Forty Recommendations.[121] Meanwhile, however, all the Central American countries were invited to join the CFATF, and three (Belize, Guatemala, and Nicaragua) have done so, bringing the group's current membership to twenty-one. The CFATF conducts peer reviews and recently launched its own topologies exercise, through which it will develop and share among its members the latest intelligence on money laundering and other financial crime techniques used in the Caribbean region and elsewhere. Of central importance to the CFATF's operation has been the financial and technical support of five FATF governments: Canada, France, the Netherlands, the United Kingdom, and the United States. Previously called sponsor governments, their role was recently formalized, and they are now referred to as "Cooperating and Supporting Nations."[122] The United Kingdom, for example, in addition to supplying financial resources, has provided the principal officer for the CFATF secretariat in Trinidad and Tobago; the U.S. Treasury has also provided support staff.

The FATF should make a concerted effort to push its other regional initiatives in the same direction. In Asia its early efforts have been channeled through the Asian Secretariat, which is part of the FATF itself and is funded by Australia's Confiscated Assets Trust Fund.[123] In 1996 further progress was made with the creation of the Asia/Pacific Group on Money Laundering.[124] This group, which has the official support of the Asia-Pacific Economic Cooperation (APEC) forum, has agreed to develop a regional plan of action to facilitate the enactment of anti–money laundering measures. However, not all members of APEC have chosen to join the group, a fact that was duly noted at the APEC ministerial meeting in April 1997.[125]

In Latin America, anti–money laundering efforts began in 1986 with the establishment of the Inter-American Drug Abuse Control Commission (known by its Spanish acronym CICAD) by the Organization of American States (OAS). OAS/CICAD provides assistance to member states in their fight against the illicit production and trafficking of drugs and related crimes. In 1992 the Commission completed model legislation on narcotics-related money laundering and asset forfeiture.[126] Another step forward was made at the Summit of the Americas Ministerial Conference on Money Laundering, which took place in Buenos Aires in November and December 1995. Participating countries agreed to implement a range of policies to combat money laundering, including mutual assessments of the type practiced by the FATF, under the control of OAS/CICAD.

Until recently, Africa was not a concern in the fight against money laundering. However, in October 1996 the FATF sponsored the first Southern and Eastern African Money Laundering Conference. The thirteen participating countries adopted a proposal, subject to confirmation by their heads of government, to establish a Southern and Eastern African FATF similar to the CFATF.[127] If, as advocated above, the FATF succeeds in converting these loose regional groupings into fully fledged FATFs, they would cover about three-quarters of the sixty-four countries identified as priority countries by the INCSR. This assumes, however, that all the countries in each region also join their regional FATF, which has not yet happened.[128]

One region not yet adequately covered is the former Soviet Union and central and eastern Europe. As OECD members, the Czech Republic, Hungary, and Poland could be asked to join the original FATF, and there is every indication that the prospect of FATF membership explains Mexico's decision not to sign the Memorandum of Understanding among CFATF members. Nevertheless, a number of important countries and regions remain left out, in particular Cyprus, India, Israel, Liechtenstein, Nigeria, Pakistan, and Russia. Their omission needs to be addressed, and there have been bilateral contacts and efforts by the FATF with some of these countries.[129]

No doubt this is an ambitious agenda for the FATF, but there is no real alternative. Relying on a regional approach not only ensures substantial structural subsidiarity during the assessment, but also allows each group to employ some functional subsidiarity. As long as it can be guaranteed that governments will adhere to the Forty Recommendations and make a serious effort to integrate them into their domestic laws and regulations, one important precondition to operationalizing internal sovereignty collectively has been met. In time the assessments, the information exchanges, and other shared experiences are likely to lead to further adaptations not only of national legal systems but of the day-to-day practice of pursuing money launderers. Moreover, as the CFATF's experience shows, the multiple regional groupings may well create some institutional competition to improve and update the recommendations, and to contribute innovative and practical ideas that support the overall public policy goal. A joint forum representing the regional groups, each of which is led by a rotating presidency, could provide the institutional foundation for a global anti–money laundering network.

But although the application of common standards will reduce the incentive for money launderers to engage in regulatory arbitrage, a global framework will not succeed unless policymakers are able to overcome the regulatory dialectic and information asymmetries that have arisen from the constantly changing strategies of criminal organizations, from financial innovation, and, most important in the global context, from the disjuncture between the illegal and legal geographies that define the scope of money laundering. As the earlier discussion of the U.S. effort has shown, the only feasible way to meet this challenge is through the creation of sophisticated financial intelligence units in each country. Fortunately, the United States is not the only country that has employed large-scale data processing capacity and artificial intelligence to detect money laundering. During the early 1990s the Traitement du Renseignement et Action contre les Circuits Financiers Clandestins (TRACFIN) in France, the Australian Transaction Reports and Analysis Centre (AUSTRAC), the National Criminal Intelligence Service (NCIS) in the United Kingdom, and the Cellule de Traitement des Informations Financieres (CTIF) in Belgium were all established for the same purpose.[130] The number of financial intelligence units worldwide has grown rapidly ever since, to seventeen by 1995.[131] Today, "[w]e are witnessing a new world-wide phenomenon, that is the establishment of financial intelligence units (FIUs) in countries throughout the globe. . . ," and ". . . there are at least 29 such units."[132]

To encourage better cooperation and coordination, the Egmont Group, a regular forum for financial intelligence units from around the world, was founded in 1995 at the initiative of Belgium and the United States.[133] The group's creation was based on a consensus among the FATF members and interested governments that improved interaction and communication among financial intelligence units would serve a broad range of common goals in the areas of information sharing, coordination of training, and legal issues. Most important, the effort to increase communication among financial intelligence units has been furthered by FinCEN's development of a secure World Wide Web site, which will "permit members of the Egmont Group to access information on FIUs, money laundering trends, financial analysis tools, and technological developments."[134]

No doubt the formation of the Egmont Group itself, but in particular the creation of a secure web site, should be considered a major step toward overcoming information asymmetries. As a second pillar of its medium-term strategy, the FATF therefore should develop a plan to promote the establishment of financial intelligence units in all member countries of the various FATFs and secure both regional and global cooperation among these units in exchanging information. To prevent this information from being disseminated too widely, structural subsidiarity should be applied as well. Thus the gathering and exchange of data could be organized at three levels: national, regional, and global. Only those data that have implications beyond the national geography would be passed on to the regional level, and likewise from the regional to the global level. In this context it somewhat ironic that, almost ten years ago, the 1988 Anti–Drug Abuse Act in the United States proposed the establishment of an International Currency Control Agency, intended "to (1) serve as central source of information and database for international drug enforcement agencies; (2) collect and analyze currency transaction reports filed by member countries; and (3) encourage the adoption, by member countries, of uniform cash transaction and money laundering statutes."[135]

How much horizontal subsidiarity will be used in both the regional groupings and the financial intelligence units remains to be seen. In light of the U.S. experience and the recent changes in the FATF, however, other governments would be well advised to adopt such an approach for their own domestic systems. No doubt initiating public-private partnerships will be more difficult once a cross-national dimension is added, but it would further improve the quality of the data. At the same time, however, horizontal subsidiarity is not critical to the functioning of the system itself. The first step in exploring such a possibility might be to set up regional groupings based on the model of the Bank Secrecy Advisory Group.

To succeed in establishing these two pillars of global anti–money laundering policy, the FATF and its member governments will have to muster the financial resources and technical assistance necessary for the regional groups and their members to fulfill their obligations and set up and run the intelligence units. It is therefore vital that the FATF develop a network of "Cooperating and Supporting Nations" that are prepared to engage those governments in need of assistance. In addition to bilateral support, the regional development banks, the United Nations, and in particular the international financial institutions (IFIs) should be involved in such a plan (for more on the IFIs see below).

However, neither pillar will achieve the desired results unless countries have sufficient incentives to participate in them. It is here, in the domain of compliance and enforcement, that the current FATF, and for that matter the CFATF, reveal their greatest weakness. Time and again FATF annual reports have stated that the task force is not an international organization. The group prides itself on its informality and efficiency. This may have been an advantage in getting countries to agree to join the FATF at a time when money laundering was only beginning to emerge as an global public policy problem and the group of countries affected by it was relatively small. Today, however, given the magnitude and scope of the problem, this position is no longer to the FATF's advantage. Rather, it has become a handicap as more and more countries free-ride on the global financial system, taking advantage of the multiple benefits that liberalized capital flows bring while contributing little to containing the dangers that they pose. As the 1996–97 FATF annual report unambiguously states, "Whilst most FATF members and a few non FATF countries have comprehensive measures in place, the vast majority of countries do not and this is where increased attention needs to be focused."[136] As far as the informality and efficiency of the FATF model goes, this point is well taken, but it is a characteristic with which *all* organizations that deal with global problems have to contend. To resolve an organizational and operational challenge by restricting membership to the point where it undermines the policy mandate itself ultimately frustrates the efforts of current members and defeats the entire purpose of the initiative. The problem must be addressed in a different manner, and structural subsidiarity is one important element.

Moreover, the fact that the FATF has little or no leverage to ensure compliance or exercise enforcement does not imply that it needs to acquire such leverage in the future. An easier and less disruptive approach might be to engage other international organizations that do have leverage and that also consider their mandate threatened by money laundering. Both the International Monetary Fund (IMF) and the World Bank fall into that category. Indeed, they will have to play a central role in the fight against money laundering if that fight is to be won. The IMF presented a study on the economic aspects of money laundering at the FATF VII plenary meeting in 1996. The IMF acknowledged the link between anti–money laundering policies and macroeconomic policies aimed at developing financial markets. The study identified numerous channels through which the negative effects of money laundering are transmitted to the broader economy and concluded that "there is considerable synergy to be gained from coordinating the two sets of policies."[137] But the Fund gave no indication that it was prepared to go beyond coordination to exploit this synergy and use its financial leverage to ensure compliance with FATF recommendations, on the basis that their neglect undermined its own policies and fulfillment of its mandate. This has to change, and a recent IMF publication leads the way in moving beyond merely recognizing the linkage to acting upon it.[138]

The international financial system should be considered a global public good. This good can only bestow its benefits on all members if it remains transparent and credible and is not abused by some for short-term gains, such as attracting ill-gotten money through lenient or poorly enforced regulations. To maintain credibility and transparency, and to allow every country equal access to the gains that the international financial system provides, it will be necessary to establish a set of minimum guidelines with respect to money laundering. In doing so, policymakers should make use of the FATF's recommendations and the experience derived from their application. At the operational level this requires that the IMF, in its work on financial sector reform in emerging markets, embrace these recommendations by establishing a set of regulations and practical policy steps, including KYC guidelines for banks, to be followed by member countries and their financial institutions, in addition to those that already focus on conventional regulatory and supervisory issues.

But the Fund has also indicated that it can go further. To enforce these rules, a variety of sanctions and other punitive measures could be applied. For example, the IMF study suggests that international legal recognition could be denied to financial operations transacted and rights acquired within countries that do not adhere to the rules. Another option would be to tax any capital flows that pass through the financial markets of countries that do not adhere to the standards. The advantage of such market-based rules is that they create incentives for individual and institutional investors to withdraw from these markets. This, in turn, eliminates the incentive for countries to engage in offensive intervention by undercutting the global standards, as they would quickly find themselves cut off from international capital markets. Furthermore, FATF members could deny banks from nonmember countries access to their domestic markets, thus virtually excluding them from the world's financial centers.

The Fund could even be part of the enforcement process. Since its official position is that money laundering is an obstacle to an effective, efficient, and stable monetary system, it could invoke Article VIII, Section 5, of its Articles of Agreement, which states that "The Fund may require members to furnish it with such information as it deems necessary for its operations, . . . , as the minimum necessary for the effective discharge of the Fund's duties."[139] Thus, to fulfill its mandate, the Fund could, in its surveillance activities, monitor the "rules governing capital flows and the capital operations in the balance of payments to facilitate the monitoring of an internationally agreed upon set of rules for capital transactions."[140]

The World Bank, too, should be concerned about the effects of money laundering on financial sector reform—an issue area to which the Bank has devoted considerable attention since the early 1990s.[141] Indeed, one Bank brief has acknowledged the need for the Bank to focus on this issue: "Emerging markets are increasingly becoming the venue for large scale money laundering operations. If left unchecked, this activity eventually will undermine the credibility of the formal financial sector. In its financial sector operations the World Bank can promote measures to counter the flow of illicit funds into the financial systems of countries and arrange for external assistance."[142] And yet the Bank's operational directive on the financial sector, while providing guidelines on a variety of regulatory, supervisory, and legal issues, both at a general level and in detail, does not address the issue.[143]

But the Bank's interest in combating money laundering should not be driven only by its concern about adverse effects on such specific endeavors as financial sector reform. Money laundering is also an important source of the continued and widespread corruption in both the public and the private sector around the world.[144] The Bank has for some time now focused on issues of good governance, but corruption has only recently become an integral and important part of that effort.[145] The Bank has made it clear that good governance, including the absence of corruption, is now considered an essential precondition for a country's effectiveness and efficiency in the application of resources and capital, including Bank loans.[146] Accordingly, it has pledged to support countries' efforts to establish good governance, and to engage in an intensive dialogue with them to induce change toward that goal. However, when that "dialogue is not fruitful," the mandate stipulates that "it inevitably affects the Bank's analysis of the country's overall development management and performance and in turn the nature and extent of Bank support for the country."[147] Given this link between Bank support and good governance and the absence of corruption, the Bank should have little trouble supporting the FATF, by integrating where applicable the Forty Recommendations in its own financial sector assistance program. This must also include a clear statement by the Bank that it can no longer hesitate to deny access to its resources to countries that fail to adopt global anti–money laundering standards and continue to free-ride on the global financial system. To demonstrate their resolve, ensure consistency, and avoid duplication, the Bank and the Fund should join forces in this effort and develop a joint approach. The Policy Framework Paper (PFP) would provide a useful coordinating mechanism.[148] However, it will also require further efforts to strengthen the principle of cross-conditionality.[149]

Since the FATF's inception, the relationship between it and the IFIs has grown closer. Bank and Fund representatives attended the early plenary sessions of the FATF on an ad hoc, observer basis and participated in some working group meetings.[150] Later these meetings also included discussions on technical assistance and mutual cooperation in the area of financial reform.[151] Thereafter the FATF reinforced its links with the IFIs and, as already mentioned, initiated a study with the Fund.[152] The latest and probably most important step came in 1997 when the president of the FATF sent letters to the president of the World Bank and the managing director of the IMF requesting their assistance in the fight against money laundering, thus acknowledging the need for external support.[153]

As the third pillar of a global public policy framework, the leverage of the World Bank and the IMF will be vital in ensuring compliance and, if necessary, in using their leverage to enforce it. Organized crime, money laundering, and widespread public and private sector corruption have the capacity to destabilize governments, undermine democratic reforms, and reverse economic progress. Failure to control these activities will not only lead to the misallocation of already scarce resources for development aid, but further undermine public support for aid as well. Whether and how both institutions embrace this call for help will depend to a considerable degree on the attitude of their most powerful members. By initiating the FATF in 1989, these governments recognized then the corrosive power of global crime on their societies and economies. Unless they move ahead now and step up the fight, they will be forced into forms of defensive intervention, which will prove much more costly.

CHAPTER 6

From Denial to Disclosure: Dual-Use Trade in a Globalizing Industry

THE PURPOSE of this case study is twofold. Its first purpose is to demonstrate that the public policy challenges of globalization reach beyond economic issues—legal or criminal. In some cases the loss of internal sovereignty due to globalization has begun to impinge directly on matters of national security. Thus, although the state's task of preserving territorial integrity may be least affected by globalization, it can no longer be considered exempt. An example is the growing inability of governments, individually or collectively, to manage and control the flow and application of dual-use goods and technologies, here referred to as dual-use items.[1] Dual-use items are defined broadly as those that can be used for productive purposes in the civilian economy as well as in the development or enhancement of offensive military capabilities.

The second purpose of the chapter is to develop an alternative framework for the operation and management of controls over dual-use items that can respond to this new environment. In doing so, the chapter draws extensively on the two previous case studies, but with one important conceptual difference. Unlike financial services and money laundering, dual-use trade is one of the few areas of the international economy where *competitive cooperation,* not *cooperative competition* (see chapter 2), has been the guiding principle for policy, shaping the interaction of states in the world political economy under conditions of interdependence. The Soviet challenge to the territorial integrity of the Western alliance

explains why the principles of competition and liberalization, and in particular free trade, played only a limited role in the policy decisions of the
Coordinating Committee for Multilateral Strategic Export Controls
(COCOM), the international institution that coordinated the denial of
dual-use items to the Warsaw Pact countries. Here the public interest in
security far outweighed the private interest in free trade. However, this
did not protect policymakers in this area from the dynamics of globalization and the challenges it presents to each country's internal sovereignty. Rather, globalization, accelerated by the end of the bipolar conflict, is forcing a modification in the preference mix between cooperation
and competition, coupled with adjustments in the organizational and
operational requirements for dual-use controls that are necessary for
those controls to remain effective.

A New Environment

The volume and geographic pattern of transfers of international arms and
dual-use items, their subsidization and even encouragement by national
governments, and the resulting proliferation were largely a reflection and an
instrument of the global political competition between the two superpowers
and their military and economic alliances. The end of the cold war does not
mean that the supply and demand for these goods will subside; it does,
however, imply that the relatively predictable and controllable environment
of the cold war period no longer exists.[2] As a result, policymakers are
dealing with a much more unstable international environment, dominated
largely by regional conflicts and internal violence, as well as by economic
and technological factors. Clearly, managing the risk emanating from the
spread of dual-use items has become much more complex.

One example is the economic pressure on the arms industry brought on
by excess capacity in global arms production, which is in turn the result
of declining military budgets. With this increased pressure, arms proliferation, in addition to being one of the principal sources of traditional security concerns, has now also become a consequence of political considerations such as unemployment, as the industry struggles to adjust to cuts at
home and the search for new markets abroad.[3] In this buyer's market, successful consolidation and downsizing of the military-industrial base
remains one of the more important elements in containing proliferation.

These changes have also begun to redefine the traditional relationship between the defense and high-technology industries and their sponsoring governments. The defense industry is progressively being transformed from an instrument of foreign policy, enjoying generous subsidies and protection, to a national liability, with the potential to cause political harm for elected officials. In the area of dual-use items, policymakers have tried with some success to moderate the implications of this development through strategies designed to increase the integration of the civilian and military sectors, and thus compensate the losses on the military side with a large and rapidly growing market for dual-use goods and technologies in the civilian economy.[4] In the United States one of the better known programs in this area is the Technology Reinvestment Project (TRP) administered by the Defense Advanced Research Projects Agency (DARPA) in cooperation with three military departments and five other federal agencies.[5] Although the direct funding of dual-use research and development (R&D) through programs such as the TRP has been criticized, and alternative strategies have been suggested, the overall goal has remained: greater integration of the civilian and military sectors.[6] Similar programs are under way in other industrialized countries.[7] Successful civilian-military integration is expected to reduce the pressure on weapons companies to find new markets and thus have a direct impact on certain aspects of dual-use proliferation.

In addition to the changing external environment, the nature of warfare and the evolution of the arms industry over the last three decades, from one that produces weapons to one that produces weapon systems, give a much greater and in some cases even a central role to functional aspects such as observation and communication and the processing of information.[8] Nowhere was this more vividly demonstrated than in the Gulf War.[9] In essence a shift from attrition-based to information-based warfare has led to a reversal of the traditional direction of technology transfer. That flow is today increasingly from the civilian to the military domain rather than vice versa, as was the case for many years. Among other things, this change has been reflected in the acquisitions patterns of military establishments. For example, the U.S. Department of Defense estimated in late 1994 that defense spending on specialized, defense-specific technologies would drop to 30 percent of the total over the coming years, with the remaining 70 percent coming from the dual-use sector.[10] According to one estimate, the Pentagon, which in the 1960s accounted for most of the U.S. market for sophisticated electronics, now makes up less than 1 percent of that market.[11]

Thus, on the supply side the debate over the risks of proliferation will no longer be restricted to matters of foreign or traditional security policy. Rather, it will penetrate deeply into the domestic political economy of each nation, affecting such issues as employment, investment, productivity, industrial policy, and corporate restructuring, and ultimately, success or failure in a globalizing industry. As a result, security and economic policy goals may well find themselves at odds.

A similar dynamic can be observed on the demand side of the proliferation equation. The end of the cold war has opened the door to addressing other aspects of international security in a more consistent, systematic, and comprehensive manner. An array of "new" security threats have mostly, for political reasons, been kept off the agenda of the international political economy or were structured by the bipolar conflict. These threats include the persistent underdevelopment and poverty of large parts of the world, the population explosion and the associated intensification of global inequity, the pollution of the global environment, the destruction of the planet's biodiversity, and the spread of epidemics, to name but a few. Their successful management will in most cases depend in part on the availability of and access to dual-use technologies such as earth-resource satellites, global positioning systems, supercomputers, new materials, and sophisticated electronic systems. Moreover, the magnitude of these problems and the urgent need to integrate much of the developing world into the global economy are likely to require, and thus permit, an unprecedented amount of technology transfer. This is one basic precondition to generating sufficient private sector investment, the only available avenue for the developing world's integration into the global economy.[12] Undoubtedly the containment of dual-use proliferation through a policy of technology denial, in light of the much-needed technology transfers necessary to respond to the "new" security threats, would be counterproductive to all countries, developed and developing alike. As on the supply side, traditional foreign policy goals come into conflict with other goals, public and private, whose strategic importance has increased considerably with the end of the cold war.

It is important to understand, however, that these more immediate changes in the external environment of dual-use trade have merely accelerated a trend toward the diffusion of dual-use goods and technologies that was already well under way.[13] The role of globalization in this process is central for two reasons. First, as discussed in chapter 1, cost pressures, increased market risk, shorter product life cycles, and intense competition have forced industry to resort to global alliance strategies such as joint R&D, licensed production agreements, subcontracting, and joint marketing. These alliances are often concentrated in those industrial sectors where the dual-use phenomenon is particularly important. Aerospace and defense, biotechnology, information technology, new materials, and semiconductors are the most obvious examples (see, for example, figure 1-2 in chapter 1).[14]

Second, cross-foreign direct investment (FDI) in dual-use industries is widespread across Europe, the United States, Japan, and, more recently, a number of emerging markets, making it increasingly difficult to attach a particular nationality to dual-use technology firms that share their knowledge freely among their subsidiaries.[15] Although the share of the total remains relatively small, there has been a steady increase in countries' R&D expenditures financed by foreign sources.[16] In addition, modern techniques for outsourcing to host countries, as well as global corporate strategies, rely increasingly on fully integrated communication networks, such as intranets (not the Internet). The success of these networks will in large part depend on the degree to which all components of a global company, wherever located, have access to the same information and possess the same technological capabilities as corporate headquarters. As a result, in the dual-use sector, and to a considerable degree also in the defense industrial sectors of the established industrial countries, the globalization of industry has led to the "internationalization of availability," radically transforming the external constraints under which antiproliferation policy and export controls operate.[17]

This trend has already had an impact on public policy. Thus the Committee on Foreign Direct Investment in the United States (CFIUS), established in 1988 to review defense-related FDI by foreign interests, has only once since its inception opposed a proposed investment.[18] The trend has also led to a sharp increase in what is known as "foreign availability," and in numerous instances U.S. procedures for assessing foreign availability have proved incapable of keeping up with the actual spread of technology.[19] Today many previously restricted technologies have been decontrolled. Following a number of positive foreign availability judgments, the general relaxation of former COCOM controls, and action by the Department of Commerce in 1993 and 1994 to lift controls on certain types of computing and telecommunications equipment, the number of goods requiring an individual validated export license has plummeted. Between 1989 and 1995, applications for such licenses fell by over 85 percent, from 71,000 to 10,000. During the same period the value of all goods exported under a validated license dropped from $116 billion to $8 billion.[20] Yet another sign of the diffusion of dual-use technology is that public policy itself is relying on open sources. DARPA's Information Systems Office recently solicited proposals for research projects under its Integrated Proliferation Prevention and Open Source Monitoring program. This research should focus on the creation and maintenance of open source data collection and dissemination, as well as research and analysis. This work is expected to lead to an integrated approach that will facilitate the development of proliferation-stemming norms in critical countries and provide U.S. policymakers with critical open source data and analysis.[21]

It is now evident that, at its root, the challenge of containing the proliferation of dual-use items is strongly reminiscent of the problems conceptualized in chapters 2 and 3. The globalization of the dual-use industry, accelerated by the end of the cold war, has called into question yet another longstanding policy equilibrium sustained by a basically fixed preference ordering of governments. In this case, however, the ordering of states' preferences was tilted strongly in favor of the public interest, that is, the national security of each country and the security of the Western alliance. The international regime through which this public good was provided was COCOM.

COCOM denied countries access to dual-use technologies by prohibiting exports to proscribed, mostly Warsaw Pact, destinations. Internal sovereignty, in this case a government's ability to enforce export control regulations, was operationalized by relying on the government's exclusive monopoly of legal authority within a given territory. The conflict between private interests (the spread of civilian applications) and the public interest (restrictions on the use of military applications) inherent in the "duality" of these items was thus never really resolved. Given the disproportionate weight attributed to the public interest, private interests were hardly reflected in the policy outcome. There were occasional differences among COCOM members regarding the relative weights to be attributed to the public and private interests.[22] However, there was widespread consensus that liberal economic internationalism, otherwise dominant under conditions of interdependence, did not apply to trade in dual-use technology except where driven by strategic security concerns. With the end of the cold war that consensus broke down, and considerable differences arose among COCOM members on the timing and substance of opening up the possibility of technology transfers to the former Soviet bloc and other countries.[23]

This strategy, and more specifically the preference ordering it was based upon, have come under considerable pressure with the end of the cold war and the globalization of industrial activity. First, in the absence of an imminent and credible threat from the Soviet Union, and with heightened economic pressures at home and from abroad, policymakers have found it increasingly difficult to justify the disproportionate emphasis on the public security interest. Private commercial interests have gained in relative terms and need to be taken into account when developing a control regime. Moreover, other public interests, under the general heading of new security threats, have also gained in importance in the foreign policy strategy of governments. Second, and maybe more important, even if governments were to maintain the same preference ordering despite pressures from the private sector and competing foreign policy goals, policymakers can no longer provide security by relying on a strategy of technology denial. Thus, even if policymakers were to insist that the *mere* absence of a nuclear, chemical, or biological threat from the Soviet Union no longer makes such a threat less likely, since now other states and nonstate actors may use such weapons, it must be recognized that globalization has made a public policy that relies on outright denial ineffectual if not redundant.

Export controls, the principal tool by which trade in technology has been denied, are becoming increasingly futile in a world that, in this domain as in international finance, no longer sees territoriality as the principal mechanism by which to structure corporate strategies and activities. As far as the transfer of intangible capital such as sensitive knowledge is concerned, the notion of a "borderless world" is no longer fiction but instead has become a reality with the Internet—and in particular with the development of intranets, private cross-border information systems that elude public control, making defensive intervention close to impossible. Controlling physical transfers of goods and technologies through defensive intervention also seems increasingly futile under conditions of globalization. In theory, border controls could regulate the flow of all dual-use items. However, as mentioned above, given the ever-increasing integration of the civilian and defense economies, such a strategy would cripple the external trade of an economy. In addition, the sheer volume of trade that can be classified as dual-use has reached proportions that would make any such effort prohibitively expensive.

Finally, any country that did impose such controls on its external trade would promptly experience a sharp decline, if not a halt, in both FDI and offers of strategic collaboration from other companies, as foreign companies would quickly exclude that market from their global strategy. In short, in light of the increasing importance of private commercial and competing public interests, as well as the globalization of industry, defensive intervention, the principal policy instrument throughout the cold war, has to be dismissed as a viable public policy for the regulation of dual-use items in the future.

Nor will offensive intervention achieve the desired results. There is little doubt that unilaterally relaxing export controls would satisfy the commercial interests of the dual-use industries, and it would give policymakers the much-needed latitude to address the aforementioned "new" security threats. But offensive intervention would quickly deteriorate into competitive deregulation of countries' export control systems. Ultimately, dual-use trade would be subject to no controls at all. In this scenario, traditional security interests would no longer carry any weight. The preference ordering of states would be completely reversed, giving absolute priority to private interests and exposing countries to a wide variety of threats from rogue states and an increasing number of nonstate actors. Although no government has proposed or advocated such a policy approach, it cannot be denied that the drive toward competitive deregulation, often initiated by national industries, has begun to shape the policies of many supplier governments.[24] Thus policymakers have tacitly supported the decontrol of exports, especially in those industrial sectors where a country has comparative advantage over its principal competitors. Competitors in other countries of course oppose such a removal of controls, because export controls artificially lower the threshold of competition. Such a dynamic has been in place for a number of years in the United States and Germany, which have targeted sophisticated computers and high-precision machine tools, respectively, for deregulation.

The Wassenaar Arrangement

It is not quite clear how the successor regime to COCOM, as currently structured, will be able to withstand these pressures of competitive deregulation. During the last few years the members of COCOM, with the participation of most of the former Eastern bloc countries, including Russia, have been engaged in the development of this successor regime. Originally called the New Forum, this group was able to agree only in early 1996, after repeated delays reflecting many fundamental differences, to set up a new control mechanism. This mechanism was called the Wassenaar Arrangement, after the Dutch town where it was negotiated.[25] The agreement has been widely hailed as a major policy success and an effective successor to COCOM, providing an "international framework to respond to the critical security threats of the post Cold War world. . . ."[26] However, a closer look at its current structure and rules leads to the conclusion that, if anything, it reflects the inability of national governments to come to an effective agreement without the pressure of a Soviet threat. Moreover, there is a considerable risk that the new regime will deteriorate into what might be best described as crawling deregulation, undermining prior multilateral control efforts and exposing its members to the threats to which dual-use proliferation gives rise.

The control effort under the Wassenaar Arrangement, which is based on a coordinated application of members' national export control policies, is based on two main pillars: a dual-use pillar and a conventional arms pillar. With respect to the dual-use pillar, members have agreed on a list of controlled products, which is divided into two tiers: tier 1, the basic list, and tier 2, the sensitive list. The latter includes advanced machine tools and semiconductor manufacturing equipment, among other items. Within tier 2 is a subset of very sensitive items, including stealth technology and cryptographic equipment.[27] Although the lists are incorporated into each country's national export control system, the decision to approve or deny transfer of any listed item remains at the discretion of each country.[28] However, members have agreed to exchange aggregate information biannually on all denials of export licenses for tier 1 items to nonmembers. Members have also agreed that denials of licenses *should* be notified individually to other members within sixty days (and preferably within thirty days) of the date of denial. In addition, aggregate information on licenses to export any tier 2 items to nonmember countries *should* be exchanged twice a year. For these sensitive items, members *should* notify, preferably within thirty days but not later than sixty days, all other members of an approval of a license that has been denied by another member for an *essentially identical transaction* during the previous three years. In addition, extreme vigilance should be exercised in any decisions to export very sensitive goods.

Development of the second pillar, which covers conventional arms, was highly controversial. It came about not least because major dual-use exporters refused to subscribe to the first pillar unless major conventional arms exporters agreed to control their exports as well. Given the focus of this study, this is not the place to discuss this second pillar in great detail. Suffice it to say that the result has been described as a minimalist approach. Countries have agreed to exchange information confidentially every six months on deliveries of weapons covered by the UN Arms Register, including details of the model and type of weapon. According to one observer, this is "scarcely a major step forward: many countries already provide data on models and types to the UN Register (where it is publicly available) already going beyond this confidential intergovernmental exchange of information."[29]

How resilient the arrangement will be depends in large part on the willingness of member countries to avoid so-called undercutting, that is, exporting a listed item after a license denial for that item has been announced by another member. A number of weak points make it unlikely that undercutting will be avoided. Six of these are briefly mentioned here. First, although the notification rule may have some sort of shaming effect, the language of the agreement states merely that members "should" notify each other, and the phrase "essentially identical" transaction leaves room for various interpretations. Both these features introduce a considerable amount of instability into the agreement. Members will never know for sure exactly what goods others are exporting and whether undercutting has taken place. Given the considerable amount of undercutting that took place during the final years of COCOM, the outlook is not good: after all, the majority of countries chose not to establish a "no undercutting" rule.

A second basic flaw of the agreement is the assumption that since all its signatories share the same broad security concerns, the agreement will lead all members to behave in the same way. This supposition is easily disproved by the fact that although the signatories were able to agree informally on their position toward four rogue states (Iran, Iraq, Libya, and North Korea), they were unable to agree on a more general list of proscribed destinations to be maintained by each country with respect to its own national export control policy. An analysis of the "sensitive destination lists" of four of the founding members of Wassenaar shows that, out of a combined number of seventy-three countries listed by Germany, Japan, the United Kingdom, and the United States, only twenty-eight countries appear on all four lists.[30] These variations could easily lead to undercutting, even though the countries have agreed on the list of sensitive goods. For example, suppose country A denies a license for export to destination X because it is on its proscribed destination list. Soon thereafter, country B issues a license for the same item to the same destination. Although country B recognizes that the item is on the sensitive list, the decision to issue the license is in part determined by the fact that the destination is not proscribed. Differences in perceptions about recipient countries may further diverge because of variations in information regarding the end use of a dual-use item. This is an issue that the Wassenaar Arrangement does not address, thus increasing the chances of national policy divergence and of undercutting even further.

Third, as currently configured, the lists do not sufficiently take into account the increased piecemealing, on the supply and the demand side, that has occurred with globalization. Thus the entire control effort could be easily undercut by disassembling a dual-use good or technology to a such degree that it slips through the control web established by the Wassenaar lists, and reassembling it on arrival in the destination country. Importing countries are not the only ones that might use this strategy. Global corporations with subsidiaries in a number of Wassenaar member countries, as well as elsewhere, could do so as well. Thus, if an export license for a particular dual-use item is denied by a Wassenaar member, and other members refuse to undercut, a company could still circumvent the control effort by shipping parts that are not proscribed from a variety of different locations inside or outside the Wassenaar geography, for reassembly by the importer. In this scenario no undercutting has taken place, nor has the company violated any Wassenaar rules. But the importing country ends up in possession of a dual-use item whose transfer had been denied by all members.

Fourth, many important suppliers of dual-use items are not participants in the Wassenaar Arrangement; among the most important are some of the Asian countries.[31] In other words, the political geography of dual-use controls does not match the economic geography of dual-use production and trade, which as described earlier has changed dramatically in recent years. This opens the possibility for outsiders to undercut insiders. Over time, pressure within the Wassenaar membership will increase to lower the threshold by introducing a foreign availability and export clause for all member countries. This would defeat the original purpose or lead countries to abandon the effort entirely.

Fifth, another avenue for undercutting stems from the fact that the conventional arms pillar of the agreement is restricted to the seven categories of the UN arms register.[32] This is all the more surprising since the Wassenaar munitions list is much broader. However, countries agreed only to use the UN register as a frame of reference for the notification process. As a result, a broad array of civilian items that would fall under the notification rules of the dual-use pillar can escape those procedures if they are so modified to be classified as types of military equipment that fall through the control net of the UN register. Examples include night vision equipment, radar, and other information and observation technologies. This is all the more ironic because, as already mentioned, this technology has become central in determining battlefield superiority and is often used to upgrade existing military hardware. Whether the actual military hardware has been registered with the United Nations is of lesser or even no relevance, since its nature and potential impact have been substantially altered.

Finally, since unlike COCOM the Wassenaar Arrangement relies on national regulations to control the flow of dual-use items, and these regulations differ in quite important ways across countries and are subject to continuous adjustment and change, the resulting uneven playing field will lead to considerable pressure from industry, raising the chances for competitive deregulation and thus undercutting. This is reinforced by the fact that the regime does not contain any formal provision for prior notification of planned sales—a point pushed hard for by the U.S. government.[33]

It is not clear how, under these circumstances, the Wassenaar Arrangement as currently structured can escape all of the pressures on it, not least in light of the competitive disadvantages that multiple regulatory standards create and the subsequent regulatory arbitrage in which corporations will surely engage through their global networks. Moreover, forces outside the dynamics of the dual-use industry over which the Wassenaar Arrangement has no influence may well lead to breakdown of the agreement. For example, speaking at the closing ceremony of the 1995 Paris Air Show, French Prime Minister Alain Juppé noted that the fall in the value of the dollar was "the equivalent of additional aid of 20% for American products."[34] In a buyer's market such indirect subsidies do not bode well for regime compliance. These and other external influences that alter the competitive advantage of different national defense and dual-use industries are likely to erode a regime that uses denial as its principal tool.

To sum up, the globalization of industry spurred by the end of the cold war has transformed the external policy environment of dual-use trade in a fundamental way. Not only are traditional security concerns being replaced by competing interests in both private (free trade) and public ("new" security) policy domains, but even those traditional security concerns which remain can no longer be adequately and efficiently met by relying on a strategy of denying technology transfers. Defensive intervention through export controls can no longer guarantee the maintenance of either internal sovereignty or ultimately of external sovereignty, nor is such intervention politically feasible. Offensive intervention would satisfy the competing interests of free trade and sustainable development but fails to assign any public value to the vital security interests of a country, thus putting its external sovereignty at risk.

The inability of both defensive and offensive intervention to respond to these challenges calls for a public policy approach that no longer relies on territoriality as the principal instrument for maintaining internal sovereignty. Operational sovereignty should be cut loose from its now-defunct point of intervention, the national border. This would permit policymakers to design the political geography of dual-use controls in a much more flexible manner, taking advantage of alternative sources of information and responding to the changing economic geography within which public policy has to operate. Instead of meeting traditional security interests through the denial of technology, the strategy would be to ensure that dual-use items are used only for civilian purposes. Such a policy would respond not only to the inability of borders to act as instruments of control, but also to those public and private interests that benefit from technology transfer and open trade. Figuratively speaking, national borders were formerly the point where supply and demand for dual-use items intersected. However, since denial was the principal instrument, control of the demand side was not relevant. With borders no longer in a position to act as a point of intervention, internal sovereignty must be operationalized elsewhere. As will be shown, such an approach focuses on both the supply and the demand side, by moving both further up- and downstream in the production and distribution of dual-use items. As in the previous case studies, horizontal subsidiarity is a core component of this new approach. Thus much will also depend on the ability of policymakers to design a set of rules that ensure a high degree of transparency and disclosure, creating a strong incentive for industry and participating governments to act in a way that supports the overall purpose.

In its current form the Wassenaar Arrangement does not meet these requirements. In many aspects the outcome of the negotiations reflects—albeit in disguised form—a preference for offensive intervention. This is not how the effort was initiated: the original structure contained important elements relating to transparency and disclosure, indicating that at least some if not all countries recognized the basic dilemma that globalization poses. Thus the control regime outlined below should not necessarily be understood as replacing the Wassenaar Arrangement, but rather as an effort at improving the control regime. Such an approach is all the more promising since all signatories to the agreement have recognized that this is an evolutionary process and that more work needs to be done to strengthen the regime.

In evaluating the proposal made below, it is important to note that no regulatory regime, however effective, can ensure that dual-use items will only be used in civilian applications. This has two implications. First, the merits of the proposal should be compared to alternative forms of controls either currently in place, such as the Wassenaar Arrangement, or other regimes. Second, governments, individually or collectively, will always retain the right to apply the ultimate form of regulation to protect themselves.[35] In other words, they retain the right to apply military force against states that deliberately and consistently seek to circumvent the agreed structure and rules.

Toward Disclosure-Based Regulation

The principal challenge for policy is to develop a structure that allows relatively uninhibited trade of dual-use items, while at the same time ensuring that these items are used only in civilian applications. Such a policy would combine the goal of providing a public good—security—with the need to be more responsive to private sector demands for an open international economy and to demands for technology transfer, reflecting the shifting weight of private and public preferences.

To be successful, policymakers must be able to reduce the risk of failure in the market for dual-use items by ensuring a degree of transparency and disclosure that will allow sufficient monitoring of the activities of private sector actors. In addition, and ultimately probably more important, a high degree of transparency will reduce the incentive to engage in illegal activities, thus reducing the need for elaborate and often expensive control efforts in the first place. It is helpful here to distinguish between direct and indirect controls. The former apply to the manufacturer and distributor of a dual-use item, the latter to other market actors who are involved in some capacity in the production, distribution, or financing of such items, and thus have access to the privileged and timely information that lies at the heart of disclosure-based regulation.[36]

Direct Controls

Risk management with respect to dual-use technologies has to be implemented at an early stage in the manufacturing process. Indeed, a priori one should not even exclude the R&D stage of a product or technology, where changes in design, material content, and other specifications could convert a dual-use into a single-use item, thus making regulation of the product superfluous or at least facilitating future control efforts, such as tagging and tracking.[37] For other stages of the product cycle such as production, distribution, marketing, and even servicing, risk management will have to make use of horizontal subsidiarity to overcome the information asymmetries already present between the regulators and the regulated. These asymmetries have grown considerably. The utility of national borders, which heretofore were the primary instrument of territorial control but also acted as the central source of information upon which the control effort was based, has declined dramatically.

Thus policymakers need to ensure a consistently high degree of transparency and disclosure of activities by companies as they relate to potential or actual sales and subsequent trade (whether intra- or extrafirm) in dual-use items. Such information would permit the gathering of data to be used in deciding whether to permit, delay, or, if necessary, deny the transfer of a dual-use item. The data gathered must provide for effective monitoring of the source, quantity, foreign destination, intermediaries, end user, and purpose of dual-use items. At a practical and technical level, such flows of information would be generated by establishing permanent electronic links between dual-use producers and distributors and the authorities charged with licensing and controlling these exports. Such links would amount to an interactive, real-time online system that allows both sides to exchange and register relevant information. Clearly such a system resembles the basic idea of the financial intelligence units described in chapter 5. However, unlike in the case of money laundering, the underlying activity to be controlled is legal. Hence there is no immediate need to rely solely on secondary sources of information. Indeed, it is of great importance that the interaction between public and private actors be as close to real-time as possible, so that proliferation can be stopped while minimizing the disturbance to international trade flows.

In 1989 the German government introduced an electronic data gathering system called Kontrolle bei der Ausfuhr (KOBRA), which provides an early model of such an electronic data infrastructure.[38] KOBRA centralizes in a single database all documents filed with German customs and with the licensing office, called the Bundesausfuhramt (BAFA). This allows the authorities to quickly compare, check, disseminate, and exchange important information regarding suspicious behavior and practices on both the supply and the demand side. The principal source of information is individual export declarations and license applications, which are scanned into the database or entered manually. Thus KOBRA can, for example, signal whether or not a stated end user for a given product is known to be involved in weapons development. It can quickly compare export documents against a checklist of known suspicious corporate intermediaries and end users, as well as against a list of those countries that may be seeking to further their weapons development programs.[39] However, the utility of KOBRA was limited because it did not provide a direct electronic link between the exporter and customs authorities. As a result, the earliest point at which the details of an export shipment are digitized, and can thus be compared against the database, is when a customs officer manually keys in data from documentation submitted by the exporter. By this time, of course, the shipment has usually left the country, and the information can only be used for future preventive efforts.[40]

Customs authorities in a number of other countries have also started to phase in more sophisticated large-scale electronic systems with the aim of achieving paperless exporting and importing. Three of the most advanced export automation systems implemented to date are Australia's Export Integration (EXIT) program, the United Kingdom's Customs Handling of Import and Export Freight (CHIEF) system, and the Automated Export System (AES) in the United States.[41] All three systems are fairly similar and contain a number of common features.[42] The utility of these systems for controlling proliferation is derived from their ability to interface with data from the country's national licensing agencies and check information supplied to customs against that supplied to the licensing agency. In the case of AES, for example, when an exporter enters his or her license information, the system automatically checks the validity of the license against current license data supplied by the Department of Commerce's Bureau of Economic Analysis and the State Department. If AES detects a problem, it will put a hold on the shipment before it is exported from the United States. Nevertheless, even with this real-time, online capability, systems such as AES still do not fully bridge the information asymmetry between exporter and regulator, and they rely to a considerable degree on the exporter's own informed compliance. For instance, AES does not automatically check whether a certain type of good, or delivery to a particular country, requires licensing. Also, although a denied parties list will eventually be built into the system, this is designed only as a convenient lookup tool for the exporter and not as a filter through which shipment details would automatically be screened.

German customs is also making the move toward paperless trade and recently unveiled plans for its own comprehensive electronic system for tracking exports and imports. Scheduled for completion in 1998, ATLAS (Automated Customs Tariff and Local Processing Application System) will bring German customs processing into line with automated systems already in place in other countries.[43] Finally, at the European level there has been an effort to coordinate the separate information technology initiatives of member states' customs authorities. The basis for this is the European Union's proposed Customs 2000 project, which encourages computerization of the various customs services in a framework coordinated at the European level, so as to ensure interconnection and compatibility between national systems.[44] An initial step in this direction has already been taken with the establishment of a joint customs information system that will use a central database to increase cooperation and the exchange of data between member states' customs authorities.[45]

These brief descriptions of a number of national systems, as well as the regional scenario for the European Union, indicate that from a technical perspective several important supplier countries are well on their way to establishing fully operational, online registries for the purpose of monitoring all exports (and imports). By taking advantage of technologies such as modern database tools, electronic data interchange (EDI), and even the Internet, these systems are for the first time able to provide near-real-time electronic access to the details of a country's international trade. Among other things this will allow the authorities, in principle, to evaluate the data for proliferation potential. In addition, despite some initial concerns about data safety and protection, the private sector has

become less resistant to such schemes; these concerns arose from the
potential for leakage of valuable information to unauthorized users,
including competitors. Authorities have established a variety of safety
measures that will make it difficult for unauthorized parties to get access
to the available information. In practice, however, a number of bureaucratic and other organizational obstacles remain, raising at least some
doubt as to the effectiveness of these systems, both nationally and within
an increasingly globalized industry.

First, in most countries the bureaucracy administering export controls
is fragmented; often it is set up in a way that promotes interagency competition rather than cooperation. In the United States, for instance, cooperation between the Customs Service and the licensing personnel at the
Departments of Commerce and State remains fragmentary.[46] Even within
the licensing community, which includes the Departments of Defense and
Energy in consultative roles, duplicative and incompatible computer
systems result in a squandering of useful intelligence information.[47] There
have been plenty of proposals to streamline and consolidate the current
regulatory structure by establishing an independent agency, but so far this
has not happened.[48] These and other problems created by bureaucratic
politics, agency maneuvering, and the familiar turf fights among admin-
istrators are also prevalent in other countries. Without considerable
improvement in this public domain, policy will continue to lose its effectiveness in the face of globalization and rapid technological evolution.

Second, although the public authorities will soon be in a better position to manage the huge amount of data and evaluate it in a timely
fashion, all systems, including those described above, as currently structured do not and cannot resolve whether the quality of the data provided
and the criteria by which the data are evaluated, as well as the risk profiles that are developed with the available information, accurately reflect
the inherent risks. As a result, important information asymmetries will
persist. Moreover, as in the case of the globalization of the financial services industry, the technology driving change in these industries has led
and will continue to lead to rapid change in both the nature and the
source of the risk, as well as in its geographic pattern. This leads to additional information asymmetries, which cannot be managed through technical means alone.

By way of comparison, just as the Basle Agreement was a valiant and
politically successful effort to deal with the changing nature of the financial services industry, so the Wassenaar Arrangement reflects the ability

of policymakers to adjust, albeit not without some delay, to the end of the cold war by including some of the most important supplier countries in the agreement. Also like the Basle Agreement, however, the Wassenaar Arrangement does not respond to the underlying forces of globalization, and in particular to the degree to which this process has undermined the operational sovereignty of national governments. A strategy based on territorial enlargement alone, although necessary, is not sufficient. As in the case of the Basle Agreement, by the time the Wassenaar agreement was struck, it was incapable of responding to the nature of the risk it was supposed to address. Unless the Wassenaar Arrangement is altered to respond directly to the globalization of dual-use industry, it will not succeed in reestablishing the operational sovereignty of national governments. Upgrading the Wassenaar Arrangement with an interactive, cross-national electronic registry would go some way toward improving the management of existing information. But it cannot improve the quality of the information itself.

The only way for policymakers to maintain a limited and therefore, from a public policy perspective, manageable level of information asymmetry is to make greater use of public-private partnerships. As in the two previous cases, this can be achieved by enlisting the active participation of those nonstate actors that have better access to timely and privileged information regarding both the flow and the potential use of dual-use items. This will allow policymakers to set workable and enforceable standards for controlling dual-use flows, as well as to keep the parameters that develop those standards up to date, as technological innovation continues to change the definition of pertinent dual-use items.

Drawing on the experience of other mixed regulatory organizations such as the National Association of Securities Dealers (NASD), and large-scale data-gathering networks such as the Financial Crimes Enforcement Network and other financial intelligence units, policymakers charged with the control of dual-use trade flows should consider establishing a similar institution that requires the registration of all companies involved in the production or transfer of sensitive dual-use goods and technology. Although it would have to be more refined and sophisticated, such a system could build on the experience gained with existing or planned systems such as AES, EXIT, CHIEF, and ATLAS, or a combination thereof. The principal function of such an institution would be to establish an automated technology transfer registry (ATTR).[49] The ATTR would take advantage of the sophisticated and powerful technology available to monitor technology transfers both within a single country and in international trade. In addition to registering and electronically tracking the flow of dual-use items, a specially designed computer program would trigger a warning if a planned transfer does not comply with the parameters set by the program.[50]

It is beyond the scope of this book to develop such criteria in detail. However, at a minimum these parameters should set forth the following: that transfers may only take place among companies registered with the ATTR; that transfers may only take place if all the required information, including destination, recipient, and end use, is furnished; that transfers must be checked against a proscribed product and destination list that includes both countries and end users and is regularly updated; and that transfers must be checked for possible piecemealing by the same supplier or across several suppliers, in a manner that allows tracking of piecemealing over long periods. If the ATTR sends a warning that one of these conditions has been violated, the transfer should be interrupted and not allowed to proceed unless cleared by the authorities.

In developing such an electronic safety net, the ATTR can make use of systems using artificial intelligence. Such systems have grown in sophistication and are no longer being applied just to financial markets but to an expanding array of businesses, such as credit card and insurance companies and health care providers, seeking protection from illegal activity.[51] The relevance of artificial intelligence for the dual-use trade becomes immediately obvious when one considers some of its recognized advantages: a capacity to learn and adapt, great flexibility, and the ability to discover patterns in a very short time. These are all attributes that lie at the core of any successful dual-use control effort that does not rely on denial.[52] Interestingly enough, such a system could be used not only to detect illegal activity, but also to disprove allegations of wrongdoing—a risk to which such systems are exposed, as companies may not refrain from making false allegations against their competitors. No doubt there are limits to the degree to which these systems could simply be transferred to the detection of dual-use violations. Thus the rules according to which such a system would operate would differ from those in the financial services or health care industries. As a first step, therefore, regulators, the private sector, nongovernmental organizations, and experts in hybrid intelligence should come together and consider the development of such a system.

In addition to monitoring the activities of its members, the ATTR could also be responsible for a number of other activities that are important to adequate risk management and can be tailored to the needs of particular dual-use industries. The registry could be responsible for updating and explaining new technology transfer regulations to companies. It could also act as an information exchange and alert suppliers to new techniques used by front companies and countries to circumvent regulations, while disseminating intelligence information that is shared by the authorities over its computer network.

Many small and medium-size companies are likely to resist such a scheme, since compliance with such a broad-based and technically sophisticated control effort is likely to have high fixed costs. To reduce that burden, small and medium-size companies could outsource to the ATTR the implementation and execution of their internal control efforts, which would be subject to a regular export control audit. Given the economies of scale involved, these services are likely to result in lower costs for each business and at the same time generate additional revenue (from the training and information services provided) for the ATTR itself to support its monitoring operations, thus reducing the fiscal burden of the entire control effort.

In designing the structure of the registry, officials should heed the experience gained in the context of the NASD. The control and enforcement division of the ATTR should be a separate and independent entity in the overall organization, and the public interest should be adequately represented in its deliberations. In addition, the experience of the NASD should remind policymakers that they cannot abandon their own responsibility to maintain a supervisory and enforcement umbrella over the mixed regulatory organization. This umbrella must give them continuous and open access to all information available, and it must create incentives, through the threat of spot checks, secret taping, and other measures, to ensure compliance and, if necessary, enforce it through the civil and criminal justice system.

This also assumes that the dual-use industry itself is prepared to adhere to the ATTR's statutes. As the NASD, having gone through the various disciplinary actions described in chapter 3, somewhat remorsefully acknowledged in its 1996 annual report, "Self-regulation works because the industry recognizes it is a *privilege* not a right."[53] This comment is a reminder that de jure internal sovereignty remains firmly in the hands of public policymakers. But it also shows that if private firms are to keep that privilege, they should contribute to the overall regulatory effort by enhancing their own internal control mechanisms so that they can fulfill the responsibilities assigned to them. Following from the previous cases, policymakers should require, in return for implementing the ATTR, that companies implement their own internal policy guidelines.

The idea of a know-your-customer (KYC) policy for dual-use trade seems a sensible one and could be developed in parallel with the ATTR. As one export control official from a large multinational corporation noted in a conversation with the author, "By far the best and most effective export controls are a company's sales and marketing agents."[54] Companies' marketing and sales divisions usually have very good information about their customers' activities. Long-established client relationships lead to insider information about the purpose of an order. Large corporations have foreign offices that are in close contact with their customers. Familiar with the historical pattern of the customer's purchases, they can judge whether an order is in any way suspicious, because of the amount requested or its timing. Yet another additional source of disclosure is companies' support personnel, such as technicians who install and service dual-use machinery and equipment on a regular basis, including the replacement of parts. These points of access provide additional information and hence an opportunity for a supplier to check on how dual-use items are actually being used.[55]

To formalize KYC policies, companies should be required to appoint a senior manager, a board member, or an executive as the company's "proliferation risk officer." That person would be responsible for the company's compliance with all national and international regulations regarding dual-use trade. In cases of proven violations, the officer could be held accountable. The risk officer would be charged with developing the company's own internal control system. The ATTR would not accept any requests for licensing unless the application contained the signature of the designated export official.[56]

One large multinational dual-use manufacturer has gone a step further. Over the last few years the Siemens corporation, the cost of whose current global control efforts has been estimated at about DM40 million (about $22 million) annually, has begun to establish an elaborate internal electronic data collection and control infrastructure. This system in many ways resembles similar efforts by financial institutions to track money laundering activity. Among other things, the system checks all potentially damaging exports against German, EU, and U.S. export control regulations. Not only is this system more sophisticated than existing national control structures; it also represents the first integrated nonterritorial control network (albeit limited to a single company) that is operated from a single center. Thus Siemens can avoid all the potential problems associated with agreements such as the Wassenaar Arrangement, which presume that national export control authorities will be able to negotiate comprehensive exchange-of-information agreements. The company plans to implement the system in overseas operations and develop an additional tool to control the end user destination. Interestingly enough, the company not only hopes to further strengthen its export control security system, but estimates that the system could save the company several million dollars, accelerate the entire internal control effort, allow human resources to be concentrated on difficult cases, and be marketed to other companies in the future.

These examples of internal risk management efforts are by no means exhaustive, and such efforts are likely to vary across industries. The intention here is to show that, in principle, there are many possible ways of improving the internal risk management structure of companies producing and trading dual-use items. One acknowledged obstacle to the establishment of these procedures is that companies often lack adequate information from their national intelligence agencies about possible illegal activities by their customers—a reverse information asymmetry. Public authorities should, in conjunction with the intelligence community, provide companies with information that will help them make better judgments about the legitimacy of their operations. To facilitate such intelligence sharing, officials at the ATTR could be briefed routinely, perhaps on a bimonthly basis, and then pass on the information obtained to companies that would find it useful in their own control efforts.[57] Such an early warning system not only would assist authorities in their effort to control multiple sourcing on the demand side, but would also help them suspend suspect business deals at an early stage, saving them the time and expense of having to cancel contracts later.

Indirect Controls

To reduce the information asymmetry further, but also to increase the incentives for dual-use producers and traders to adhere to the norms of the ATTR, policymakers should rely on other market participants to provide information, thus creating a multisource data network that also draws on independent data. It should come as no surprise that financial institutions will be central to this effort. Recall from chapter 5 that when the Financial Action Task Force updated its original Forty Recommendations, it also broadened their scope to include non-drug-related criminal activities, including illicit trade in arms and dual-use items. The incidents involving the Bank of Credit and Commerce International (BCCI) and the Atlanta branch of the Banca Nazionale del Lavoro revealed that money laundering is essential in facilitating this type of illegal trade.[58] The ATTR would no doubt greatly benefit from being able to request information on potential money laundering activities.

Financial institutions themselves need to expand their KYC policies to include the proliferation threat as well, by tracking certain types of data that have proved valuable in detecting illegal dual-use trade. These include, for example, financial transfers from a proscribed destination, especially when the funds go to companies or other end users that have a history of violating export control laws. Such monitoring, in turn, requires a variety of internal adjustments to a bank's project finance and foreign trade and exchange departments. Given that most of these payments are made electronically, the tagging of country, company, and even product codes need not be a very costly or elaborate procedure.

Similarly, when preparing a loan or underwriting a stock or bond issue, a financial institution has access to detailed information about its intended purpose. The bank could establish specific guidelines for providing credit or underwriting bonds or equity for projects, either in a particular country or of a specific nature. Evaluation of this information could reveal a project's proliferation potential at a very early stage. To ensure that they receive adequate information, financial institutions could in turn request that the borrowers themselves prepare a report on the proliferation potential of the project. Bank employees in the relevant divisions can be sensitized to the problem through training seminars and be kept informed of new developments in regular meetings with ATTR staff. Since many of these national and international payments are made through foreign branches or foreign correspondent banks, cooperation with them is also important to success. As intermediaries, banks are in a unique position to inform authorities about incoming and outgoing payments for possible illegal activities; their involvement may prevent the transaction from being concluded.[59] To further support banks' efforts, the regulatory authorities should, as in the case of direct controls, work with intelligence services to provide financial institutions with all the information that may help them to detect money laundering.

Financial institutions could also support nonproliferation by pursuing a socially responsible investment strategy. The screening of investment portfolios to ensure that funds are not invested to produce weapons goes as far back as the 1960s.[60] By the mid-1990s $639 billion, or almost 10 percent of all assets under management in the United States, were in some type of responsibly invested portfolio.[61] In addition, in such areas as environmental protection and labor standards, there is a growing emphasis on the use of market instruments to create incentives for the private sector to adhere to international norms and standards.

With respect to dual-use trade, greater emphasis on consumer choice comes in the form of investor responsibility. This is yet another form of a public-private partnership through which society at large can support its own interest and thus broaden the principles of disclosure-based regulation by becoming involved in policy implementation. During the last decade, investors have become increasingly interested in ascertaining the uses to which their funds will be applied and the activities of firms in which they invest.[62] The Securities Act of 1933 and the Securities Exchange Act of 1934 provide the legal basis for such an interest.[63] The Securities and Exchange Commission (SEC) itself has stated that any information for which there is a "substantial likelihood that a reasonable investor would attach importance in determining whether to buy or sell the securities registered" must be made available.[64] This principle has been confirmed by the U.S. Supreme Court.[65] Investors should require disclosure both about companies' involvement in dual-use production and trade, and about their history of compliance with nonproliferation and export control regulations. In support of such efforts, investors can make use of organizations such as the Investor Responsibility Research Center (IRRC), the Council on Economic Priorities, the Ethics Institute, and the Social Investment Forum, all of which have long and quite successful records in promoting greater public and corporate engagement in public policy.[66] Moreover, investment banks and brokerage houses have set up special funds for customers that prefer not to invest in any production or sales of arms at all.[67] Finally, institutional investors could implement a policy of withdrawing investments, domestic and international, from companies found guilty of violating the supply-side controls.

The mixed regulatory regime outlined here is a response to the increasing inability of governments to monitor and control a globalizing dual-use industry. If implemented properly and enforced vigorously, these direct and indirect controls would go far to reduce the growing information asymmetry confronting policymakers. The transparency that the controls create would permit the principle of disclosure to realize its full potential, ensuring that the private sector has the necessary incentives to adhere to the norms upon which the regime is based, while making failure to comply easy to detect and enforce, provided the resolve to detect and enforce is there. Unfortunately there is a risk that the proposed ATTR is being understood for what it is *not*—a mere supplementary data registry to an existing regime. Such a misunderstanding may occur because the policy implications of a greater reliance on horizontal subsidiarity and the replacement of the principle of regulation by denial with regulation through disclosure are not being given sufficient attention. Thus the proposal to establish an ATTR has recently been criticized in a report by the RAND Corporation because "the system begs the question of what the defining criteria should be for a regime designed to effectively control or proscribe transfers of destabilizing . . . dual-use technologies. In other words, the proposed registry would be a means of assisting implementation of a control regime, rather than constituting a regime."[68] This assertion is correct if one continues to assume that the basic control mechanism remains denial. It is incorrect, however, if the basic mechanism is disclosure. This error points to some basic misunderstandings that demand clarification.

Dual-use technologies are not "destabilizing" in themselves—their military application is. A regime based on denial has to *assume* that dual-use technologies are destabilizing because it has no means of verifying how they are used. Although this was a reasonable policy maxim during the era of bipolar conflict, the end of the cold war and in particular the advent of globalization have made a denial-based regime, except with regard to a few highly sensitive technologies, unrealistic and unwise in light of other pressing global issues. Rapid technological evolution, borderless communication, and continued liberalization of international economic transactions make efforts to establish criteria to proscribe transfers a waste of time and resources, creating a false sense of security. As an alternative, disclosure-based regulation coupled with public-private partnerships represents a regime in and of itself, and not just a data support structure, although such a structure is no doubt an important element in overcoming information asymmetry—an issue that regulation by denial does not even attempt to address. Under a disclosure-based regime, dual-use technologies would be "stabilized" by disclosing their application, ensuring adherence to agreed-upon standards. In addition, stability established through disclosure is qualitatively superior to stability established through denial. Disclosure-based regulation not only has a better chance of preventing market failure (that is, proliferation), but also permits other interests—public and private—associated with dual-use trade to be realized, thus responding to their changing weight in framing the debate on this global policy issue.

From National to Global Dual-Use Controls

The previous section argued that a greater reliance on public-private partnerships, coupled with mandated disclosure rules, can compensate for the failure of territorially based public policy efforts. However, the two previous case studies leave little doubt that this approach will only work if the political geography of technology transfer controls can match the economic geography of dual-use production and trade. Apart from being ineffective, unilateral controls, whether direct or indirect, will face strong political opposition for reasons of competitiveness.[69] Unless a country has a monopoly over a particular dual-use item, which is rarely the case today, unilateral controls will lead to regulatory arbitrage on the demand side. This not only disregards private interests by excluding firms from lucrative dual-use markets, but also fails to meet the public interest, as proliferation takes place in any case.[70] Moreover, in the medium term, governments that have imposed controls unilaterally will be pressured to adjust their regulatory standards downward as industry threatens to relocate to a more lenient regulatory environment. This threat would have to be taken seriously in circumstances of high unemployment and increasing competition for investment in high-technology industries. If regulatory standards are adjusted downward, however, it will lead to offensive intervention by others, ultimately undermining the entire control effort.

This takes the discussion right back to the weakness of the Wassenaar Arrangement, namely, that in the final analysis the principal participating countries were unable to commit themselves to a set of effective and, more important, enforceable standards. There is, however, one central difference: in the case of Wassenaar, the burden of coming to an agreement was placed solely on governments. This framed the negotiations in the traditional context of intergovernmental bargaining, subject to a multitude of often conflicting national pressures, bilateral commitments, and international obligations.[71] Under these circumstances, and against the background of the unpleasant experience of the final years of COCOM and the overall macroeconomic environment in most of the Wassenaar countries, the New Forum could not be expected to make any serious breakthrough. In addition, bureaucratic politics and institutional pride in established and supposedly proven national controls created resistance on behalf of each national control bureaucracy, making the operational-ization of internal sovereignty outside the context of one country's polit-ical geography an elusive goal.

Introducing horizontal subsidiarity would mitigate these influences and raise the prospects for greater cooperation among governments. By engaging the private sector to a greater degree in the various stages of policymaking, especially the development of a framework for imple-mentation, policymakers could step back from this process and insulate themselves from conflicting domestic interests. They could instead focus on their primary mandate, the formulation and implementation of inter-nal sovereignty. At the same time, the business community would be confronted with the challenge to develop its own control mechanisms, putting aside or at least deemphasizing competition and giving greater attention to cooperation. Research on the growing number of corporate alliances shows that companies can quite easily combine elements of competition and cooperation in their overall strategies—an important precondition for successful mixed regulation.[72]

There is no doubt that the majority of corporations active in global dual-use production and trade would benefit from, and should support, the establishment of a common public policy framework within which every-body can compete freely but fairly, and that promises considerable cost savings in administering dual-use controls. Finally, greater horizontal subsidiarity will make it more difficult for the corporate community to hide behind the alleged incompetence and narrowmindedness of national bureaucracies and political elites when explaining failure to come to an agreement. In one likely scenario, for example, horizontal subsidiarity will stimulate the formation of cross-national private sector coalitions in favor of an agreement that exposes bureaucratic and institutional rivalries (including those generated by dispersed national export control structures, such as in the United States) that have little to do with the issue at hand but prevent it from being resolved. After all, those immediately affected by a policy have a greater interest in its success than does some remote bureaucracy, which may even go out of business as a result.

In the final analysis, therefore, applying horizontal subsidiarity not only reduces information asymmetries between the public and the private sector but, as argued in chapter 3, is a central structural ingredient that is necessary for global public policy to succeed. It allows a decoupling of the operational from the formal aspects of internal sovereignty, thus permitting a greater congruence between the political and the economic geographies of dual-use technology transfers. Nevertheless, despite all of these advantages, a cross-national ATTR will not come about by itself. Rather, its development should follow a two-track strategy that combines the advantages of a shorter-term regional initiative, as in the case of the FATF, with the longer-term vision of a global technology transfer regime.

A Transatlantic Initiative

For a regional ATTR to succeed, it should be embedded in an economic environment and a political context in which countries have endorsed the notion that, in a growing number of public policy issues, an effort to operationalize internal sovereignty policy must go beyond territorially defined solutions, and in which officials have accepted the fact that public-private partnerships play a major contributing role. Current relations between the United States and the European Union provide such a context. First, as was shown in chapter 1, the United States and Europe represent the world's most deeply integrated economic area, the core of the global economy. Second, the European Union now has a common regime for the control of dual-use items, which would facilitate cooperation with the United States. Third, in November 1996 the European Union and the United States initialed a customs cooperation agreement, one of whose objectives is to establish "mechanisms of exchange of information between customs authorities, with a view to fighting commercial fraud."[73]

Finally, and most important from a political perspective, the United States and the European Union decided, at their biannual summit in Madrid in December 1995, to establish a New Transatlantic Marketplace (NTM).[74] The goal of the NTM is to create a common or at least mutually recognized public policy framework for the transatlantic economy. In developing the agenda for the NTM, policymakers sought the close cooperation and substantive input of the corporate community by launching an initiative that became known as the Transatlantic Business Dialogue (TABD).

The purpose of the TABD was to encourage the private sector to participate in the development of a common public policy framework.[75] The process generated many useful and constructive ideas, which had a considerable influence in shaping the initiatives begun under the new marketplace concept, and which continue to shape the process of deep integration across the Atlantic.[76] The TABD is subdivided into fifteen issue groups, one of which is in charge of export controls. The group has expressed its support for the Wassenaar Arrangement and has made a few other useful suggestions for streamlining transatlantic export controls. It has not, however, generated any practical concepts or policy proposals on how to move beyond the current system.[77] The TABD and, in particular, the export controls issue group would be an ideal forum in which to debate the prospects for a transatlantic ATTR. Backed by their leading domestic companies and industry associations and a number of other important dual-use manufacturers in Europe and the United States, the group should initiate such a dialogue between private and public sector actors.[78]

Since complete harmony cannot be expected within the corporate community, this core group must take a leadership role in developing the structure of such an institution and convince others to participate.[79] One possible refinement would be to start the initiative in an industry that promises success. A small number of participating firms, a limited number of dual-use items in need of control, strong cross-investment, and many strategic transatlantic alliances are all characteristics that define such an industry. To ensure broad public representation and participation, however, other interested parties need to be given access. The experience of the NASD, discussed in chapter 3, is one reason, and policymakers should heed the organizational restructuring of the NASD in the wake of the Rudman Report. But the purpose of including other interests in this debate is not to favor one group over another; rather, the experience from integration in Europe (EU) and North America (NAFTA), and more recently at the multilateral level, has shown that, in the long run, insufficient public participation results in a democratic deficit, which hurts and ultimately undermines the process of deeper economic integration.

A Global Vision

Nevertheless the proposed creation of a regional ATTR is no more than a near-term strategic choice aimed at initiating a longer-term process. Recall from chapter 4 the positive impact that the U.S.-U.K.

alliance on risk-based capital adequacy had in getting the Basle process back on track; today the Bank for International Settlements is in the process of accepting new members, whose participation is vital if the organization is to fulfill its mandate. Similarly, forming a technology cartel of the principal supplier countries should be seen as the first building block of what should evolve into a global technology transfer regime. Such a regime can develop along two dimensions, which are not mutually exclusive but complementary. As part of the regional ATTR, and following the example of Siemens mentioned above, ATTR members that are host countries of dual-use multinationals could require these corporations to adopt internal, corporate-wide (that is, nonterritorial) control practices that internalize, where applicable, the standards of the ATTR. This would broaden the reach of the ATTR beyond its formal geographic definition and contribute to the control effort. Recall, moreover, that the Basle Committee witnessed a market-driven diffusion of its capital adequacy standards as banks from countries outside the G-10 internalized these norms. On this model, the ATTR should invite corporations from nonmember countries to adopt its standards. Successful global public policy in this domain requires that the individual company, not the country where it operates, accept the norms. Governments only took on that function because territoriality was until recently the best institutional form within which to enforce such norms.

Clearly, however, such a strategy can only be considered supplemental. A much more important but also more challenging goal that any global effort must entail is to enlist the support and participation of other countries. After all, one of the real advantages of the ATTR is that it permits the free flow of many dual-use items and thus provides opportunities for large-scale technology transfer to industrializing countries. This is only possible because disclosure-based regulation can achieve a high degree of transparency, allowing policymakers to collect sufficient information to ensure compliance, while at the same time developing behavioral patterns on the part of the private sector that conform to the norms of the regime. For such a policy to become fully operational, disclosure must be universal. The automated data registries and evaluation schemes suggested above will only be as good as their reach is long. Ideally, it should be possible to match data with respect to type, quantity, destination, and stated use on the supply side with the same information on the demand side, as well as with any intermediary involved in the distribution of the dual-use item.

Such a global effort faces numerous hurdles, some of which the previous case study has already addressed. Whenever possible, structural and functional subsidiarity should be used, and the option of multiple regional initiatives should be explored, as a means of overcoming these hurdles. Still, many countries lack the necessary infrastructure to participate in such a regime. A regulatory system structured on the model of the ATTR presumes a bureaucracy with a level of professionalism and expertise that today only a handful of countries around the globe can claim. It also requires a sophisticated and expensive electronic infrastructure, which is unlikely to be a top priority in a country's strategy for sustainable development. Beyond enabling countries to participate in such a regime, it will be necessary to ensure that they have sufficient incentives to participate in it. This can be achieved by a variety of inducements, the purpose of which is to make sure that the costs (political and economic) of free riding are greater than their benefits. Such inducements should be, first and foremost, positive. As one recent analysis of a variety of international agreements suggests, noncompliance is the "deviant rather than the expected behavior," and it is "endemic rather than deliberate."[80] This would call for an approach that deemphasizes the early use of coercion and formal enforcement and instead puts much greater weight on the role of positive inducements, such as financial and technical aid, to ensure disclosure.[81] As already discussed in chapter 5, a strong case can be made that the international financial institutions and the regional development banks could play a significant role in supporting compliance.[82] Like the global financial system, the international trading system is best characterized as a global public good, whose provision requires adherence to a set of norms and standards by those who want to make use of it.

No doubt critics will reject such a linkage, arguing that adding yet another item to the international financial institutions' growing list of tasks contributes to goal congestion.[83] Their agenda is already overcrowded, these critics argue, and cannot absorb another concern. Initially, and in particular from an institutional perspective, this argument sounds convincing. Yet on closer inspection it appears that these critics may be confusing goals with instruments. The goal of the World Bank, for example, has been and continues to be development, and more recently *sustainable* development. Supporting the provision of national and global public goods, however, is not an end in itself but another instrument in achieving the Bank's goal. If anything, the fact that the

Bank is broadening its set of instruments to achieve what many would consider a rather complex task—sustainable development—is a reassuring sign that the institution has adopted a richer notion of social and economic evolution. Concern regarding the institutional implications is proper. But it would be fallacious to compromise the substantive issues regarding sustainable development and the provision of global public goods for the sake of institutional convenience and politics. As the case of money laundering has shown, supporting the provision of global public goods does not require that the international financial institutions themselves get involved in the management of global public policy. It does, however, require that they support its cause.

A number of other criticisms are likely to be put forward against a global technology transfer regime. Three in particular stand out and require further elaboration. First, if an ATTR is to be made operational and in particular enforceable, the data supplied to it by the participants must be verifiable. Second, disclosure-based regulation and intrusive verification procedures involving the private sector raise anxieties about the confidentiality of proprietary information. Third, any regulatory regime that requires the participation of a large number of countries raises concerns about the equitable participation of its members.

Fortunately, there is no need to go very far in the search for ways to address each of these issues. All three have already been addressed in the context of the Chemical Weapons Convention (CWC), which came into force on April 29, 1997, and which as of late fall 1997 had been signed by 168 countries and acceded to by 106.[84] This is not the place to discuss the history and substance of the CWC, but it does serve as a useful model for addressing these three concerns when designing a global regime in the domain of dual-use technology: a Convention on the Transfer of Dual-Use Technologies (CTDT).

VERIFICATION. The CWC contains a number of unprecedented and innovative verification mechanisms. These highly intrusive mechanisms to verify compliance create such a high degree of transparency among those that join that the presumption of intent to harm is very low or nonexistent, which in turn creates confidence in the regime. In addition, however, these mechanisms create the proper policy environment for collective action. Refusal to join indicates a desire to cover up, which presumes the intent to do harm.

The convention has two goals. First, it requires the declaration and destruction of chemical weapons stockpiles and production facilities. Although very important to the CWC, this dimension is of lesser importance for this discussion. Second, the CWC requires verification that states are not attempting to initiate or resume chemical weapons production or storage. Indeed, the verification of nonproduction is at the core of the CWC and faces the same challenges that a dual-use control effort does. Although members retain the right to produce and use toxic chemicals for a variety of civilian (that is, commercial) purposes, they have to ensure that these chemicals are used only for purposes not prohibited under the convention.[85]

To complete its mandate, the CWC has established an elaborate, powerful, and intrusive structure with which to monitor all production and acquisition of a variety of chemicals by its members. This leads to a significant reduction in the information asymmetry and permits policymakers to operationalize internal sovereignty. The instruments of verification include declarations and inspections. Declarations require countries to provide detailed information about chemicals being produced, consumed, imported, or exported.[86] In addition, information has to be provided on the purposes for which these chemicals are being obtained or processed, and on the production facilities where processing takes place.

To ensure that these declarations are correct, the CWC gives regulators the right to inspect the facilities where the activity in question occurs. Inspections are of two kinds: routine and challenge. The purpose of routine inspections is to verify annual declarations and to deter violations. It allows inspectors to search documents, take photographs, and interview personnel in the facility being inspected. Challenge inspections may be conducted when an evaluation of the data generated by the annual declarations and the routine inspections, by intelligence information, or from other potential sources gives rise to suspicion of violation. These inspections can take place anywhere on the territory of a suspected member, including private homes and government facilities. A challenge inspection can only be blocked if three-quarters of the members of the CWC's Executive Council consider it "frivolous, abusive or clearly beyond the scope of this convention."[87] Challenge inspections are not refusable, they can apply to declared and undeclared facilities, and the country must be informed no more than twelve hours before the arrival of the inspection team.[88]

The CWC is not based on denial but instead operates on the principle of disclosure-based regulation, not least because the chemicals for which it requires disclosure are widely available. Two different principles of disclosure have been used: voluntary or regular disclosure (corresponding to the routine inspections) and mandatory or irregular disclosure (corresponding to the challenge inspections). Although the data are collected in somewhat different fashion, and the reporting is not done in real time, the information generated is similar to that which would be generated under a global ATTR. The annual declarations provide a comprehensive picture of global trade in the chemicals listed in the Annex on Chemicals in the Convention. Imports can be matched with exports, and potential piecemealing and other risk profiles can be checked against the data collected. This information is supplemented with data on production, consumption, processing, and so forth. After a few years in operation, time-series analyses can be added. A CTDT would no doubt face greater technical challenges, both in data collection and with respect to evaluation, but as argued earlier, these challenges can be met with the application of innovative techniques such as hybrid intelligence and online registries, which will soon be operational in a number of countries.

The information to be evaluated by the CTDT can be further improved by applying a variety of safeguards, tagging, and end-use verification techniques. The sophistication of these methods continues to grow. As an information resource, tagging is particularly effective, because modern weapons systems often represent aggregations of a variety of dual-use technologies from a variety of locations.[89] Tagging supplements the information submitted in the declarations and enhances the transparency of the regime, thus further encouraging adherence to the norms by both corporations and governments. In general, it is possible to distinguish between preventive verification technologies such as tags and seals, and forensic technologies, which are used to detect illegal use after it occurs. Tags can range from simple devices such as bar codes, which rely on a preprinted pattern or set of instructions, to more complex "smart" electronic tags that are able to detect their own surroundings. For example, microtaggants are microscopic particles consisting of several layers of a highly cross-linked polymer. Each layer has its own color, and the resulting color sequence can be translated into a numeric series according to the color codes used with electrical resistors. Additional magnetic or fluorescent layers can be included to help in detection and retrieval of the taggants.[90] Chemical tags are developed by altering an isotope within a chemical compound. Much as in the case of a microtaggant, the altered isotope will act as a fingerprint, linking the chemical of which it is a part to a manufacturer or point of origin. One company that has pioneered this technique has developed a process for integrating heavy isotopes of hydrogen into chemical compounds. Once the isotope is included in the compound, it can easily be detected by mass spectroscopy or gas chromatography. One proposed application of this technology has been the marking of crude oil and other potential environmental pollutants, which could then be traced to their source.[91]

Passive electronic tags contain microcircuits that allow storage of information such as an identification number, an inventory number, or a set of instructions. The tag is "passive" in that it does not have its own power supply and, in effect, remains asleep until charged or triggered by a reading device, which directs radio or microwave signals at it. Commonly, these radiofrequency (RF) tags have read-only capabilities, and the information on them cannot be updated. RF tags have already been used widely in a variety of tracking, stock taking, and inventory functions.[92] The Lawrence Livermore National Laboratory has developed a high-security RF tag to be used to identify sensitive items such as nuclear warheads, tanks, and chemical and biological munitions.[93] The tags have the advantage of being virtually tamper-proof and impossible to remove without detection. They are also small (the size of a penny) and can operate in a largely unattended mode, without the benefit of permanent, commercial power sources, for a period of ten years. One proposed use for these secure tags has been in the development of a system for monitoring the movements and operational activities of treaty-limited items throughout eastern Europe, the former Soviet Union, and the United States.[94] The backbone of this system would be the U.S. Department of Energy's Transcom Tracking System, currently used to monitor the movement of nuclear materials within the United States. In the treaty verification system, secure tags would be attached to treaty-limited items and interrogated periodically by fixed, ground-based RF transmitters. Information from the tag would be relayed from the RF device by satellite to a monitoring facility in the United States.

A further step in tag technology has been the development of "active" electronic tags that contain their own power source and have read and write capability, so that their instructions can be updated. One advantage of this type of tag is that it can be linked with various forms of sensors. Thus, attaching the tag to a temperature sensor would provide information not only on the location of a tagged item but also on the temperature of its environment. Similarly, a tag equipped with an acceleration sensor could show if an item has been dropped, and one equipped with a photosensor could detect whether a box has been opened.[95] Modified versions of tags can be used as seals, to verify, for example, that an object has not been opened or detached from another object. The seal uses a fiber of plastic or glass to carry pulses of light out of the seal, around a loop, and back to the seal. Any change in the amount of time it takes for a pulse of light to travel through the loop will indicate that the seal has been moved or tampered with. In addition, critical parts of the seal can be enclosed in an airtight chamber at a pressure different from that of the atmosphere. The pressure is monitored to detect attempts to defeat the seal. All of these tagging devices could be used in conjunction with a worldwide application of the Global Positioning System to provide a rather comprehensive picture of the whereabouts, movements, tampering and alteration, and final use of dual-use items.

The usefulness of forensic technologies such as video monitoring is more widely known and has most recently been highlighted by the United Nations Special Commission (UNSCOM) experience in Iraq.[96] In an effort to detect Iraqi misuse of technology, UNSCOM has placed an extensive network of remote video cameras in a number of Iraqi industrial facilities.[97] Video images can be either stored on a tape or transmitted on demand via satellite from the monitored site to the Baghdad monitoring center.[98] Other forensic technologies used to collect data are satellite and aerial reconnaissance, mass spectrometers and gamma ray detectors to detect radioactive matter in dual-use machinery,[99] millimeter wave-detectors and air sampling devices that are placed in or downwind from a chemical production facility to determine which chemicals are being produced, and environmental monitoring technologies that analyze small samples of soil, air, or biota that might provide indications of clandestine activity. Significantly, these samples do not have to be taken within the immediate vicinity of a suspect facility.

Which of these verification devices are to be used, and where and under what circumstances, needs to be determined. It may be decided that some will only be used for particularly sensitive dual-use items, whereas others may be justified only after a country or company has violated the rules. The important point here is that the experience of the CWC shows that countries are willing to submit to a set of rather intrusive verification procedures, and that recent technological developments can contribute significantly to their success. This is not explained by some magical change in countries' interests, leading them to give up their sovereignty. On the contrary, countries have understood that the only way they can maintain their internal and, ultimately, their external sovereignty is to operationalize it through collective action, which requires the degree of disclosure and cooperation that the CWC displays and that a CTDT would have to embrace as well.

CONFIDENTIALITY. The CWC's extensive and intrusive system of verification raises questions not only about the continued centrality of territoriality as an organizing principle of the international system. The annual declarations, the routine inspections, and in particular the challenge inspections also represent an infringement upon proprietary and often confidential information held by the private sector.[100] The implications go beyond short-term competitive concerns, however. Unless individual companies and corporate alliances can be assured of enjoying some monopoly rents, and thus of reaping the benefits from their investment in R&D (which is particularly high in the dual-use domain), they will refrain from investing. Their failure to invest would have long-term structural implications for the economy and society at large.[101] Therefore, in order to gain the support of the private sector that is essential for any disclosure-based regulatory structure, mechanisms must be developed to reassure corporations that the information collected by a CTDT will be treated with utmost confidentiality. Given that any effective verification scheme must be cross-national, the danger of a breach of confidentiality is high, especially for those countries that are the leading innovators in dual-use technologies. The need for confidentiality is not mitigated by a greater reliance on horizontal subsidiarity. On the contrary, some might argue that it is better to entrust the public sector with the collected information. This reinforces the need to create a strong, independent regulatory body within the CTDT, as discussed in chapter 3 in the context of the NASD experience, as even the private sector now has an interest in its integrity and professionalism. Finally, successful protection of proprietary information is also vital to sustain disclosure-based dual-use controls themselves. Only a few well-publicized revelations of breaches of confidentiality would rapidly erode the support of the private sector and the general public. What has to be avoided at all costs is a situation that forces companies to choose between violating the disclosure requirements and failing to protect valuable information.

The CWC has put in place an elaborate structure to protect proprietary information from getting into the wrong hands. This can happen at either of two levels: the systemic or macro level, or the subsystemic or micro level.[102] The former refers to the possibility of government agencies being forced by existing laws to divulge confidential information in their possession. The Freedom of Information Act in the United States comes to mind. The latter refers to the deliberate and illegal divulging by individuals of information derived from the declarations or collected during the inspection and verification process. Given this study's primary focus on the micro level and the operational structure of disclosure-based regulation, the macro dimension is not discussed here. However, there is no doubt that it requires careful attention.[103]

At the micro level, policymakers, realizing the need for cooperation from and, in the final analysis, approval by the private sector, made extensive use of horizontal subsidiarity during the agenda setting and policy formulation phases of the CWC.[104] Public-private partnerships existed domestically, as national industry organizations, such as the Chemical Manufacturers Association in the United States and the Verband der Chemischen Industrie in Germany, advised government negotiators on the issue of confidentiality. But they also existed in a multilateral context and were given a boost by the Government-Industry Conference against Chemical Weapons in 1989, which brought together public officials from sixty countries whose chemical companies represent 95 percent of the world's chemical production capacity.[105]

The CWC's confidentiality provisions are oriented to both actors and processes and are laid out in the Convention's Confidentiality Annex.[106] The majority of the requirements relating to actors fall on the Organization for the Prohibition of Chemical Weapons (OPCW), which houses the CWC's Executive Council and its Technical Secretariat, both of which are part of the disclosure arrangements. The OPCW and, in particular, the Technical Secretariat are subject to myriad requirements related to access, treatment, and storage of information at various levels of confidentiality, according to a classification scheme that is applied uniformly across the membership. The CWC also provides a detailed guide for the employment and conduct of personnel in the Technical Secretariat. Mandated procedures include such obvious ones as individual secrecy for five years after termination of employment, but also more innovative measures. For example, it is the responsibility of the Secretariat to inform a country about the proposed clearance of a person who will have access to that country's declarations; this notification must take place at least thirty days before the clearance goes into effect. Employee performance evaluations must give specific attention to the employee's record in protecting confidential information. The second set of actor-oriented provisions are directed at country members of the CWC. Parties to the convention must follow strict guidelines as to the handling of confidential information, especially as it relates to information provided by other members, and may be asked to provide details as to their handling of such information.

Process-oriented provisions deal with the procedural and behavioral aspects of the routine and challenge inspections. Thus the OPCW must fulfill a variety of pre- and postinspection requirements. These, for example, allow facilities to be inspected to take necessary confidentiality precautions and establish stringent guidelines for the transport and analysis of samples. Similarly, inspectors are required to conduct themselves in the least intrusive manner consistent with the effective and timely execution of their mission. Finally, the convention has established procedures for cases where a breach of confidentiality is suspected. The existing provisions to protect the illegal handling of proprietary information probably will need further improvement and strengthening. For example, there is today no effective remedy for a country or a company that has been the victim of such illegalities.[107] Moreover, given the novelty of this form of agreement, there is a steep learning curve, and further adjustments will be required as the CWC evolves.

Important from the perspective of this study is the fact that the existing confidentiality provisions of the CWC, as well as the various suggestions to improve them, provide a rich and fertile ground for developing similar arrangements for a CTDT. The precise nature of the confidentiality provisions is likely to differ. One reason is that declarations to the ATTR will be made continuously rather than at discrete intervals, and the volume of the information will be much larger. For the most part, however, these are primarily procedural and technical challenges that architects of an ATTR should be able to handle. The most important conclusion that can be drawn from the experience of the CWC with respect to the issue of confidentiality is that, if approached in the right manner, the ATTR and its equally stringent disclosure requirements do not have to fall victim to opposition from what could easily become its most powerful opponent, the private sector.

EQUITY. There is a risk that many developing countries will reject the convention as an attempt by the industrial countries to control their access to technology—in other words, as a technology cartel. To avoid such a stigma, architects of the CTDT must ensure that negotiations to establish the convention are open to all interested parties, including countries, regional and international organizations, private companies and their associations, and nongovernmental organizations. Each type of participant would have a distinct role to be determined, but only states or regional organizations with jurisdictional powers over such issues would have decisionmaking authority. A second and ultimately more important element in ensuring equity is the structure of the CTDT's governing body. This structure must be equitable with respect to both geographical and industry representation, and the body must be accessible to all that have ratified the convention, yet it must also reflect the disproportionate but legitimate interests of those countries that dominate the global dual-use industry and are therefore most significantly affected by the convention.

The Executive Council of the CWC is structured in a way that meets all three requirements while at the same time maintaining its operational and decisionmaking capacity. Each country has one vote on the council. The council's forty-one seats are occupied by countries from five different regions, which together cover the world.[108] Accessibility is assured by the provision that each country that ratifies the convention has the right to serve on the council and will do so on a rotating basis. Countries are elected to the council by their regional peers and serve for two years. To give due regard to the importance of the chemical industry in the council and the countries that bear the greatest implementation burden, a prespecified number of members representing the most significant national chemical industries from each region must as a rule be represented on the council.

For example, of the nine seats assigned to Africa, three will be occupied by the countries with the most significant chemical industries. These three states enjoy quasi-permanent status, as they can only lose their seats if another African country overtakes them in the ranking of the region's chemical industries. However, because the ranking is done within regions, geography still plays an important role. For example, each of the three most significant chemical industries in Africa will surely be smaller than the industry that ranks sixth in the group that includes western Europe and the United States (a group that has five quasi-permanent members and also includes Canada and Australia).[109] The fact that some states have quasi-permanent status also reduces the number of seats open for rotation—in the case of Africa, for example, to six. Together these elements fulfill the requirements of equitable geographic distribution and industrial representation.

The council's decisionmaking is based on majority rule; individual members have no veto power. Matters of substance are decided by a two-thirds majority. Procedural issues are decided by a simple majority.[110]

Clearly, the equitable architecture of the CWC Executive Council reflects the fact that a large number of countries participated in its creation. This is one central reason for the widespread support that the CWC enjoys. Nonsignatories include Libya, Iraq, and North Korea. Their abstention should not come as a surprise. On the contrary, it is proof of one of the virtues of the treaty, namely, that it is effectively isolating and shaming those countries, further eroding what little support is left for them within the international community, a point often missed by critics of the Convention.[111]

International isolation will also help when positive inducements to adhere to the disclosure requirements of a CTDT fail and countries have to consider enforcing the convention. A variety of negative inducements are available, the most important of which is economic sanctions. Many have argued that the success of sanctions in the past has been at best mixed, although more recent evidence suggests a somewhat better record.[112] Moreover, any evaluation of the effect of sanctions suffers from the same problem that other studies of deterrence encounter, namely, "the empirical bias of failures being more obvious than successes."[113]

Still, many problems remain. Countries are often unable to reach a political consensus on whether to impose, and later to maintain, sanctions. Sanctions are difficult to implement effectively, given the large number of countries that must cooperate.[114] Companies can profit from sanctions-busting—by sidestepping an embargo, for example—and violations are difficult to verify. Sanctions also can backfire: instead of improving the target country's behavior, they may make the country more determined to fight back, especially if it succeeds in gaining self-sufficiency and is able to circumvent the effects of the sanctions. In addition, the harshest impact of sanctions often falls not on the governing elite or the military, whose behavior they are intended to change, but on innocent civilians and, in particular, the poor. Moreover, rather than substituting for the use of force, sanctions may precipitate it since embargoes often have to be enforced by military action which could evolve into a conflict "that the sanctions were meant to avoid."[115] Finally, sanctions are also often resisted by economic interests in the sanctioning countries, since they hurt exporters and possibly importers as well.[116]

Two policy implications follow from this analysis. First, a collective decision to impose sanctions alone will not suffice. Rather, throughout the period that they are in effect—which in many cases is open ended— sanctions require constant nurturing to be effective, both as far as the sanctioners and the sanctions are concerned. Regarding the former, much greater attention must be given to enforcement.[117] This requires that all participating countries have the capacity—legal, technical, and adminis- trative—to implement them. The success of enforcement will also depend on the ability of the sanctioning countries collectively to com- pensate those participating countries that are poor and suffer dispropor- tionately from the imposition of sanctions. This requires resources des- ignated specifically for that purpose.

Close cooperation with the private sector and with nongovernmental organizations is also essential. Greater use of personalized sanctions, such as the freezing or even confiscation of assets of the target country's elites, will in many cases be more effective than punishing a collective, when the majority has little influence over policy. Successful enforce- ment also requires an effective umbrella organization that can coordinate the enforcement process. Here it is important to signal to the target country that options are available to negotiate an end to the sanctions. Thus governments that for historical, geographic, economic, or other reasons have close ties to the target country should be designated as mediators, to keep channels of communication open and search for ways to resolve the dispute.

Second—and this is a related point, given the difficulties of imple- mentation and enforcement—sanctions should be applied only when *all* noncoercive possibilities have been exhausted. This puts the burden back on positive inducements. In addition, disclosure rules must be widely accepted, reemphasizing the central role of equity, and they must be well developed, systematically structured, and implementable, essentially establishing an international norm or standard that justifies their enforce- ment. The justification for sanctions is thus derived from the fact that a country's failure to comply with the norms can *only* be interpreted as an open and deliberate rejection of participation in the global public policy effort. Such rejection not only undermines the ability of other govern- ments to operationalize their internal sovereignty, but in turn represents a direct threat to the external sovereignty of all those that do participate and submit themselves to the agreed international regulatory standards. Rejection in such circumstances justifies the harsh measures that successful sanctions represent.

Finally, sanctions only work if the target can be easily identified and remains fixed. Countries meet these criteria, but sanctions work much less well against nonstate actors or groups such as terrorists (unless the terrorists are state-sponsored, but this has become much less common).[118] The increasingly nonterritorial nature of terrorism is amplified by the fact that it relies upon and feeds off of nonterritorial structures. Such networks pertain to technology transfer (as discussed in this chapter), the processing and dissemination of information, financial intermediation, transport, and last but not least, research and development, discussed previously. Terrorists use these networks often without the knowledge of the state from which they operate.[119] This must raise at least some doubt about the effectiveness of sanctions for an increasingly important category of threats that most countries will have to confront. If anything, it places the burden on effective management and control of global networks, which have been the focus of this study.

No doubt the range of negative inducements will vary, depending on the issue to be addressed by global public policy. As far as proliferation is concerned, this must include military action. Market failure in the global dual-use industry not only indicates a diminution of internal sovereignty but has the potential to threaten a country's external sovereignty and, where deemed necessary, should be answered in kind.

To sum up, the purpose here is not to develop a detailed structure and operational guidelines for a technology transfer regime. Many of the technical, legal, and even political issues have been discussed only in rudimentary form. All require a much more detailed and in-depth treatment. Rather, the goal is to demonstrate that, even in the traditional domain of national security, globalization has transformed the public policy environment to such a degree that governments need to reformulate some of the basic assumptions on which public policy is predicated. This does not necessarily imply that traditional means such as military force and other forms of coercion such as sanctions no longer have any utility. Rather they need to be placed in a larger, integrated menu of policy tools and should only be used after noncoercive measures have failed. However, unless policy responds adequately to the new environment in which they have to operate, these noncoercive means will fail, leaving governments little choice but to fall back on coercion. The growing and increasingly indiscriminate use of sanctions attests to that.

Critics of the ideas spelled out here will argue that such an ambitious undertaking will never work. But unless a serious attempt is made, we will never find out. Moreover, as chapter 2 argued, states' interests in the international system are changing under conditions of globalization—toward competitive cooperation. This is an important transformation that needs to be taken into account before rejecting the proposal on those grounds. Critics of the proposal should also be prepared to offer what they think are better alternatives. The management of complex risks can never follow absolute principles but must be based on comparing alternatives and choosing the best from among them.[120]

CHAPTER 7

Conclusion

DURING THE PAST five decades the international system was dominated by the competition of two antithetical political geographies and economic systems. The nature of this competition and the threat that it posed were such that states put an overwhelming emphasis on external sovereignty in defining their security, and the institutional and functional infrastructure that they built to address public policy issues followed from that definition. Territorial government was the logical and preferred choice to operationalize governance, both domestically and internationally. However, the cold war overshadowed other less visible, but no less important, changes in the international system. Its peaceful but sudden ending and the continued and accelerating pace of globalization have raised the management of internal sovereignty, previously relegated to domestic politics, to a transnational policy issue. This has left nation-states in a race to catch up with the changing composition of external and internal challenges that shape today's international relations.

Nevertheless, we continue to see an overemphasis on external sovereignty and its institutions, while the management of internal sovereignty in most instances remains the prisoner of territoriality. If international cooperation is to generate concrete solutions to the challenge of globalization, managing external sovereignty alone will not suffice. International cooperation must be redefined to include the administration of internal sovereignty. This need to exercise internal sovereignty in a nonterritorial setting led us to ask the question posed in the title of this book: *Governing without Government?*

There is general consensus that global government is not only utopian but also undesirable; thus it cannot be the answer. However, two recent contributions to the debate on globalization suggest two possible avenues for the future of governance in the face of globalization. One perspective sees an ever growing role of nonstate actors (corporations and nongovernmental organizations alike) and international organizations leading to a "power shift" in the international system and challenging states' traditional monopoly over matters of governance.[1] This perspective is rejected by the other one. Rather the "real new world order" does not represent "a shift away from the state—up, down, and sideways—to supra-state, sub-state, and, above all, nonstate actors" but envisions a state that is disaggregated into its functional parts (such as the executive, the legislature, courts, and independent agencies).[2] These parts "are networking with their counterparts abroad, creating a dense web of relations that constitutes a new transgovernmental order" in which the state continues to play a dominant and traditional role.[3]

This book suggested yet another perspective; one that combines the two visions outlined above. This study concludes that they actually can be mutually reinforcing. Thus for the foreseeable future governments will remain the core constituent elements of global governance. Governing the global economy *without* governments is not an option. Yet for global governance to succeed, governments will also have to enlist the active cooperation of nonstate actors. As the case study of global financial regulation showed, greater cross-national cooperation among functionally equivalent or comparable state actors plays a vital function in reducing the information asymmetries generated by globalization. Moreover, with globalization continuing to progress, policymakers will have to expand and formalize their cross-national contacts in other policy domains including transnational criminal activities, such as money laundering and global security issues as in the case of dual-use proliferation, and other public policy issues traditionally subject to territorial governance. The formation of transgovernmental networks is a necessary condition for global governance to succeed, but it is not sufficient.

The history of capital adequacy regulation showed that the creation of transgovernmental networks such as the Basle Committee alone will no longer be able to fully cope with an increasingly dynamic and heterogenous global economic environment. Rather it suggests that nonstate actors can and should play an important role not only in the formulation but also the implementation of global public policy. These actors have a direct stake in the outcome of global governance. Equally important is the fact that their range of activity is not bound by a particular territory. In addition, not only will the better information, knowledge and understanding possessed by these actors of increasingly complex, technology-driven, and fast-changing public policy issues generate greater acceptability and legitimacy of global public policy, but public-private partnerships will also produce a more efficient and effective policy process. Moreover, horizontal subsidiarity encourages mutual learning among national public policy systems and openness to change—a vital precondition for global public policy to succeed. Finally, international organizations can and should play a strong and leading role in fostering and facilitating the emergence of global public policy networks, promoting better knowledge to anticipate issues that demand global public policies, and acting as intermediaries between the public and private sectors to ensure that adequate information is available to meet global challenges.

The specific mix between state, nonstate, and multilateral actors will vary depending on the particular policy issue at hand. The structure of public-private partnerships may also change over time in response to policy failures that require corrective action or to political pressure. Indeed one can interpret the recent growth of transgovernmental links among state actors as a public (state) reaction to a real or perceived power shift toward private (nonstate) actors. Governments are collectively reasserting their role in an emerging network of global governance. These public-private dynamics rather than state-to-state interactions will have a growing importance in the global politics to come.

Undoubtedly there will be opposition to public-private partnerships. Nongovernmental organizations will continue to raise questions about the degree of trust given to the private sector in executing public functions. However, they should consider that the loss of internal operational sovereignty has already resulted in a democratic deficit, and they should recognize the new opportunities that public-private partnerships offer. The business community also will resist the intrusiveness of the necessary disclosure rules and shun the required internal adjustments, but business leaders should consider the alternative policy responses discussed in previous chapters that permit states to maintain internal sovereignty.

To preserve their legitimacy, governments will feel they have little choice but to fall back on offensive or defensive intervention or a combination of both. Such strategies should not be dismissed as politically inoperable. Rather, they are attractive because they provide policymakers with the appearance of control while inducing a feeling of security in the population at large. It is no secret that the popularity of these policies has increased considerably since the early 1990s, as political opportunists in many countries have built on the widespread fear and insecurity brought on by the declining effectiveness of internal sovereignty, thus forcing governing elites on the defensive.

The medium- and longer-term consequences of these strategies, however, are rarely taken into consideration. First, neither strategy can effectively respond to globalization; these strategies can only succeed once the achievements of interdependence have been reversed. Second, both forms of interventionism reemphasize territoriality as an ordering principle of international relations, despite decades of efforts to achieve integration and the end of the cold war. But unless policymakers are given a viable alternative, governments may soon be forced to engage in defensive or offensive interventions, or both together, as the continued loss of internal operational sovereignty leads to a further erosion of the belief in the institutions of democratic governance and, ultimately, to the breakdown of the political and social consensus that internal sovereignty is supposed to uphold.

Global public policy will not necessarily erase the danger of a democratic deficit. On the contrary, by decoupling the process and practice of internal sovereignty from its territorial base, global public policy runs the risk of undermining popular sovereignty and thus the democratic character of policymaking even further. Thus it is of central importance to understand that globalization has led to a situation where democratic theory and the concept of pluralism can no longer be operationalized exclusively in the context of a territorially defined polity. Democratic governance must instead find new avenues, institutions, and instruments that reach beyond the current political geography of the nation-state. No doubt it is here that the concept of global public policy will be tested most and will need further work.[4] However, if the prospect of a democratic deficit is taken seriously, particularly by national governments, then applying the principles of subsidiarity broadly and rigorously will avoid top-heavy, centralized decisionmaking and allow individuals to participate in global public policymaking to a greater degree than they do now. This will provide an effective response to the increasing popular resentment toward deeper economic integration.

Keeping up with the Times

The geographic and sectoral reach of globalization remains limited. International relations at the end of the twentieth century is therefore best characterized by a coexistence of interdependence and a globalization that cuts across both countries and industrial sectors. As far as countries are concerned, globalization has come to dominate interstate relationships among established industrial nations where questions of internal sovereignty and its associated security themes have emerged as a decisive force in structuring their relations. The increasing focus on nontariff barriers in transatlantic relations, ranging from financial regulation to health, environmental, and safety standards, is a telling example. Furthermore, territorial conflict among these countries has been rendered all but impossible for now.

The same cannot yet be said about interstate relationships in the industrializing world, where interdependence continues to play an important role.[5] Here external sovereignty, along with territoriality, remains an important determinant in foreign policy and the definition of security. However, we can now see that integrating much of the developing world into the global economy brings not just economic benefits but immediate consequences for security as well. The more progress that can be made with their integration, the less emphasis there will be on external sovereignty, and thus on territoriality, as a source of conflict.[6]

In relations between developed and developing countries, the coexistence of interdependence and globalization is reflected in the changing mandate of international organizations such as the World Trade Organization (WTO), which no longer focuses exclusively on free trade (cooperative competition) but has been pressed by the industrialized countries to pursue this goal with an eye on environmental protection and minimum labor standards (competitive cooperation). The contending demands of interdependence and globalization will have a decisive influence on the future structure and mandate of international organizations and will be a defining characteristic of North-South relations in the years to come, as evidenced in the debate over efforts to cut global greenhouse gas emissions.

The dynamics of interdependence and globalization may also be observed within economic sectors, for example in financial services. Even as the industrialized countries, through the International Monetary Fund (IMF), the WTO, and the Organization for Economic Cooperation and Development (OECD) are encouraging other, mostly developing, nations to deregulate and liberalize their financial markets, they themselves are engaged in an effort to establish a global public policy framework that deals with the consequences of the deregulation and liberalization in their own financial services industries during the last three decades.

Co-managing the challenges created here by interdependence and globalization raises a number of important policy issues. First, whereas certain aspects of the liberalization and deregulation of financial services are dealt with primarily in the WTO, the IMF, and to some degree the OECD, regulatory and supervisory issues are covered by other institutional fora such as the Bank for International Settlements (BIS), the International Organization of Securities Commissions (IOSCO), and the Joint Forum, as well as a variety of regional organizations. Greater coordination and cooperation between the institutions of competition and those of cooperation, which in effect are operating on opposite sides of the same coin, would not only help ease the transition from an interdependent to a global world economy, but also make that transition more efficient. Ideally both functions would be located in one and the same institution, to reduce the turf fights that will undoubtedly arise as institutions compete over the global public policy portfolio. These turf fights have already begun in the financial services area.

Second, it must be asked whether deregulation at the national level and reregulation at the global level should be dealt with sequentially, as they have been in most cases to date. Considering that interdependence and globalization are causally related and can be strategized as an integrated whole, there is no reason why both policy steps cannot be brought closer together or even implemented simultaneously. A united effort would help to avoid bureaucratic overlap and turf fights among international institutions and permit a more integrated approach toward the dual challenge of domestic liberalization and global public policy. Asia's financial crisis in the fall of 1997 is a reminder that many economies will face this challenge in the years to come.

Implications for International Security

The conceptual distinction between interdependence and globalization has deeper implications that reach beyond the organizational and technical aspects of global public policy and place new demands on the management of international security. If the architects of international security and its institutions are to generate concrete solutions for the twenty-first century, managing external sovereignty as the sole paradigm for international relations will no longer suffice. International security requires a two-dimensional definition, embracing its external-collective, or territorial, as well as its internal-individual, or human, dimension. This will not be easy.

The shifting demands on those charged with maintaining international security will transform the domestic politics of security policy. In most cases the challenges emanating from globalization cannot be considered a threat to the collective security of a country, nor do they challenge the territorial integrity of nation-states. The threats are more diffuse and selective, and seldom directed at an entire country. Instead they tend to affect specific groups and, in some cases, a few individuals. These threats emanate not from territorial states but from nonstate actors, using integrated, nonterritorial global networks in such domains as information processing and communications, finance, technology, and transport to realize their ambitions. Such threats will be more difficult to anticipate and measure; still harder will be mustering support for a collective national response. Policy coalitions to counter them will cut across territorial boundaries and form around functional spaces, bringing the very concept of "national" security itself into question.

Introducing internal sovereignty as a transnational security issue will also have wide ranging institutional implications. Maintaining external sovereignty, in the final analysis, depends on the ability of a government to exclude, whereas preserving internal sovereignty ultimately depends on its ability to include. Creating a set of institutional structures and mechanism that can combine the two in a meaningful and constructive way defines the challenge for international relations in the years to come. Most recently, this challenge has manifested itself in the controversy over expansion of the North Atlantic Treaty Organization (NATO). Opponents (east and west) of NATO enlargement focus on external sovereignty, emphasizing the territorial character of the policy and its potential implications. Proponents have gone great lengths to deemphasize territoriality. NATO itself no longer refers to its initiative as an "expansion" but as an "adaptation." Indeed, by focusing on such themes as democracy and civil society, NATO's future mission has in part been redefined as promoting internal sovereignty, or at least preventing its breakdown.

But to ask whether NATO should or should not be enlarged may be to ask the wrong question. Given the organization's historical significance, institutional inertia, bureaucratic resistance, and the lack of concrete alternatives, the political bias is strongly in favor of enlargement, regardless of its repercussions on Russia. Moreover, if NATO is not enlarged, it will not be because a better vision for European and global security has emerged, but rather because in this policy domain, too, defensive intervention has gained the upper hand—an outcome that opponents of NATO expansion would consider to be even worse. The real question is whether the current NATO members are prepared to choose the right mix of external and internal sovereignty, one that reflects the changing composition of European and global security demands and the fact that many of those demands, including internal violence, proliferation, organized crime, terrorism, drug trafficking, and environmental pollution, can no longer be resolved without Russia's participation. The Russia-NATO Permanent Joint Council and a variety of other recent initiatives involving Russia are based on the principle of inclusion. They should be given every opportunity to succeed so that one day they will be considered as the first building blocks of a new European and global security structure.

But the growing need for inclusiveness reaches far beyond NATO. As the data on FDI and corporate alliances in chapter 1 show, large parts of the world economy remain excluded from globalization. Given the rising importance of internal sovereignty in international relations, this suggests a strategic vision that places the international financial institutions, such as the IMF, the World Bank, regional development organizations, and the United Nations, at the center of future arrangements for international security, while putting new programmatic demands on them. The World Bank has already begun to shift its attention toward aspects of internal sovereignty, including good governance, poverty reduction, environmental protection, and, more recently, the prevention of internal violence; it should continue to direct its resources and powers towards that end. The IMF, too, has begun to focus its attention on such matters as the regulation and supervision of the global financial system, money laundering, tax collection, and other aspects of internal sovereignty. In fact, both institutions have gone further. Examining the economic consequences of excessive military spending, they have on occasion questioned the devotion of resources to the preservation of external sovereignty by countries that can no longer finance even such rudimentary elements of internal sovereignty as basic health care and education.

If these programmatic changes are to continue and to succeed, these international organizations must be able to internalize the principles of global public policy. Unless they make greater use of horizontal subsidiarity, they will not be able to respond swiftly and decisively to the challenges that globalization generates. Unless they become more open and transparent, they will not attain the degree of accountability and legitimacy that the management of internal sovereignty requires. It is true that nongovernmental organizations have become a central force in realizing vertical (global versus local) and horizontal (state versus nonstate) subsidiarity, but it is too early to determine the outcome of what must be considered a modest, although important, change in that direction.

The problem with the current debate over the reform of the international financial institutions is that it focuses too much on how much power these institutions should have, and not enough on their accountability. The more accountable they are, the more power they can be allowed, and certainly they will need more power if they are to fulfill their mandate in the global economy. Five decades ago these institutions were given a mandate to promote interdependence. Their future lies with the promotion of globalization and global public policy itself. Unless member governments are willing to grant the necessary revisions of their charters, it will be very difficult for these institutions to pursue this new mandate, providing further support for their critics.

One of the defining characteristics of internal sovereignty is its inclusive character. To date, globalization has not performed too well on that account. Nationally, governments struggle to remain inclusive in the face of growing unemployment and rising poverty even as globalization calls for the radical transformation of their economic structures. At the level of the world economy, "globalization" does not yet accurately describe economic reality: large parts of the world economy remain shut out from the process. They risk being excluded from the growth dynamic that deeper integration brings; such exclusion would further heighten already staggering levels of global inequality. But under conditions of deep integration, exclusion no longer implies isolation. Many global public policy issues simply cannot be resolved without the active participation and cooperation of the developing world. The success of global public policy, and thus the success of globalization itself, will depend on the degree to which it can promote inclusiveness. The magnitude of this task cannot be underestimated: during each of the next three to five decades a billion people will be added to the world population, 95 percent of whom will fall within the lowest 20 percent of the global distribution of income and wealth.[7] This worsening of global inequality will further sharpen the North-South divide.

For globalization to succeed, transfers of capital, both tangible and intangible, to the developing world will continue to be sorely needed. The bulk of these transfers will be channeled through the private sector, and the dramatic change already seen in the composition of financial flows to the industrializing world attests to that. In 1990, 44 percent of all long-term financial flows to developing countries came from private sources, the remainder being public financial flows. By 1996, the share of private financial flows had increased to 86 percent.[8] The bulk of North-South transfers will continue to come from the private sector. But if global public policy is to succeed, the governments of developing countries will have to participate in it. Among other things, this presumes that these countries have the institutional infrastructure and the bureaucratic capacities in place to exercise internal sovereignty which in many instances is not the case.[9] Renewed calls for development assistance may seem vain given the difficulty some have in rationalizing foreign aid after the cold war. However, as this study has shown, resource transfers to promote global financial stability, fight international money launderers, suppress the military application of dual-use technologies, and meet other goals of global public policy are in truth neither "foreign" nor "aid," but rather an investment that generates a return and that return is shared by all.

Toward Global Public Policy

The interventionist strategies discussed in this book cannot be disregarded, since their use is on the rise. They no longer exclude such drastic versions of interventionism that rely either on a country's unilateral projection of internal sovereignty upon others or the attempted reassertion of internal sovereignty through territorial secession. External sovereignty will once again come to dominate relations among states, increasing the risk of territorial conflict.

The alternative scenario, global public policy, requires political leadership and institutional change, both of which are in short supply. It also requires the willingness and close cooperation of private and nongovernmental actors to share responsibility in exercising public policy.

In particular, the degree to which the global corporate community is ready and able to take on some of the public policy functions in conjunction with other nonstate actors will be decisive in determining success. This blurring of the public and private spheres, once clearly demarcated domains whose origin dates back to the end of the feudal era, is an indication of the powerful social force that globalization represents. At its root lies the fact that modern territorial sovereignty as an organizing principal of political and social life is becoming contested.[10] But, as has been argued in this essay, it is the *territoriality* of sovereignty as an instrument of public policy that is becoming contested, not the concept of sovereignty itself. The latter will only face a crisis if public policy cannot replace territoriality with a functional equivalent that is better equipped to meet the challenges of globalization.

Considering the data on globalization, there can be little doubt that the world economy is characterized by a growing number of global corporate networks. The current state of global governance, however, at best resembles a loose set of cross-national policy patchworks conspicuous for its missing links and unnecessary overlaps. Given the evolutionary, often hybrid nature of social and in particular integrative processes, this should not come as a surprise. Nevertheless, for global public policy to become a viable and workable alternative to interventionism, it is time for governments to step in and ensure that these patchworks can evolve into networks of governance that can operationalize internal sovereignty in the global economy. Their first step would be to commission a global governance audit. The purpose of such an audit is to map these patchworks responding to global obligations and responsibilities along different dimensions including the functional, financial, institutional, and structural.

The next step toward a global public policy network is to fill the most important gaps and establish the missing links identified in each policy domain. At least three separate but related initiatives are necessary to achieve that goal. First, national bureaucracies, not just the top leadership, need to establish permanent channels of communication to facilitate the exchange of information on cross-border economic activity. The experience of financial regulation and its recent failures evidenced in the case of Barings and Daiwa Banks have confirmed the urgency of such an initiative, and some progress has been made during the last few years. But this networking needs to go far beyond the domain of global capital markets. In addition to these regularized forms of communication, periodic meetings among policymakers to share experiences, techniques, and lessons learned should prove highly valuable. Both forms of inter-action will create a sense of trust and shared purpose that provide some substance to the concept of "international community," a term that continues to suffer from vacuity. Second, in the multilateral domain greater cooperation—not competition—is required among international institutions. This avoids unnecessary and wasteful dupli-cation of activities. An agreed-upon division of labor on global gover-nance issues can contain the growing number of turf fights that have erupted in recent years. The December 1996 agreement on collaboration and cooperation between the IMF and the WTO is a welcome start. But as the World Bank's experience in the former Yugoslavia has shown, such institutionalized exchange of information and coordination of activ-ities must extend from humanitarian and to security organizations, such as NATO or the Organization for Security and Cooperation in Europe, which are increasingly confronted with other dimensions of eroding internal sovereignty.

Finally, while multigovernmental networks represent a necessary pre-condition for global public policy, they are by no means sufficient. Unless governments and international organizations sufficiently promote and even facilitate the formation of cross-national structures of interest formation, aggregation, and representation and are subsequently pre-pared to engage these structures in the operationalization of internal sov-ereignty, the core feature of global public policy—public-private part-nerships—cannot come to fruition. In policy areas such as environmental protection, humanitarian assistance, and, to some degree, financial regu-lation, support for such structures has grown. But too often this support has come as a hasty reaction to a crisis and was not part of a proactive, well-executed strategy. In addition, it is those cross-national social net-works, representing the foundation of a global civil society and ensuring that internal sovereignty can be operationalized not only in a nonterrito-rial context but also on popular terms, that are vital to the legitimacy and accountability of global public policy.

Back to the Future

Going beyond the immediate policy arena, it is difficult to ignore the fact that international relations, and the international system itself, are at a crucial crossroads. The fusion or blurring of the public and private spheres, which at least since the Industrial Revolution and the end of feudalism have been clearly demarcated and contested spaces, is only one of many signs that contemporary social systems find themselves at a threshold of similar historical magnitude. At the root of this transformation lies the fact that sovereignty is becoming contested, both as a concept and as an instrument for public policy. But here, too, it is important to be specific. First, it is the *territoriality* of sovereignty, and therefore the nation-state, that is being contested, not necessarily sovereignty itself. The latter will face a crisis only if public policy cannot replace territoriality with a functional equivalent that is better equipped to meet the specific challenges of globalization. Second, the challenges faced today by the nation-state are primarily challenges to internal, not external sovereignty. Both distinctions are central to the conceptual framework developed in this book, and both are important elements in a strategy of response. They are also instructive when probing further into the future, including the future of the nation-state itself.

External and internal sovereignty are not unrelated. The primary reason for distinguishing between them today is the success of the nation-state, during the transition from feudalism to capitalism, in establishing itself as the dominant and ultimately sole institutional form exercising internal sovereignty.[11] It was able to do so only by invoking external sovereignty, which guaranteed a monopoly of power over a territory, its resources, and its people. Today, as has been shown, such power can no longer be guaranteed. With globalization, internal sovereignty can no longer be operationalized through a reliance on territoriality. This deprives external sovereignty of its functional value. Where global public policy is fully operational, external sovereignty has lost its meaning. In a growing number of public policy areas, exporting anarchy to the international system, as Thomas Hobbes did, will no longer guarantee safety and stability at home. The nation-state as an *externally* sovereign actor in the international system will become an institution of the past.

But this will only happen if internal sovereignty also finds a new operational context—global public policy. This requires political elites, in part, to dissociate themselves from territory and create a more dynamic and responsive organizational and institutional context. *Anarchy is no* *longer just the outcome of, but also the cause for state interests in the international system.* Whether and for how long the evolving hybrid that results is still called "state" should be of lesser concern. Political geography and its institutions have changed many times over the centuries, relying to varying degrees on the concept of territory and a single central power to administer sovereignty. The nation-state is one relatively recent form of governance, and there is no reason to believe that it has a claim to perpetuity. Similarly, it has been shown that the meaning of sovereignty as a concept in international relations has changed over time, which can affect our understanding of international relations.[12] But while the territorial state as an abstraction may eventually become redundant, the principles and values that govern democracies should not. Steps should be taken now to support and accelerate the notion of global public policy, so that our societies will be better equipped to respond to the demands of globalization.

Notes

INTRODUCTION

1. Zbigniew Brzezinski, *Out of Control: Global Turmoil on the Eve of the Twenty-First Century* (Scribners, 1993), p. x.

2. Charles William Maynes, "Bottom-Up Foreign Policy," *Foreign Policy,* vol. 104 (Fall 1996), pp. 35–53.

3. Richard N. Haass, "The Next Secretary of State," *Washington Post,* November 7, 1996, p. A21.

4. G. John Ikenberry, "The Myth of Post–Cold War Chaos," *Foreign Affairs,* vol. 75, no. 3 (May-June 1996), pp. 79–91.

5. Indeed in some areas it had already unraveled long before the end of the cold war. Thus students of the international *economic* system were somewhat astonished when President George Bush proposed the concept of a "new world order." Not only was there no indication that any of the accompanying policy pronouncements changed the way in which the international *economic* order was organized, but more important, and in contrast to traditional security issues, many would have argued that, at least as far as monetary relations are concerned, the *old* economic order had ended long since, with the collapse of the Bretton Woods system in the early 1970s.

6. On the importance of information and information technology in precipitating the collapse of the Soviet Union see Scott Shane, *Dismantling Utopia: How Information Ended the Soviet Union* (Chicago: Ivan R. Dee, 1994). On the broader implications of the international economy for the Soviet economy see Matthew Evangelista, "Stalin's Revenge: Institutional Barriers to Internationalization in the Soviet Union," in Robert Keohane and Helen V. Milner, eds., *Internationalization and Domestic Politics* (Cambridge University Press, 1996), pp. 159–85.

7. Marshal Nikolai Ogarkov to Leslie Gelb, as reported in Gelb, "Who Won the Cold War?" *New York Times,* August 20, 1992, p. A27. I am grateful to my colleague Clifford Gaddy for alerting me to this quote.

8. Klaus Schwab and Claude Smadja, "Start Taking the Backlash against Globalization Seriously," *International Herald Tribune,* February 1, 1996, p. 8; see also Dani Rodrik, *Has Globalization Gone Too Far?* (Institute for International Economics, 1997); "Sense and Nonsense in the Globalization Debate," *Foreign Policy,* vol. 107 (Summer 1997), pp. 19–36; and Group of Lisbon, *The Limits to Competition* (MIT Press, 1995).

9. See, for example, Jerry Mander and Edward Goldsmith, eds., *The Case against the Global Economy: And a Turn toward the Local* (San Francisco: Sierra Club Books, 1996); Richard J. Barnet and John Cavanagh, *Global Dreams: Imperial Corporations and the New World Order* (Simon & Schuster, 1994); William Greider, *One World, Ready or Not: The Manic Logic of Global Capitalism* (Simon & Schuster, 1997); Barry K. Gillis, ed., "Globalization and the Politics of Resistance," *New Political Economy,* vol. 2, no. 1 (March 1997, special issue).

10. Martin Wolf, "The Dilemma of Inequality," *Financial Times,* July 23, 1996, p. 16; Thomas L. Friedman, "Don't Leave Globalization's Losers Out of Mind," *International Herald Tribune,* July 18, 1996; see also Vincent Cable, "The World's New Fissures: Identities in Crisis," *Demos Paper* 6 (London: Demos, 1994); and Vincent Cable, "The Diminished Nation-State: A Study in the Loss of Economic Power," *Daedalus,* vol. 124, no. 2 (Spring 1995), pp. 23–53.

11. The term *chaos-theorists* is from Yahya Sadowski, *The Myth of Global Chaos* (Brookings, forthcoming 1998). Some of the more prominent exponents of chaos theory are Graham E. Fuller, *The Democracy Trap: The Perils of the Post–Cold War World* (Dutton, 1991); Robert D. Kaplan, "The Coming Anarchy," *Atlantic Monthly,* (February 1994), pp. 44–76; Benjamin R. Barber, *Jihad vs. McWorld: How the Planet Is Both Falling Apart and Coming Together—And What This Means for Democracy* (New York Times Books, 1995); Samuel P. Huntington, *The Clash of Civilizations and the Remaking of World Order* (Simon & Schuster, 1996).

12. For an overview of these trends see United Nations Development Programme, *Human Development Report 1996* (Oxford University Press, 1996), p. 11. See also Khozem Merchant, "World 'Heads for Grotesque Inequalities,'" *Financial Times,* July 16, 1996, p. 4.

13. On the global information village see, for example, Claude Moisy, "Myths of the Global Information Village," *Foreign Policy,* vol. 107 (Summer 1997), pp. 78–87.

14. Merchant, "World 'Heads for Grotesque Inequalities.'" Data are from UNDP, *Human Development Report 1996,* pp. 11, 13. Some question a comparison of wealth and income, but, as noted in the *Human Development Report 1996,* p. 13, "a contrast of wealth alone, if it were possible, would be even starker."

15. *Webster's Third New International Dictionary of the English Language, Unabridged,* s.v. "public policy." (Springfield, Mass.: 1961), p. 1836.

16. For detailed definitions of these categories see Theodore Lowi, "American Business, Public Policy, Case-Studies, and Political Theory," *World Politics,* vol. 16,

no. 4 (1964), pp. 677–715. These are by no means artificial divisions. According to Lowi, "these categories are not mere contrivances for purposes of simplification . . . These areas of policy or government activity constitute real arenas of power. Each arena tends to develop its own characteristic political structure, political process, elites, and group relations," pp. 689–90.

17. See, for example, Dani Rodrik, *Has Globalization Gone Too Far?* (Washington: Institute for International Economics, 1997).

18. Except where noted to the contrary, statistics in this study referring to the OECD do not include its newest members: the Czech Republic, Hungary, the Republic of Korea, Mexico, and Poland.

19. OECD, Industry Committee, *Symposium on the Globalization of Industry: Government and Corporate Issues* (Paris, 1994), p. 2.

20. A search of the ABI Inform Database, which covers 800 professional publications, academic journals, and trade magazines on economic and business affairs, produced no book or article title from 1971 with the words *global* or *globalization*; a similar search for 1995 found almost 1,200 entries.

21. In an otherwise very helpful volume on the issue of globalization, Holm and Sørensen, for example, define globalization as "the intensification of economic, political, social and cultural relations across borders." Hans-Henrik Holm and Georg Sørensen, "Introduction: What Has Changed?" in Holm and Sørensen, eds., *Whose World Order: Uneven Globalization and the End of the Cold War* (Boulder, Colo.: Westview Press, 1995), p. 1. See also Anthony G. McGrew and others, *Global Politics: Globalization and the Nation-State* (Cambridge: Polity Press, 1992). McGrew states that globalization "implies an intensification in the levels of interaction, interconnectedness or interdependence between states and societies which constitute the world community," p. 23. Curiously, however, he also states that "globalization does not mean that the world is not becoming more economically interdependent," p. 23. Riccardo Petrella uses that same definition in his otherwise useful discussion of the topic. See Riccardo Petrella, "Globalization and Internationalization: The Dynamics of the Emerging World Order," in Robert Boyer and Daniel Drache, *States against Markets: The Limits of Globalization* (New York: Routledge, 1996), pp. 64–66. See also David Held, "Democracy, the Nation-State and the Global System," *Economy and Society,* vol. 20, no. 2 (May 1991), p. 144.

22. Max Weber, *Economy and Society: An Outline of Interpretive Sociology*, edited by Günther Roth and Claus Wittich (University of California Press, 1978).

23. This by no means should imply that private sector actors are necessarily and always engaged in a deliberate effort to undermine internal sovereignty by adjusting the geography of corporate networks. Rather, each corporate geography follows a set of fundamentally different organizational logics. Political systems, at least in their contemporary form as nation-states, are boundary-maintaining systems. Indeed, their legitimation, both internal and external, is derived from their ability to maintain boundaries. Markets, on the other hand, although initially dependent for their creation upon political power and economic networks, are not defined by, or at least do not depend on, the presence of boundaries. See Friedrich Kratochwil, "Of Systems, Boundaries, and Territoriality: An Inquiry into the Formation of the State System," *World Politics,* vol. 39, no. 1 (October 1986), pp. 27–52.

CHAPTER 1

1. For a broader discussion of globalization see, for example, Roland Robertson, "Mapping the Global Condition: Globalization as the Central Concept," *Theory, Culture & Society,* vol. 7 (1990), pp. 15–30; Anthony D. King, *Culture, Globalization, and the World System* (Binghamton, N.Y.: Department of Art and Art History, State University of New York at Binghamton, 1991); Anthony Giddens, *The Consequences of Modernity* (Stanford University Press, 1990) and *Modernity and Self-Identity: Self and Society in the Late Modern Age* (Stanford University Press, 1991); Anthony D. Smith, "Toward a Global Culture," *Theory, Culture & Society,* vol. 7 (1990), pp. 171–91; Jan Aart Scholte, "From Power Politics to Social Change: An Alternative Focus for International Studies," *Review of International Studies,* vol. 19 (1993), at http://www.cup.org/journals/jnlscat/ris/ris.html.

2. A search of the ABI Inform Database, which covers 800 professional publications, academic journals, and trade magazines on economic and business affairs, produced no title with the words *global* or *globalization* for 1971; by 1995 the number had risen to almost 1,200.

3. For an overview of this issue see R. J. Barry Jones, *Globalisation and Interdependence in the International Political Economy: Rhetoric and Reality* (London: Printer Publishers, 1995). According to Jones (p. 3), "the idea of globalization has assumed much of the role played by the concept of interdependence in the study of the international political economy in the late 1980's and early 1990's."

4. For a good overview see Winfried Ruigrok and Rob van Tulder, *The Logic of International Restructuring* (New York: Routledge, 1995), especially chapter 6; "Globalization and Production," see also Berkeley Roundtable on the International Economy (BRIE), *Globalization and Production,* BRIE Working Paper 45 (Berkeley, Calif.: University of California, 1992).

5. Charles Oman, *Globalisation and Regionalisation: The Challenge for Developing Countries* (Paris: Organization for Economic Cooperation and Development, 1994).

6. Organization for Economic Cooperation and Development (OECD), *Globalisation of Industry: Overview and Sector Reports* (Paris, 1996), p. 15; see also Thomas Hatzichronoglou, "Globalisation and Competitiveness: Relevant Indicators," STI Working Paper 5, OECD/GD(96)43 (Paris, 1996).

7. See Oman, *Globalisation and Regionalisation;* see also Kevin Done, "Tomorrow, the World," *Financial Times,* April 22, 1994, p. 17, on Ford Motor Company's new global strategy; on the implications for local or national companies see Peter Martin, "No More Cosy Backyards," *Financial Times,* March 7, 1996, p. 18.

8. Kenichi Ohmae, *The Borderless World: Power and Strategy in the Interlinked Economy* (London: Fontana, 1990); see also Thomas Friedman, "Big Mac II," *New York Times,* December 11, 1996, p. 27.

9. The term *global web* comes from Robert B. Reich, *The Work of Nations: Preparing Ourselves for 21st Century Capitalism* (New York: A.A. Knopf, 1991); see also Manuel Castells, *The Rise of the Network Society* (Cambridge, England: Blackwell, 1996), especially chapter 3, "The Network Enterprise: The Culture, Institutions, and Organizations of the Informational Economy"; United Nations Conference on

Trade and Development (UNCTAD), *World Investment Report 1993: Transnational Corporations and Integrated International Production* (United Nations, 1993); BRIE, *Globalization and Production*.

10. Hatzichronoglou, "Globalisation and Competitiveness," p. 9.

11. Note that a global strategy does not by itself lead to greater centralization. On the contrary, it may well lead to further decentralization of decision making, even though these decisions are made against the background of a global strategy.

12. See Castells, *The Rise of the Network Society*.

13. OECD, *Globalisation of Industrial Activities,* Report to Ministers, OECD/GD(94)60 (Paris, 1994).

14. The concept of globalization used here covers a broad spectrum of industrial activities. Thus global strategies differ across industries and even between firms in the same industry. See OECD, Industry Committee, "Symposium on the Globalisation of Industry: Government and Corporate Issues," DSTI/IND(94)15 (Paris, 1994).

15. Nobuo Tanaka and Graham Vickery, "Introduction: Perspectives on Globalisation," *STI Review,* no. 13 (December 1993), pp. 7–12.

16. Paul R. Krugman, "Growing World Trade: Causes and Consequences," *Brookings Papers on Economic Activity, 1:1995.*

17. See Linda Aguilar, "A Current Look at Foreign Banking in the U.S. and Seventh District," *Economic Perspectives*, vol. 19, no. 1 (Federal Reserve Bank of Chicago, January/February 1995), p. 21, and George N. Yannopoulos, "The Growth of Transnational Banking," in M. Casson, ed., *The Growth of International Production* (London: George Allen and Unwin, 1983), pp. 236–57; see also Diane Page and Neal M. Soss, "Some Evidence on Transnational Banking Structure," *Staff Papers* (Comptroller of the Currency, 1980); and Ralph Bryant, *International Financial Intermediation* (Brookings, 1987).

18. Gregory Millman, *The Vandal's Crown: How Rebel Currency Traders Overthrew the World's Central Banks* (New York: The Free Press, 1995), chapter 4.

19. On variations across industries see OECD, *Globalization of Industrial Activities: Four Case Studies. Auto Parts, Chemicals, Construction and Semi Conductors* (Paris, 1992), and *Globalization of Industry, Overview and Sector Reports* (Paris, 1996). On national variations see I. Nonanka, "Managing Globalization as a Self-Renewing Process: Experiences of Japanese MNCs," in Christopher A. Bartlett, Yves L. Doz, and Gunnar Hedlund, eds., *Managing the Global Firm* (London: Routledge, 1990), pp. 69–94; Wayne Sandholtz and others, *The Highest Stakes: The Economic Foundations of the Next Security System* (Oxford University Press, 1992); UNCTAD, *World Investment Report 1993*; Martin Carnoy, *The New Global Economy in the Information Age* (Penn State University Press, 1993); Peter Evans, *Embedded Autonomy: States and Industrial Transformation* (Princeton University Press, 1995); Louis W. Pauly and Simon Reich, "National Structures and Multinational Corporate Behavior: Enduring Differences in the Age of Globalization," *International Organization,* vol. 51, no. 1 (Winter 1997), pp. 1–30; see also the differing perspectives in Suzanne Berger and Ronald Dore, eds., *National Diversity and Global Capitalism* (Cornell University Press, 1996).

20. See, for example, Jaideep Anand and Andrew Delios, "Competing Globally: How Japanese MNCs Have Matched Goals and Strategies in India and China,"

Columbia Journal of World Business, vol. 31, no. 3 (Fall 1996), pp. 51–62; "The Discreet Charm of the Multicultural Multinational," *The Economist,* July 30, 1994, pp. 57–58.

21. World Trade Organization, Economic Research and Analysis Division and Statistics and Information Systems Division, *International Trade Trends and Statistics* (Geneva, 1995); see also Paul Bairoch, *Economics and World History: Myths and Paradoxes* (University of Chicago Press, 1993), especially table 3.3, p. 40.

22. On reciprocity see Robert Keohane, "Reciprocity in International Relations," *International Organization,* vol. 40 (Winter 1986), pp. 1–27. It is true that tariff barriers also stimulated overseas engagement by multinationals, mostly through greenfield investments. However, these subsidiaries, for the most part, produced for the local market and were fully integrated into the overall global strategic management concept. As such, this is yet another difference between economic interdependence and economic globalization.

23. See Geza Feketekuty, *The New Trade Agenda* (Washington: Group of Thirty, 1992); see also OECD, *New Dimensions of Market Access in a Globalising World Economy* (Paris, 1995); Sylvia Ostry, "New Dimensions of Market Access," Occasional Papers 49 (Washington: Group of Thirty, 1995). The term "behind-the-border issues" was coined by Miles Kahler, *Regional Futures and Transatlantic Relations* (European Communities Studies Association, 1995). For further discussion of the term, see Wolfgang H. Reinicke, *Deepening the Atlantic: Toward a New Transatlantic Marketplace?* (Gütersloh, Germany: Bertelsmann Foundation Publishers, 1996).

24. See, for instance, Marie-France Houde, *International Direct Investment: Policies and Trends in the 1980's* (Paris: OECD, 1992).

25. Hatzichronoglou, "Globalisation and Competitiveness," p. 7.

26. OECD, "Symposium on the Globalisation of Industry."

27. John B. Goodman and Louis W. Pauly, "The Obsolescence of Capital Controls? Economic Management in an Age of Global Markets," *World Politics,* vol. 46 (October 1993), pp. 55–60.

28. For a detailed list of these measures see Morris Goldstein and Michael Mussa, "The Integration of World Capital Markets," IMF Working Paper 93/95 (December 1993), pp. 2–4.

29. Eric Helleiner, *States and the Reemergence of Global Finance: From Bretton Woods to the 1990's* (Cornell University Press, 1994), p. 146.

30. For an overview see OECD, "Technology and Globalisation," in *Technology and the Economy: The Key Relationships* (Paris, 1992), pp. 209–36. For more background see François Chesnais, "Technical Cooperation Agreements between Firms," *STI Review,* vol. 4 (December 1988), pp. 52–119; Luc Soete, "Technology in a Changing World: Policy Synthesis of the OECD Technology and Economy Programme" (Maastricht, Netherlands: MERIT/TEP, 1991); see also Castells, *Rise of the Network Society,* especially chapters 1 and 2.

31. Christopher Lorenz, "End of a Corporate Era," *Financial Times,* March 30, 1995, p. 19.

32. Charles Oman, "The Policy Challenges of Globalisation and Regionalisation," Policy Brief 11 (Paris: OECD, 1996).

33. See also OECD, *Globalisation of Industry: Overview and Sector Reports*, pp. 41–43.

34. Carnegie Bosch Institute, "Managing International Research and Development," Working Paper 94-8 (Pittsburgh, November 1993).

35. See, for example, Robert D. Pearce, *The Internationalization of Research Development by Multinational Enterprises* (New York: St. Martin's Press, 1990); OECD, Working Party No. 9 of the Industry Committee on Industrial Statistics, *The Impact of Foreign Investment on Domestic Economies of OECD Countries*, DSTI/EAS/IND/WP9(93)6 (Paris, June 21, 1993); John Cantwell, *Technological Innovation and Multinational Corporations* (Oxford: Basil Blackwell, 1989). For a somewhat different perspective see Pari Patel and Keith Pavitt, "Large Firms in the Production of the World's Technology: An Important Case of 'Non-Globalization'," *Journal of International Business Studies,* vol. 22, no. 1 (First Quarter 1991), pp. 1–21. These authors argue that not only has the control of R&D remained central, but so has its operation. On some of the limitations of the Patel and Pavitt study see OECD, "Technology and Globalisation," pp. 225–26.

36. Manuel Castells and Peter Hall, *Technopoles of the World: The Makings of the 21st Century Industrial Complexes* (London: Routledge, 1994).

37. Luc Soete, "Technology and the Economy in a Changing World," paper prepared for the OECD International Policy Conference on Technology and the Global Economy, 1991.

38. A. S. Prasada Reddy and Jon Sigurdson, "Emerging Patterns of Globalisation of Corporate R&D and Scope for Innovative Capability Building in Developing Countries" *Science and Public Policy,* vol. 21, no. 5 (October 1994), pp. 283–304.

39. UNCTAD, *World Investment Report 1994: Transnational Corporations, Employment and the Workplace* (United Nations, 1994), pp. 3–35. All dollar figures are stated as current U.S. dollars except where noted otherwise.

40. UNCTAD, *World Investment Report 1997: Transnational Corporations, Market Structure and Competition Policy* (United Nations, 1997), annex, table B.1, pp. 303–07.

41. UNCTAD, *World Investment Report 1997*, p. xv.

42. UNCTAD, *World Investment Report 1995: Transnational Corporations and Competitiveness* (United Nations, 1995), pp. 7–9; see also Baring Securities, *The Financial Silk Road. . . A Fifth Wave of Global Money: Cross Border Equity Flows*, vol. 1 (London, July 1995), p. 17.

43. UNCTAD, *World Investment Report 1997,* p. xv; World Trade Organization, *WTO Focus*, no. 18 (April 1997), p. 2.

44. See OECD, *Impact of Foreign Investment on Domestic Economies of OECD Countries.*

45. Statistics on FDI and M&As rely on different methodologies and are not directly comparable. In addition, FDI includes reinvested earnings and intrafirm loans, which do not count as M&As, whereas figures for M&As include portfolio investments and domestically raised capital, which cannot be counted as FDI.

46. See KPMG, "The Value of Global Cross-Border Mergers and Acquisitions," (February 1997), at http://www.kpmg.com; see also UNCTAD, *World Investment Report 1997*, pp. 9–10.

47. Oman, "The Policy Challenges of Globalisation and Regionalisation," p. 12; on M&As in the financial services industry, see UNCTAD, *World Investment Report 1996: Investment, Trade and International Policy Arrangements* (United Nations, 1996), pp. 10 and 15, and annex table 9.

48. For a detailed analysis of recent investment trends in the OECD and their policy implications see Houde, *International Direct Investment: Policies and Trends in the 1980's*, pp. 13–18; OECD, *Financial Market Trends*, no. 64 (Paris, June 1996), pp. 37–61. Since the early 1990s this pattern has again been altered somewhat, as a number of East Asian economies have attracted large shares of FDI.

49. For an examination of these trends see J. H. Dunning, "Changes in the Level and Structure of International Production: The Last One Hundred Years," in M. Casson, ed., *The Growth of International Production*, and *Explaining International Production* (London: Unwin Hyman, 1988), as cited in David Levy, "International Production and Sourcing: Trends and Issues," *STI Review*, no. 13 (December 1993), p. 55.

50. U.S. Department of Commerce, "US Direct Investment Abroad: Detail for Historical-Cost Position and Related Capital Income Flows, 1994," *Survey of Current Business*, vol. 75, no. 8 (August 1996), table 18, p. 115.

51. Benjamin Gomes-Casseres, *The Alliance Revolution: The New Shape of Business Rivalry* (Harvard University Press, 1996); Joel Bleeke and David Ernst, eds., *Collaborating to Compete: Using Strategic Alliances and Acquisitions in the Global Marketplace* (New York: John Wiley & Sons, 1993); Michael L. Gerlach, *Alliance Capitalism: The Social Organization of Japanese Business* (Berkeley, Calif.: University of California Press, 1992); Lynn Krieger Mytelka, ed., *Strategic Partnerships: States, Firms and International Competition* (Rutherford, N.J.: Fairleigh Dickinson University, 1991); OECD, "Technology and Globalisation," pp. 226–33; John Hagedoorn, "Strategic Technology Partnering During the 1980s: Trends, Networks, and Corporate Patterns in Non-Core Technologies," *Research Policy*, vol. 24 (March 1995), pp. 207–31.

52. See OECD, Industry Committee, "Symposium on the Globalisation of Industry: Government and Corporate Issues." See also B. Gomes-Casseres, "International Trade, Competition and Alliances in the Computer Industry," in David Yoffie, ed., *The Dynamics of Global Competition* (Harvard Business School, 1993).

53. See, for example, Deigan Morris and Michael Hergert, "Trends in International Collaborative Agreements," *Columbia Journal of World Business* (Summer 1987), pp. 15–21; see also C. Freeman and J. Hagedoorn, "Globalization of Technology: A Report for the FAST Programme" (Brussels: Commission of the European Communities, June 1992); "Multinationals Are Back in Fashion," *The Economist*, March 27, 1993, pp. 5–8 of insert.

54. Vanessa Moulder, "Today's Friend, Tomorrow's Foe," *Financial Times*, October 2, 1995, p. 14.

55. The Cooperative Agreements and Technology Indicators (CATI) database maintained by MERIT is based on literature sources such as newspapers, journal articles, books, and specialized journals that report on business events. The CATI database includes only interfirm agreements that contain some form of technology transfer or joint research.

56. National Science Board, *Science and Engineering Indicators 1996* (GPO, 1996), chapter 4. See also http://www.nsf.gov/sbe/srs/seind96/ch4_intn.htm#pl.

57. National Science Board, *Science and Engineering Indicators 1996,* chapter 4.

58. On the globalization of small and medium-size enterprises see UNCTAD, *Small and Medium Sized Transnational Corporations, Role Impact and Policy Implications* (United Nations, 1993); OECD, *Globalisation of Economic Activities and the Development of SMEs: Working Party of the Industry Committee on Small and Medium Sized Enterprises,* DSTI/IND/PME(95)3 (Paris, 1995).

59. OECD, *Science and Technology Policy Outlook—1991* (Paris, 1991); John Hagedoorn, "Organizational Modes of Inter-Firm Cooperation and Technology Transfer," *Technovation,* vol. 10, no. 1 (February 1990), pp. 17–30.

60. World Trade Organization, *International Trade, Trends and Statistics 1996* (Geneva, 1996), p. 15.

61. It has been estimated that the intrafirm and intraindustry trade (the latter a measure of trade strongly associated with international sourcing) in the OECD countries alone accounts for about 70 percent of global trade.

62. Increasingly, Adam Smith's concept of absolute advantage is again taking on importance, not least because some of the assumptions underlying the concept of comparative advantage, in particular factor immobility, no longer hold. A global company often operates independently of the factor endowment of its own national environment. See J. R. Markusen, "Factor Movements and Commodity Trade as Complements," *Journal of International Economics,* vol. 13 (1983), pp. 341–56, and "The Boundaries of Multinational Enterprises and the Theory of International Trade," *Journal of Economic Perspectives,* vol. 9, no. 2 (Spring 1995), pp. 169–89; see also J. R. Markusen and A. Venables, "Multinational Firms and the New Trade Theory," Working Paper 5036 (Cambridge, Mass.: National Bureau of Economic Research, 1995).

63. OECD, *Intra-Firm Trade: Trade Policy Issues,* 1 (Paris, 1993), p. 25.

64. For a more detailed discussion on the relationship between exchange rates and intrafirm trade see Jane Sneddon Little, "Intra-Firm Trade: An Update," *New England Economic Review,* (May/June 1987), pp. 46–51.

65. For an overview of IFT data and their limitations see Bernard Michael Gilroy, "Intra-Firm Trade," *Journal of Economic Surveys,* vol. 3, no. 4 (1989), pp. 325–43, and F. Steb Hipple, *Multinational Companies in United States International Trade: A Statistical and Analytical Sourcebook* (Westport, Conn.: Quorum Books, 1995).

66. On transfer pricing see, for example, Alan M. Rugman and Lorraine Eden, eds., *Multinationals and Transfer Pricing* (London: Croom Helm, 1985); Robin Murray, ed., *Multinationals Beyond the Market: Intra-Firm Trade and the Control of Transfer Pricing* (John Wiley & Sons, 1981). For evidence on tax avoidance see J. T. Bernard and R. J. Weiner, "Multinational Corporations, Transfer Pricing and Taxes: Evidence from the U.S. Petroleum Industry," Working Paper 3013 (Cambridge, Mass.: National Bureau of Economic Research, 1989); and Sanjaya Lall, "Transfer-Pricing by Multinational Manufacturing Firms," *Oxford Bulletin of Economics and Statistics,* vol. 35, no. 3 (1973), pp. 173–95. For a different perspective see Shabtai Donnefeld and Thomas J. Prusa, "Monitoring and Coordinating in MNCs: Implications for Transfer Pricing and Intra-Firm Trade," *Journal of Economic Integration,* vol. 10, no. 2

(1995), pp. 230–55; for a firm-level perspective on transfer pricing see Ernst & Young, *Risk Reduction and Advanced Pricing Agreements* (New York, 1995).

67. Raymond J. Mataloni, Jr., "U.S. Multinational Companies: Operations in 1995," *Survey of Current Business*, vol. 77, no. 10 (October 1997), p. 50; Mahnaz Fahim-Nadir and William J. Zeile, "Foreign Direct Investment in the United States," *Survey of Current Business*, vol. 77, no. 6 (June 1997); and William J. Zeile, "U.S. Intrafirm Trade in Goods," *Survey of Current Business,* vol. 77, no. 2 (February 1997), p. 24.

68. For a thorough discussion of this issue see Office of Technology Assessment (OTA), *Multinationals and the U.S. Technology Base* (September 1994); and Lawrence Chimerine, Andrew Z. Szamosszegi, and Clyde V. Prestowitz, Jr., *Multinational Corporations and the US Economy* (Washington: Economic Strategy Institute, 1995).

69. Mataloni, "U.S. Multinational Companies," p. 50; Fahim-Nadir and Zeile, "Foreign Direct Investment in the United States," p. 48.

70. OTA, *Multinationals and the U.S. Technology Base,* pp. 129–53.

71. Zeile, "U.S. Intrafirm Trade in Goods," p. 26.

72. Zeile, "U.S. Intrafirm Trade in Goods," p. 26.

73. See OECD, *Intra-Firm Trade: Trade Policy Issues,* p. 20; Japan External Trade Organization, *White Paper on Foreign Direct Investment 1996* (Tokyo, 1996), table 18.

74. Krugman, "Growing World Trade," pp. 333–34.

75. Krugman, "Growing World Trade," p. 334.

76. Oman, "Policy Challenges of Globalisation and Regionalisation," pp. 20–23.

77. OECD, *The OECD Jobs Study: Evidence and Explanations, Part I—Labour Market Trends and Underlying Forces of Change* (Paris, 1995), p. 114–116.

78. Bank for International Settlements, *65th Annual Report: 1 April 1993–31st March 1994* (Basle, Switzerland, June 12, 1994), p. 175.

79. International Monetary Fund (IMF), *International Financial Statistics 1996* (Washington, 1996), CD-ROM (Dataware Technologies).

80. The proportion varies for different national markets. In the United States the share is quite low, with foreign investors accounting for only 10 percent of total equity trading in 1993, whereas in countries such as France and the Netherlands it often surpasses 50 percent of total market volume.

81. Note, however, that the "foreign" investor may actually be a national of the country that issued that debt, who makes the transaction through a foreign intermediary for tax or other reasons.

82. Board of Governors of the Federal Reserve System, *Federal Reserve Bulletin*, vol. 83, no. 7 (July 1997), table 1.41, p. A27.

83. See Richard J. Herring and Robert E. Litan, *Financial Regulation in a Global Economy* (Brookings, 1995), pp. 29–43; Jeffrey A. Frankel, *On Exchange Rates* (MIT Press, 1993); Bruce Kasman and Charles A. Pigott, "Interest Rate Divergences among the Major Industrial Nations," *Federal Reserve Bank of New York Quarterly Review,* vol. 13, no. 3 (Fall 1988), pp. 28–44; Charles A. Pigott, "International Interest Rate Convergence: A Survey of the Issues and Evidence," *Federal Reserve Bank of New York Quarterly Review,* vol. 18, no. 4 (Winter 1993–94), pp. 24–37.

84. OECD, "The New Financial Landscape: Forces Shaping the Revolution in Banking, Risk Management and Capital Markets" (Paris, 1995), pp. 38–39.

85. The growth in portfolio flows has been fairly equally divided between cross-border investments in bonds and in equities, although the internationalization of bond markets, spurred by the issuance of large amounts of sovereign debt during the 1980s, occurred somewhat earlier.

86. Lowell L. Bryan and Diana Farrell, *Market Unbound: Unleashing Global Capitalism* (New York: John Wiley & Sons, 1996), pp. 201–15.

87. See, for instance, the epilogue in Martin Mayer, *The Bankers: The Next Generation* (New York: Truman Tally Books, 1997).

88. McKinsey Global Institute, *The Global Capital Market* (Washington, 1994), p. 15.

89. See Goldstein and Mussa, "Integration of World Capital Markets," table 2, p. 6.

90. For U.S. pension funds diversification is not just optional, but is in fact mandated by the Employees Retirement Income Security Act of 1974 (ERISA).

91. In 1986, for instance, Japanese insurance company and pension fund trust accounts were permitted to raise their holdings of foreign-currency-denominated assets, and in 1988 the postal savings system was allowed to increase the share of foreign assets in its portfolio. In Canada the ceiling on foreign holdings for pension funds was raised from 10 percent to 20 percent in 1990. See IMF, *International Capital Markets: Developments, Prospects and Policy Issues* (September 1994), p. 129, for further examples.

92. Norma Cohen, "US Pension Funds Increase Foreign Investments," *Financial Times,* March 11, 1994, p. 18.

93. Figures provided by the Investment Company Institute, Washington.

94. Based on a 3 percent share of the total assets of U.S. mutual funds in 1992, which then stood at $1.6 trillion.

95. OECD, "The New Financial Landscape," pp. 38–39.

96. Bryan and Farrell, *Market Unbound,* p. 67.

97. Note that the OECD study on which the table is based did not contain data on cooperative agreements in these industrial sectors.

98. Richard O'Brien, *Global Financial Integration: The End of Geography* (New York: Council on Foreign Relations Press, 1992).

99. See also Robert Wade, "Globalization and Its Limits: Reports of the Death of the National Economy Are Greatly Exaggerated," in Suzanne Berger and Ronald Dore, eds., *National Diversity and Global Capitalism* (Cornell University Press, 1996), pp. 60–88.

100. See OECD, *Technology and the Economy: The Key Relationships* (Paris, 1992); and Reinicke, *Deepening the Atlantic,* for an earlier discussion of this point. One commentator recently referred to this phenomenon as "truncated globalization" or "triadization"; see Petrella, "Globalization and Internationalization," p. 77.

101. Oman, "The Policy Challenges of Globalisation and Regionalisation," p. 29.

102. Pier Carlo Padoan, "Globalization and European Regional Integration," paper presented at a conference on "Globalization: What It Is and Its Implications," Universidade de São Paulo, May 23–24, 1996.

103. As in the case of overall FDI, this activity was especially concentrated in the 1980s, with the OECD economies accounting for 95 percent of all cross-border deals between 1986 and 1989. See Baring Securities, *The Financial Silk Road,* vol. 2, p. 50, table 31.

104. Chris Freeman and John Hagedoorn, "Convergence and Divergence in the Internationalization of Technology," in John Hagedoorn, ed., *Technological Change in the World Economy* (Aldershot, England: Edward Elgar Publishing, 1995), pp. 34–57.

105. OECD, "Recent Trends in Foreign Direct Investment," *Financial Market Trends,* no. 61 (Paris, June 1995). Indeed, recently some doubts have been voiced about the sustainability of the investment boom in Southeast Asia. Foreign acquisitions and joint ventures involving China actually fell by one-third in 1995.

106. The ten countries, in descending order of the size of their FDI inflows, were China, Brazil, Singapore, Indonesia, Mexico, Malaysia, Poland, Argentina, Peru, and Chile. UNCTAD, *World Investment Report 1997,* annex table B.1, pp. 303–07.

107. In addition, an important part of this investment represents internally generated Chinese funds sent abroad to be reinvested under more favorable conditions.

108. UNCTAD, *World Investment Report 1993,* table I.4, p. 16; and *World Investment Report 1997,* annex table B.1, pp. 303–07.

109. World Bank, *Global Economic Prospects and the Developing Countries* (Washington, 1997), p. 14.

110. Gross foreign equity trading is the sum of all purchases and sales of foreign equity, either in the form of foreign purchases and sales of domestic equities or purchases and sales of foreign equities listed in the domestic market (for example, American depository receipts). Baring Securities, *The Financial Silk Road,* vol. 2, p. 18.

111. Bank for International Settlements, *International Banking and Financial Markets Developments* (Basle, Switzerland, 1996).

112. Baring Securities, *The Financial Silk Road,* vol. 2, pp. 24 and 30.

113. See Bank for International Settlements, *International Banking and Financial Markets Developments.*

114. The term is from Robert Brooke Zevin, "Are World Financial Markets More Open? If So Why and With What Effects?" (Helsinki: United Nations University/ World Institute for Development Economics Research, June 13, 1989).

115. On financial markets see, for example, David D. Hale, "The Atlantic Community in an Age of Global Economic Integration," in Chicago Council on Foreign Relations, *Is the Atlantic Widening?* (Chicago, 1995), pp. 96–174; on trade see, for example, Krugman, "Growing World Trade," pp. 327–62.

116. See Zevin, "Are World Financial Markets More Open?"; Charles Kindleberger, "The New Multinationalization of Business," *Asean Economic Bulletin,* no. 5 (1988), pp. 113–24; Paul Hirst and Grahame Thompson, *Globalization in Question: The International Economy and the Possibilities of Governance* (Cambridge, England: Polity Press, 1996); John Pitt, "Emerging Markets: Strategy, *Financial Times,* February 12, 1996, p. 25; "Back to the Future," *The Economist,* October 7, 1995, Survey, pp. 5–6; Wade, "Globalization and Its Limits," pp. 60–88.

117. Arthur Irving Bloomfield, *Patterns of Fluctuation in International Investment Before 1914* (Princeton University Press, 1968), p. 1; John Maynard Keynes, *The Economic Consequences of the Peace,* reprint (New York: Penguin Books, 1988).

118. Bairoch, *Economics and World History,* p. xiv; Paul Bairoch and Richard Kozul-Wright, "Globalization Myths: Some Historical Reflections on Integration, Industrialization and Growth in the World Economy," UNCTAD/OSG/DP/113 (United Nations, March 1996).

119. See also UNCTAD, *World Investment Report 1994,* chapter 3.

120. In the United States, for instance, exports of services were equal to approximately 2.9 percent of GDP in 1992 (at current prices). *Economic Report of the President 1996,* appendix tables B-1, B-102.

121. Philip Turner, "Capital Flows in the 1980s: A Survey of Major Trends" in *BIS Economic Papers* 30 (Basle: BIS, April 1991).

122. This was reflected in relatively narrow interest rate differentials across countries, with only small differences in rates being required to finance balance of payments imbalances, and in the fact that short-term capital flows were not dominated by expectations of exchange rate changes as they are today, creating the massive trading volumes in the foreign exchange markets.

123. It is estimated that by 1914 three-quarters of the United Kingdom's foreign investment position was in public and public utility investment, of which the majority was in railroads in the United States, Argentina, and India. See Joseph Bisignano, "The Internationalization of Financial Markets: Measurement, Benefits, and Unexpected Interdependence," in *Cahiers economiques et monétaires* 43 (Paris: Banque de France, 1994), p. 21.

124. The primary sector accounted for 55 percent of the total stock of FDI in 1913. Another 30 percent was accounted for by transportation, trade, and distribution, and only 15 percent by manufacturing. See John H. Dunning, "Changes in the Level and Structure of International Production," in M. Casson, *The Growth of International Business,* p. 89.

125. See also Krugman, "Growing World Trade."

126. In the case of trade, it is estimated that 17 percent of exports from western Europe were sent to the developing world between 1800 and 1938, of which about half were directed to colonial empires. For some countries, however, and in certain product categories, these proportions were often considerably higher. The United Kingdom, for instance, shipped 40 percent of all its exports and 67 percent of its cotton textile exports to the developing world during this period. See Bairoch, *Economics and World History,* pp. 72–79. For more on colonialism and international trade see Ephraim Kleiman, "Trade and the Decline of Colonialism," *Economic Journal,* vol. 86 (1976), pp. 459–79.

127. Cleona Lewis, *Debtor and Creditor Countries: 1938–1944* (Brookings, 1945), p. 48.

128. Thus the European countries (and the United States) either totally prohibited the import of yarn or manufactured cotton or imposed duties ranging from 30 to 80 percent, yet British textile goods could enter the Indian market with no duties at all. Bairoch, *Economics and World History,* p. 89.

129. See, for example, Angus Maddison, *The World Economy in the 20th Century* (Paris: OECD, 1989); Mic Panic, *National Management of the International Economy* (London: St Martin's Press, 1988); John Henderson, "International Economic Integration: Progress, Prospects and Implications," *International Affairs,* vol. 68 (1992), pp. 633–53.

130. OECD, *Financial Market Trends* 64 (Paris, June 1996), p. 46.

131. OECD, *Globalisation of Industrial Activities: Background Report.*

132. OECD, "Symposium on the Globalisation of Industry," p. 5.

133. OECD, "Technology and Globalisation," p. 209.

134. Hatzichronoglou, "Globalisation and Competitiveness," p. 14.

CHAPTER 2

1. See Jean Marie Guehenno, *The End of the Nation-State,* trans. Victoria Elliot (University of Minnesota Press, 1995); Kenichi Ohmae, *The End of the Nation-State: The Rise of Regional Economies* (Free Press, 1995).

2. Stephen Krasner, "Sovereignty: An Institutional Perspective," *Comparative Political Studies,* vol. 21, no. 1 (April 1988), p. 76; see also Nicholas Colchester, "Goodbye, Nation-State. Hello . . . What?" *New York Times,* July 17, 1994, p. 17.

3. Jessica T. Mathews, "Power Shift," *Foreign Affairs,* vol. 76, no. 1 (January/February 1997), pp. 50–66; Peter J. Spiro, "New Global Communities: Nongovernmental Organizations in International Decision-Making Institutions," *Washington Quarterly,* vol. 18, no. 7 (Winter 1995), pp. 45–56; see also Raymond Vernon, "Transnational Corporations: Where Are They Coming from, Where Are They Headed?" *Transnational Corporations,* vol. 1, no. 2 (August 1992), pp. 7–35.

4. For a cogent summary of this view, see "The Myth of the Powerless State," *The Economist,* October 7, 1995, pp. 15–16.

5. For an early exposition of this argument see David Cameron, "The Expansion of the Public Economy," *American Political Science Review,* vol. 72, no. 4 (1978), pp. 1243–61; for a more recent exposition, addressing the rising popular resentment against globalization, see Dani Rodrik, "Why Do More Open Economies Have Bigger Governments?" Working Paper 5537 (Cambridge, Mass.: National Bureau of Economic Research, April 1996); Dani Rodrik, "Trade, Social Insurance, and the Limits to Globalization," Working Paper 5905 (Cambridge, Mass.: National Bureau of Economic Research, January 1997); and Dani Rodrik, *Has Globalization Gone Too Far?* (Washington: Institute for International Economics, 1997).

6. Krasner, "Sovereignty: An Institutional Perspective," pp. 66–94.

7. See Theodore Lowi, "American Business, Public Policy, Case Studies, and Political Theory," *World Politics,* vol. 16 (1964), p. 689.

8. Robert O. Keohane and Joseph S. Nye Jr., "Power and Interdependence Revisited," *International Organization,* vol. 41, no. 4 (1987), pp. 725–53.

9. For a general discussion see David Baldwin, "Interdependence and Power: A Conceptual Analysis," *International Organization,* vol. 34 (1989), pp. 471–506; R. J. Barry Jones and Peter Willetts, *Interdependence on Trial: Studies in the Theory and Reality of Contemporary Interdependence* (New York: St. Martin's, 1984); P. A. Reynolds and R. D. McKinlay, "The Concept of Interdependence: Its Uses and Misuses," in Kjell Goldmann and Gunnar Sjöstedt, eds., *Power, Capabilities, Interdependence: Problems in the Study of International Influence* (Sage, 1979). On complex interdependence see Robert O. Keohane and Stanley Hoffmann, "Institutional Change in Europe in the 1980s," in Robert O. Keohane and Stanley Hoffmann, eds., *The New*

European Community: Decisionmaking and Institutional Change (Boulder, Colo.: West-view Press, 1991), pp. 1–39; Keohane and Nye, "Power and Interdependence Revisited."

10. Robert O. Keohane and Joseph S. Nye, Jr., *Power and Interdependence: World Politics in Transition* (Little, Brown, 1977), pp. 8, 12–19. The notion of increased national sensitivity to external (economic) developments was first intro-duced by Richard N. Cooper, *The Economics of Interdependence: Economic Policy in the Atlantic Community* (McGraw-Hill, 1968).

11. This distinction was first made by Bull, who calls the two concepts "norma-tive" and "factual" sovereignty. See Hedley Bull, *The Anarchical Society: A Study of Order in World Politics* (Columbia University Press, 1977), p. 8. The distinction has recently been elaborated by Keohane, who distinguishes between "formal" and "operational" sovereignty. See Robert O. Keohane, "Sovereignty, Interdependence, and International Institutions," Working Paper 1 (Harvard University, 1991).

12. Joel Krieger, ed., *The Oxford Companion to Politics of the World* (Oxford University Press, 1993), p. 851.

13. Bull, *The Anarchical Society,* p. 8.

14. John Gerard Ruggie, "Continuity and Transformation in the World Polity: Toward a Neorealist Synthesis," *World Politics,* vol. 35, no. 2 (January 1983), p. 276. See also Ruth Lapidoth, "Sovereignty in Transition," *Journal of International Affairs,* vol. 45, no.2 (1992), pp. 325–46, for a good historical overview of the concept of sovereignty and its meanings.

15. Martin Wight, *International Theory: The Three Traditions,* edited by Gabriele Wight and Brian Porter (Holmes & Meier, 1992), pp. 2–3.

16. The classic work here is Jean Bodin, *Six Books of the Commonwealth* (Harvard University Press, 19962). Bodin defined citizenship as subjection to a sov-ereign. See George Holland Sabine, *A History of Political Theory,* 4th ed. (Hinsdale: Dryden Press, 1973), chap. 20; see also Max Adams Shepard, "Sovereignty at the Crossroads: A Study of Bodin," *Political Science Quarterly,* vol. 45 (Columbia Uni-versity, 1930), pp. 580–603.

17. See Max Weber, *Economy and Society: An Outline of Interpretive Sociology,* edited by Guenther Roth and Claus Wittich (University of California Press, 1978).

18. Krasner, "Sovereignty: An Institutional Perspective," pp. 66–94.

19. David Dessler, "What's at Stake in the Agent-Structure Debate," *Interna-tional Organization,* vol. 43, no. 3 (Summer 1989), pp. 441–74.

20. John Gerard Ruggie, "Territoriality and Beyond: Problematizing Modernity in International Relations," *International Organization,* vol. 47, no. 1 (Winter 1993), pp. 139–74. As Ruggie correctly points out, in reality this exclusion cannot be total, for this would imply no contact among states. Over the years this contact has grown and developed into an extensive set of bilateral, plurilateral, and multilateral rela-tionships that allow externally sovereign states to interact with each other.

21. Alexander Wendt, "Anarchy Is What States Make of It: The Social Con-struction of Power Politics," *International Organization,* vol. 46, no. 2 (1992), pp. 395–421.

22. The distinction between internal and external sovereignty is also helpful in examining other issues in international relations. Yugoslavia provides an example. Although some progress has been achieved in establishing external sovereignty for

the successor states of the former Yugoslavia, much work remains to be done to consolidate their internal sovereignty. If this fails, so will the ongoing efforts at sustaining external sovereignty for each successor state. At a more general level, it is probably accurate to assume that, in the evolution of the modern state in western Europe, internal sovereignty preceded the establishment of external sovereignty. In many of the former European colonies, on the other hand, external sovereignty, often imposed from without, was much more developed than its internal counterpart, which in many cases remains weak. See Robert H. Jackson and Carl G. Rosberg, "Why Africa's Weak States Persist: The Empirical and the Juridical in Statehood," *World Politics,* vol. 35, no. 1 (1982), pp. 1–24; Robert H. Jackson, *Quasi-States: Sovereignty, International Relations and the Third World* (Cambridge University Press, 1990). See also Francis Deng and others, *Sovereignty as Responsibility: Conflict Management in Africa* (Brookings, 1996).

23. Ruggie, "Territoriality and Beyond," pp. 139–74.

24. As Wendt points out, "the commitment to and the salience of particular identities vary, but each identity is an inherently social definition of the actor grounded in the theories which actors hold about themselves and one another and which constitute the structure of the social world." Wendt, "Anarchy Is What States Make of It," pp. 395–421.

25. On this debate see, for example, *International Security,* vol. 20, no. 1 (Summer 1995), entire issue; Baldwin, "Interdependence and Power"; John Mearsheimer, "Back to the Future: Instability in Europe after the Cold War," *International Security,* vol. 13 (Summer 1990), pp. 5–56; Robert O. Keohane, *International Institutions and State Power: Essays in International Theory* (Boulder, Colo.: Westview Press, 1989); Joseph M. Grieco, "Anarchy and the Limits of Cooperation: A Realist Critique of the Newest Liberal Institutionalism," *International Organization,* vol. 42 (Summer 1988), pp. 485–507; Robert O. Keohane, ed., *Neorealism and Its Critics* (Columbia University Press, 1986).

26. The standard work on neorealism is Kenneth N. Waltz, *Theory of International Politics* (Addison-Wesley, 1979).

27. For the distinction between structure and process see Wendt, "Anarchy Is What States Make of It"; on the importance of process for cooperation see Robert Axelrod, *The Evolution of Cooperation* (Basic Books, 1984), and Kenneth A. Oye, ed., *Cooperation under Anarchy* (Princeton University Press, 1986).

28. This explains the liberals' frequent references to the prisoner's dilemma game.

29. Grieco, "Anarchy and the Limits of Cooperation," pp. 485–507.

30. Wendt, "Anarchy Is What States Make of It." Wendt does acknowledge that a number of neoliberals have attempted to include theories of complex learning and adaptation in their writings, but argues that "they lack a systematic theory on how such change occurs," p. 393.

31. For a distinction between absolute and relative gains see Grieco, "Anarchy and the Limits of Cooperation," pp. 485–507.

32. Stephen D. Krasner, "Structural Causes and Regime Consequences: Regimes as Intervening Variables," in Stephen D. Krasner, ed., *International Regimes* (Cornell University Press, 1983), p. 2.

33. Highlighting this difference between absolute and relative sovereignty should

be the neoliberal rebuttal to the neorealist critique that neoliberals neglect to differentiate between absolute and relative gains—a critique eloquently advanced by Grieco, "Anarchy and the Limits of Cooperation." Thus neoliberals are concerned about relative notions of power, a concern that is embodied in the principle of reciprocity.

34. On "embedded liberalism" see John Gerard Ruggie, "International Regimes, Transactions, and Change: Embedded Liberalism in the Postwar Economic Order," and Stephen D. Krasner, "Structural Causes and Regime Consequences: Regimes as Intervening Variables," both in Stephen D. Krasner, ed., *International Regimes* (Cornell University Press, 1983); the importance of domestic coalitions and interest formation in the context of the regimes literature has been demonstrated by Robert Putnam, "Diplomacy and Domestic Politics: The Logic of Two-Level Games," *International Organization,* vol. 42 (Summer 1988), pp. 427–60.

35. John A. C. Conybeare, "Public Goods, Prisoners' Dilemma and the International Political Economy," *International Studies Quarterly,* vol. 28 (March 1984), pp. 5–22. If and to what degree individual governments use their internal sovereignty to ensure broad-based distribution of the gains is an open question. Rodrik also makes this point when he discusses the social implications of globalization, stating that trade not only increases income but also redistributes it among industries, regions, and individuals. "Therefore, a principled defense of free trade cannot be constructed without addressing the question of the fairness and legitimacy of these distributional 'costs.'" See Dani Rodrik, "Sense and Nonsense in the Globalization Debate," *Foreign Policy,* vol. 107 (Summer 1997), p. 28.

36. Grieco, "Anarchy and the Limits of Cooperation," pp. 485–507.

37. Holm and Sørensen also make such an effort. See Hans-Henrik Holm and Georg Sørensen, "Introduction: What Has Changed?" and "International Relations Theory in a World of Variation," in Holm and Sørensen, eds., *Whose World Order?* pp. 1–17 and 187–206.

38. Paul Hirst and Grahame Thompson, "The Problem of 'Globalization': International Economic Relations, National Economic Management and the Formation of Trade Blocs," *Economy and Society,* vol. 21, no. 4 (November 1992), pp. 357–96; see also Paul Hirst and Grahame Thompson, *Globalization in Question: The International Economy and the Possibilities of Governance* (Cambridge, England: Polity Press, 1996).

39. Stephen J. Kobrin, "An Empirical Analysis of the Determinants of Global Integration," *Strategic Management Journal,* vol. 12 (1991), pp. 17–31.

40. See Ruggie, "Territoriality and Beyond," pp. 139–74. Ruggie adapted the use of this term from Friedrich Kratochwil, "Of Systems, Boundaries, and Territoriality," pp. 27–52.

41. For more on the concept of information asymmetry, see the case studies.

42. The Internet and in particular electronic commerce have not only accelerated that process considerably, but have also given small individual consumers and small producers access to the global marketplace.

43. Kratochwil, "Of Systems, Boundaries, and Territoriality," pp. 27–52.

44. See, for example, Hendrik Spruyt, "Institutional Selection in International Relations," *International Organization,* vol. 48, no. 4 (1994), pp. 527–57.

45. Of course, this is not to say that, in a democracy, public policy has never been

sensitive to the interests of competing groups, including that of the private sector. In a democracy, "voice" has been and should always be the principal instrument by which different interest groups, including the private sector, shape domestic policy-making. Thus, as discussed above, for example, the voice of the dominant private sector coalitions has been a central factor in determining the path of international economic interdependence and conditioning the positions of governments in international economic regimes. Globalization has changed this dynamic by making the option of "exit" not only a viable and sometimes more convenient option, but also in many cases the necessary, even the natural strategy. For more on exits, see Albert O. Hirschman, *Exit, Voice and Loyalty: Responses to Decline in Firms, Organizations, and States* (Harvard University Press, 1970).

46. Marc Granovetter, "Economic Action and Social Structure: The Problem of Embeddedness," *American Journal of Sociology,* vol. 91 (November 1985), pp. 481–510.

47. James S. Coleman, "Introducing Social Structure into Economic Analysis," *American Economic Review,* vol. 74 (May 1984), pp. 84–88.

48. The balancing of public and private interests is, of course, not free of conflict. Yet all social actors are in agreement that a certain basic framework, be it of a legal, political, or even social nature, is not only compatible with but even desirable when operating in a market environment. Nowhere has this become more apparent than in the recent process of systemic transformation in the former Eastern bloc.

49. One commentator has taken the argument even further: "The nightmare for politicians is that they are held responsible for their national economies but have fewer ways of affecting the economy's direction. Responsibility without power can be as corrupting as power without responsibility." See E. J. Dionne, "All Politics Is Now Global," *Washington Post,* July 13, 1993, p. A15. Another has linked it to the declining attractiveness of public service. "The [U.S.] congressional exodus may reflect a sense that what governments do matters less in a world than it is used to because the map of power is being redrawn; not the distribution of power among nations but between national governments on the one hand and non-governmental entities . . . on the other." See Jessica T. Mathews, "Exodus of Authority," *Washington Post,* January 22, 1996, p. A19.

50. Edward Mortimer, "Surfeit of Good Things: The right to vote can be meaningless if the real choices are left to the market and those elected are powerless to act," *Financial Times,* February 28, 1996, p. 16.

51. The inability of the interdependence literature to focus on the internal dynamics that arise in response to increased interdependence has recently been acknowledged. "Missing from this [interdependence] literature, however, was a systematic analysis of how interdependence affected domestic politics." Milner and Keohane, "Internationalization and Domestic Politics," p. 7.

52. Ruggie, "Territoriality and Beyond," p. 172.

53. The distinction between "somewhere else" and "another place" comes from Ruggie, "Territoriality and Beyond," pp. 139–74.

54. Wendt, "Anarchy Is What States Make of It," pp. 395–421.

55. Recall the earlier point that external sovereignty is unsustainable in the longer term if internal sovereignty cannot be maintained, either by democratic or by

other means. Historically, internal sovereignty has preceded external sovereignty and has been more important as a constitutive force during the process of state formation.

56. The argument presented here gives strong support to Wendt's analysis, which states that socialization, which is the interaction of states over time, will change states' identities and interests. Yet Wendt had to concede that the strength of his argument depends on "how important interaction among states is for the constitution of their identities and interests." Wendt, "Anarchy Is What States Make of It," p. 423. As far as globalization goes, interaction is, of course, vital, since it is the only way to preserve internal sovereignty.

57. Keohane recently acknowledged that his and Nye's analysis in *Power and Interdependence* was limited to the international level, and thus that they "had to view interests [of states] as formed largely exogenously, in a way unexplained by our theory . . . [yet] changes in the definitions of self interest . . . kept appearing in our case studies." Keohane and Nye, "Power and Interdependence Revisited," p. 739.

58. Note that this is different from the notion of declining external sovereignty under the neoliberal paradigm of cooperative competition. There sovereignty was said to decline in absolute terms but remain the same in relative terms. Here external sovereignty has lost its meaning. These are no longer interactions between separate territorial entities.

CHAPTER 3

1. Peter Sutherland, former director general of the WTO. See Guy de Jonquieres, "Sutherland Urges Policy Framework: WTO Director General Warns of a 'Returning Tide of Protectionism,'" *Financial Times,* January 30, 1995, p. 4.

2. C. Fred Bergsten, "The World Economy after the Cold War," *California Management Review* vol, 34, no. 2 (Winter 1992), pp. 51–65, and Guy de Jonquieres "Tackling Trade Barriers: Transnational Businesses are Having to Contend with Ever More Obstacles," *Financial Times,* October 6, 1995, p. xix; see also J. Nogues, A. Olechowski, and L. A. Winters, "The Extent of Nontariff Barriers to Industrial Countries' Imports," *World Bank Economic Review,* vol. 1 (1986), pp. 181–99; on antidumping see Congressional Budget Office, *How the GATT Affects U.S. Antidumping and Countervailing-Duty Policy* (Washington, September 1994); see also Nancy Dunne, "White House Urged to Reduce Use of Antidumping Measures," *Financial Times,* December 8, 1994, p. 7.

3. Mark Clough, "Shadow Cast over WTO," *Financial Times,* April 15, 1997, p. 16.

4. "Disputes Reach Century Mark," *WTO Focus,* no. 21 (August 1997), p. 1.

5. See George Parker, "Goldsmith Aims to be Britain's Answer to Perot: Politics is too serious to be left to politicians, the billionaire Referendum party leader tells supporters," *Financial Times,* July 1, 1996, p. 7; for Goldsmith's position on these issues see Sir James Goldsmith, *The Trap* (New York: Carroll & Graf, 1995); on the situation in France see Suzanne Berger, "The Coming Protectionism: Trade and Identity in France," in Gregory Flynn, ed., *Remaking the Hexagon: The New France in the New Europe* (Westview Press, 1995), pp. 195–210; on Austria see Brigitte Bailer-Galanda, *Haider wörtlich: Führer in die Dritte Republik* (Vienna: Löcker, 1995).

6. Robert Z. Lawrence, *Single World, Divided Nations? International Trade and the OECD Labor Markets* (Brookings, 1996); Adrian Wood, *North-South Trade, Employment, and Inequality: Changing Fortunes in a Skill-Driven World* (Oxford University Press, 1994). See also Robert Z. Lawrence and Robert E. Litan, "Globaphobia: The Wrong Debate over Trade Policy," *Brookings Policy Brief*, no. 24 (September 1997) and related cites, p. 8.

7. This list reflects Buchanan's agenda perhaps more than others. See, for example, Patrick J. Buchanan, "An American Economy for Americans," *Wall Street Journal*, September 5, 1995, p. 14; "Nothing Timid about My Nationalism," *Washington Post*, October 30, 1995, p. 17; and "It's about Our Way of Life," *Washington Post*, November 7, 1993, p. 1. Nader advocates political reform to open the decisionmaking process on foreign policy issues such as trade agreements to the broader public. See "Ralph Nader, Throwback to the Future," *The Economist*, March 30, 1996, p. 36; Leslie Kaufman, "America's New Mr. International," *International Economy*, vol. 5, no. 4 (July-August 1991), pp. 35–37.

8. "Buchanan's Protectionism Slows Trade Agenda," *Congressional Quarterly*, March 2, 1996, pp. 532–36. Two bills introduced in 1995 were geared toward a reversal of the trade liberalization agenda. The NAFTA Accountability Act (H.R. 978/S.1514) provides, among other things, for U.S. withdrawal from the North American Free Trade Agreement (NAFTA) unless certain conditions are met. The WTO Dispute Settlement Review Commission Act (H.R.78) would establish a commission to review all WTO dispute settlement cases where the final report is adverse to the United States. See also Nancy Dunne, "Alarm over Protection with New Bite in '97," *Financial Times*, February 26, 1996, p. 5. In a speech on November 3, 1995, Senator Bob Dole (R-Kan.) announced his opposition to any new trade deals until results from NAFTA and the Uruguay Round were in. See Ben Wildavsky, "The Insider's Insider," *National Journal*, vol. 27, no. 46 (November 18, 1995), pp. 2852–55; see also "The Struggle for the Soul of a Changing GOP," *Congressional Quarterly*, April 6, 1996, pp. 941–48, and "Deficit Looks Tiny as Issue," *New York Times*, February 14, 1996, p. 1.

9. "Deficit Looks Tiny as Issue," p. 1.

10. See, for example, Ralph Nader, "Trade in Secrets," *Washington Post*, October 6, 1996, p. 31; on world government see "Sovereignty and the WTO," *Washington Post*, May 10, 1994, p. A16.

11. Buchanan, "Nothing Timid about My Nationalism," p. 17.

12. See, for example, the testimony of Lori Wallach, director, Public Citizen's Global Trade Watch, in *Future Direction of U.S. Trade Policy*, Hearings before the Subcommittee on Trade, House Ways and Means Committee, 105 Cong., 1 sess. (GPO, 1997).

13. Cerny has called this the "competition state." See Philip G. Cerny, *The Changing Architecture of Politics: Structure, Agency and the Future of the State* (Sage, 1990), especially chapter 8.

14. Edward Luttwak, *The Endangered American Dream: How to Stop the United States from Becoming a Third World Country and How to Win the Geo-Economics: Struggle for Industrial Supremacy* (Simon & Schuster, 1993); Lester Thurow, *Head to Head: The Coming Economic Battle among Japan, Europe and America* (Morrow,

1992); Jeffrey E. Garten, *A Cold Peace: America, Japan, Germany and the Struggle for Supremacy* (Times Books, 1992); see also Samuel Huntington, "Why International Primacy Matters," *International Security,* vol. 17, no. 4 (Spring 1993), pp. 68–83.

15. See "Tax Competition," *OECD: Financial, Fiscal, and Enterprise Affairs,* on the OECD's Internet web site at http//www.oecd.org/daf/fa/taxcomp.htm; see also Jim Kelly, "OECD Task Force Seeks to Curb Tax Competition," *Financial Times,* January 13, 1997, p. 20; and "Living with Tax Rivalry," *Financial Times,* January 14, 1997, p. 17.

16. OECD, *Cross Country Study on Subsidies* (Paris, 1995).

17. Nancy Dunne and Michael Cassell, "Big Brother Lends a Hand: The U.S. and UK governments Are Trying to Help Companies Win Business in India," *Financial Times,* February 15, 1995, p. 20. See also Jeffrey E. Garten, "Business and Foreign Policy," *Foreign Affairs,* vol. 76, no. 3 (May/June 1977), pp. 67–79.

18. Guy de Jonquieres, "Waging a War for U.S. Business," *Financial Times,* June 3, 1994, p. 6; see also "Clinton & Co Looks for Business: Administration Is Fighting for More Foreign Orders," *Financial Times,* February 24, 1994, p. 7.

19. In the spring of 1994 the French government appeared to have secured the contract for the European consortium Airbus Industrie but was rejected after U.S. intervention. See William Drozdiak, "French Resent U.S. Coups in New Espionage," *Washington Post,* February 26, 1995, p. 1; see also "Airliners for the Saudis," *Washington Post,* February 18, 1994, p. 24.

20. AT&T publicly acknowledged that political pressure was a factor. See Andrew Adonis, "Rivals Say They Underbid AT&T for Saudi Deal," *Financial Times,* May 12, 1994, p. 3.

21. Robert S. Greenberger, "Foreigners Use Bribes to Beat U.S. Rivals in Many Deals, New Report Concludes," *Wall Street Journal,* October 12, 1995. According to the report, for every $1,000 of gross national product, the United Kingdom spent about 25 cents on export promotion, France and Japan about 17 cents, and the United States only 3 cents.

22. For some background see Jeff Augustini, "From Goldfinger to Butterfinger: The Legal and Policy Issues Surrounding Proposals to Use the CIA for Economic Espionage," *Law and Policy in International Business,* vol. 26 (Winter 1995), pp. 459–95; Dennis DeConcini, "The Role of U.S. Intelligence in Promoting Economic Interests," *Journal of International Affairs,* vol. 48 (Summer 1994), pp. 39–57.

23. On economic espionage in the United States see, for example, Peter Schweizer, "The Growth of Economic Espionage, America Is Target Number One," *Foreign Affairs,* vol. 75, no. 1 (January-February 1996), pp. 9–14; John J. Fialka, *War by Other Means: Economic Espionage in America* (Norton, 1997). The incidents involving the United States relate to various activities in France and Japan where the Central Intelligence Agency and the National Security Agency eavesdropped on conversations between Japanese bureaucrats and automobile executives during bilateral negotiations over auto parts trade.

24. Greenberger, "Foreigners Use Bribes to Beat U.S. Rivals in Many Deals," p. A3.

25. Companies can lower their taxable income by moving operations or through transfer pricing. When a firm pays inflated prices for components imported from a subsidiary in a low-tax country, it can shift taxable profits to that country and so lower its tax bill. A government may respond to this strategy through unitary taxa-

tion, which determines the taxable profits of a firm operating in its jurisdiction by prorating the firm's total profits according to the share of, for example, its total assets located in the jurisdiction. For some background on this issue see Robert Tannenwald, "The Pro's and Con's of Worldwide Unitary Taxation," *New England Economic Review* (July-August 1984), pp. 17–28; Massimo Agostini, "U.S. Perspectives of Worldwide Unitary Taxation," *Dickinson Journal of International Law,* vol. 7, no. 2 (Winter 1989), pp. 213–27; Steven D. Erdahl, "Supreme Court Upholds California's Unitary Taxation of Foreign Multinationals," *Journal of Corporate Taxation,* vol. 22, no. 1 (Spring 1995), pp. 3–35; Rick Wartzman, "Politics and Policy: California Tax Dispute Forces Clinton to Choose between Vote-Rich State and Trading Partners," *Wall Street Journal,* August 19, 1993, p. A12. The Helms-Burton Act imposes sanctions on the U.S. parents of foreign affiliates that do business with Cuba. See James Whisenand, "US Aims to Isolate Cuba and Threatens Free Trade," *International Financial Law Review,* vol. 15 (May 1996), pp. 22–24; "On the Meaning of the Helms-Burton Law," *Political Affairs,* vol. 75 (July 1996), pp. 11–12; "Planes' Downing Forces Clinton to Compromise on Sanctions," *Congressional Quarterly Weekly Report,* vol. 54 (March 2, 1996), p. 54.

26. On regionalism in Europe see, for example, John Newhouse, "Europe's Rising Regionalism," *Foreign Affairs,* vol. 76, no. 1 (January-February 1997), pp. 67–84. It is interesting to note that shortly after it became clear that the October 1995 secession referendum in Quebec had failed, the separatist leader Jacques Parizeau blamed "money and the ethnic vote" for the loss. See Charles Trueheart, "Premier to Resign in Quebec; Separatists Promise Renewed Campaign," *Washington Post,* November 1, 1995, p. A1. The Northern League, or Lega Nord, is a right-wing separatist movement centered in northern Italy under the leadership of Umberto Bossi. The movement was very successful earlier this decade when it captured 23 percent of the vote in the national elections of 1992, but it has recently suffered a number of setbacks.

27. There are a few exceptions, such as the so-called escape clause of the GATT. See, for example, Gary C. Hufbauer and Howard F. Rosen, "Trade Policies for Troubled Industries," Policy Analysis in International Economics 15 (Washington: Institute for International Economics, 1986). When and how a country retaliates is likely to depend on its size. Small, open economies will find it more difficult to retaliate, especially if the target country offers a large market. But even small countries will not tolerate a consistent violation of international principles.

28. Buchanan, "An American Economy for Americans," p. 14.

29. "War among the states" refers to the escalating competition between states to lure business through preferential tax breaks and other incentives. See Melvin L. Burstein and Arthur J. Rolnick, "Congress Should End the Economic War among the States," *The Region* (Federal Reserve Bank of Minneapolis, March 1995); "The Economic War for Sports and other Businesses," *The Region* (Federal Reserve Bank of Minneapolis, special issue, June 1996), pp. 35–36. In 1996 the Ohio Senate passed a resolution requesting federal assistance in halting competition among states. See Charles Mahtesian, "Saving the States from Each Other: Can Congress Dictate an End to the Great Smokestack Chase?" *Governing,* vol. 10 (November 1996), p. 15. According to the *New York Times,* in its drive to attract Mercedes-Benz to the state,

Alabama spent $200,000 per job created. See Allen R. Myerson, "O Governor, Won't You Buy Me a Mercedes Plant?" *New York Times,* September 1, 1996, p. 1.

30. As quoted in de Jonquiers, "Waging a War for US Business"; on European retaliation see David Buchan, "French Attack Clinton on Aircraft Sales," *Financial Times,* March 2, 1994, p. 6; Quentin Peel, "Bonn Urged to Promote Exports More Vigorously," *Financial Times,* October 12, 1993, p. 7.

31. Theodore H. Moran, "An Economics Agenda for Neorealists," *International Security,* vol. 18, no. 2 (1993), p. 214.

32. Vincent Cable, "What Is International Economic Security?" *International Affairs,* vol. 71, no. 2 (April 1995), pp. 305–24.

33. Paul Krugman, "Competitiveness: A Dangerous Obsession," *Foreign Affairs,* vol. 73, no. 2 (March-April 1994), pp. 28–44; see also Krugman, "The Illusion of Conflict in International Trade," *Peace Economics, Peace Science, and Public Policy,* vol. 3 (Winter 1995), pp. 9–18.

34. See, for example, Pietro S. Nivola, *Regulating Unfair Trade* (Brookings, 1993).

35. See OECD, *Multilateral Agreement on Investment: Progress Report,* OECD/GD(96)78 (Paris, 1996).

36. Thomas J. Prusa, "The Trade Effects of US Antidumping Actions," Working Paper 5440 (Cambridge, Mass.: National Bureau of Economic Research, 1996).

37. Local content rules require that a firm use a certain amount of domestically produced inputs in the production of its final output. For background information see G. M. Grossman, "The Theory of Domestic Content Protection and Content Preference," *Quarterly Journal of Economics,* vol. 96 (1981), pp. 538–603; T. H. Moran and C. S. Pearson, "Tread Carefully in the Field of TRIP Measures," *The World Economy,* vol. 11, no. 1 (1988), pp. 119–34; M. Mussa, "The Economics of Content Protection," Working Paper 1457 (Cambridge, Mass.: National Bureau of Economic Research, 1984); OECD, "Trade Related Investment Measures: An Overview of Characteristics, Incidence and Effects," TC/WP (87) 78 (1987).

38. As quoted in Nancy Dunne, "Congress Urged to Reject R&D Proposal," *Financial Times,* August 18, 1994, p. 4.

39. For a discussion of some of these differences and their implications for deeper integration between the United States and Canada see R. Kent Weaver, "Domestic Political Structures and the Management of Complex Interdependence," Brookings, August 1996.

40. For an earlier argument along these lines see James N. Rosenau and Ernst-Otto Czempiel, eds., *Governance without Government: Order and Change in World Politics,* Cambridge Studies in International Relations 20 (Cambridge University Press, 1992).

41. *Webster's Third New International Dictionary,* s.v. "sovereignty."

42. Centre for Economic Policy Research, *Making Sense of Subsidiarity: How Much Centralization for Europe?* (London, November 1993).

43. The Tenth Amendment to the U.S. Constitution reads, "The powers not delegated to the United States by the Constitution, nor prohibited by it to the states, are reserved to the states respectively or to the people." In the Treaty on the European Union the relevant section is Article G (3b), which reads, "The Community shall act

within the limits of the powers conferred upon it by this Treaty and of the objectives assigned to it therein. In areas which do not fall within its exclusive competence, the Community shall take action, in accordance with the principle of subsidiarity, only if and in so far as the objectives of the proposed action cannot be sufficiently achieved by the Member States and can therefore, by reason of the scale or effects of the proposed action, be better achieved by the Community." *Treaty on the European Union* (Luxembourg: Office for Official Publications of the European Communities, 1992). For more on the concept of subsidiarity see, for example, Rudolf Hbrek, ed., *Das Subsidiaritätsprinzip in der Europäischen Union—Bedeutung und Wirkung für ausgewählte Politikbereiche* (Baden-Baden: Nomos, 1995); Centre for Economic Policy Research, *Making Sense of Subsidiarity.*

44. For some background on soft law see Tadeusz Gruchalla-Wesierski, "A Framework for Understanding Soft Law," *McGill Law Journal,* vol. 30 (1984), p. 37; C. M. Chinkin, "The Challenge of Soft Law: Development and Change in International Law," *International and Comparative Law Quarterly,* vol. 38 (October 1989), pp. 850–66.

45. For an earlier discussion of structural and functional subsidiarity see Wolfgang H. Reinicke, *Building a New Europe: The Challenge of System Transformation and Systemic Reform* (Brookings, 1992).

46. Wolfgang H. Reinicke, "Democratic Legitimacy and Transparency of Multilateral Institutions," paper presented at a symposium on "Longer-Term Multilateral Cooperation: Managing a Globalizing Economy," sponsored by the European Commission, DG-I (Brussels, December 8, 1993).

47. Some policymakers may welcome the possibility of regulatory arbitrage, so that outmoded public policies can be eliminated through a process of competitive deregulation, and policymakers can externalize the political costs by blaming it on other countries. This is a dangerous strategy because it only fuels existing antiglobalization sentiment. Getting rid of unnecessary and cumbersome public policies, however, could be one of the goals of global public policy itself.

48. See Jessica T. Mathews, "Power Shift," *Foreign Affairs,* vol. 76, no. 1 (January-February 1997), pp. 50–66; James Cameron and Ruth Mackenzie, "State Sovereignty, Non-Governmental Organizations and Multilateral Institutions," paper prepared for the Council on Foreign Relations Study Group on Sovereignty, Non-State Actors and a New World Politics, January 30, 1995. Nongovernmental organizations were, however, "less successful in ensuring that their goals were reflected in the convention," according to Jill Jäger, "The Lessons, Impacts and Implications of the Role of Non-State Actors in the Climate Treaty," paper presented to the Council on Foreign Relations Study Group on Sovereignty, Non-State Actors and a New World Politics, March 1995.

49. For a discussion of the potential role of foundations in this process see Wolfgang H. Reinicke, "Cooperation among Foundations," in Volcker Then, ed., *The Work of Operative Foundations: Strategies—Instruments—Perspectives* (Gütersloh, Germany: Bertelsmann Foundation Publishers, 1997). A prominent example from the United States is foundations. For some background see Lester M. Salamon and Helmut K. Anheier, *The Emerging Nonprofit Sector: An Overview* (Manchester University Press, 1996).

50. Exemplary here is the U.S. Environmental Protection Agency's program to trade rights to sulfur dioxide emissions, which has reduced annual emissions by about 50 percent at two-thirds of the costs of previous regulation.

51. For some background material see Leo M. Loll and Julian G. Buckley, *The Over-the-Counter Securities Markets*, 4th ed. (Prentice Hall, 1981); *The NASDAQ Handbook: The Stock Market for the Next 100 Years* (Chicago: Probus, 1992); NASD, *National Association of Securities Dealers: An Introduction* (Washington, 1992). On mixed regulation see, for example, Franklin R. Edwards, "Futures Markets in Transition: The Uneasy Balance between Government and Self-Regulation," *Journal of Futures Markets*, vol. 3, no. 2 (1983), pp. 191–202; Todd E. Petzel, "Self Regulation and Futures Markets: Benefits from Technology Gains," in Anthony Saunders and Lawrence White, eds., *Technology and the Regulation of Financial Markets: Securities, Futures, and Banking* (Lexington, Mass.: Lexington Books, 1986).

52. The NASD was created in 1938 under the Maloney Act, as an amendment to the Securities Exchange Act of 1934.

53. David Garvin, "Can Industry Self-Regulation Work?" *California Management Review*, vol. 25, no. 4 (Summer 1983), pp. 46–47; Marianne K. Smythe, "Government Supervised Self-Regulation in the Securities Industry and the Antitrust Laws: Suggestions for an Accommodation," *North Carolina Law Review*, vol. 62 (1984), p. 503.

54. These data include records of any denial of membership or registration and of any disciplinary action taken against, or sanction imposed upon, a broker; records of any denial, suspension, expulsion, or revocation of membership or registration of any member, broker, or dealer with whom the broker was associated; and records of any arrests, indictments, or convictions for any other misdemeanor. Detailed records of all NASD-registered representatives are maintained in the NASD's Central Registration Depository (CRD) system, which the public can consult using a toll-free telephone number. See John F. Wasik, "How to Check out a Broker," *Barron's*, vol. 71, no. 2 (January 14, 1991), p. 24; "Investigating Broker' Histories Is Easier, But Not Foolproof Yet," *Wall Street Journal*, October 4, 1991, p. 1. The database maintains files on more than 5,700 firms and 417,000 individuals who are currently active. "NASD Slaps Increasingly Stiff Penalties on Stockbrokers Who Cheat Customers," *Wall Street Journal*, February 4, 1991, p. 6.

55. The system records all over-the-counter stock transactions; between 1978 and 1995 the annual volume of shares traded through NASDAQ increased from 3.7 billion to 101.2 trillion. See "Computer Cop Stakes out OTC Trading," *Computer World*, June 11, 1990, p. 25. The system has been under development for more than twenty years, and the NASD has an almost continuous mandate to improve and expand its capacity. John Desmond, "Mapping the Real, Comparing to Real: NASD Pursues Top-Down Development to Save Time, Money," *Software*, vol. 12, no. 1 (January 1992), pp. 46–47; "Network Security Lacking at Major Stock Exchanges," *Network World*, September 16, 1991, pp. 23–24.

56. The system is called Stock Watch Automated Tracking (SWAT). During 1996 (through November 30) the system monitored approximately 346,000 trades and 230,000 price quotes on average each day. The historical trading patterns of over 5,400 NASDAQ member firms are recorded on the system. In 1995 SWAT was aug-

mented by the Research and Data Analysis Repository (RADAR), which was designed to increase the system's speed and flexibility.

57. Each day the model issues as many as eighty to ninety alerts. The system then ranks the alerts according to how suspicious the activity appears. At the same time, news stories appear on the analysts' screens, fed to their workstations by a subsystem that monitors dispatches from four commercial wire services and automatically picks out those mentioning NASDAQ companies. Relevant news stories are automatically downloaded to a database, from which analysts can retrieve current and past news stories or headlines using the company's trading symbol. See "Computer Cop Stakes out OTC Trading," p. 25.

58. By measuring the relationship between set parameter values and case outcomes through logistic regression analysis, the system can identify which indicators are the most significant, suggest parameter settings that best discriminate between true exceptions and reasonable activity patterns, and reflect the composite effect of a set of indicators to ensure that a critical mixture of smaller effects is duly detected. See Samuel G. Davis and J. Keith Ord, "Improving and Measuring the Performance of a Securities Industry Surveillance System," *Interface,* vol. 20, no. 5 (September-October 1990), p. 40.

59. In addition, in 1995 disciplinary action initiated and acted upon by the NASD's compliance and arbitration committees, which are composed of industry members, led to nine firms' being suspended and eight firms' being expelled from membership, respectively; 196 individuals were suspended and 412 individuals were barred from the industry. NASD, *1995 Annual Report to Members* (Washington, 1996), p. 3; see also Davis, Samuel, and Ord, "Improving and Measuring the Performance of a Securities Industry Surveillance System," p. 33.

60. Also known as the Christie-Schultz study, the report presented evidence of what the authors claimed was price fixing by market makers. Central to their contention was the observation that market makers seemed to be quoting prices only in even eighths (excluding 1/8 and 3/8, etc.), thereby ensuring minimum spreads of a quarter point. The only explanation the authors could find for this pricing practice was collusion among a cartel of market makers to keep spreads artificially wide. As further evidence, the authors noted that, after publication of their initial paper, spreads in some large stocks suddenly narrowed. See William G. Christie and Paul H. Schultz, "Why do NASDAQ Market Makers Avoid Odd-Eighth Quotes?" *Journal of Finance,* vol. 49, no. 5 (December 1994), pp. 1813–40. Market makers have also come under scrutiny for a number of other irregular practices. They have been accused of not immediately disclosing large transactions that could affect stock prices; such behavior would be in contravention of NASD rules. Market makers are also suspected of offering better prices to other market makers than to investors. If true, this might represent a violation of a broker's legal obligation to his or her customers.

61. See, for example, Maggie Urry, "Questions over Youth's Behavior," *Financial Times,* August 23, 1995, p. 9; Jerry Knight, "Who's Being Helped?" *Washington Post,* September 3, 1995, p. H1; Jeffrey Taylor and Molly Baker, "U.S. Sets Target Date for NASDAQ Inquiry," *Wall Street Journal,* June 2, 1995, p. C1; Jeffrey Taylor and Molly Baker, "SEC Weighs Filing Disciplinary Case against NASD on Alleged Dealer Abuses," *Wall Street Journal,* July 10, 1995, p. A4.

62. Warren Getler and William Power, "Street Insiders Set to Review NASDAQ Market," *Wall Street Journal,* November 21, 1994, p. C1.

63. See, for example, George Graham and Maggy Urry, "NASDAQ Set for Overhaul of System," *Financial Times,* September 20, 1995, p. 5, London edition; Jerry Knight, "Panel Advocates Changes in NASDAQ," *Washington Post,* September 20, 1995, p. C1.

64. As the report noted, the NASD has a staff of 26 attorneys and 365 examiners in its regional branches to handle complaints involving more than half a million people working in 57,000 brokerage offices. This has led to a situation where some NASD regional offices do not even make a follow-up phone call to some investors who file complaints accusing brokers of violating stock market rules or federal securities laws. See Jerry Knight, "NASD Orders Investor Complaints Probed," *Washington Post,* September 29, 1995, p. B1.

65. Jerry Knight, "NASD to Be Split into Two Units," *Washington Post,* November 18, 1995, p. F1.

66. William Power, "NASDAQ To Have Fewer 'Public' Directors Than Expected, But Percentages Will Rise," *Wall Street Journal,* September 27, 1995, p. A4; Jerry Knight, "NASD to Give Public Bigger Oversight Role," *Washington Post,* November 1, 1995, p. F1.

67. At present it is projected to increase from $76 million in 1994 to $100 million in 1996, with further increases expected. Linda Bransten, "Boost for Tech Stocks Leads Equities Higher," *Financial Times,* May 16, 1996, p. 41.

68. Jerry Knight, "NASD Wants Schapiro to Head New Regulatory Subsidiary," *Washington Post,* November 10, 1995, p. B1.

69. Jeffrey Taylor and William Power, "Rule Changes on OTC Quotes; Public Would Be Given Same Access to Prices NASDAQ Dealers Have," *Wall Street Journal,* September 25, 1995, p. A4; "Wall Street Formally Gets New NASDAQ Rules," *Wall Street Journal,* September 28, 1995, p. C1.

70. United States of America before the Securities and Exchange Commission, Securities Exchange Act of 1934, Release no. 37538/August 8, 1996, Administrative Proceeding File No. 3-9056; for the full report see SEC, *Report Pursuant to Section 21(a) of the Securities and Exchange Act of 1934 Regarding the NASD and the NASDAQ Market* (Washington, August 8, 1996). On the NASD's effort to soften the SEC's criticism see Deborah Lohse and Jeffrey Taylor, "NASD Is Urging SEC to Tone Down Criticism in Accord," *Wall Street Journal,* July 25, 1996, p. C24.

71. See United States of America before the Securities and Exchange Commission, Release no. 37538.

72. Attorney General Janet Reno at a news conference. See Maggie Urry, "NASDAQ Securities Firms Avoid Price-Fixing Charges," *Financial Times,* July 18, 1996, p. 12.

73. Deborah Lohse and Anita Raghavan, "Your Money Matters: Will NASDAQ Accord lead to Better Prices for Investors?" *Wall Street Journal,* July 18, 1996.

74. For some of the reactions to the various settlements see Jerry Knight, "NASD to Be Split into Two Units, New Agency," *Washington Post,* November 18, 1995, p. F1; Jerry Knight, "Panel Advocates Changes in NASDAQ," *Washington Post,* September 20, 1995, p. C1; Brett D. Fromson, "Settlement Ends NASDAQ Price Probe," *Washington Post,* July 18, 1996, p. A1.

75. Wolfgang H. Reinicke, *Deepening the Atlantic: Toward a New Transatlantic Marketplace?* (Gütersloh, Germany: Bertelsmann Foundation Publishers, 1996).

76. On the problem of information asymmetries and ways to reduce them see Wolfgang H. Reinicke, "Cooperative Security and the Political Economy of Nonproliferation," in Janne E. Nolan, ed., *Global Engagement: Cooperation and Security in the 21st Century* (Brookings, 1994), pp. 175–234.

77. On the importance of business in gathering technical information, see Garten, *A Cold Peace,* p. 71.

78. For an earlier, brief exposition of disclosure-based regulation see Wolfgang H. Reinicke, "From Denial to Disclosure: The Political Economy of Export Controls and Technology Transfer," in Francine R. Frankel, ed., *Bridging the Nonproliferation Divide: The United States and India* (University Press of America, 1995), pp. 269–86.

79. "Sovereignty and the WTO," *Washington Post,* p. A16.

80. In doing so, however, one should be careful not to reject all solutions that fall short of an ideal model of democracy, which does not exist and never has existed even at the domestic level. A more fruitful approach is to follow Dahl's concept of polyarchy, and identify important indicators of democracy that should be embedded in the operational and administrative structures of international institutions. See Robert Dahl, *Polyarchy: Participation and Opposition* (Yale University Press, 1971); on measuring polyarchy and its indicators see Michael Coppedge and Wolfgang H. Reinicke, "Measuring Polyarchy," *Studies in Comparative International Development,* vol. 25, no. 1 (Spring 1990), pp. 51–72.

81. Ralph Nader, "Trade in Secrets," *Washington Post,* October 6, 1994, p. A31; Ralph Nader and Lori Wallach, "GATT, NAFTA, and the Subversion of the Democratic Process," in Jerry Mander and Edward Goldsmith, eds., *The Case against the Global Economy: And for a Turn toward the Local* (San Francisco: Sierra Club Books, 1996); see also "The World Trade Organization at 27 Months: A Sampling of the Damage and Dangers So Far," *Public Citizen's Global Trade Watch,* April 1997.

82. For more information on the role of nongovernmental organizations, see Ann Marie Clark, "Nongovernmental Organizations and Their Influence on International Society (Transcending National Boundaries)" *Journal of International Affairs,* vol. 48, no. 2 (Winter 1995), pp. 507–25; Robert Livernash, "The Growing Influence of NGOs in the Developing World," *Environment,* vol. 34, no. 5 (June 1992), pp. 12–20; Shirin Sinnar, "Mixed Blessing: The Growing Influence of NGOs," *Harvard International Review,* vol. 28, no. 1 (Winter 1996/1997), pp. 54–57; Hugo Slim, "To the Rescue: Radicals or Poodles?" vol. 53, no. 8–9 (August 1997), pp. 209–17; Peter J. Spiro, "New Global Communities: Nongovernmental Organizations in International Decisionmaking Institutions (Sovereignty at Bay)" *Washington Quarterly,* vol. 18, no. 1 (Winter 1995), pp. 45–57; Thomas G. Weiss and Leon Gordenker, *NGOs, the UN, and Global Governance* (Boulder, Colo.: Lynne Rienner, 1996).

CHAPTER 4

1. For some background information and overview of these challenges, see Wolfgang H. Reinicke, "Regulatory Challenges of Global Financial Integration: The Basle

Agreement and Beyond," paper prepared for the Council on Foreign Relations Study Group on Sovereignty, Non-State Actors, and a New World Politics, April 27, 1995.

2. Strictly speaking, private sector financial institutions are nongovernmental organizations. Since these institutions are the only private sector organizations that have become involved in the debate on global public policy, and to avoid confusion with other nongovernmental organizations, they are referred to here as nonstate actors.

3. The Group of Ten (G-10) countries are Belgium, Canada, France, Germany, Italy, Japan, the Netherlands, Sweden, United Kingdom, and the United States. The objectives of the Basle Committee are to provide a forum for bank supervisory officials to exchange information about their regulatory structures, and to strengthen collaboration among national authorities in their supervision of international banking. The committee acts as an advisory body whose recommendations require unanimous agreement of its representatives. It has no power to require implementation of its agreements in the laws or regulations of its member nations. However, U.S. federal bank supervisory agencies, as well as bank supervisory agencies in other countries, have committed themselves to work to implement the principles established by the committee.

4. For the text of the Accord, see Basle Committee on Banking Supervision, *International Convergence of Capital Measurement and Capital Standards* (Basle: Bank for International Settlements, July 1988).

5. George Blunden, "International Co-operation in Banking Supervision," *Quarterly Bulletin* (Bank of England, September 1977), vol. 17, pp. 325–29.

6. The most important of these bank failures were those of the Herstatt Bank in the Federal Republic of Germany and the Franklin National Bank in the United States.

7. Peter Cooke, "Developments in Co-operation among Banking Supervisory Authorities," *Quarterly Bulletin* (Bank of England, June 1981), vol. 21, p. 238; Blunden, "International Co-operation in Banking Supervision."

8. These principles are embedded in two agreements referred to as the original and the revised Basle Concordat. The original concordat, adopted in December of 1975, represented an important step toward greater international supervisory cooperation. However, it suffered from a number of deficiencies, which became apparent after 1978 and culminated in a conflict among regulatory authorities over culpability in the collapse of Banco Ambrosiano's Luxembourg subsidiary in 1983. Regulators reacted quickly and adopted a revised concordat, with more precise guidelines for supervision, in June 1983. For more on the topic see Richard Dale, "Basle Concordat: Lessons from Ambrosiano," *Banker,* vol. 133, no. 691 (September 1983), pp. 55–60, and "Safeguarding the International Banking System," *Banker*, vol. 132, no. 678 (August 1982), pp. 49–56.

9. Basle Committee on Banking Supervision, *Minimum Standards for the Supervision of International Banking Groups and Their Cross Border Establishments* (Basle, July 1992), in *Compendium of Documents Produced by the Basle Committee on Banking Supervision, Volume Three—International Supervisory Issues*, April 1997, pp. 23–28.

10. Pierre Jaans, "Measuring Capital and Liquidity Adequacy for International Banking Business," *Record of Proceedings*, International Conference of Banking Supervisors, London, July 5–6, 1979; J. J. Norton, "The Work of the Basle Supervi-

sors Committee on Bank Capital Adequacy and the July 1988 Report on International Convergence of Capital Measurement and Capital Standards," *International Lawyer,* vol. 23, no. 1 (Spring 1989), pp. 245–69.

11. Blunden, "International Co-operation in Banking Supervision," p. 326.

12. Michael C. Keeley, "Bank Capital Regulation in the 1980s: Effective or Ineffective?" *Economic Review* (Federal Reserve Bank of San Francisco, Winter 1988), no. 1, pp. 3–20.

13. Larry D. Wall, "Capital Requirements for Banks: A Look at the 1981 and the 1988 Standards," *Economic Review* (Federal Reserve Bank of Atlanta, March-April 1989), vol. 74, pp. 14–29; Alan Marcus, "The Bank Capital Decision: A Time Series-Cross Section Analysis," *Journal of Finance,* vol. 38 (September 1983), pp. 1217–32. Among the large commercial banks, the proportion of bank capital to total assets declined from around 10 percent in the early 1950s to 5 percent by the mid-1970s. Federal Financial Institutions Examination Council, *Capital Trends in Federally Regulated Financial Institutions* (Washington, 1980); Yair E. Orgler and Benjamin Wolkowitz, *Bank Capital* (New York: Van Nostrand Reinhold Co., 1976).

14. More than twenty banks with assets of over $50 million failed during the 1970s. Among them were four banks with assets of over $1 billion. The Bank of Commonwealth in Detroit, U.S. National Bank in San Diego, Franklin National Bank in New York, and Security National Bank in Hempstead, New York, were either aided or merged to prevent failure (in the cases of Commonwealth and Security National) or taken over by other banking institutions following foreclosure (U.S. National and Franklin National). The FDIC's bailout in April 1980 of the First Pennsylvania Bank, with over $8.4 billion in assets, raised the total assets of banks requiring assistance to over $20 billion. Sherman J. Maisel, ed., *Risk and Capital Adequacy in Commercial Banks* (University of Chicago Press, 1981); Joan Edelman Spero, *The Failure of the Franklin National Bank: Challenge to the International Banking System* (Columbia University Press, 1980).

15. Wall, "Capital Requirements for Banks," pp. 14–29.

16. The nine largest U.S. banks had lent over 140 percent of their capital, or $30 billion, to Argentina, Brazil, and Mexico.

17. *International Debt,* Hearings before the Subcommittee on International Finance and Monetary Policy of the Senate Committee on Banking, Housing, and Urban Affairs, 98 Cong., 1 sess. (Government Printing Office, February 17, 1983), p. 239.

18. In February 1983 the First National Bank of Bellaire, Texas, successfully challenged the regulators' authority to impose explicit capital requirements and to issue a cease-and-desist order if the bank did not comply.

19. *International Financial Markets and Related Matters*, Hearings before the House Committee on Banking, Finance, and Urban Affairs, 98 Cong., 1 sess. (GPO, December 21, 1983).

20. *International Financial Markets and Related Problems,* Hearings before the Senate Committee on Banking, Housing, and Urban Affairs, 98 Cong., 1 sess. (GPO, February 2, 1983).

21. *International Debt*, Hearings; *International Financial Markets and Related Problems,* Hearings.

22. International Lending Supervision Act of 1983, Pub. L. no. 98-181, sec. 908 (b)(3)(C), 97 Stat. 1281 in *United States Statutes at Large Containing the Laws and Concurrent Resolutions Enacted during the First Session of the 98th Congress of the United States of America 1983*, vol. 97 (GPO, 1985).

23. Norton, "The Work of the Basle Supervisors Committee on Bank Capital Adequacy"; Jeffrey Bardos, "The Risk-Based Capital Agreement: A Further Step Towards Policy Convergence," *Quarterly Review* (Federal Reserve Bank of New York, Winter 1987–88), vol. 12, no. 4, pp. 26–34; Basle Committee on Banking Regulations and Supervisory Practices, *Report on International Developments in Banking Supervision 1983* (Basle, 1984).

24. Bank for International Settlements, *Fifty-Sixth Annual Report 1985–1986* (Basle, June 9, 1986); David Lascelles, "The Battle to Keep Tabs in the Face of Rapid Change," *Financial Times,* April 21, 1986, p. I15. When banking supervisors from around the world met for their fourth international conference in October 1986, capital adequacy was the major theme. Stressing the importance of convergence toward higher standards of capital adequacy, H. J. Müller, chairman of the Basle Committee and executive director of the Netherlands' central bank, presented the current status of the Basle Committee's work on this issue. See H. J. Müller, "Capital and Risk," paper presented to the Fourth International Conference of Banking Supervisors, Amsterdam, October 22–23, 1986.

25. Press Release, Fourth International Conference of Banking Supervisors, Amsterdam, October 22–23, 1986; David Lascelles, "World Bankers Debate Regulation," *Financial Times,* October 22, 1986, p. 38.

26. Bardos, "The Risk-Based Capital Agreement"; Basle Committee on Banking Regulations and Supervisory Practices, *Report on International Developments in Banking Supervision 1983.*

27. Statement of Carleton R. Haswell, Senior Vice President, Chemical Bank, in *Review of the International Lending Supervision Act of 1983,* Hearings before the Subcommittee on International Finance and Monetary Policy of the Senate Committee on Banking, Housing, and Urban Affairs, 99 Cong., 2 sess. (GPO, June 25, 1986).

28. David S. Holland, "Foreign Bank Capital and the United States Federal Reserve Board," *International Lawyer,* vol. 20, no. 3 (Summer 1986), pp. 785–818.

29. British regulators were in the midst of revising their own system of capital regulation and were eager both to move forward with the implementation of a revised rule and to address the issue of competitive inequality. In the fall of 1986, regulators in the United States and the United Kingdom agreed to develop a common approach to the issue of capital adequacy. Given the importance of New York and London as international banking centers, regulators felt that an agreement on a uniform risk-based capital framework implemented in both countries would represent a major step forward toward international convergence. Bardos, "The Risk-Based Capital Agreement."

30. The agreement is reprinted in *Quarterly Bulletin* (Bank of England, February 1987), vol. 27, no. 1, pp. 87–93; for an in-depth discussion of the agreement see the Federal Reserve Board's staff report in "US-British Proposal for Risk-Based Capital," three-part series, *American Banker* (January 14, 15, 20, 1987), respectively, p. 9, 4, and 32. One reason for this rapid convergence of supervisory perspectives was that the Federal Reserve had considered, and thus was familiar with, the risk-based capital

approach the Bank of England had adopted when it revised its own risk-weighting scheme in early 1986. However, observers also admitted that no one had expected the conclusion of an agreement within such a short time. They concurred that the agreement reflected the concern and the increasing urgency felt by regulatory authorities in the two countries over the soundness of global financial markets, as well as pressure from the private sectors in the two countries to deal with the competitive inequalities arising from regulatory inequities in a single global financial market.

31. For further discussion of the accord, see Allen Murray-Jones and David Spencer, "The US/UK Proposal on Capital Adequacy," *International Financial Law Review,* vol. 6, no. 9 (1987), pp. 20–23; Steve Mintz, "International Banking: United States–United Kingdom Capital Adequacy Agreement," *Harvard International Law Journal,* vol. 28, no. 2 (Spring 1987), pp. 499–506. Not all member countries of the Basle Committee, let alone the committee itself, were enthusiastic about the bilateral accord. According to Cooke, the agreement at first appeared to be counterproductive to the multilateral objectives of the Basle Committee. See Peter Cooke, "International Convergence of Capital Adequacy Standards," in Edward Gardener, ed., *The Future of Financial Systems and Services: Essays in Honor of Jack Revell* (St. Martin's Press, 1990), pp. 310–35. Markus Lusser, the vice chairman of the governing board of the Swiss National Bank, saw the agreement as " . . . political pressure by the economic superpowers. . . . [A]t least in the representative of a small country the agreement between the United Kingdom and the United States arouses somewhat mixed feelings. . . . Should the example set a precedent and the strategy of the two powers be extended to other fields of harmonizing banking supervision — as a substitute, so to speak, for internationally negotiated compromises — then the willingness to co-operate internationally could suffer damage in the long run. In view of the problems that need to be solved, this would be a harmful development." Speech delivered in Boppard am Rhein, Germany, March 13, 1987.

32. *Risk-Based Capital Requirements for Banks and Bank Holding Companies,* Hearings before the Subcommittee on General Oversight and Investigations of the House Committee on Banking, Finance, and Urban Affairs, 100 Cong., 1 sess. (GPO, 1987), p. 9.

33. It was clear to the U.S. and British regulators that some compromise was necessary, and they indicated to the other countries that they were willing to make some adjustments to accommodate other regulatory regimes, reflecting different national perspectives on capital and its regulation. For example, Gerald Corrigan, president of the Federal Reserve Bank of New York, which had been instrumental in achieving the accord, stated only a few weeks after the agreement that "it is an approach which can be easily adapted to future developments as they occur." Remarks before the Overseas Bankers Club Annual Banquet, London, February 2, 1987.

34. Basle Committee on Bank Supervision, *Risk-Based Capital Requirements for Banks and Bank Holding Companies* (Basle, April 30, 1987). The Committee was aware that the United States and the United Kingdom were trying to come to an agreement with Japan, and there was some fear that once a trilateral agreement had been reached, other countries' banks could be barred from the three most important financial centers, which would be a major blow to their ability to remain competitive. They therefore pressured their governments to cooperate internationally. See also Markus Lusser, speech delivered in Boppard am Rhein, March 13, 1987.

35. As mentioned previously, each country had its own definition of regulatory capital. Each definition reflected a different set of country-specific accounting practices, banking activities, and supervisory philosophies. Moreover, the slightest change in the definition of capital could greatly affect measured capital ratios within the banking system and thus alter the market's perception of the financial strength of banking organizations in that system.

36. Japanese banks maintain sizable unrealized gains on their equity positions. These unrealized gains have traditionally been realized when necessary to offset losses. In fact, Japanese regulators had recently introduced new capital guidelines to bring their capital standards more in line with those of the other major industrialized countries. The new guidelines also explicitly recognized these gains (also referred to as hidden reserves) as a form of capital and allowed banks to include 70 percent of unrealized gains as capital. Other member countries did not recognize hidden reserves at all, which created a major obstacle to early conclusion of an agreement. Under the guidelines issued in May 1986, Japanese banks were required to raise their capital-to-asset ratios to 4 percent by 1992. Banks with overseas branches were required to raise their capital-to-asset ratios to 6 percent by April 1987. General Accounting Office, *Market Access Concerns of U.S. Financial Institutions in Japan*, GAO/NSIAD-88-108BR (Washington, 1988); Bardos, "The Risk-Based Capital Agreement."

37. In response to Japan's efforts in the mid-1980s to capture a share of the U.S. financial market, both on the corporate and on the consumer side, U.S. and Japanese regulatory authorities had agreed on a set of financial disclosure measures required for banks on one country applying to set up subsidiaries in the other. Invoking this agreement, the Federal Reserve in early 1987 demanded that five Japanese banks supply such information. More important, the Federal Reserve asked the banks to furnish data on their capital structures in line with the capital adequacy rules and definitions of primary capital on which the U.S. and U.K. bank regulators had agreed.

38. Cooke, "International Convergence of Capital Adequacy Standards."

39. Bank for International Settlements, *Fifty-Seventh Annual Report 1986–87* (Basle, 15 June 1987), p. 87.

40. This represented a clear shift away from a sole emphasis on competition in international financial markets toward a focus on the equivalent need for cooperation. This was notwithstanding the fact that cooperation as a process occurred on competitive terms (see below for more information).

41. A consultative paper was issued for banking associations from the member countries, supervisory authorities outside the G-10 countries, and other interested parties. Basle Committee on Banking Regulations and Supervisory Practices, *Report on International Developments in Banking Supervision*, no. 6 (Basle, 1987).

42. Pub. L. 98-181, November 30, 1983, Section 908(3)(C).

43. Robert Guenther, "Banking—A Special Report: Big U.S. Banks May Have to Shrink to Satisfy New Capital Standards," *Wall Street Journal*, April 7, 1988.

44. "Banks Across Borders," *Washington Post*, May 8, 1988, p. B6.

45. It has been represented through individual financial institutions and their trade associations (both domestic, such as the American Bankers Association, and international, such as the Institute of International Bankers and the Institute of Inter-

national Finance, as well as through such organizations as the Group of Thirty, which has achieved clout and legitimacy in the policymaking process thanks to its diverse membership, comprised of former public sector officials, academic experts, and representatives of the private sector. In the United States there were some differences in preferred policy between small and large commercial banks, but they did not directly influence the negotiations in the Basle Committee.

46. The lower the risk weight attached to an asset type, the less capital a bank has to hold when it holds assets of that type. An asset assigned a weight of zero percent is therefore more attractive for a bank to hold than an asset that produces an identical return but carries a risk weight of 50 or 100 percent. By attaching a weight of zero percent to debt issued by member governments of the Organization for Economic Cooperation and Development, the Basle Accord—whether deliberately or not—created a bias in favor of public (in other words, their own) debt. Mortgages, on the other hand, were assigned a weight of 50 percent. For these to be equally attractive for banks to hold, they had to generate a much higher return than government debt. This ultimately made mortgages more expensive for customers. Some have also argued that risk-weighting schemes do not favor traditional loans, which is disadvantageous to medium-size companies. See Ethan Kapstein, *Supervising International Banks: Origins and Implications of the Basle Accord* (Princeton University Press, 1991), p. 29.

47. Wolfgang H. Reinicke, "Democratic Legitimacy and Transparency of Multilateral Institutions," paper prepared for a seminar on "Longer-Term Multilateral Cooperation: Managing a Globalizing Economy," sponsored by the European Commission, Directorate General I (Brussels, December 8, 1993).

48. Wolfgang H. Reinicke, "Integrating the World Economy: Economics Is Not Enough," in Klaus Schwab, ed., *Overcoming Indifference: Ten Key Challenges in Today's Changing World* (New York University Press, 1995), pp. 224–28.

49. In setting the secondary capital requirement, countries were free to use as many or as few of the noncore elements as they wished. If they preferred, countries could even use additional core capital to fulfill the requirement.

50. Some problems have arisen in the interpretation of the agreement, however. First, regarding the composition of tier-two capital, "investment bankers and others have not been slow in designing new capital instruments designed for inclusion in tier 1 or tier 2." Basle Committee on Banking Regulations and Supervisory Practices, *Report on International Developments in Banking Supervision,* no. 7 (Basle, 1988), p. 12. Although the committee agreed that in most instances the interpretation could be left to national supervisors, a number of cases may have led to conflict due to the creation of competitive inequalities. This led members to set up "mechanisms for reaching agreed solutions."

51. U.S. regulators had long debated the issue of capital adequacy among themselves, but there was substantial disagreement among the Federal Reserve, the Office of the Comptroller of the Currency, and the FDIC about the details of policy. This situation led to the familiar interagency bureaucratic and regulatory competition, in which Congress was unable or unwilling to intervene. On bureaucratic competition among regulators see Wolfgang H. Reinicke, "Consolidation of Federal Bank Regulation?" *Challenge,* vol. 37, no. 3 (May-June 1994), pp. 23–29. For a detailed analy-

sis of the domestic politics of capital adequacy regulation see Wolfgang H. Reinicke, *Banking, Politics and Global Finance: American Commercial Banks and Regulatory Change, 1980–1990* (Aldershot, England: Edward Elgar Publishing, 1995).

52. This is notwithstanding the fact that far broader measures will be necessary to ensure financial stability. See Edward J. Kane, "Difficulties of Transferring Risk-Based Capital Requirements to Developing Countries," Policy Research Working Paper 1244 (Washington: World Bank, January 1994); Claudia Dziobek, Olivier Frécaut, and María Nieto, "Non-G-10 Countries and the Basle Capital Rules: How Tough a Challenge is it to Joint The Basle Club?" IMF Paper on Policy Analysis and Assessment (Washington, 1995).

53. As the Committee's 1990 report states, "The market itself has imposed its own disciplines. Banks have found a distinct advantage in being able to satisfy the rating agencies and the market generally that their capital was adequate in terms of the final Basle standard . . . ." Basle Committee on Banking Regulations and Supervisory Practices, *Report on International Developments in Banking Supervision,* no. 9 (Basle, 1990), p. 11.

54. Wolfgang H. Reinicke, "Globalization, Public Policy and the Private Sector: Are They Compatible?" paper prepared for the annual meeting of the World Economic Forum (Davos, Switzerland, January 30, 1995).

55. Edward Kane, "Accelerating Inflation, Technological Innovation, and the Decreasing Effectiveness of Banking Regulation," *Journal of Finance,* vol. 36 (May 1981), pp. 355–67.

56. Johann Wilhelm Gaddum, "Financial Conglomerates—a Challenge for Supervisors," address to the Sixth International Conference of Bank Supervisors, Frankfurt, October 10–12, 1990, p. 72.

57. John Gapper, "Self-Calculation of Risks for Banks Is Urged by Watchdog," *Financial Times,* April 13, 1995, p. 22.

58. Among the seven largest U.S. money center banks, interest income declined, on average, from 70 percent of total revenue at the end of 1987 to less than 50 percent at the end of 1993. By contrast, income from trading activities more than doubled, from about 6 percent to over 13 percent, and fee income increased from 12 percent to about 18 percent. By the end of 1992 the notional principal of interest rate swaps held off the balance sheet by these banks amounted to $1.7 trillion, almost double their total balance sheet assets. These changes reflected the increasing concentration of bank activities in over-the-counter derivative transactions. See David Folkerts-Landau and Takatoshi Ito, *International Capital Markets: Developments, Prospects, and Policy Issues* (Washington: International Monetary Fund, August 1995).

59. Credit risk considers the possibility that a counterparty might default on its obligations; market risk is that due to unexpected general market price and interest rate changes; operational risk is that due to human error, fraud, or the lack of internal controls.

60. Basle Committee on Banking Supervision, "The Prudential Supervision of Netting, Market Risks and Interest Rate Risk" (Basle, April 1993); Basle Committee on Banking Supervision, "The Supervisory Recognition of Netting for Capital Adequacy Purposes" (Basle, April 1993); Basle Committee on Banking Supervision, "The Supervisory Treatment of Market Risks" (Basle, April 1993); Basle Committee

on Banking Supervision, "Measurement of Banks' Exposure to Interest Rate Risk" (Basle, April 1993).

61. In particular, private sector critics objected to the proposal of a standardized framework to be adopted by all banks. For a summary of these often highly technical criticisms see Folkerts-Landau and Ito, *International Capital Markets,* pp. 138–41; see also Gapper, "Self-Calculation of Risks for Banks Is Urged by Watchdog."

62. Basle Committee on Banking Supervision, "Proposal to Issue a Supplement to the Basle Capital Accord to Cover Market Risks" (Basle, April 1995); Basle Committee on Banking Supervision, "An Internal Model-Based Approach to Market Risk Capital Requirements" (Basle, April 1995); Basle Committee on Banking Supervision, "Planned Supplement to the Capital Accord to Incorporate Market Risks" (Basle, April 1995). At the same time, however, banks would be required to use a common approach to measure risk, the so-called value-at-risk approach. Value-at-risk is an estimate, to a certain level of confidence, of the maximum possible loss in value of a portfolio or financial position over a given period of time. The Group of Thirty had previously recommended such an approach. See Group of Thirty, *Derivatives: Practices and Principles* (Washington, 1993). However, many different models and estimation methods can be used to calculate value-at-risk. See Folkerts-Landau and Ito, *International Capital Markets,* pp. 141–43.

63. Essentially VAR models measure the sensitivity of a bank to losses from past market movements and use complex computer models to assess the probability of such losses occurring in the future, taking into account correlations in the performance of different financial instruments. (This is the technique used by banks to try and diversify risk by offsetting involvement in one market with a roughly equal involvement in other markets that historically perform in the opposite fashion.)

64. John Gapper, "Basle Model for Banking Safeguards," *Financial Times,* April 13, 1995, p. 31.

65. These estimation parameters are more stringent than those used by banks themselves (a 95 percent probability and a one-day holding period).

66. Laurie Morse, "ISDA Says BIS Risk Model Plans Should Be Revised," *Financial Times,* August 4, 1995, p. 26.

67. Basle Committee on Banking Supervision, "Overview of the Amendment to the Capital Accord to Incorporate Market Risks" (Basle, January 1996), p. 2. Most of the quantitative standards remained intact and thus gave regulators sufficient power to continue to exercise control over banks. Basle Committee on Banking Supervision, "Amendment to the Capital Accord to Incorporate Market Risks" (Basle, January 1996).

68. Basle Committee on Banking Supervision, "Overview of the Amendment to the Capital Accord to Incorporate Market Risks," p. 2. The Committee also demonstrated some flexibility on the use of the plus factor: "The Committee believes that the approach adopted strikes a balance between recognition of the potential limitations of backtesting and the need to put in place a clear and consistent framework that contains incentives to ensure that banks model market risk with integrity. At the same time, the Committee recognizes that the techniques for backtesting are still evolving, and it is committed to incorporating new developments in this area into its framework." See Basle Committee on Banking Supervision, "Overview of the Amend-

ment," p. 5; see also Basle Committee on Banking Supervision, "Supervisory Framework for the Use of 'Backtesting' in Conjunction with the Internal Models Approach to Market Risk Capital Requirements" (Basle, January 1996).

69. George Graham, "Bank Regulators in Capital Rules Row," *Financial Times,* December 13, 1995, p. 4.

70. Gapper, "Basle Model for Banking Safeguards," p. 31.

71. Gapper, "Basle Model for Banking Safeguards," p. 31.

72. Indeed, commenting on the stringency of the outsourcing in the present case, some banks indicated that they would not take advantage of the new approach, and thus rejected the horizontal subsidiarity that was offered to them.

73. Leeson's superiors in London claimed that he was probably involved in a scheme to profit from Barings' demise. An increasing amount of evidence, however, paints a different picture. Investigators sent to Singapore by the Bank of England found no evidence of anyone building a single, large short position against the bank. In fact, it was discovered that the former Barings employee had traded with a number of parties. A more plausible explanation is that Leeson might have been selling call and put options on the Nikkei, betting that the Japanese equities market would fluctuate within a stable range. In the wake of the January 1995 Kobe earthquake, however, the Nikkei moved out of its normal trading range, forcing Leeson to buy contracts to support the market. His exposure increased from less than 5,000 contracts on January 13 to 20,000 by February 17. When Leeson's scheme collapsed, Barings accounted for nearly 20 percent of the open interest in the contract on the exchange and exceeded the level of holdings of the next largest market participant by almost eightfold.

74. Richard Lapper, "The Barings Crisis: Dealers Puzzled over Unusual Futures Strategy—Leeson's Trading Logic," *Financial Times,* March 1, 1995, p. 2.

75. John Gapper, Nicholas Denton, and Peter Marsh, "The Barings Crisis: Chairman's Fraud Allegations Challenged," *Financial Times,* March 1, 1995, p. 2. For at least two reasons, Barings should have known the true extent of Leeson's trading. First, there was the huge $7 billion unmatched position that Leeson took on the Osaka and Singapore exchanges. Brokers in those markets were aware that Barings was amassing large positions. Second, Barings' treasury in London advanced the firm's Singapore operations an estimated £580 million to cover margin calls on Leeson's positions as they fell in value with the Japanese market. The cash transfers should have alerted the bank's directors to the situation. In fact, the transfer of funds had led one banker to speculate that someone in the London office must have been funding the intercompany balance and that Leeson could not have covered up the cash movements as well as the contracts themselves.

76. At that time the head of Barings Securities operations in Singapore alerted the firm's management in London to the potential dangers of having Leeson manage both trading and settlement. In March 1992 he wrote to the head of equities in London, "My concern is that we are in danger of setting up a structure which will subsequently prove disastrous and with which we will succeed in losing either a lot of money or client goodwill or probably both." As quoted in Nikki Tait, "The Barings Crisis: Failure Is Blamed on Management in London," *Financial Times,* March 6, 1995, p. 2. The fact that Leeson had no gross position limits on proprietary trading operations made the potentially dangerous management structure even worse.

77. Richard Lapper, "Work Ahead for Quality Controllers: International Banks Have Some Way to Go in Improving Management of Trading Risks," *Financial Times,* April 12, 1995, p. 19.

78. See Group of Thirty, *Derivatives: Practices and Principles*; for a critical review of current efforts to improve internal risk management see General Accounting Office, *Financial Derivatives: Actions Needed to Protect the Financial System,* GGD-94-13 (Washington, May 18, 1994); see also the response by the International Swaps and Derivatives Association, *The GAO Report on Financial Derivatives: Good Facts and Bad Conclusions* (New York, May 27, 1994); and the GAO's rebuttal in the form of testimony by James Bothwell, Director, Financial Institutions and Markets Issues, in Hearings before the Subcommittee on Environment, Credit, and Rural Development of the House Committee on Agriculture, 103 Cong., 2 sess. (GPO, June 14, 1994).

79. Among other things, these standards call for an independent risk control unit, active involvement of the board of directors and senior management in risk control, the allocation of significant resources to risk control, a routine that ensures compliance with all the steps taken, and a regular and independent review in the context of a bank's internal audit process. See, for example, Basle Committee on Banking Supervision, "Risk Management Guidelines for Derivatives" (Basle, July 1994).

80. See Basle Committee on Banking Supervision, "Overview of the Amendment to the Capital Accord to Incorporate Market Risks," pp. 39–43.

81. According to one expert, banks are at least five years away from having "perfect all-singing and all-dancing systems which integrate the front and back office across all business areas." Lapper, "Work Ahead for Quality Controllers," p. 19.

82. For the recommendations see Group of Thirty, *Derivatives: Practices and Principles.* For the survey results see Group of Thirty, *Derivatives: Practices and Principles—Follow-up Surveys of Industry Practice* (Washington, December 1994).

83. Basle Committee on Banking Supervision, "Overview of the Amendment to the Capital Accord to Incorporate Market Risks," pp. 6–7.

84. Richard C. Breeden, "Deterring Fraud in the Derivatives Business: What Needs to be Done," address at the International Swaps and Derivatives Association (ISDA) conference on "Derivatives, Disclosure and Financial Contracting," Washington, February 22, 1995. The Federal Accounting Standards Board, an industry organization that establishes voluntary codes of conduct for disclosure and transparency on a wide range of financial matters, would also have to invest considerably more time and resources to improving and updating its standards. See, for example, Clark M. Anstis, *Illustrations of Financial Instruments Disclosures* (Norwalk, Conn.: Federal Accounting Standards Board, December 1994); American Institute of Certified Public Accountants, *Derivatives: Current Accounting and Auditing Literature,* report prepared by the Financial Instruments Task Force of the Accounting Standards Executive Committee (Jersey City, New Jersey, 1994). I am grateful to Philip S. Spellberg for highlighting this point.

85. Although global in scope in principle (functional subsidiarity), architects of such an organization should make use of structural subsidiarity by creating national chapters that would be in charge of many of the operational aspects of mixed regulation.

86. Such training seminars are currently held by a number of accounting firms and industry organizations such as the ISDA. For somewhat similar proposals by the Group of Thirty which emphasize a greater degree of self-regulations, see Group of Thirty, *Global Institutions, National Supervision and Systemic Risk* (Washington, June 1997); George Graham, "Global Banks Plan Self-Regulation Scheme," *Financial Times*, June 4, 1997, p. 3; George Graham, "When Bankers' Hearts Beat a Little Faster: Report Points to How Global Financial Services Could Regulate Themselves," *Financial Times*, June 6, 1997, p. 3.

87. "The 'Invisible Hand': How Market Forces Discipline Financial Contracting," address by Peter Hancock, Managing Director and Head of Global Derivatives, J. P. Morgan, at the ISDA conference on "Derivatives, Disclosure and Financial Contracting," Washington, February 22, 1995.

88. In its defense, SIMEX argued that Barings had been a consistently large player in the futures market. In addition, it seems that Leeson had been able to meet every margin payment requested by SIMEX up to the time of Barings' default. Last but not least, Barings was viewed in Singapore as a well-established and respected market participant. All this may be true, but the fact that SIMEX did contact Barings indicates that there was considerable concern, which at a minimum should have also been passed on to the bank's principal regulator.

89. In general, there seems to have been a lack of transparency on the SIMEX exchange. The Osaka exchange regularly publishes a weekly table of brokers in Japan with the largest exposures in the futures market, but the Singapore exchange publishes no analogous report. Gerard Baker and Emiko Terazono, "The Barings Crisis: Everyone Knew of the Trades But No One Understood Them," *Financial Times*, February 28, 1995, p. 3.

90. SIMEX has promised a range of tougher controls. For example, traders will now have to be relicensed annually and will have to supply character references. It will also ensure that dealers do not take charge of settlement and that proprietary traders do not handle customers' business. Peter Montagnon and Kieran Cooke, "Prompt Treatment for Futures Shock: Singapore Has Moved Fast to Mend Its Reputation after the Barings Havoc," *Financial Times*, March 3, 1995, p. 17.

91. Folkerts-Landau and Ito, *International Capital Markets*, p. 28.

92. The novelty of financial conglomerates depended of course on the degree to which domestic financial markets were segmented along functional lines. In the United States, for example, functional consolidation both within the lending industry (commercial banks, savings and loans, credit unions, and so on) and across other financial services (securities and insurance) has been evolving slowly since the late 1970s and has been a constant concern of regulators and Congress. Germany, on the other hand, with its universal banking system, where different financial services can be offered and performed by the same institution subject to a few general regulations, has not experienced such a debate (although universal banking has come under recent attack for other reasons).

93. Basle Committee on Banking Regulations and Supervisory Practices, *Report on International Developments in Banking Supervision*, no. 9 (Basle, 1994). The report differentiates between "financial conglomerates" and "mixed conglomerates," the latter offering not only financial services but also certain nonfinancial or even

commercial services. Still, many of the same supervisory problems would also be found in mixed conglomerates. See also Claudio E. V. Borio and Renato Filosa, "The Changing Borders of Banking: Trends and Implications," *BIS Economic Papers,* no. 43 (Basle: BIS, December 1994). The emergence of such conglomerates would have been impossible without the deliberate deregulatory actions of governments to encourage the despecialization of financial institutions. Here, too, the challenges that governments currently face are a consequence of earlier policies that had widespread support. At the same time, it should be acknowledged that these policies were often the result of intense political pressure from a private sector that, in the face of a glob-ally integrated market, could no longer compete with institutions in less stringently regulated jurisdictions. This was especially the case in the United States, where large commercial banks have long lobbied, with varying degrees of success, for the func-tional deregulation of the financial services industry, in particular in the areas of commercial and investment banking. See Reinicke, *Banking, Politics and Global Finance,* chapters 5 and 6.

94. For a detailed list of risks, see Basle Committee on Banking Regulations and Supervisory Practices, *Report on International Developments in Banking Supervi-sion,* no. 8 (Basle, 1992), pp. 61–63.

95. Statement by Richard C. Breeden in *Oversight Hearing on Derivative Finan-cial Markets,* Hearings before the Subcommittee on Telecommunications and Finance of the House Committee on Energy and Commerce, 103 Cong., 2 sess. (GPO, May 10, 1994), p. 6.

96. For a summary of the group's findings see Basle Committee on Banking Reg-ulations and Supervisory Practices, *Report on International Developments in Banking Supervision,* no. 9.

97. This could be achieved either by consolidated supervision, where capital requirements of the parent company are applied to the consolidated group's assets and liabilities, or through a so-called solo-plus approach, where the solo supervision of each corporate entity is complemented by groupwide risk assessment.

98. Basle Committee on Banking Regulations and Supervisory Practices, *Report on International Developments in Banking Supervision,* no. 9, p. 56.

99. As late as April 1995, Padoa-Schioppa stated that there was currently "no possibility of joining forces" but that he hoped that a solution could be found within two years. See Gapper, "Basle Model for Banking Safeguards," p. 31.

100. Basle Committee on Banking Supervision and the Technical Committee of the International Organisation of Securities Commissions, "Public Disclosure of the Trading and Derivatives Activities of Banks and Securities Firms" (Basle, November 1995).

101. For more information on the Joint Forum, see Basle Committee on Banking Supervision, *Report on International Developments in Banking Supervision,* no. 10 (Basle, June 1996), p. 49; David Folkerts-Landau and Takatoshi Ito, *International Capital Markets: Developments, Prospects, and Key Policy Issues* (Washington: IMF, 1996), pp. 154–55.

102. As quoted in Richard Lapper, "Regulators Aim to Gird the Globe: Enthusi-asm Is Growing for an International Framework for Supervising Financial Markets," *Financial Times,* July 10, 1995, p. 16.

103. Seventy countries are members of IOSCO, represented by their securities regulators. Nine associate members are securities regulators either from countries already represented in the first group or from offshore financial centers. Apart from these government representatives, IOSCO also has thirty-five private sector industry associations and stock exchanges as affiliate members, who lack voting rights but are part of the working groups that make operational recommendations.

104. Breeden, *Oversight Hearing on Derivative Financial Markets*, p. 35.

105. The candidates are the Banco Central do Brasil, the People's Bank of China, the Hong Kong Monetary Authority, the Reserve Bank of India, the Bank of Korea, Banco de México, the Central Bank of Russian Federation, the Saudi Arabian Monetary Agency, and the Monetary Authority of Singapore. Future potential candidates are, among others, Argentina and Chile.

106. Gillian Tett, "A Changing World and EMU Challenge Old Banking Order: An Expanded Membership of the 'Central Bankers' Bank' Could Raise More Questions Than It Answers," *Financial Times*, September 11, 1996, p. 6.

107. William Hall and Gillian Tett, "BIS Seeks to Boost Market Role," *Financial Times*, September 10, 1996, p. 1.

108. Basle Committee on Banking Supervision, *Core Principles for Effective Banking Supervision* (Basle, September 1997), p. 1.

109. Basle Committee on Banking Supervision, *Core Principles for Effective Banking Supervision*, p. 2.

110. George Graham, "Focus on a Set of Core Principles: Most Central Bankers Believe the Prize of a Global Standard Is Worth Paying For," *Financial Times*, September 19, 1997, pp. 14, 15. See also Morris Goldstein and Philip Turner, "Banking Crises in Emerging Economies: Origins and Policy Options," *BIS Economic Papers,* no. 46 (Basle: BIS, October 1996); Patrick Honohan, "Banking System Failures in Developing and Transition Countries: Diagnosis and Prediction," *BIS Working Papers,* no. 39 (Basle: BIS, January 1997); Kane, "Difficulties of Transferring Risk-Based Capital Requirements to Developing Countries,"; Dziobek, Frécaut, and Nieto, "Non-G-10 Countries and the Basle Capital Rules."

111. George Graham, "New Banking Standards Set for Approval," *Financial Times*, September 22, 1997, p. 4.

CHAPTER 5

1. Given this study's emphasis on the economic dimension of global public policy, this chapter considers only crime as business and thus does not directly examine the rise of international terrorism. Whereas the primary concern of the former is profits, the goal of the latter is political—indeed, terrorism often seeks to destroy the very system from which organized crime benefits. It cannot be excluded, however, that these two types of crime may also be complementary. This is especially true of non-state-sponsored terrorism, which requires a source of funding other than the state. For more on this issue see R. T. Naylor, "The Insurgent Economy: Black-Market Operations of Guerilla Organizations," *Crime, Law, and Social Change,* vol.

20, no. 1 (July 1993), pp. 13–51; M. Amir, "Political Terrorism and Common Criminality: Some Preliminary Considerations," *Violence, Aggression and Terrorism,* vol. 1, no. 4 (1987), pp. 377–78; see also United Nations Economic and Social Council (ECOSOC), Commission on Crime Prevention and Criminal Justice, "Links between Transnational Organized Crime and Terrorist Crimes," *Report of the Secretary General,* E/CN.15/1996/7 (New York, 1996).

2. The United Nations, for example, started to focus on international crime as early as 1955. See, for example, United Nations, Secretariat, Department of Economic and Social Affairs, *First United Nations Congress on the Prevention of Crime and the Treatment of Offenders,* sales no. 1956.IV.4 (New York, 1956). More recently, efforts to fight global crime at the UN level were strengthened with the creation, in 1992, of the Commission on Crime Prevention and Criminal Justice under the UN Economic and Social Council. This commission replaced the Committee on Crime Prevention and Control. For more background see *The United Nations and Crime Prevention* (New York: United Nations, 1996).

3. Lawrence H. Summers, deputy secretary of the treasury, address at the Financial Action Task Force plenary session, Washington, June 26, 1996.

4. According to ECOSOC, *Report and Recommendations of the International Conference on Preventing and Controlling Money Laundering and the Use of the Proceeds of Crime: A Global Approach* (Courmayeur, Italy, 1994). See also statement by Secretary General Boutros Boutros-Ghali at the World Ministerial Conference on Organized Transnational Crime, Naples, November 21–23, 1994. E/CONF.88/7. July 12, 1994.

5. Vincent Boland, "Crime and Drug Trafficking Earned 1,000bn by Last Year," *Financial Times,* February 14, 1997, p. 1. For an overview of transnational crime see Phil Williams and Ernesto Savona, eds., *The United Nations and Transnational Organized Crime* (London: F. Cass, 1996).

6. The term *crime multinationals* has been used by, among others, former Secretary General of the United Nations Boutros Boutros-Ghali. See, for example, his statement at the opening of the World Ministerial Conference on Organized Transnational Crime, Naples, Italy, November 21–23, 1994.

7. Phil Williams, "Transnational Criminal Organizations: Strategic Alliances," *Washington Quarterly,* vol. 18, no. 1 (Winter 1995), pp. 57–72.

8. Money laundering is defined here broadly as the disguising or concealing of illicit income in order to make it appear legitimate.

9. Financial Action Task Force on Money Laundering (FATF), *Annual Report 1995–1996,* as found on the Internet at http://www.oecd.org/faff/annual95.htm.

10. Gerhard O. W. Müller, former director of the UN Congress for the Prevention of Crime and the Treatment of Offenders, statement at a workshop on "The Global Struggle against Organized Crime" at the 27th International Management Symposium, St. Gallen, Switzerland, May 26–28, 1997.

11. Office of Technology Assessment (OTA), *Information Technologies for the Control of Money Laundering,* OTA-ITC-630 (Government Printing Office, September 1995), p. 119.

12. David Andelman, "The Drug Money Maze," *Foreign Affairs,* vol. 73, no. 4 (July/August 1994), pp. 94–108.

13. Department of State, Bureau for International Narcotics and Law Enforcement Affairs, *International Narcotics Control Strategy Report* (Washington, March 1997), p. 398.

14. A recent example of a country engaging in such offensive intervention is the Seychelles. The country's Economic Development Act, passed in November 1995, provides immunity from prosecution to anyone investing $10,000 in the country, as long as the investor did not commit a drug violation in the Seychelles. See Beth A. Simmons, "Compliance with Non-Binding Legal Accords: The Case of Money Laundering," paper prepared for the American Society for International Law's Study on Global Change and Nonbinding Legal Accords, Washington, May 17, 1997.

15. For an overview see Kirk W. Munroe, "The Extraterritorial Reach of the United States Anti-Money Laundering Laws," pp. 290–303, and William Parker, III, "Nowhere to Run, Nowhere to Hide: The Long Arm of U.S. Law Enforcement," pp. 304–18, both in Barry Rider and Michael Ashe, eds., *Money Laundering Controls* (Dublin: Round Hall Sweet and Maxwell, 1996).

16. For a discussion of extraterritoriality in the struggle against money laundering see Kirk W. Munroe, "Surviving the Solution: The Extraterritorial Reach of the United States," paper presented at the Canada–United States International Money Laundering Conference, Windsor, Ontario, May 1–3, 1996.

17. Peter Andreas, "U.S.-Mexico: Open Markets, Closed Border," *Foreign Policy*, no. 103 (Summer 1996), pp. 51–69.

18. Jonathan J. Rusch, "Hue and Cry in the Counting House: Some Observations on the Bank Secrecy Act," *Catholic University Law Review*, vol. 37, no. 2 (Winter 1988), p. 467.

19. Pub. L. 102–550, 106 Stat. 3672.

20. See Elliot H. Berman, "Knowing Your Customer and Reporting Suspicious Transactions: Designing and Implementing a Compliance Program," paper presented at the Canada–United States International Money Laundering Conference, University of Windsor, Ontario, May 1–3, 1996, p. 2. The act also mandated new compliance procedures and required staff training for banks, as well as heavy sanctions against defecting institutions. According to an OTA report, "the huge volume of CTRs [currency transaction reports] now far exceeds the resources that law enforcement agencies have for investigating them." OTA, *Information Technologies for the Control of Money Laundering*, p. 37.

21. Until recently, wire transfers were almost completely unregulated, and virtually no information (including even the originator's identity) followed the transfer to the receiving institution. They thus provided anonymity. Not surprisingly, wire transfers have become the primary means of laundering funds. CHIPS is the primary system for processing international U.S. dollar transfers. It serves 132 foreign and domestic banks, representing thirty-three countries, and is operated by the New York Clearing House Association. Fedwire is the primary domestic transfer system operated by the Federal Reserve. SWIFT is the principal international service for wire transfer message traffic that initiates funds transfers. It has more than 2,600 member institutions in sixty-five countries. See General Accounting Office (GAO), *Money Laundering: A Framework for Understanding U.S. Efforts Overseas*, GGD-96-105 (Washington, May 24, 1996), Appendix IV:1.

22. For more details see Maureen Murphy, *The Riegle Community Development and Regulatory Improvement Act of 1994, Titles III–VI: Paperwork Reduction, Regulatory Improvement, Money Laundering,* CRS Report for Congress (Washington, September 2, 1994); and Ezra C. Levine and James C. Duff, "Congress Takes Aim at Non-Bank Financial Institutions," *Legal Times,* August 29, 1994, p. 21.

23. For an overview of national developments see the national assessments contained in FATF, *Annual Report 1995–1996* and *Annual Report 1996–1997,* and Department of State, *International Narcotics Control Strategy Report* (Washington, 1996). On Australia see also United Nations, *Report of the Secretary-General on the Control of the Proceeds of Crime,* E/CN.15/1996/3 (New York, 1996), sections 12–16; on Canada see sections 20–26 of the report just cited; John L. Evans, "International Money Laundering: Enforcement Challenges and Opportunities," *Southwestern Journal of Law and Trade in the Americas,* vol. 3 (Spring 1996), pp. 4–8.

24. See, for example, Scott Sultzer, "Money Laundering: The Scope of the Problem and Attempts to Combat It," *Tennessee Law Review,* vol. 63, no. 1 (Fall 1995), pp. 143–237.

25. These concerns were the result of certain provisions in the Right to Financial Privacy Act of 1978, which generated questions in the banking community about the type of customer information that could be disclosed in reporting a suspicious transaction. See GAO, *Money Laundering: Needed Improvements for Reporting Suspicious Transactions Are Planned,* GGD-95-156 (Washington, May 30, 1995), pp. 13–14; G. Philip Rutledge, "Bank Secrecy Laws: An American Perspective," *Dickinson Journal of International Law,* vol. 14, no. 3 (1996), pp. 601–11.

26. For example, the Bank of Boston was fined $500,000. See Sultzer, "Money Laundering," p. 158.

27. Bruce Zagaris, "Dollar Diplomacy: International Enforcement of Money Movement and Related Matters—A United States Perspective," *George Washington Journal of International Law and Economics,* vol. 22, no. 3 (1989), pp. 468–74.

28. Sultzer, "Money Laundering," p. 176.

29. Lisa A. Barbot, "Money Laundering: An International Challenge," *Tulane Journal of International and Comparative Law,* vol. 3, nos. 1 and 2 (Spring 1995), p. 184; see also John J. Fialka, "Politics and Policy: Obscure Treasury Unit Helps DEA Uncover Money-Laundering Scheme," *Wall Street Journal,* December 31, 1996, p. 32.

30. Gerald L. Hilsher, "Money Laundering: The Banker's Role as Watchdog," *Issues in Bank Regulation,* vol. 13 (Fall 1989), p. 16.

31. Hilsher, "Money Laundering," p. 16.

32. Department of the Treasury, *Minimum Security Devices and Procedures: Reports of Crimes and Suspected Crimes and Bank Secrecy Act Compliance,* 53 Fed. Reg. 7882 (1988).

33. For example, the two-track reporting mechanism for CRFs and the modified CTRs confused bank personnel, who often did not know whether to file one or the other form, or both. In any case, filing the CRF was often an administrative headache, sometimes requiring banks to send the same form to up to six separate regulators. Ticking the "suspicious" box on the CTR presented its own problems, because there was no room on the form to comment on the nature or context of the suspicious activity. See GAO, *Money Laundering,* chapters 1 and 2.

34. Stanley E. Morris, remarks before the American Bankers Association and American Bar Association Money Laundering Enforcement Seminar, Washington, October 28, 1994, p. 2.

35. Dominic Bencivenga, "Suspicious Activity: Reporting Rules Rely on Bank's Good Judgment," *New York Law Journal,* vol. 215, no. 65 (April 4, 1996), p. 5.

36. Howard W. Goldstein, "Money Laundering Regulations," *New York Law Journal,* vol. 216, no. 18, July 25, 1996, p. 5.

37. OTA, *Information Technologies for the Control of Money Laundering,* p. 7.

38. See the testimony by Henry R. Wray, director, administration of justice issues, GAO, in GAO, *Money Laundering: The Volume of Currency Transaction Reports Filed Can and Should Be Reduced* GAO/T-GGD-94-113 (Washington, March 15, 1994).

39. The language is from 31 U.S.C. 5313(d), which was codified by section 2 of the MLSA of 1994.

40. FinCEN, "Treasury Secretary Announces Bank Secrecy Act Advisory Group," *News Release*, March 10, 1994.

41. Stanley E. Morris, statement in Hearings before the House Subcommittee on General Oversight and Investigations of the House Banking and Financial Services Committee, 105 Cong., 1 sess., March 19, 1997.

42. FinCEN, "New Bank Reporting Rule to Cut Paperwork by 20 Percent," *News Release*, April 17, 1996.

43. Morris, statement before the House Subcommittee on General Oversight and Investigations.

44. GAO, *Money Laundering: Progress Report on Treasury's Financial Crimes Enforcement Network*, GGD-94-30 (Washington, November 8, 1993) p. 2; see also OTA, *Information Technologies for the Control of Money Laundering,* chapter 3; Patrick Symmes, "Caught in the Net," *Washington City Paper,* August 9, 1996, pp. 18–29.

45. FinCEN is organized by major activity: tactical support, strategic analysis, systems integration, and resource management. It has a staff of about 200, including 87 intelligence analysts and 23 agents. Thirty-four of its staff are detailed from law enforcement agencies.

46. The BSA requires CTRs for any transaction through a financial institution over $10,000; financial institutions are also now required to maintain records of transactions over $3,000 for five years. The purpose of the CTR is to preserve the paper trail of the money launderer from the originating account to the final destination. CTRs represent over 95 percent of the 52 million BSA reports filed as of May 1993. The Suspicious Activity Report (SAR), which has replaced the older Criminal Referral Form (CRF), is used to report known or suspected criminal offenses and transactions that involve money laundering. Whereas the CRF was filed with a number of different agencies, creating the usual confusion and turf fights, the SAR is filed with FinCEN only. Financial institutions are required to submit SARs only for transactions over a $5,000 threshold. The institution must keep records of the transaction for five years and maintain the equivalent of the original document. A safe-harbor clause in the BSA protects banks from prosecution by their clients for reporting suspicious activity in good faith. See GAO, *Money Laundering: Progress Report on Treasury's Financial Crimes Enforcement Network.*

47. The system is designed to facilitate coordination and cooperation among law enforcement agencies, and thus avoid overlap, and to identify persons who have been previously investigated.

48. For a complete list see OTA, *Information Technologies for the Control of Money Laundering* (GPO, September 1995), p. 45.

49. The FAIS can easily detect attempts to break down large sums of money into many transactions of just under $10,000 in an attempt to avoid the CTR filing (a technique referred to as smurfing). For a more detailed discussion of the FAIS see Ted E. Senator and others, "The Financial Crimes Enforcement Network AI System (FAIS)," *AI Magazine* (Winter 1995), pp. 21–39.

50. Senator and others, "The Financial Crimes Enforcement Network AI System (FAIS)," p. 35.

51. Morris, remarks before the American Bankers Association and American Bar Association Money Laundering Enforcement Seminar, p. 14.

52. Berman, "Knowing Your Customer and Reporting Suspicious Transactions," p. 3.

53. Berman, "Knowing Your Customer and Reporting Suspicious Transactions," p. 3.

54. See statement of Sara Redding Wilson, senior corporate counsel, Signet Banking Corporation, discussing the legislative history of the BSA, in *Federal Government's Response to Money Laundering,* Hearings before the House Committee on Banking, Finance, and Urban Affairs, 103 Cong., 1 sess. (1993), pp. 200–01 at 722.

55. See Board of Governors of the Federal Reserve System, *Bank Secrecy Act Manual* (Washington, January 1995), section 601.0.

56. Matthew R. Hall, "An Emerging Duty to Report Criminal Conduct: Banks, Money Laundering, and the Suspicious Activity Report," *Kentucky Law Journal*, vol. 84, no. 3 (1995–96), p. 659. For a detailed description of the various exemptions, see 31 U.S.C. § (5313), 1994.

57. See Matt Schulz, "Charges against Citibank Put Spotlight on Laundering Rules," *American Banker,* June 13, 1996, p. 13; and "Anti-Laundering Rules Stuck in Neutral," *American Banker,* June 20, 1996, p. 11.

58. Boris F. Melnikoff, Senior Vice President, Wachovia Corporation, statement on behalf of the American Bankers Association at the Financial Services Forum, sponsored by the FATF, Paris, January 1996.

59. OTA, *Information Technologies for the Control of Money Laundering,* p. 54.

60. OTA, *Information Technologies for the Control of Money Laundering,* p. 54.

61. OTA, *Information Technologies for the Control of Money Laundering,* p. 37.

62. The most relevant legislation is the Comprehensive Environmental Response Compensation and Liability Act (CERCLA) of 1980, also known as Superfund, which was strengthened in 1984 and amended in 1986 and 1988 to tighten the standards. For some background see Eleanor H. Erdevig, "Lenders and Environmental Policies," *Economic Perspectives* (Federal Reserve Bank of Chicago, November/December 1991), vol. 15, pp. 2–12; Peter Reuter, *The Economic Consequences of Expanded Corporate Liability: An Exploratory Study* (Santa Monica, Calif.: RAND, November 1988); Peter Huber, "Environmental Hazards and Liability Law," in Robert E. Litan and Clifford Winston, eds., *Liability: Perspectives and Policy* (Brookings, 1988), pp. 128–54; see also GAO, *Superfund: Actions Needed to Correct Long-Standing Contract Management Problems,* GAO/TRCED-92-78 (Washington, July 8, 1992).

63. David Lascelles, "Only Clean and Green Borrowers Need Apply," *Financial Times,* March 27, 1992, p. 19.

64. Stephen Labaton, "Bank Liability for Toxic Sites," *New York Times,* April 18, 1991, p. D2.

65. See, for example, Bruce Smart, ed., *Beyond Compliance: A New Industry View of the Environment* (Washington: World Resources Institute, 1992). For a different perspective on the industry see Kenny Bruno, *The Greenpeace Book of Greenwash* (Washington: Greenpeace International, 1992).

66. For example, Environmental Compliance Services Inc., of Exton, Pennsylvania, provides such services; see the company's information package; see also "Out of the Muck: A Banker's Guide," *American Banker,* April 27, 1992, p. 2A.

67. Ron Noble, then president of the FATF. See "International Task Force Meets to Discuss Improved Efforts to Fight Money Laundering," *BNA's Banking Report* (Washington: Bureau of National Affairs, July 1, 1996), vol. 67, p. 26.

68. FATF, *FATF-VIII Money Laundering Typologies Exercise Public Report* (Paris: OECD, 1997).

69. For a more detailed discussion of these and other techniques, see Timothy D. Wagner, director, Financial Investigations Division, U.S. Customs Service, "Exploitation of International Trade by Money Launderers," paper presented to the Canada–United States International Money Laundering Conference, University of Windsor, Ontario, May 1–3, 1996. See also Mario Possamai, senior investigator, Lindquist Avey MacDonald Baskerville, Inc., "Money Laundering: A Canadian Perspective," paper presented to the Canada–United States International Money Laundering Conference, University of Windsor, Ontario, May 1–3, 1996.

70. See World Trade Organization, *Regionalism and the World Trading System* (Geneva, 1995), p. 1.

71. ECOSOC, "Review of Priority Themes, Control of the Proceeds of Crime," *Report of the Secretary General,* (Vienna, May 21–31, 1996), p. 84.

72. For an overview of these issues see Department of the Treasury, "An Introduction to Electronic Money Issues," paper prepared for a Department of the Treasury conference "Toward Electronic Money and Banking: The Role of Government," Washington, September 19–20, 1996; Group of Ten, "Electronic Money: Consumer Protection, Law Enforcement, Supervisory and Cross Border Issues" (Basle: Bank for International Settlements, April 1997); FATF, *FATF-VIII Money Laundering Typologies Exercise Public Report*; Stephen J. Kobrin, "Electronic Cash and the End of National Markets," *Foreign Policy,* no. 107 (Summer 1997), pp. 65–77; Ellen Leander, "Finance's Top Cops," *Global Finance,* vol. 10, no. 10 (October 1996), pp. 26–32.

73. An example is the Mondex card, introduced on a trial basis in certain parts of the United Kingdom. The card is loaded with e-money by the card issuer, Mondex Ltd., and can then be used to purchase a variety of goods and services. The stored e-money can also be transferred between cardholders through the use of an electronic purse.

74. For a summary of the debate see the National Research Council's report on cryptography's role in the information society. Kenneth W. Dam and Herbert S. Lin, eds., *Cryptography's Role in Securing the Information Society* (Washington: National Academy Press, 1996).

75. Morris, remarks before the American Bankers Association and American Bar Association Money Laundering Enforcement Seminar, p. 5.

76. Matthew R. Hall, "An Emerging Duty to Report Criminal Conduct," pp. 643–83, here p. 661. For more information Hall cites in his footnote 127: Steven A. Bercu, "Toward Universal Surveillance in an Information Age Economy: Can We Handle Treasury's New Police Technology?" *Jurimetrics Journal,* vol. 34 (Summer 1994), pp. 383–450; Matthew N. Kleinman, "The Right to Financial Privacy versus Computerized Law Enforcement: A New Fight in an Old Battle," *Northwestern University Law Review,* vol. 86, no. 4 (Summer 1992), pp. 1169–1228. See also Anthony L. Kimery, "Big Brother Wants to Look into Your Bank Account (Any Time It Pleases)," *Wired,* Issue 1.6 (December 1993); Symmes, "Caught in the Net."

77. Notwithstanding, two such projects, "Operation Gateway" and the "Deposit Tracking System," have been proposed, although the latter is not immediately for FinCEN purposes. See Kimery, "Big Brother Wants to Look into Your Bank Account."

78. This achievement was confirmed in the 1996–97 FATF annual report, which states that the "U.S. commitment to combating money laundering at all levels of government is outstanding." See FATF, *Annual Report 1996–1997,* at 60.

79. Members of the Interagency Coordination Group include the Criminal Investigation Division of the Internal Revenue Service, the U.S. Customs Service, the U.S. Postal Service, the Drug Enforcement Administration, the Department of Justice, the Federal Bureau of Investigation, and FinCEN.

80. Wolfgang H. Reinicke, "Interdependence, Globalization and the Emergence of Legally Nonbinding Accords," paper prepared for the American Society of International Law's Study on Global Change and Nonbinding Legal Accords, Washington, May 17, 1997.

81. Pub. L. 100-690, sec. 4702, (2)(A), (B) as found in United States Congress, *United States Statutes at Large Containing the Laws and Concurrent Resolutions Enacted during the Second Session of the One-Hundredth Congress of the United States of America 1988 and Proclamations* (GPO, 1990), vol. 102, part 5, p. 4291.

82. Switzerland, which is not a regular member of the United Nations, has also signed the convention.

83. See the preamble to Basle Committee on Banking Regulations and Supervisory Practices, *Prevention of Criminal Use of the Banking System for the Purpose of Money-Laundering* (Basle, December 1988).

84. Robert Peston, "Basle Code to Avoid Repeat of BCCI Case," *Financial Times,* July 7, 1992, p. 3; titled "Minimum Standards for the Supervision of International Banking Groups and Their Cross-Border Establishments," the code is a revision of the 1975 and 1983 concordats established in response to the failure of the Herstatt Bank and the Banco Ambrosiano, in an attempt to deal with the issue of host-versus home-country responsibility in a global financial market.

85. According to the code, supervisory authorities should cooperate on "all prudential matters pertaining to international banks, and, in particular, in respect of the investigation of documented allegations of fraud, criminal activity, or violations of banking laws. In addition, both the Committee and its members will continue their efforts to reduce impediments to the sharing of information among supervisory

authorities." Federal Reserve Board, "Press Release: Basle Minimum Standards," July 6, 1992, p. 2; for more on information sharing see Basle Committee on Banking Supervision, *Exchange of Information between Banking and Securities Supervisors* (Basle, April 1990) and *Exchanges of Information between Supervisors of Participants in the Financial Market Place* (Basle, April 1990).

86. IOSCO, *Report on Money Laundering: Meeting of the Technical Committee of the IOSCO in Quebec, July 7–8, 1992* (Montreal, 1992).

87. "Council Directive of June 10, 1991 on the Prevention of the Use of the Financial System for the Purpose of Money Laundering," *Official Journal of the European Communities*, 91/308/EEC, no. L166/77 (Brussels, June 28, 1991). Within four years of its enactment, the European Commission noted that the directive required updating. The Commission identified a considerable number of "weak points" in the current system due to changes in the financial marketplace, the growing role of nonfinancial institutions in money laundering, and the growing use of money laundering for non-drug-related offenses. See Commission of the European Communities, "First Commission's Report on the Implementation of the Money Laundering Directive," 91/308/EEC to be submitted to the European parliament and to the Council of Ministers (Brussels, March 3, 1995). The Commission is currently working on the revisions and is expected to present an updated directive no later than March 1998.

88. To its credit, the Commission has not shied away from its determination to ensure that the directive is adopted. It recently publicly reprimanded Austria for failing to comply, threatening to take the matter to the European Court of Justice. See European Commission, "Infringement Procedure: Money Laundering Commission to Send Reasoned Opinion to Austria," IP/96/557 (Brussels, July 2, 1996). Barring any further changes, this case will be referred to the European Court of Justice, since Austria has rejected the Commission's complaint.

89. Council of Europe, "Convention on Laundering, Search, Seizure and Confiscation of the Proceeds of Crime" (Luxembourg, November 1990). An additional twelve members have signed the Convention.

90. *BNA's Banking Report,* July 24, 1989, pp. 145–46. See also GAO, *Money Laundering: A Framework for Understanding U.S. Efforts Overseas*; OECD, *OECD Financial Action Task Force on Money Laundering* (Paris, February 7, 1990).

91. The FATF membership does not include the most recently admitted members of the OECD: Mexico, Czech Republic, Hungary, Poland, and South Korea (by order of accession to the OECD).

92. Since the handover of Hong Kong to the People's Republic of China on July 1, 1997, Hong Kong remains a full attending and participating member of the FATF and is known as Hong Kong, China.

93. Until 1994 the FATF was organized into a plenary and three core working groups focusing on legal issues (law enforcement, legal systems, etc.), financial issues (money laundering techniques, regulatory issues), and external relations (links to other countries and international organizations). The working group structure was abandoned during FATF V (1993–94) to give the plenary group greater weight in the discussion and policy decisions, while maintaining the option to create ad hoc groups to carry out specific tasks approved by the plenary.

94. GAO, *Money Laundering: A Framework for Understanding U.S. Efforts Overseas,* letter 7.1.

95. FATF, *Annual Report 1995–1996,* at 19.

96. FATF, *Annual Report 1995–1996,* at 19.

97. Peer evaluation is conducted by the member countries, and the resulting confidential report is discussed with the member under review. The final report gives a confidential assessment of how well the member is adhering to the recommendations and identifies areas needing further work. For a more detailed description see FATF, *Annual Report 1991–1992,* at 31.

98. See FATF, *Annual Report 1996–1997,* at 37. By the end of the eighth round, six second-round evaluations had been completed.

99. By the end of FATF VIII, eight such evaluations had been completed.

100. FATF, *Annual Report 1996–1997,* at 38.

101. FATF, *Annual Report 1995–1996,* at 60–61.

102. FATF, *Annual Report 1996–1997,* at 32.

103. FATF, *Annual Report 1996–1997,* at 32.

104. OECD, *News Release,* September 19, 1996. At a plenary meeting, the FATF agreed to apply its Recommendation 21, which requires financial institutions to give special attention to business relations and transactions with persons, companies, and financial institutions domiciled in Turkey. Whenever these transactions have no apparent economic or visible lawful purpose, their background and purpose should, as far as possible, be examined, and the findings established in writing and made available to supervisors, auditors, and law enforcement agencies. After Turkey responded by enacting a number of laws, the application of Recommendation 21 was lifted. But Turkey did not follow up by issuing regulations to operationalize the laws. If those regulations are not issued by the time the plenary session meets again in September 1997, the sanctions will be reapplied.

105. See FATF, *Annual Report 1995–1996,* Annex I, at 4–7.

106. See *OECD Letter,* vol. 5, no. 8 (October 1996); FATF, *Annual Report 1995–1996,* at 28–29.

107. FATF, *Annual Report 1995–1996,* at 28.

108. For a discussion of the study's results see FATF, *Annual Report 1996–1997,* at 24–27.

109. FATF, *Report on Money Laundering Typologies 1996–1997,* (Paris: OECD, 1997).

110. FinCEN, "FATF Report Highlights Money Laundering Trends," *News Release* (Washington, February 6, 1997). For more information see FATF, *Report on Money Laundering Typologies 1996–1997,* at 13.

111. The original members were the G-7 countries plus Australia, Austria, Belgium, Luxembourg, the Netherlands, Spain, Sweden, and Switzerland. In 1990 they were joined by nine new members—Denmark, Finland, Greece, Hong Kong, Ireland, New Zealand, Norway, Portugal, and Turkey—and two regional groupings: the European Commission and the Gulf Cooperation Council. In 1991 two additional members, Iceland and Singapore joined. On the issue of political pressure see Andelman, "The Drug Money Maze," p. 105.

112. FATF, *Annual Report 1991–1992,* at 96.

113. FATF, *Annual Report 1993–1994,* at 23.

114. Thus the FATF VI annual report states that the task force "began . . . a review of its policy on expansion of the membership of the FATF . . . " which "will be taken forward in FATF-VII." See FATF, *Annual Report 1994–1995,* at 1. On the controversy surrounding this decision see John L. Evans, "International Efforts to Contain Money Laundering," paper presented at a seminar on "Money Laundering: Joining Forces to Prevent It," Bankers Club, Mexico City, April 8, 1997.

115. FATF, *Annual Report 1996–1997,* at 111.

116. Department of State, *International Narcotics Control Strategy Report,* p. 36.

117. Between 1996 and 1997 alone, the State Department upgraded twenty-two countries into the priority groups, whereas only four were downgraded. See Department of State, *International Narcotics Control Strategy Report,* pp. 33–34.

118. The strategy is based on three prongs: advocating the widest possible implementation of FATF policies by nonmembers through education and monitoring; prioritizing efforts both geographically and by sector; and focusing cooperation on regional and international organizations. For more detail see FATF, *Annual Report 1995–1996,* at 64; and FATF, *Annual Report 1996–1997,* at 85.

119. For an overview see CFATF, *Annual Report 1995–1996.*

120. Some of the nineteen recommendations go further than and extend the original forty. They cover such issues as the power to confiscate assets, certain privacy privileges between lawyers and clients, and the extension of reporting requirements to nonfinancial institutions. In some ways the CFATF recommendations anticipated changes made to the FATF recommendations only later, in 1996. For a list of the CFATF recommendations see FinCEN, *Compendium of International Anti–Money Laundering Conventions and Agreements,* 2d ed. (Washington, January 1996), pp. 63–66.

121. Five countries (Dominica, Guyana, St. Kitts & Nevis, Suriname, and Venezuela) did not sign because they were not present. Three countries (Colombia, Jamaica, and Mexico) were present but elected not to sign.

122. See CFATF, *Joint Statement of Cooperation and Support for the Caribbean Financial Action Task Force* (San Jose, Costa Rica, October 10, 1996), pp. 9–10.

123. To date, the Asia Secretariat's main functions have been to conduct missions to nonmember countries in the Asian region and to organize an annual symposium on money laundering in the region.

124. Members include Australia, Bangladesh, Chinese Taipei (Taiwan), Hong Kong, Japan, New Zealand, People's Republic of China, Philippines, Singapore, Sri Lanka, Thailand, the United States, and Vanuatu. See FATF, *Annual Report 1996–1997,* at 99.

125. "[W]e welcome the establishment of the Asia-Pacific Group on Money Laundering of which several APEC economies are members. We pointed out however that money laundering is a global phenomenon and in this regard, we encourage all other economies to join in a determined global effort to effectively address it." See "Joint Ministerial Statement," Asia-Pacific Economic Cooperation, *Fourth APEC Finance Ministers Meeting, Cebu, Philippines, 5–6 April 1997,* section 25.

126. See Inter-American Drug Abuse Control Commission, CICAD, "Model Regulations Concerning Money Laundering Offences Connected to Illicit Drug Trafficking and Related Offences" (Washington, 1990).

127. FATF, *Annual Report 1996–1997,* at 100 and 101.

128. In the case of the Asian region this will be most challenging, since China, Indonesia, Korea, and Malaysia are not members of the Asian FATF.

129. Most of these countries have been in contact with the FATF or with national authorities. India, for example, has expressed an interest in enacting legislation and possibly establishing a financial intelligence unit. See Department of State, *International Narcotics Control Strategy Report,* p. 21.

130. For more on AUSTRAC see Greg Tucker, "Money Laundering, Banks and the Duties of Inquiry and Disclosure," *Journal of Banking and Finance Law and Practice,* vol. 6, no. 3 (September 1995), pp. 181–94; AUSTRAC, *Annual Report,* various years; John J. Fialka, "Computers Keep Tabs on Dirty Money: Chinese Puzzle Uncovered by Australian Team's Software," *Wall Street Journal,* May 8, 1995, p. 9C; on TRACFIN, see Douanes & Droits Indirects, *La Lutte contre le Blanchiment des Capitaux: L'Action de Tracfin, Role de Tracfin* (Paris, 1995); on the NCIS see NCIS, *Annual Report,* various years; NCIS Pamphlet on the International Division; "Britain's National Criminal Intelligence Service," www.alternatives.com/crime/crimuk.html; see also Mark Yost, "Chasing Criminals at Cyberspeed," *Wall Street Journal,* May 23, 1996, p. 14.

131. "Financial Intelligent Units Proliferate around the World," *Money Laundering Alert,* vol. 6, February 1, 1995, p. 7.

132. Morris, statement before the House Committee on Banking, pp. 9–10.

133. The group held its initial meeting, co-hosted by the United States and Belgium, in Brussels in June 1995.

134. Morris, statement before the House Committee on Banking, p. 10.

135. Pub. L. 100-690, section 4701, as found in United States Congress, *United States Statutes at Large 1988,* vol. 102, Part 5, pp. 4290–91.

136. FATF, *Annual Report 1996–1997,* at 18.

137. Peter J. Quirk, "Macroeconomic Implications of Money Laundering," *IMF Working Paper,* 96/66 (Washington, June 1996), p. 29; see also, by the same author, "Money Laundering: Muddying the Macroeconomy," *Finance and Development,* vol. 34, no. 1 (March 1997), pp. 7–9.

138. Vito Tanzi, "Money Laundering and the International Financial System," *IMF Working Paper,* 96/55 (Washington, May 1996). As Tanzi points out, it is noteworthy that the idea for this proposal came from the IMF's managing director himself, Michel Camdessus; Vito Tanzi, "Money Laundering and the International Financial System," paper presented at the 14th Annual Dialogue Conference on "Money, Finance, and Monetary Policy in the Global Economy: Challenges to National Governments and the International Monetary System," Hong Kong, January 19–23, 1997. In fact the idea goes back all the way to 1994, when it was first presented at an international conference on money laundering in Courmayeur, Italy; see also Stephanie Flanders, "Cleaning up the Global Economy," *Financial Times,* August 26, 1996, p. 7.

139. IMF, *Articles of Agreement of the International Monetary Fund* (Washington, 1944), Article VIII, Section 5.

140. Tanzi, "Money Laundering and the International Financial System," pp. 13–14.

141. See, for example, World Bank, *Private Sector Development Seminar: The Financial Sector: World Bank Seminar Presented to the Executive Directors* (Washington, March 1994); G. Caprio and L. Summers, "Finance and Its Reform beyond Laissez-Faire," Working Paper 1171, Financial Sector Development Department, World Bank (Washington, August 1993); R. Listfield and F. Montes-Negret, "Modernizing Payment Systems in Emerging Economies," Working Paper 1336, Financial Sector Development Department, World Bank (Washington, August 1994).

142. David Scott, "Money Laundering and International Efforts to Fight It," *FDP Note* (World Bank Publication), no. 48 (May 1995).

143. World Bank, *Operational Directive OD 8.30: Financial Sector Operations* (Washington, February 1992). In all fairness it should be noted that even the most developed countries did not show much concern about money laundering legislation in their own financial systems until the early 1990s.

144. Andelman, "The Drug Money Maze."

145. Good governance encourages governments to create the legal and institutional framework for transparency, predictability on the part of officials, and competence in the conduct of public affairs and the management of economic development. See World Bank, *Governance and Development* (Washington, 1992), p. 1; see also World Bank, *Managing Development: The Governance Dimension* (Washington, 1991); Carol Lancaster, "Governance and Development: The Views from Washington," *IDS Bulletin,* vol. 24, no. 1 (1993); see also Mick Moore and Mark Robinson, "Can Foreign Aid Be Used to Promote Good Government in Developing Countries?" *Ethics and International Affairs,* vol. 8 (1994), pp. 141–58; World Bank, *Governance: The World Bank Experience* (Washington, 1994). In the fall of 1996 the Bank outlined a major new strategy for combating corruption. The initiative has three main planks, involving better oversight of the Bank's own programs, technical assistance to countries that ask for help in fighting corruption, and countering international business corruption through fostering the use of voluntary codes. See "Transparency International Supports World Bank Initiative," *Transparency International Newsletter,* December 1996; Peter Eigen, "Combatting Corruption around the World," *Journal of Democracy,* vol. 7, no. 1 (January 1996), pp. 158–68; World Bank, *World Development Report: The State in a Changing World* (Washington, 1997), especially chapter 6.

146. This implies the need to improve public sector management, ensure economic and financial accountability, maintain predictability in applying rules and regulations, and ensure the availability of and access to information about the economy.

147. World Bank, *Governance and Development,* p. 1.

148. The PFP is currently used to coordinate Bank and Fund operations in the context of the structural adjustment facility (SAF), enhanced structural adjustment facility (ESAF), and systemic transformation facility (STF) and could be expanded, with a few modifications, to include the aspect of passive prevention. For more on the PFP see Jacques J. Polak, *The World Bank and the International Monetary Fund: A Changing Relationship* (Brookings, 1994).

149. Sidney Dell, "The Question of Cross Conditionality," *World Development,* vol. 16, no. 5 (May 1988), pp. 557–68.

150. FATF, *Annual Report 1991–1992,* at 12 and Annex II, section II, at 4.

151. FATF, *Annual Report 1991–1992*, Annex III, at C2.

152. FATF, *Annual Report 1994–1995*, at 99.

153. FATF, *Annual Report 1996–1997*, at 90.

CHAPTER 6

1. Although technology for the development of nuclear weapons should be subject to the same controls as for dual-use items, it is recognized that this effort alone will not suffice to contain nuclear proliferation.

2. However, there has been a notable decline in military expenditures around the world since 1989, with a concomitant drop in the international arms trade. By the end of 1993 the value of trade in arms had declined to $22 billion, its lowest level since the early 1970s and 70 percent below its near-record peak in 1987 ($74 billion). Arms sales agreements began to rise again, however, in 1993 to $39 billion, from $29 billion in 1992. See U.S. Arms Control and Disarmament Agency, *World Military Expenditures and Arms Transfers, 1993–1994* (Washington: Government Printing Office, 1995).

3. For an excellent discussion of these issues see Jacques S. Gansler, *Defense Conversion: Transforming the Arsenal of Democracy* (MIT Press, 1995).

4. Such integration can occur in any of three domains: research and development, engineering and production, or equipment (parts, materials, and software). See Gansler, *Defense Conversion,* p. 87.

5. For some background see National Economic Council, National Security Council, and Office of Science and Technology Policy, "Second to None: Preserving America's Military Advantage through Dual-Use Technology" (Washington, February 9, 1995). See also Gansler, *Defense Conversion,* especially chapters 6, 8, and 12; Rose Marie Ham and David C. Mowery, "Enduring Dilemmas in U.S. Technology Policy," *California Management Review,* vol. 37, no. 4 (1995), pp. 89–107; Lewis M. Branscomb, ed., *Empowering Technology: Implementing a U.S. Strategy* (MIT Press, 1993), especially chapter 3; John A. Alic, *Beyond Spinoff: Military and Commercial Technologies in a Changing World* (Harvard Business School Press, 1992). Responding to congressional criticism that the TRP was industrial policy by the back door, the administration's fiscal 1997 budget replaced the program with the Dual-Use Applications Program (DUAP), which will focus only on technologies of potential use to the military. DUAP is expected to deepen the integration of the defense industrial base with the civilian economy even further. A number of other dual-use programs, such as those involving research and development in high-performance computing, materials and electronic processing, and electronic modules, have also been supported. Earlier dual-use programs such as the Very High Speed Integrated Circuits (VHSIC) program and the Strategic Computing Initiative have had a more narrow focus. For a brief description of VHSIC see Wayne Sandholtz and others, *The Highest Stakes: The Economic Foundations of the Next Security System* (Oxford University Press, 1992), pp. 130ff.

6. Critics of the direct subsidy approach have argued that adopting commercial standards in place of military specifications may allow weapons producers to incor-

porate civil components on a more widespread basis than under the DARPA approach. See Congressional Budget Office, *Reducing the Deficit: Spending and Revenue Options* (Washington, August 1996), p. 150. Another well-known example of civil-military integration was the program to support the development and production of flat-screen computer displays.

7. On such programs in Japan see Kensuke Ebata, "Co-operation for Weapon Technology Transfers and Technological/Economic Development," in United Nations, UNDIR, *Arms and Technology Transfers: Security and Economic Considerations among Importing and Exporting States* (New York, 1995), pp. 177–203.

8. Oliver Morton, "The Information Advantage" (survey of defense technology), *The Economist* (June 10, 1995), p. 6; Yves Boyer, "The Proliferation of Conventional Arms and Dual-Use Technologies," in Yves Boyer and others, *Europe and the Challenge of Proliferation,* eds. Paul Cornish, Peter van Ham and Joachim Krause, *Chaillot Paper* 24 (Paris: Institute for Security Studies of Western European Union, May 1996), pp. 22–32.

9. Ashton Carter, William Perry, and John D. Steinbruner, *A New Concept of Cooperative Security* (Brookings, 1992).

10. John M. Deutch, "Transatlantic Armaments Cooperation: The United States' Point of View," *International Défense & Technologie* (November 1994), p. 12, cited in Boyer, "The Proliferation of Conventional Arms and Dual-Use Technologies," pp. 28–30.

11. "The Information Advantage," pp. 5–7.

12. World Bank, *World Development Report 1992: Development and the Environment* (Washington, 1992); see also United Nations Conference on Trade and Development, *Periodic Report 1990: Policies, Laws and Regulations on Transfer, Application and Development of Technology,* UNCTAD/ITP/TEC/16 (New York, 1992); UN General Assembly Resolution 44/228; United Nations, *Arms and Technology Transfers.*

13. For an overview of technology diffusion see Michael Moodie, "Beyond Proliferation: The Challenge of Technology Diffusion," *Washington Quarterly,* vol. 18, no. 2 (1995), pp. 183–202; see also Wolfgang H. Reinicke, "Cooperative Security and the Political Economy of Nonproliferation," in Janne E. Nolan, ed., *Global Engagement: Cooperation and Security in the 21st Century* (Brookings, 1994), pp. 175–234.

14. On the semiconductor industry see Organization for Economic Cooperation and Development (OECD), *Globalization of Industrial Activities* (Paris, 1992); on global strategic alliances in the semiconductor market, see Steven Butler and Louise Kehoe, "Partners Thank Each Other for the Memory: Growing Trend towards Global Alliances in the Semiconductor Industry," *Financial Times,* July 14, 1992, p. 17; Paul Blustein and John Burgess, "High-Tech's Global Links: Costs Unite Former Rivals," *Washington Post,* July 16, 1992, p. A4.

15. For some examples see Boyer, "The Proliferation of Conventional Arms and Dual-Use Technologies," pp. 22–32.

16. National Science Board, *Science and Engineering Indicators 1996* (GPO, 1996). Among other things, this trend is due to the fact that, with rising competition, product development—an intrinsically global process—has gained in emphasis over basic research, which remains more confined to particular national environments.

17. See, for example, OECD, "Technology and Globalization," in *Technology and the Economy: The Key Relationships* (Paris, February 1992); Thomas Hatzichronoglou, *Globalisation and Competitiveness: Relevant Indicators* (Paris: OECD, 1996); Janet M. Muroyama and H. Guyford Stever, eds., *Globalization of Technology: International Perspectives, Proceedings of the Sixth Convocation of the Council of Academics of Engineering and Technological Sciences* (National Academy Press, 1988). For an overview of the defense-related issues see "The Commercial Implications of Exporting and Importing Military Technology: A Review of the Issues," CRS Report 90-409 SPR (Congressional Research Service, August 24, 1990). On the internationalization of the defense industry see Ethan B. Kapstein, "International Collaboration in Armaments Production," *Political Science Quarterly,* vol. 106, no. 4 (Winter 1991–92), pp. 657–76; Aron L. Friedberg, "The End of Autonomy: The United States after Five Decades," *Daedalus,* vol. 120, no. 4 (Fall 1991), pp. 69–90; Theodore Moran, "The Globalization of America's Defense Industries: Managing the Threat of Foreign Dependence," *International Security,* vol. 15, no. 1 (Summer 1990), pp. 57–99. This spread of availability was further spurred, both in scale and in geographic scope, by an increasing reliance on so-called offset arrangements, which are "industrial compensation practices mandated by many foreign governments when purchasing defense systems." For example, Kuwait, Saudi Arabia, South Korea, Taiwan, Turkey, and others all have offset guidelines for arms imports, leading to a further diffusion of dual-use technologies. See U.S. Department of Commerce, *Export Administration Annual Report,* February 1996, p. II-44. Such arrangements include licensed production or mandatory co-production agreements, transfer of intangibles, setting up production lines, countertrade, and others. See U.S. Department of Commerce, Bureau of Export Administration, Office of Strategic Industries and Economic Security, Strategic Analysis Division, *Offsets in Defense Trade, A Study Conducted under Section 309 of the Defense Production Act of 1950, As Amended* (Washington, May 1996). For a more critical perspective see Lora Lumpe, Director, Arms Sales Monitoring Project, Federation of American Scientists, "Economic Costs of Arms Exports: Subsidies and Offsets," in Hearings before the Subcommittee on Foreign Operations of the Senate Appropriations Committee, 104 Cong., 1 sess. (May 23, 1995).

18. In five cases, including most recently the attempt in 1992 by the French-owned Thomson group to buy out LTV's missile business, the prospect of a negative ruling by the CFIUS prompted the foreign investor to withdraw its proposed acquisition.

19. According to Section 5 of the Export Administration Act (EAA), foreign availability exists when any good or technology is available from a non-U.S. source in sufficient quantity and of comparable quality to make the requirement of a validated U.S. license useless. A major weakness of the EAA provision, in particular in the area of chemical and biological weapons, is that experience in the case of weapons of mass destruction suggests that the quality condition imposed in the EAA is flawed. Chemical weapons can and have been produced with far less sophisticated technology, making current foreign availability provisions ineffective. See also National Academy of Sciences, *Finding Common Ground: US Export Controls in a Changed Global Environment* (Washington: National Academy Press, 1991), p. 255. The diffusion of modern technology also presents a challenge to traditional efforts at

arms control and nonproliferation, as countries will try to compensate for quantitative restrictions through technological innovation.

20. As a result of the drop in both licensing activity and requests for foreign availability assessments, and as part of an overall reorganization of the Department of Commerce, the Office of Foreign Availability was abolished in October 1994, with most of its functions assumed by the Office of Strategic Industries and Economic Security.

21. "DARPA Officials Act to Fight Proliferation," *Defense News,* September 23–29, 1996, p. 2.

22. The case most often cited is the pipeline dispute between the United States and Europe in the early 1980s. See, for example, Bruce W. Jentelson, *Pipeline Politics: The Complex Political Economy of East-West Energy Trade* (Cornell University Press, 1986). There were also differences among the allies regarding overall strategy toward the Soviet Union.

23. For more on this issue see below. See also Wolfgang H. Reinicke, "Political and Economic Changes in the Eastern Bloc and Their Implications for COCOM: West-German and European Community Perspectives" (Washington: National Academy of Sciences, 1990).

24. One example is the tightening of Germany's export controls in 1989, in response to revelations that, among others, German firms aided in the construction of a chemical weapons plant in Rabta, Libya, and their subsequent relaxation in light of more lenient EU-wide regulations that created a competitive disadvantage for German industry with respect to its European counterparts.

25. *The Wassenaar Arrangement on Export Controls for Conventional Arms and Dual-Use Goods and Technologies, Initial Elements, as Adopted by the Plenary of 11–12 July 1996.*

26. Lynn E. Davis, under secretary of state for arms control and international security affairs, "The Wassenaar Arrangement," address at the Carnegie Endowment for International Peace, Washington, January 23, 1996. Davis does, however, acknowledge that the agreement falls short of U.S. goals in some important areas.

27. See *The Wassenaar Arrangement on Export Controls for Conventional Arms and Dual-Use Goods and Technologies, List of Dual-Use Goods and Technologies and Munitions List,* August 1, 1996.

28. Thus, unlike under COCOM, Wassenaar participants have no veto power over other members' transfers.

29. Owen Greene, "Launching the Wassenaar Agreement: Challenges for the New Arms Export Control Regime," *Safer World,* Briefing, March 1996, p. 6.

30. Another six appear on only three of the lists, twenty-two on only two lists, and seventeen on only one list. See Owen Greene, "Developing an Effective Successor to COCOM," *Safer World* (September 1995) and "Successor to COCOM: Options and Dilemmas," *Safer World* (March 1994).

31. Susan Willett, *Martial Arts: Transfers of Arms and Military Technology to East Asia* (London: Centre for Defence Studies, May 1996).

32. These categories are battle tanks, armored combat vehicles, large-caliber artillery systems, combat aircraft, attack helicopters, warships, and missiles and missile launchers.

33. Theresa Hitchens, "Experts Tout Post-CoCom Regime, Despite Shortfalls," *Defense News,* January 29–February 4, 1996, p. 8.

34. As quoted in Boyer, "The Proliferation of Conventional Arms and Dual-Use Technologies," p. 32.

35. For a general framework of foreign policy as regulation, see Richard N. Haass, *The Reluctant Sheriff: The United States after the Cold War* (Council on Foreign Relations Press, 1997).

36. Ultimately, it is of course arbitrary to try to establish a fixed point where supply turns into demand as far as the trail of a dual-use item is concerned, especially when third countries and trading companies play a role in the path of distribution.

37. For a discussion of these issues in the area of nuclear proliferation see Harald Müller and others, "Gläserne Labors? / Möglichkeiten der Rüstungskontrolle in Forschung und Entwicklung," HSFK-Report 1/1995 (Frankfurt am Main: Hessische Stiftung Friedens und Konflikt-Forschung, 1995). In another case, central banks and the private sector are currently engaged in an effort to alter the technology of color photocopiers so as to make them incapable of producing counterfeit money. See Hans Joachim Pick, "Präventionsmöglichkeiten zur Verhinderung von Banknotenfälschungen aus der Sicht der Deutschen Bundesbank" (Frankfurt am Main: Deutsche Bundesbank, April 1994). Yet another option is the so-called logic bomb, developed for purposes of information warfare, which could be implanted in the electronics of a dual-use item and triggered if it is used for military purposes. According to one report, the Central Intelligence Agency has already developed booby-trapped computer chips that can be inserted into a weapons system that a foreign arms manufacturer might ship to a potentially hostile country. The technique is called chipping. See Mark Thompson, "Onward Cyber Soldiers," *Time,* August 21, 1995, pp. 38–44.

38. Developed in response to a number of well-publicized illegal transfers from Germany to Iraq, Iran, and Libya, KOBRA was designed to aid the federal customs office in monitoring Germany's exports. For a brief description see *Verfahrenkurzbeschreibung, KOBRA,* Rechenzentrum der Bundesfinanzverwaltung bei der Oberfinanzdirektion Frankfurt am Main, November 1, 1995. KOBRA became fully functional in April 1991. See *VSF-Nachrichten,* N 1391 (March 13, 1991). Originally intended to cover all customs offices, the system today covers approximately 200 out of 500 of these offices. The more elaborate plans had to be scaled back in light of the costs of German unification. However, the 200 registries are placed in strategic areas where the risk of illegal activity is particularly high.

39. These lists of dual-use items have been developed by the Customs Criminological Institute (Zollkriminalamt, or ZKA). They focus primarily on high-technology goods and the chemical industry. The ZKA is the principal institution involved in analyzing the data collected, and it investigates and prosecutes violations in conjunction with the intelligence services.

40. Despite the system's limitations in terms of both geographic coverage and real-time supply of information, German authorities concluded that it has been successful in preventing, if not entirely eliminating, shipments of illegal dual-use items. The fact that KOBRA covered only 40 percent of all customs offices was less of a problem than often argued, as it was implemented in those regions with heavy concentrations of dual-use industries.

290   NOTES

41. See Australian Customs Service, "EXIT Fact Sheet" (Canberra, October 1994); "CHIEF Fact Sheet," U.K. Customs and Excise website, Operations Compliance Directorate 4A, www.open.gov.uk/customs/chief/hompage.htm; U.S. Customs Service, "Automated Export System Fact Sheet" (Washington, October 1996).

42. Before delivering any merchandise to a carrier or shipper, the exporter or its agent transmits predeparture commodity information to the customs system. The system in turn sends back a message linking the information to a unique export transaction number. In the Australian system this is called an export clearance number. This number is then passed on to the carrier, who uses it when compiling the shipping manifest, which is itself then transmitted to the customs system. Once the system has cross-checked the two filings and determined that everything is in order, it sends the carrier an "OK to load" message, whereupon the merchandise can be exported.

43. See Bundesministerium der Finanzen, *IT-Verfahren ATLAS: Kurzbeschreibung* (October 1996). Significantly, by requiring that exporters file electronically, ATLAS will also overcome the major shortcomings of KOBRA mentioned earlier.

44. "Proposal for a European Parliament and Council Decision Adopting an Action Programme for Community Customs (Customs 2000)," *Official Journal of the European Communities,* C 346/04 (Luxembourg, December 23, 1995), pp. 4–9.

45. See the Council Act of 26 July 1995 drawing up the convention on the use of information technology for customs purposes, *Official Journal of the European Communities,* C 316/33 (Luxembourg, November 27, 1995), pp. 33–42.

46. See *Export Controls: License Screening and Compliance Procedures Need Strengthening,* GAO/NSIAD-94-178 (General Accounting Office, June 14, 1994); *Export Controls: Actions Needed to Improve Enforcement,* GAO/NSIAD-94-28 (General Accounting Office, December 30, 1993).

47. See *The Federal Government's Export Licensing Process for Munitions and Dual-Use Commodities,* Final Report of the Office of the Inspector General at the U.S. Departments of Commerce, Defense, Energy, and State (Washington, 1993); Marcy Agmon and others, *Arms Proliferation Policy: Support to the Presidential Advisory Board* (RAND Corporation, 1996).

48. See, for example, the proposal by Senator Jake Garn (R-Ut.). *Export Administration Act of 1992,* S.2519, April 2, 1992; see also *Congressional Record,* S.4826, April 2, 1992; *Strengthening the Export Licensing System,* House Committee on Government Operations, 102 Cong., 1 sess. (GPO, 1991); "Export Controls," CRS Issue Brief, IB91064 (Congressional Research Service, March 27, 1992); National Academy of Sciences, *Finding Common Ground.*

49. For an earlier brief discussion of the ATTR see Reinicke, "Cooperative Security and the Political Economy of Nonproliferation."

50. The UN-mandated inspection for Iraq has made great progress in the tracking and monitoring of dual-use items.

51. For an overview see Suran Goonatilake and Philip Treleaven, eds., *Intelligent Systems for Finance and Business* (John Wiley & Sons, 1995); Suran Goonatilake and Sukhdev Khebbal, eds., *Intelligent Hybrid Systems* (John Wiley & Sons, 1995). Visa and American Express, for example, are using such systems to detect credit card fraud, with great success. During a six-month trial run in the early 1990s, Visa's

Cardholder Risk Identification Service (CRIS) saved the company $40 million by cutting down on fraud. See Vanessa Houlder, "War on Suspicious Payments," *Financial Times,* February 7, 1995, p. 15. American Express was one of the first companies to develop commercial expert systems to handle large volumes of data. See Robert S. Didner, "Intelligent Systems at American Express," in Goonatilake and Treleaven, eds., *Intelligent Hybrid Systems,* pp. 31–37.

52. As far back as 1994, fraud investigators at the London Stock Exchange started to test so-called hybrid intelligence systems in an effort to crack down on insider trading. The Monitoring Insider Trading and Regulatory Surveillance (Monitars) system combines neural networks (a computing device that exhibits similarities to the structural and functional characteristics of nerve cells in the human brain) with fuzzy logic (a mechanism for dealing with imprecise information) and genetic algorithms (derived from biological evolution). See Vanessa Houlder, "Tackling Insider Dealing with Fuzzy Logic," *Financial Times,* September 29, 1994, p. 16. After a number of remarkable successes during the test period, the exchange has now formally adopted the system, and installment started in late 1996. The tracking device, renamed the Intelligent Alert System (IAS), although operating in concert with the existing system, called Imass (Integrated Monitoring and Surveillance System), is considerably more powerful. It evaluates and prioritizes incoming alerts, relates them to specific persons, and looks at historical patterns for as long as five years once they have been established. The investigation of insider trading referred to required the searching of more than 2.8 million records, which took less than a minute. See Nuala Moran, "Stock Exchange Gets Fuzzy Logic," *Financial Times,* September 4, 1996, p. 8.

53. NASD, *Annual Report 1995,* p. 25. Emphasis added.

54. Confidential interview, November 27, 1996.

55. In the United States, the Blue Lantern program moves in this direction by establishing prelicense checks (PLCs) and postshipment verification (PSVs) of defense exports. A PLC is an effort to predetermine the reliability of overseas recipients and to ensure that the proposed use of the commodity or technical data in question is consistent with the normal business of the recipient. A PSV is used to confirm that the export has in fact been received by the designated end user and that it is being used in accordance with the terms and provisions of the approved license. The Enhanced Proliferation Control Initiative, implemented by the Bush administration in the wake of the Gulf War, is another example. However, neither program ensures close enough cooperation between the public and the private sector for regulators to gather all the information that might be useful.

56. Since 1991, Germany's export control regulations require the designation of such an official.

57. A number of countries, including Germany and the United States, have already initiated such exchanges.

58. See, for example, "Iraq's Campaign to Acquire and Develop High Technology," CRS Report 92-611 F (Congressional Research Service, August 3, 1992); Robert E. Powis, *The Money Launderers: Lessons from the Drug Wars—How Billions of Illegal Dollars Are Washed through Banks & Businesses* (Chicago: Probus Publishing Company, 1992), chapter 6; Jennifer W. MacDonald, "Following the Money to Iraq," *Journal of Commerce,* September 14, 1992, p. 8A.

59. See, for example, Matthew C. Gruskin, "Invading the Private Sector," *Corporate Law and Practice Course Handbook Series,* no. 202 (New York: Practicing Law Institute, 1976).

60. Dale Chaney and Jacqueline Emigh, "Green Marketing Strategies," *American Banker,* vol. 157, no. 80 (April 27, 1992), p. A6.

61. Social Investment Forum, *After South Africa, Responsible Investment Trends in the United States* (Washington, 1995). The argument that these funds generally have lower returns has proved questionable as well. See Patrick McVeigh, "Successful Investments for the Socially Conscious," *Wall Street Journal,* April 25, 1997, p. A15; Nancy Dunne, "Green Policies Attract Investment," *Financial Times,* January 28, 1997, p. 4; see also "When Foreign Investors Pay for Development," *World Watch* (May–June 1997), pp. 8–17.

62. Capital presently invested in socially screened funds amounts to some $8 billion. "The growth in options for mutual fund investors parallels the growth in social investing in general, and represents an increasing willingness on the part of both investors and financial professionals to screen potential investments using social as well as financial criteria." Trex Proffitt, "Ethical Investment Funds Proliferate; Set Tenor for Social Investing in the 1990s," *IRRC News for Investors,* December 1990, p. 234. Among the many recently published guides to socially responsible investing are Amy L. Domini and Peter D. Kinder, *Ethical Investing—How to Make Profitable Investments without Sacrificing Your Principles* (Reading, Mass.: Addison-Wesley, 1984); Myra Alperson and others, *The Better World Investment Guide* (Prentice Hall, 1991).

63. Companies that raise capital through publicly offered securities must file various reports that disclose to the Securities and Exchange Commission and to shareholders all "material" information, financial and otherwise. The term "material" is not clearly defined, and this has led to many prolonged disputes. See Michael V. Seitzinger, "Securities Law: Environmental Disclosures," CRS Report 91-422a (Congressional Research Service, May 12, 1991).

64. 17 C.F.R. Par. 240.12b-2, *Basic Inc. v. Levinson.* See website at www.westpub. com/montgomery/108sct978.htm.

65. "[D]isclosure, and not paternalistic withholding of accurate information, is the policy chosen and expressed by Congress. We have recognized time and time again, a 'fundamental purpose' of the various securities acts, was to substitute a philosophy of full disclosure for the philosophy of caveat emptor and thus to achieve a high standard of business ethics in the securities industry." *Basic Inc. v. Levinson,* 108 S.Ct. 984-985 (1988).

66. The IRRC is a nonprofit research organization founded by and for institutional investors. Registered as an investment adviser with the SEC, it compiles information about corporations' policies and businesses on a regular basis. Other services include the Corporate Governance Service, which tracks corporate governance and financial performance; the Global Shareholder Service, which provides information on corporate practices, shareholder issues, and shareholder rights in other countries; and the Environmental Information Service, which tracks business and the environment; in addition, the IRRC will conduct research on more specific topics as requested by clients. See Investor Responsibility Research Center, *Annual Report*

1991 (Washington, 1991). For a listing of socially screened mutual funds and their comparative performance, see, for example, Council on Economic Priorities, *Research Report* (New York, February 1994), p. 6.

67. So-called ethical funds started in the early 1980s. A British fund called the Stewardship Unit Trust, with £105 million under management, is the largest of these funds. Among other things, it avoids companies in the armaments industry. Since the late 1980s, "green funds" such as NPI Global Care and Sovereign Ethical have become increasingly popular. See Daneshkhu Scheherazade, "Why This May Be the Time to Turn Green," *Financial Times,* May 30, 1992, p. 3. In 1996 the Overseas Private Investment Corporation set up an International Environmental Investment Fund to attract investors for projects in developing countries with sound environmental purposes. See Paula L. Greene, "Investors Mixing with Environment," *Journal of Commerce,* September 6, 1991, p. 3A; see also Jamie Heard, "Investor: An Idea Whose Time Has Come?" *Journal of Portfolio Management,* vol. 4 (Spring 1978), pp. 12–14.

68. Agmon and others, *Arms Proliferation Policy: Support to the Presidential Advisory Board*, p. 66.

69. The strongest criticism made by German companies against the new, more stringent export control laws was directed at the fact that they do not apply to their European competitors. This creates a severe disadvantage for German firms in light of the creation of a single European market by the end of 1992. See Wolfgang H. Reinicke, "European Community Export Controls Beyond 1992," *Brookings Review,* vol. 10, no. 3 (Summer 1992), pp. 22–25.

70. Of course, the same company may end up making the sale through a foreign affiliate; this suggests that industry resistance may be limited under conditions of globalization.

71. The different demands on negotiators emanating from the international and the domestic environment were first discussed in Robert Putnam, "Diplomacy and Domestic Politics: The Logic of Two-Level Games," *International Organization,* vol. 42 (Summer 1988), pp. 427–60.

72. See, for example, Benjamin Gomes-Casseres, *The Alliance Revolution: The New Shape of Business Rivalry* (Harvard University Press, 1996).

73. "The European Union and the United States Initial Agreement on Customs Cooperation and Mutual Assistance in Customs Matters," *European Union Press Releases,* no. 66/96 (November 7, 1996), as found at www.eurunion.org/news/index.htm.

74. For some background see Wolfgang H. Reinicke, *Deepening the Atlantic: Toward a New Transatlantic Marketplace?* (Gütersloh, Germany: Bertelsmann Foundation Publishers, 1996); Christoph Bail, Wolfgang H. Reinicke, and Reinhardt Rummel, eds., *Perspectives on Transatlantic Relations* (Baden-Baden: Nomos Verlagsgesellschaft, 1997).

75. The initiative was launched with a jointly developed questionnaire sent to companies on both sides of the Atlantic by the U.S. government and the European Commission.

76. "Brown-Brittan-Bangemann Joint Statement Inviting Madrid Summit to Implement Recommendations by Business Leaders," *Agence Europe,* November 15,

1995, p. 8. For the U.S. proposals see TABD, *US Working Group Papers I-IV* (draft), October 23, 1995.

77. The group's 1996 Chicago declaration calls for establishing an "expert consultative committee" to review export controls and ensure transparency in their implementation, so as to maintain a level playing field. See TABD, "Chicago Declaration," November 9, 1996.

78. The four organizations are Phillips, Bayer, Motorola, and the Chemical Manufacturers Association.

79. At the first official meeting of the TABD in November 1995 in Seville, Spain, disagreements between the two business communities emerged not only with respect to specific sectoral issues that one side or the other wanted to address, but also with respect to more fundamental issues that produced rival agendas. See Guy de Jonquieres and Lionel Barber, "Business Meets to Revive US-EU Ties," *Financial Times,* November 10, 1995, p. 6; David White, "US Shows United Front across the Divide," *Financial Times,* November 13, 1995, p. 2.

80. Abram Chayes and Antonia Handler Chayes, "On Compliance," *International Organization,* vol. 47, no. 2 (1993), pp. 175–206. For a more comprehensive treatment see Abram Chayes and Antonia Handler Chayes, *The New Sovereignty: Compliance with International Regulatory Agreements* (Harvard University Press, 1995).

81. David A. Koplow and Philip G. Schrag, "Carrying a Big Carrot: Linking Multilateral Disarmament and Development Assistance," *Columbia Law Review,* vol. 91, no. 5 (June 1991), pp. 993–1059.

82. Wolfgang H. Reinicke, "Cooperative Security and the Political Economy of Non-Proliferation," in Nolan, *Global Engagement*; and "From Denial to Disclosure: The Political Economy of Export Controls and Technology Transfer," in Francine Frankel, ed., *Bridging the Non-Proliferation Divide: The United States and India* (University Press of America, 1995).

83. See, for example, Francisco Sagasti and John Stremlau, "The World Bank and the International Financial Institutions: What Role in Conflict Prevention?" paper prepared for FORO Nacional/International AGENDA: Peru and the Carnegie Commission for Preventing Deadly Conflict, Lima and Washington, May 1996.

84. *Convention on the Prohibition of the Development, Production and Stockpiling and use of Chemical Weapons,* corrected version in accordance with Depository Notification C.N.246.1993.TREATIES-5 and the corresponding Procès-Verbal of Ratification of the original of the Convention, issued on August 8, 1994.

85. *Convention on the Prohibition of the Development, Production and Stockpiling and Use of Chemical Weapons,* Article VI, (1).

86. Chemicals to be controlled are categorized into three lists according to their suitability for chemical weapons and for legitimate commercial use.

87. *Convention on the Prohibition of the Development, Production and Stockpiling and Use of Chemical Weapons,* Article IX, (17).

88. The inspection team must be transported to a declared facility within twenty-four hours, or to an undeclared facility within thirty-six hours. Access to the site to be inspected must be provided no later than 108 hours after arrival of the team in the country. See *Convention on the Prohibition of the Development, Production and*

Stockpiling and Use of Chemical Weapons, Annex on Implementation and Verification, Part X (6), (13)–(15), (39).

89. Agmon and others, *Arms Proliferation Policy.*

90. A. Maureen Rouhi, "Government, Industry Efforts Yield Array of Tools to Combat Terrorism," *Chemical and Engineering News,* vol. 73, no. 30 (July 24, 1995), pp. 10–19. The best-publicized potential use of microtaggants has been in the context of explosive compounds. Mixed into smokeless powder, TNT, fertilizer, or plastic explosives, taggants act as fingerprints identifying the source or manufacturer of the substance. A number of taggants will remain intact even after the explosion of these substances. To date, only Switzerland has passed legislation that requires explosives to contain a marker substance that allows reliable determination of origin after detonation. Efforts in the United States to institute similar regulations, most recently in the wake of the 1995 Oklahoma City bombing, have consistently been derailed by lobbying from the National Rifle Association. See John Schwartz, "Technology Used to Tag Explosives Gets Second Look after Bombing," *Washington Post,* May 7, 1995, p. A8. Following the 1988 bombing of a Pan Am 747 jet over Lockerbie, Scotland, fifty countries, including the United States, signed the Convention on the Marking of Plastic Explosives for the Purpose of Detection. The treaty, which requires incorporation of any of four detection agents into plastic explosives, was ratified by the U.S. Senate in November 1993. To date, however, only twenty-three of the thirty-five national ratifications required for the treaty to enter into force have taken place.

91. See "Excuse Me, Captain, Is This Your Oil Spill?" *New Scientist,* vol. 143, no. 1938 (August 13, 1994), p. 20.

92. Applications have included the tagging of animals, criminals, cars, trash cans, and articles of clothing. The U.S. military has even initiated a system that uses RF tags to monitor the movement of supplies.

93. D. G. Gritton and others, *Tag Technology R&D Final Report: Secure Electronic Tags,* Report UCRL-ID-112709 (Livermore, Calif.: Lawrence Livermore National Laboratory, University of California, March 1993).

94. Y. Cai and others, *User Interface Program for Secure Electronic Tags,* Report ANL-95/16 (Argonne, Ill.: Argonne National Laboratory, 1995).

95. Jenny Luesby, "On the Right Track: Electronic and Radio Tags Are Poised to Transform Consumers' Lives," *Financial Times,* July 4, 1995, p. 16.

96. UNSCOM was formed pursuant to Security Council Resolution 687 (1991). It mandated the Special Commission to "carry out immediate on-site inspection of Iraq's biological, chemical and missile capabilities, based on Iraq's declarations and the designation of any additional locations by the Special Commission itself." See S/RES/687 (1991), section (b)(i).

97. Typically these cameras are encased in a tamper-proof housing, have an auxiliary power supply, and are connected to motion sensors. One of UNSCOM's successes was to expose Iraq's widespread use of piecemealing in its acquisition of Scud missiles.

98. See Jonathan B. Tucker, "Remote Monitoring of Dual-Capable Biological Facilities in Iraq," *Politics and the Life Sciences,* vol. 14, no. 2 (August 1995), pp. 247–54.

99. This equipment was used by the International Atomic Energy Administration to determine that North Korea had embarked on a program to develop nuclear weapons.

100. Confidential business information includes formulas, drawings, patterns, techniques, price codes, customer lists, studies, and much else. See Office of Technology Assessment, *The Chemical Weapons Convention: Effect on the United States Chemical Industry* (Washington: GPO, 1993); Burrus M. Carnahan, "Chemical Arms Control, Trade Secrets, and the Constitution: Facing the Unresolved Issues," *International Lawyer,* vol. 25, no. 1 (Spring 1991), pp. 167–86. Although a variety of international treaties and agencies such as the World Intellectual Property Organization deal with the protection of intellectual property, and the issue has been at the top of the agenda of the World Trade Organization, they do not deal with this issue. For some background on intellectual property protection see Kenneth W. Dam, "The Growing Importance of International Protection of Intellectual Property," *International Lawyer,* vol. 21, no. 3 (Summer 1987), pp. 627–38.

101. On the other hand, one might argue that the growing number of strategic alliances and the increasing internationalization of R&D have somewhat mitigated the threat of a breach of confidentiality at this stage in the product cycle.

102. For a discussion of the differences between the two see Barry Kellman, David S. Gualtieri, and Edward E. Tanzman, "Disarmament and Disclosure: How Arms Control Verification Can Proceed without Threatening Confidential Business Information," *Harvard International Law Journal,* vol. 36, no. 1 (Winter 1995), pp. 71–126.

103. Kellman, Gualtieri, and Tanzman, "Disarmament and Disclosure," pp. 114–25.

104. On the role of business in the development of the CWC, see, for example, Amy Smithson, "Implementing the Chemical Weapons Convention: Counsel from Industry," *Report No. 10* (Washington: Henry L. Stimson Center, January 1994); Business Executives for National Security, *Making Americans Safer: The Case for the Chemicals Weapons Convention (CWC)* (Washington, Spring 1996).

105. OTA, *Chemical Weapons Convention,* p. 10.

106. *Convention on the Prohibition of the Development, Production and Stockpiling and Use of Chemical Weapons, Annex on the Protection of Confidential Information.*

107. See Kellman, Gualtieri, and Tanzman, "Disarmament and Disclosure," pp. 114–25, for a critique and proposals for improvement.

108. Nine seats are allotted to Africa, nine to Asia, five to eastern Europe, seven to Latin America and the Caribbean, and ten to a group that includes western Europe and North America. The forty-first member is chosen on a rotating basis from Asia or from Latin America and the Caribbean.

109. Note, however, that the United States has reached a political agreement within its group that it "will have a permanent seat on the Executive Council." See *Chemical Weapons Convention: Message from the President of the United States,* Treaty Doc. 103-21 (GPO, 1993), p. 49.

110. The question of whether an issue is substantive or not is itself treated as an issue of substance, and hence subject to a two-thirds majority, unless the Executive Council changes that rule, which also requires a two-thirds majority.

111. See, for example, George F. Will, "A Feel-Good Treaty," *Washington Post*, September 8, 1996, p. 6.

112. Probably in response to their increased use by policymakers, scholarly interest in sanctions has grown considerably and produced a series of valuable overviews and analyses. See Chayes and Chayes, *The New Sovereignty*; David Cortright and George A. Lopez, eds., *Economic Sanctions: Panacea or Peacebuilding in a Post–Cold War World?* (Boulder, Colo.: Westview Press, 1995); Lisa Martin, *Explaining International Economic Sanctions* (Princeton University Press, 1992); Gary Clyde Hufbauer, Jeffrey J. Schott, and Kimberly Ann Elliott, *Economic Sanctions Reconsidered,* 2nd ed. (Washington: Institute for International Economics, 1990); Donald L. Losman, "Good Intentions Gone Bad: Punitive Trade Embargoes Are Appealing, but They Don't Achieve Our Goals," *Washington Post,* October 6, 1996, p. C3.

113. Bruce W. Jentleson, "Economic Sanctions: Post–Cold War Policy Challenges," working paper prepared for the Committee on International Conflict Resolution, National Research Council, June 17, 1996, p. 11.

114. For an interesting argument that somewhat qualifies this commonly accepted generalization and holds that unilateral sanctions can have some effect despite global economic integration, see Kenneth A. Rodman, "Sanctions at Bay? Hegemonic Decline, Multinational Corporations, and U.S. Economic Sanctions since the Pipeline Case," *International Organization,* vol. 49, no. 1 (Winter 1995), pp. 105–37.

115. Daniel N. Nelson, "Seeking International Consensus," *Foreign Service Journal,* vol. 67, no. 11 (November 1990), pp. 26–27.

116. Sanctions on Yugoslavia, for example, had considerable adverse effects on neighboring countries. See Milan Ruzicka, "Embargo on Yugoslavia Echoes through Balkans," *Journal of Commerce,* August 16, 1993, p. 1A, 8A.

117. John Stremlau, *Sharpening International Sanctions: Toward a Stronger Role for the United Nations, A Report to the Carnegie Commission on Preventing Deadly Conflict* (New York: Carnegie Corporation of New York, November 1996).

118. U.S. Department of State, *Patterns of Global Terrorism, 1995* (Washington: GPO, April 1996).

119. Wolfgang H. Reinicke, "Combating Terrorism: What Works? What Doesn't?" statement to a Policy Impact Panel hosted by the Council on Foreign Relations, Washington, October 11, 1996.

120. Charles Perrow, *Normal Accidents: Living with High Risk Technologies* (New York: Basic Books, 1984).

CHAPTER 7

1. Jessica T. Mathews, "Power Shift," *Foreign Affairs*, vol. 76, no. 1 (January/February 1997), pp. 50–66.

2. Anne-Marie Slaughter, "The Real New World Order," *Foreign Affairs*, vol. 76, no. 5 (September/October 1997), pp. 183–97.

3. Slaughter, "The Real New World Order," p. 184.

4. Karl Kaiser raised this issue over twenty-five years ago by distinguishing between international and transnational politics. See Karl Kaiser, "Transnational Pol-

itics: Toward a Theory of Multinational Politics," *International Organization*, vol. 25, no. 4 (Autumn 1971), pp. 790–817. For a more recent treatment of this subject, see David Held, *Democracy and the Global Order* (Stanford University Press, 1995).

5. This is not to underestimate the importance of the many regional integration projects now under way, such as MERCOSUR (the Southern Common Market) in South America, the proposed ASEAN free trade area, and the SADC (Southern African Development Community). All are important efforts at reducing the emphasis on external sovereignty and should be strongly encouraged and supported.

6. Thus, even in the Middle East, where territoriality continues to dominate the definition of security, efforts are under way to reduce the emphasis on external sovereignty and the potential for violent conflict. At the forefront of these efforts are institutions such as the Middle East Development Bank, which is now officially registered with the United Nations and has been authorized by Congress.

7. World Resources Institute, United Nations Environment Program, and United Nations Development Program, *World Resources 1994–5* (Oxford University Press, 1994), pp. 28–30.

8. World Bank, *Private Capital Flows to Developing Countries: The Road to Financial Integration* (Oxford University Press, 1997), p. 5.

9. Robert Jackson called this "positive sovereignty," the active ability to act and collaborate domestically and internationally, as opposed to negative sovereignty, the mere passive freedom from outside interference. Robert H. Jackson, *Quasi-States: Sovereignty, International Relations and the Third World* (Cambridge University Press, 1990), pp. 26–31.

10. For some background, see R. B. J. Walker Saul H. Mendlovitz, eds., *Contending Sovereignties: Redefining Political Community* (Lynne Rienner Publishers, 1990), especially chapter 9; R. B. J. Walker, "Sovereignty, Identity, Community: Reflections on the Horizons of Contemporary Practice," pp. 159–85; see also Thomas J. Biersteker and Cynthia Weber, eds., *State Sovereignty as Social Construct* (Cambridge University Press, 1996).

11. See, for example, Hendrik Spruyt, "Institutional Selection in International Relations," *International Organization*, vol. 48, no. 4 (Autumn 1994), pp. 527–57.

12. J. Samuel Barkin and Bruce Cronin, "The State and the Nation: Changing Norms and the Rules of Sovereignty in International Relations," *International Organization*, vol. 48, no. 1 (Winter 1994), pp. 107–30.

Index

Accountability, democratic, 114–15, 226
Advantage, comparative, 24, 240n62
Adversarial cooperation, 61, 62
Alliances, international, 22–23, 24f
American Bankers Association, 150
Anarchical Society, The, 56
Anarchy: international markets, 71; sovereignty and, 57, 59–60, 230–31, 247n30
Annunzio-Wylie Anti-Money Laundering Act of *1992,* 140–41, 151, 274n20
Anti-Drug Abuse Act of *1988,* 140, 144, 167
Arms proliferation, 197; dual-use items and, 174–75, 189, 285n1; military downsizing and, 174, 285n2; Wassenaar Agreement, U.N. Arms Register and, 182, 183–84, 288n32
Artificial intelligence, 148, 166, 192, 290–91n51–52
Asian Secretariat, 164, 282n123
Asia-Pacific Economic Cooperation (APEC) forum, 164–65, 282n125
Asia/Pacific Group on Money Laundering, 164, 282n124
ATLAS (Automated Customs Tariff and Local Processing Application System), 189, 290n43
ATTR (automated technology transfer registry), 191–95, 290n49, 291n57; artificial intelligence and, 192; compliance/enforcement

separation, 193; confidentiality and, 212; global vision for, 202–17; money laundering and, 195–96; new technology transfer regulations and, 193, 203; small/medium-size companies and, 193; transatlantic initiative, 201–02
Australia, 166; Confiscated Assets Trust Fund, 164; Export Integration (EXIT) program, 188, 290n42
Austria, 76

Backtesting: capital adequacy, 121, 267n65; money laundering, 149
Banca Nazionale del Lavoro, Atlanta branch, 196
Bank failures, 104, 106, 260n6, 260n8, 261n14. *See also* Barings collapse
Bank for International Settlements (BIS), 111, 203, 223
Bank of Credit and Commerce International (BCCI) collapse, 104, 157, 196
Bank of England, 109–10, 124, 262–63n29–31
Bank Secrecy Act of *1970* (BSA), U.S., 140. *See also* Currency Transaction Report (CTR)
Bank Secrecy Advisory Group, 146, 150, 168
Banking centers, offshore, 43
Banks, money laundering requirements and, 140–41

299